History of the Church Volume 2

You are holding a reproduction of an original work that is in the public domain in the United States of America, and possibly other countries. You may freely copy and distribute this work as no entity (individual or corporate) has a copyright on the body of the work. This book may contain prior copyright references, and library stamps (as most of these works were scanned from library copies). These have been scanned and retained as part of the historical artifact.

This book may have occasional imperfections such as missing or blurred pages, poor pictures, errant marks, etc. that were either part of the original artifact, or were introduced by the scanning process. We believe this work is culturally important, and despite the imperfections, have elected to bring it back into print as part of our continuing commitment to the preservation of printed works worldwide. We appreciate your understanding of the imperfections in the preservation process, and hope you enjoy this valuable book.

HISTORY OF THE CHURCH,

TRANSLATED FROM THE GERMAN

OF THE

REV. J. J. IG. DÖLLINGER, D.D.

PROFESSOR OF THEOLOGY
IN THE ROYAL UNIVERSITY OF MUNICH,

BY THE

REV. EDWARD COX, D.D.

OF ST EDMUNDS COLLEGE, OLD HALL GREEN, HERTS

VOLUME THE SECOND.

LONDON:
PUBLISHED BY C. DOLMAN, 61, NEW BOND STREET,
AND BY T JONES, 63, PATERNOSTER ROW

1840.

LONDON
C RICHARDS, PRINTER, 100, ST MARTIN'S LANE

CONTENTS OF VOL. II.

PERIOD THE SECOND,

FROM THE REIGN OF CONSTANTINE TO THE SIXTH GENERAL COUNCIL.

CHAPTER THE FIRST

EXTERNAL HISTORY OF THE CHURCH

SECTION	PAGE
I.—Conflict of Christianity with Idolatry in the Roman Empire — Constantine. Julian. Fall of Paganism	1
II.—Controversies with the Pagans —The Christian Apologists	7

CHAPTER THE SECOND

THE CHURCH BEYOND THE ROMAN EMPIRE AMONGST THE GERMANS IN THE BRITISH ISLES MUHAMMEDANISM

I —Christianity in the East, and amongst the Germans	10
II —Christianity in the British Isles —Introduction of Christianity into Ireland —St Patrick —St Columba, the Apostle of the Picts —The Irish Church	19
III.—The British Church —Conversion of the Anglo-Saxons —The first ages of the Anglo-Saxon Church	35
IV —Controversies in Britain and Ireland concerning the time of the celebration of Easter and the form of the tonsure	58
V —Christianity in Germany, and in the adjacent countries	71
VI —Muhammedanism and its Founder	87

CHAPTER THE THIRD.

THE SCHISMS AND HERESIES TO THE END OF THE FOURTH CENTURY.

I —The Schism of the Donatists	97
II —The Arian Controversies —1 Down to the Council of Sardica	102
III —The last period of Arianism —The Luciferian and Meletian Schisms —The Macedonians	116
IV —Photinus and Apollinaris —The Priscillianists —Minor Sects —Individual Heretics	122
V —Controversies on the Doctrines of Origen	129

CHAPTER THE FOURTH

HERESIES AND CONTROVERSIES ON GRACE AND THE INCARNATION, FROM THE BEGINNING OF THE FIFTH CENTURY TO THE END OF THE PERIOD

I —Pelagianism	135
II.—Semipelagians	144
III —Nestorianism —The Council of Ephesus	148

IV.—Eutyches.—The Latrocinium —The Council of Chalcedon — The Monophysites —The Henoticon . . 162
V —Renewal of the Origenist Controversy —The Controversy on the Three Articles (Tria Capitula) —The Fifth General Council —Schism . 177
VI.—Internal History of the Monophysites —Controversies and Sects amongst them —The Nestorians 189
VII.—The Monothelites 194

CHAPTER THE FIFTH

CONSTITUTION AND GOVERNMENT OF THE CHURCH DURING THE SECOND PERIOD

I —Relation of the Civil power to the Church . 204
II —Succession of the Roman Pontiffs 212
III.—The Supremacy . . 219
IV —The Patriarchal and Metropolitan Constitution in the West 233
V.—Patriarchal and Metropolitan authority in the East —The Patriarchs of Constantinople . . . 245
VI —Bishops and their Dioceses —Chorepiscopi and Parish Priests — The other Clergy . . . 255
VII —Formation of Ecclesiastical Relations in the new Churches of Germany.—The Church in the kingdoms of the Franks and the West Goths . . 264
VIII —Celibacy 272
IX.—Ascetics and Anchorets —The origin of Monasteries.—Spread of the Monastic Institute in the East and West —The Benedictine Order. —Cloisters of Nuns . . 275
X.—Collections of Canons —Books of Ecclesiastical Law in the Greek and Latin Churches . . 287

THE SACRAMENTS, WORSHIP AND DISCIPLINE OF THE ANCIENT CHURCH, DURING THE FIRST SEVEN CENTURIES, OR THE FIRST AND SECOND PERIODS

XI —The Catechumenate, Baptism, and Confirmation . 291
XII.—The Liturgies of the Ancient Church . . 299
XIII —Order of the Divine Worship —The Mass of the Catechumens, and the Mass of the Faithful . . 307
XIV —Administration of the Holy Eucharist. its Elements —Various kinds of Masses.—Communion under one kind —The Agapè . 318
XV.—Penance.—The Confession of Sins —Absolution . 327
XVI.—Extreme Unction.—Orders and Matrimony 340
XVII.—Discipline of the Secret 346
XVIII —Churches.—Altars —Images.—The Cross 348
XIX.—The Feasts and Fasts of the Church . . 355
XX —Daily Prayer —Honour paid to the Saints and to their Relics.—Benedictions —Ecclesiastical Hospitality —Burials —Excommunication . . 364

HISTORY OF THE CHURCH.

PERIOD THE SECOND.

FROM THE REIGN OF CONSTANTINE TO THE SIXTH GENERAL COUNCIL—FROM 313 TO 680 *

CHAPTER THE FIRST.†
EXTERNAL HISTORY OF THE CHURCH.

SECT. I.—CONFLICT OF CHRISTIANITY WITH IDOLATRY IN THE ROMAN EMPIRE.—CONSTANTINE: JULIAN: FALL OF PAGANISM.

CONSTANTINE, although nurtured on the bosom of Paganism, had inherited the kindly disposition, we may perhaps call it the predilection, of his father, Constantius, in favour of the religion of the Christians. These sentiments were soon converted into a decided inclination, and finally into a firm belief in the divinity of the same religion. The change was effected, according to his own declaration, which we find in Eusebius, by the miraculous appearance in the heavens of a resplendent cross, which was accompanied by a promise

---

* The writers of Ecclesiastical History, Socrates, Sozomen, Theodoret, Philostorgius, Evagrius, Rufinus, Sulpicius Severus: the Profane Historians, Ammianus Marcellinus, Zosimus, Orosius, Procopius, Agathias.—The Chronicon Paschale. The Chronicles of Prosper, Idacius, Victor of Tununum, Marcellinus. The Chronography of Theophanes. The Acts of the Councils. The Imperial laws in the Codex Theodosianus and Codex Justinianus. The works of the Fathers of the Church, during this period.

† Eusebius de Vita Constantin.. Juliani Opera, ed. Ez. Spanhemius,

of victory. This occurred in the year 311, during his campaign against Maxentius. In the following year Constantine, who was now lord of the western division of the Roman empire, and Licinius, who was sole ruler of the east, promulgated a decree, granting toleration to all religions. This was the first imperial decree promulgated in favour of the Christians: in 313 it was followed by the edict of Milan, which secured to the Christians in particular the free exercise of their religion. A series of laws, during the following year, bestowed upon them many and great advantages. Constantine freed all ecclesiastical persons from the burden of the public offices of the state, and from the payment of all personal taxes: he confirmed the judicial authority of the bishops—abolished the laws against those who lived in celibacy—permitted churches to receive presents and legacies—enforced the observance of the Sunday—maintained many Churches and ecclesiastics, and erected many temples to the honour of the true God. But, in the meantime, Licinius, who beheld in Constantine a dangerous rival, and an abettor of the Christians, persecuted the faithful within his own dominions. The war which in 323 broke out between the two emperors, was, in reality, a religious war. Licinius fell in the contest, and with him fell Paganism. The conqueror, under whose sway the whole empire of Rome now lay united, declared himself, in the most unequivocal manner, a professor of the Christian religion; and expressed his desire and his hope that all his subjects would imitate his example. He caused his sons to be educated as Christians, and placed Christians in the most important offices of the

---

Lips 1696, Libanii Orationes, ed. Reiske, Altenburg, 1791; Themistii Orationes, ed Harduin, Paris, 1684.

Fr. Gusta, Vita di Constantino il Grande, Fuligno, 1786; J. E. F. Manso, Leben Constantin's de Gr. Breslau. 1817, (De la Bléterie) Vie de l' Empereur Julien, Amst. 1735, 2 vols., Jondot, Histoire de l' Emp. Julien, Paris. 1817, 2 vols, A Neander, Ueber den Kaiser Julianus und sein Zeitalter (The Emperor Julian and his Times), Leipzig, 1812; Rudiger, De Statu et Conditione Paganorum, sub Imperatoribus post Constantinum Magnum, Vratislav, 1825.

empire: to the ancient capital of the dominions of heathen Rome, he opposed a Christian metropolis, at Byzantium, now called, from him, Constantinople: he paused not in his attacks upon paganism, which he even designated as a superstition of by-gone times. He commanded the heathen temples, in many places, to be closed, or to be converted into churches; in other cities they were destroyed, and the idols of the gods broken into pieces or removed. He employed every means within his power to induce the idolaters to embrace the new faith; and it appears that towards the close of his reign, he published an universal prohibition which forbade the public worship of the gods: the law, however, was never enforced. But it must strike us with wonder when we learn, that, with all this zeal, Constantine should have continued out of the Church until the end of his life. He received baptism during his last illness, in the year 337, at a castle near Nicomedia.

His three sons, Constantine, Constantius, and Constans, who divided the empire amongst themselves, proceeded with greater severity and impetuosity in the extirpation of idolatry. A law, published in 341, commanded that "superstition should cease, and the folly of the sacrifices should be destroyed;" and when Constantius, in 353, became sole emperor by the death of his brothers, and the defeat of the usurper Magnentius, he prescribed the cessation of sacrifices to the heathen deities under pain of death. But the number of idolaters was yet too great, and their power too strong, to suffer Constantius to bring this sanguinary decree into operation, although he renewed it in the year 356. Whilst he destroyed, or gave away the temples, he could not take the government of the most celebrated schools, nor, consequently, the education of youths of the highest rank, from the most heathen-minded sophists of the age.

By the influence of these sophists, and by his connexion with the Platonists of Asia Minor, Julian, a youth of great talent, the nephew of Constantius, was led to the determination to destroy Christianity, and to employ the authority and power to which he was to succeed, in the restoration of polytheism throughout the Roman empire. Heathenism was to be ennobled and remodelled according to the ideas of the Neoplatonics, with whom Julian had associated himself. Hatred against Constantius, who was not guiltless of the murder of Julian's nearest relations, and the long necessity, which he had endured of simulating an adherence to the Christian religion, embittered him against it; and when the legions in Gaul proclaimed him emperor, and the death of Constantius in 361 placed him on the throne of the empire, he delayed not to commence at once the annihilation of Christianity, and the re-establishment of idolatry. Warned, however, by the experience of past ages, he wished to avoid direct bloody persecution; but he did not punish the violence of the heathen populace, who sacrificed many Christians to the fury. He took from the clergy and the churches the privileges which his predecessors had granted to them: he promised to all Christian sects equal toleration, with the view to engage them in continual strifes and contests: he excluded all Christian teachers from public instruction, that the Christian youth might remain in ignorance, or be compelled to frequent the schools of Pagan masters. To hasten the return of the Christians to heathenism he left no means untried; and during his short reign this defection was as ordinary an occurrence of every day, as the conversion of the idolaters had been under the preceding emperors. Thousands, for the same external motives, and for their own temporal interest, which had before made them Christians in name, now renounced their faith, and returned again to idolatry. But in vain did he seek to animate the pagan priests and the pagan people: in vain did he as *Pontifex Maximus* give the example of the most ardent zeal in the worship of the gods; for the religious enthusiasm of polytheism was extinct and could not be resuscitated. Neither could he effect his purpose by the introduction of Christian usages, hymns, sermons, cloisters, the discipline of penance and almshouses, into the practices of paganism. With his early death, in 363, the whole of his artificial work, which he had raised with great labour and design, fell of itself to pieces. It would have been well, perhaps, had he lived to witness how a mighty undertaking against Christianity could end in the glorious triumph of that religion. To refute the divine prophecies, which foretold the perpetual desolation of Jerusalem, and to disgrace the Christian Church, by opposing to it the temple, the priesthood, and the ancient sacrifices of the law, he commenced the restoration of the temple; but earthquakes and flames of fire, which repeatedly burst from the earth, either killed or severely injured the workmen, and obliged the Jews and Pagans, who had united in this work, to desist at length from their vain attempt.

Jovian, the successor of Julian, was a Christian, but gave freedom of religion to the heathens: the same was done by Valentinian I in the west, and by Valens in the east. Both, however, at a later period, prohibited the sacrifices of animals.

Idolatry had now greatly diminished in cities and towns, and as those, who still adhered to it, resided chiefly in villages *(Pagi)* and hamlets, they were known by the name of *Pagani;* a word which first occurs in a law of Valentinian, in 368. Gratian (375-383) caused the altar and the statue of the Goddess of Victory to be removed from the Roman Forum, and deprived the priests and the temples of their privileges, revenues, and possessions. The representations, which were made by the idolatrous part of the Roman senate, to him and to his successor Valentinian II, to obtain the restoration of these goods, were met and powerfully refuted by the great Saint Ambrose, archbishop of Milan. But the most decisive step towards the destruction of idolatry, was taken by Theodosius the Great, who, in 379, became emperor of the east, and was, from 392 to 395, sole ruler of the entire empire, which was then united for the last time. He forbade those sacrifices of animals, which were slain that from their entrails might be learned the secrets of futurity; and he permitted, chiefly at the instigation of religious men, that many temples of the gods should be destroyed. It was in vain that Libanius addressed to him his discourse in defence of the temples, and of the religious practices of the people in the villages. At Alexandria, the pagans, by an insurrection in which blood was shed, gave occasion to the destruction of the Serapeum and their other temples. In 392 an edict appeared, which interdicted the sacrifices and idolatrous worship, in all its branches, by threats of the severest punishment. Arcadius and Honorius, the sons of Theodosius, followed the example of their father. In 399, Honorius commanded the destruction of all the temples which still remained in the country. Those which were in the cities were allowed to stand, as works of art and as public ornaments. In the east, Theodosius the younger expressed himself, in an edict of the year 423, as if he doubted the existence of any idolaters in his empire; but long after his time their number was still considerable: hence were the laws against their religious rites from time to time renewed, and in 529 and 534, Justinian sent forth edicts, threatening the punishment of death to all who should practise these rites. Many remnants of paganism, however, were found in the manners and public life of the people: the exhibitions of gladiators were not discontinued until the year 404, when the hermit Telemachus was murdered, as he endeavoured to prevent them: the Lupercalia were celebrated as late as 495; and their suppression, when at length it was completed, was a subject of great discontent to many of the Roman nobles and senators.

SECTION II.

CONTROVERSIES WITH THE PAGANS—THE CHRISTIAN APOLOGISTS.*

THE emperor Julian wrote a long, a bitter, and an empassioned work, filled with misrepresentations against the Christian religion. The contents of this work we learn from the refutation which was written by St. Cyril of Alexandria. The imperial controvertist ridiculed the books of the Old Testament, which, he said, were composed of fables, and of representations of the Deity unworthy of his divine nature : he discovered that Jesus Christ had performed no wonderful or great works, and that he was first deified by John the Baptist. He asserted that the first Christians had been the most wicked of men, and that those of his own days were but little better : he opposed the universal dominion of the Romans, and the splendid literature of the Greeks, as the fruits of polytheism, to the sterility and weakness of Christianity. It is probable that about the same time was published the *Dialogue* of Philopater, written in the style of Lucian, against the doctrine of the trinity. But the great barrier of paganism was the Platonic-Pythagorean school of philosophy, which held its chief seats at Athens and at Alexandria, until it fell away in the latter place in the fifth century, and was destroyd in the former in the sixth, by the emperor Justinian. Its doctrines, which had been ennobled by the admixture of Christian elements, constituted the

---

* Cyrillus Alex. contra Julianum Lib x ;—Lactantii Opera, ed. Lebrun et Langlet, Dufresnoy, Paris, 1733, 2 vols 4to.;—Jul. Firm Maternus, De Errore Prof. Relig. Lug. Bat. 1709 ;—Euseb Cæsareens, Præparatio Evangelica, et Ejusdem, Demonstratio Evangelica, Colon. 1688, fol.;—Athanasii Opera, ed Montfaucon, Paris, 1698 , Augustinus, De Civitate Dei , Theodoreti, Græc. Affectuum Curatio, opp ed Schulze, tom iv., Zachæi Christiani et Apollonii Philosophi Consultatio, apud D'Achery, Spicileg. tom. i

faith of the most learned heathens of the age. Rejecting the ancient, absurd system of polytheism, they admitted the unity of the Supreme Being, the first great principle of all things. The gods, the genii, the demons, and the heroes, merited, as these philosophers taught, divine honours, although they stood far beneath the most high God, and performed the office of mediators between God and mortals. The Greek fables, and the whole of the Greek mythology, were to be considered as allegorical veils, beneath which secret doctrines and profound significations were concealed. Even the ancient heathen doctrine of fate was repudiated by these philosophers, and the precepts of morality were multiplied and made more pure by the adoption of Christian principles. Thus arose a system of religion, which was embraced by many, composed of heathen and Christian constituents, as may be seen in the writings of Ammianus Marcellinus, and of Chalcidius. Others, on the contrary, such as Libanius and Eunapius, persevered in the most bitter animosity against the Christians and their religion. The most frequent objections of these heathens against Christianity were, on the one side, the honour, or as they named it, the idolatry, which was offered to the martyrs and their relics; in comparison with which, the respect which they paid to their heroes and demons was much more noble and proper: on the other side they objected the misery of the times, the decay and consequent weakness of the Roman empire, which was deserted by the gods, as soon as the worship of Christ had been permitted to enter. To many Gentiles of this age, a God appearing in the form of a servant, and expiring on a cross, was a stumbling block over which they could not pass. Some contrasted the immoral lives of many Christians to their pretended morality—others declared that a difference in the forms of religion was necessary for the prosperity of religion: hence God concealed himself from men, and hence also those acted more according to reason, who remained in the religion in which they had been born.

During the fourth and fifth centuries many works of different writers appeared in the defence of Christianity, and in the exposition of the errors of Paganism. About the year 320, Lactantius wrote his *Divine Institutions*, and Eusebius of Cæsarea his *Evangelical Preparation*, and *Evangelical Demonstration*. Some years later St. Athanasius edited his two Treatises against the Gentiles, and on the Incarnation of the Word. In 345, Firmicus Maternus endeavoured to excite the emperors to the destruction of paganism, by presenting to them an awful picture of the crimes and immoralities of the idolaters: towards the close of the same year, St. Augustine, incited by the complaints of the pagans, that all the miseries of the age were to be attributed to Christianity, composed his great work, *On the City of God.* St. Cyril, of Jerusalem, soon after refuted the work of the emperor Julian; and lastly, in the year 430, Theodoret published his *Remedy for the Errors of Heathenism.*

CHAPTER THE SECOND.

THE CHURCH BEYOND THE ROMAN EMPIRE AMONGST THE GERMANS IN THE BRITISH ISLES· MUHAMMEDANISM.*

SECTION I.—CHRISTIANITY IN THE EAST AND AMONGST THE GERMANS.

THE people of Armenia,—the first who, as a nation, embraced the faith of Christ,—were indebted for their conversion to the zeal of St. Gregory the Illuminator, who was descended from the family of the Armenian kings, and was educated in Cappadocia. He returned to his native land towards the end of the third century, where, after a long imprisonment, he preached the Christian religion to his countrymen, and in a short time converted the king Tiridates, and the greater part of the nation. In 302, he was consecrated, at Cæsarea, metropolitan of Armenia, by the bishop Leonteus. With the assistance of Greek and Syrian priests, he continued the conversion of the people, and fully established ecclesiastical order and discipline. But internal wars impeded the progress of religion. Some adhered obstinately to their ancient idolatry—others fell back from Christianity; and when the Persians, invited by treacherous Armenians, overran a large portion of the country in 368, destruction threatened

---

* Agathangeli Acta S. Gregorii in Actis SS. Septbr. VIII. 321-400; Mosis Choroenensis Hist. Arm. ed. G. et W Whiston, Arm et Lat Lond. 1736, History of Armenia, by F. Chamich, translated by J. Audall, Calcutta, 1827; Lebeau, Hist. du Bas Empire, rev corr et augmentée d'après les historiens Orientaux, par M. de St. Martin, Paris, 1824-34, Acta Martyrum Orientalium ed. St Evod. Assemanus, Rome, 1748, Joh. Sim Assemani, Bibliotheca Orientalis, Romæ, 1726, fol. tom. II. III.

to root up the newly implanted religion. It was not however, destroyed; but the total dependence of Armenia, as a province of Persia, from the year 390, and more particularly from the year 429, gave to the Persians every opportunity of oppressing the Christian religion, and of introducing in its place the Persian fire-worship. Jezdedscherd II, in 450, commanded the people of Armenia to receive the religion and the rites of Persia. Seven hundred magi were sent into the country, with orders to raze to the earth all the churches that they should find there, or to convert them into fire-temples. The Christians opposed force to force; but the superior power of their enemies prevailed: many suffered the death of martyrs, and the nation obtained in the struggle the free exercise of the Christian religion. Repeated oppressions and repeated persecutions, in 482 and 497, provoked repeated resistance; and in 564, the attempt of the Persians to force upon the Christians the doctrines of Zoroaster produced a bloody war, during which Armenia was for years laid desolate. In the year 428, the Armenians received from the diligent zeal of their great patriarch, the holy Sahag, and of his friend the holy Mesrob, who formed the Armenian alphabet, a faithful translation of the holy Scriptures.

Christianity advanced, also, about the same time, amongst the people living north of Armenia, in the vallies of the Caucasus. As early as 326, the Faith of Christ was made known to the Iberians by a Christian female: from them the faith was transmitted to the Albanians, and to other tribes dwelling near them. The Lazi, the Tzanni, and the Albasgi, received the gospel through their connexion with the eastern parts of the Roman empire.

The Christian religion had made great progress in the Persian empire, in the middle of the fourth century, particularly amongst the numerous Syrian tribes in the extreme provinces; when the religious hatred of the fire-worshippers, and political animosity, which accused the Christians of a treasonable alliance with the eastern

Romans, raised a most cruel persecution. In the year 343, the primate of the Persian Church, Simeon Barsaboe, archbishop of Ctesiphon and Seleucia, and one hundred other bishops and priests, were, by command of King Sapor, put to death;* and on the same day which witnessed the sufferings and triumph of these martyrs, a royal edict condemned to the same punishment, all Christians, without distinction of rank or sex. This edict was afterwards made to affect more especially the clergy, the monks and nuns; and yet the number of those who suffered, whose names were known, amounted, according to Sozomen, to sixteen thousand. Apostate Christians were made the executioners of their more holy brethren. Sciadustes and Barbuscemin, the immediate successors of the blessed Simeon, with many other ecclesiastics and virgins, suffered death. The Church of Seleucia was left, for twenty years after their martyrdom, without a chief pastor. When the persecution had continued, with some intermissions, for thirty-six years, it was renewed, in 379, with redoubled violence, by an edict which threatened all Christians, without exception, with the most cruel torments and the most painful deaths. "It is folly," said the edict, "to desire to have any other religion than that of the great king." The repose which the Christians enjoyed, by the indulgence of Jezdedscherd, was broken in 418 by the indiscreet zeal of Abdas, bishop of Susa, who destroyed a fire temple, an action which cost him his life, and was the cause of new severities against the faithful. During the reign of Bahram V, the persecution again burst forth, and for thirty years the Christians were subjected to the most awful tortures which refined cruelty could devise. Amongst other sufferers, Jacob, one of the principal courtiers of the monarch, was condemned to have his body cut in pieces, under which suffering he lived in anguish for many days. Under Jezdedscherd II, the persecution

---

* See the account of this martyrdom in Alban Butler's *Lives of the Saints*, April 17

continued, until the year 450. Soon after this period the Nestorians, with the assistance of the idolaters, made themselves masters of the Church in Persia ; and, as no connexion between them and the Greeks was apprehended, they obtained, from the pagan rulers of the country, protection and security.

In Abyssinia or Axumitic Ethiopia, a youth of Tyre, named Frumentius, opened the way for the introduction of Christianity. In 326, Frumentius went to Alexandria to inform St. Athanasius of the success which had attended his first efforts : the holy patriarch consecrated him the first bishop of the Ethiopians, and sent him back to complete the work which he had so happily commenced. He fixed his see in the capital city, Axuma ; he baptized the king Aizana, and in a short time converted to the faith the greater part of his subjects. The Church of Abyssinia continued in a state of subjection to the Church of Alexandria : it received ordinarily its metropolitans from the patriarch, and at a late period fell with its parent into the heresy of the Monophysites. The Nubians and the Blemians, in the sixth century, embraced Christianity, deformed, indeed, by the same heresy : their Church was also a filiation of the Church of Alexandria ; in the tenth century it ceased to exist, but the Church of Abyssinia continued through succeeding ages.

In southern Arabia, in the kingdom of the Hamdscharen, or Homerites, the faith was planted by Theophilus, who had been sent thither by the emperor Constantius ; it was prevented from extending over the whole country only by the number and power of the Jews. At the beginning of the sixth century the Homerites were governed by a Jewish king, named Dunaan, who exerted himself unceasingly to extirpate Christianity ; and after the capture of the almost entirely Christian city Megran, in 523, he put to death, either by burning or decapitation, more than four thousand of its Christian inhabitants. The Abyssinian king, Elesbaan, marched to the assistance of his brethren in the faith : he engaged and defeated the Jews under Damaan, in

Jemen. From that period Christian sovereigns ruled in Jemen, until it was compelled to surrender, first to the arms of the Persians, and later to the power of Muhammed. The Homeritic Church, although its founder Theophilus was an Arian, either did not adopt his heresy, or soon abandoned it; but during the Persian domination, and by the influence of the Persian Nestorians, Nestorianism insinuated itself and poisoned its faith. In the central and northern provinces of Arabia, particular tribes had received the Christian religion as early as the fourth and fifth centuries; and Hira, which was situated to the south-west of Babylon, had its own Christian kings.

On the coasts of India there were, in the fourth century, Christian communities, founded by Persians, and composed chiefly of Persian Christians, although the tradition of the country takes back the foundation of its Church to the apostle St. Thomas. These provinces received Christianity as it was delivered to them by their Persian Nestorian instructors. Even in China, there existed Christian Churches in the seventh century. Of the introduction of Christianity, or rather of Nestorianism, into China, we are informed by an inscription written in the Chinese and Syriac languages, which was found in 1625, near Siganfu, in the Chinese province Ehen-Si. The monument, on which this inscription was discovered, was erected in the year 781, in the time of the Nestorian patriarch Ananjesu, by Jezdbwzid, priest and chorepiscopus, at Chumdar, the capital of the Chinese kingdom, who was the son of a priest, who had come from Balch, in Tocharistan, a part of Turchestan. It relates that, in 636, a preacher of the gospel, Olopuen, (in Syriac Saballah) brought from Ta-Thsin, that is the Roman empire, the true doctrines and the holy books in which these doctrines were contained, to China: the emperor who then reigned, in the year 639, received these doctrines with joy, and commanded a church to be built. Under the protection of the succeeding emperor, Christianity made rapid advances, until the Bonzas exerted all their power, from

PERIOD THE SECOND. 15

the year 699 to 713, to degrade and to destroy it; but in the year 719 this persecution ceased, through the favour of the emperor Ivensunchi, and the priests, John and Kielie, restored the Church and the fear of God. The emperor placed statues of his five predecessors in the church, and his successor ordered many other churches to be erected. This history of Christianity in China is contained in the Chinese portion of the inscription: the Syriac part mentions the names of seventy persons who preached the faith of Christ in China after the year 636.*

The religion of the ancient Germans was a simple and rude worship of nature and of the stars: together with the sun and the moon, trees, rivers, fountains, rocks, hills, and vallies, were the objects and scenes of their adoration. They practised augury, and pretended to foretell coming events by the flight of birds. In sacrifice they offered their first fruits, they immolated to their gods animals, and more especially horses. They offered also human victims, particularly captives and malefactors, and the execution of the latter was esteemed by them a sacred act of religion. The most general veneration was given to those deities whose names have been preserved in designating the days of the week—of Wodan, in whose honour *Wednesday* was dedicated; of Thor, the god of thunder, who gave his name to *Thursday;* and Freia, or Hertha, the mother of the earth, whose memory was recorded in *Friday.*

The Goths were the first of the Germans who surrendered themselves to the Christian religion. Sprung from the distant Scandinavian north, they

---

* For a full description of this monument, see Kircher's China Illustrata; Renaudot, Anciennes Relations des Indes et de la Chine, Paris, 1718; Assemani, Biblioth. Orient. III. p II. 538; Déguigne's Essay on the Christians in China in the Seventh Century, 1769. The genuineness of this document, although formerly much disputed, cannot, as S. Martin (Lebeau VI. 69) remarks, now be questioned. Had it been, as it was asserted to have been, a forgery of the Jesuits. we must say that the Jesuits, in 1630, possessed a knowledge of the Nestorian Church of Persia, which none of their contemporaries possessed, and which only a few since that period have obtained.

appeared about the year 215, on the left bank of the Danube. In their predatory excursions into the Roman provinces, they seized and carried away captive some Roman Christian subjects, by whom they were subjected, in turn, to the faith of Christ. At the council of Nice, we find, amongst the assembled fathers, a bishop of the Goths named Theophilus. But by their connexion with the Arian emperor Valens, in 375, the western Goths, under Fridigern, adopted the Arian heresy, in its mitigated form. Their bishop, Ulfilas, who was by descent a Cappadocian, and who had been led to Arianism in the court of the emperor, gave them an alphabet formed from the Greek model, and soon after a translation of the Scriptures. In the meantime, however, many of the Goths continued true to the Catholic faith, or were converted from idolatry; some persevered in the religion of their fathers; and the west-Gothic chieftain, Athanaric, persecuted his Christian subjects. From the western Goths Arian Christianity extended to the east Goths, and to the Gepidi, and from them to the Alans, to the Vandals, and to the Suevi. When the German tribes formed new states in the western provinces of the Roman empire, they treated the religion of the Romans, whom they conquered, with respect and honour: the Vandals and some of the west Gothic kings formed the only exception to this practice. The east Goths, in their expeditions into Italy, took with them their Arian errors, but during the entire period of their rule in Italy, from 486 to 525, the Italians adhered steadfastly to their faith. Theodoric was wise enough, during the whole of his long and celebrated reign of thirty-six years, to respect, and even to defend, the Church of his Catholic subjects.

The Burgundians, who, in 411, settled in the Roman provinces of higher Germany, were Catholics, until their king, Gundebald, the ruler of a powerful kingdom on the banks of the Rhone and Saone, introduced Arianism amongst them, about the year 490. A conference on religious subjects, which was held in the year 500, between the Catholic bishops and Arians, led to no beneficial results; but Gundebald, induced by the persuasion of Avitus, bishop of Vienne, returned in heart, though fear withheld him from a public profession, to the Catholic faith, and in 517, his son, Sigismund, re-established the same throughout his dominions.

The Suevi, under their heathen king, Rechila, who died in 448, founded a kingdom in Spain. Rechiar, the successor of Rechila, was a Catholic; but, in 496, Remismund propagated Arianism, which continued to flourish until 560; when Theodemir, whose son had been healed by the prayers of St. Martin of Tours, brought back the Suevi to the faith of the Church. In the year 585 the kingdom of the Suevi was united to that of the West-Goths, as in 534. Burgundia had been joined to the kingdom of the Franks. The West-Goths had subjected to their power the southern provinces of Gaul; but when in 470 their Arian king, Eurich, oppressed the Catholics, and persecuted the clergy, they lost their Gallic possessions, which were regained from them by the Franks. In Spain the Gothic monarchs left the Church in its liberty, until Hermenegild, the son of Leowigild, embraced the Catholic faith, in 578, and opposed himself in arms to the violence of his father. He was conquered; and as he refused, with the greatest constancy, to return to the errors which he had abandoned, he was condemned to death.* Leowigild sought to amalgamate the faith of the Catholics and Arians, and persecuted those Catholic bishops and priests who resisted his designs. His son, Reccared, participated in the opinions of his martyred brother. When he ascended the throne, he publicly professed his belief in the Catholic faith, and induced the greater part of his subjects, and many heretical bishops, to renounce the errors of the Arians. In 589, he assembled a national synod at Toledo, to secure the firm establishment of the Catholic religion in his kingdom.

---

* The Church commemorates his martyrdom on the 13th of April.

Different was the conduct of the Vandals, who having acquired possession of the Roman province of northern Africa, in 455, governed it as the most bitter and most cruel enemies of the Catholics. Under Geiserich the Catholics were deprived of their churches —their bishops were banished—some were tortured even unto death; but under his son and successor, Huneric, (477-484) the severity of the persecution became more intense; he caused 4,976 of the faithful to be transported to the most desolate of the sand desarts, where many of them languished and died. In 484, he procured a conference between Catholic and Arian bishops, the only effect of which was to afford him another pretext for proceedings of cruelty. Three hundred and forty-eight bishops were exiled, of whom many died under the harsh treatment that was inflicted on them: a vast multitude of ecclesiastics and laics, men and women, were cruelly mutilated or executed; to others, Arian baptism was administered by force. Some Catholics, at Tipasa, suffered the loss of their tongues, but miraculously recovered the faculty of speech. King Guntamund (485-496) showed great leniency towards the Catholics; but Thrasamund, who succeeded him, (496-523) wished to constitute Arianism again as the dominant religion: he drove the Catholics from their churches, banished one hundred-and-twenty bishops, and forbade the consecration of others. Kilderich, who had been compelled by Thrasamund to declare upon oath, that when king he would not recall the banished bishops or open the churches, performed these acts of humanity and justice before he took formal possession of the throne. Under Gilamer, the Vandal kingdom of the Eastern Romans was destroyed, and the Catholic Church in Africa was left in full liberty until the end of the seventh century. When the inroads of infidel Arabs laid the north of Africa waste, Christianity also was swept away before them.

The Lombards, who, from the year 568, ravaged the greater part of Italy, were chiefly Arians. but the oppressions under which the Italians suffered, during their sway, appear to have had no foundation in a difference of religion. Theodelinda, the daughter of the Duke of Bavaria, who went into Italy to be espoused to king Anthasis, was the means of propagating the true faith amongst many of the Lombards; and the kings, Agilulf, Aripert, and Grimvald, succeeded in banishing Arianism for ever from their dominions.

Thus the Franks were the only Germanic family that preserved the faith inviolate as they had received it. The Salic Franks had established themselves in the northern parts of the Roman Gaul. Their chieftain, Clovis, was baptised in 496, by Remigius, bishop of Rheims, in fulfilment of a vow which he had made in a battle with the Alemanni; with him three thousand Franks declared themselves Christians. His conversion gained for him the friendship of the Roman Gauls, and of those who were subjected to the Arian West-Goths and Burgundians. He was enabled to extend his power over nearly the whole of Gaul, and at his death, in 511, he left to his sons an extensive and a powerful kingdom.

SECTION II.

CHRISTIANITY IN THE BRITISH ISLES.—INTRODUCTION OF CHRISTIANITY INTO IRELAND.—SAINT PATRICK.—SAINT COLUMBA, THE APOSTLE OF THE PICTS.—THE IRISH CHURCH.*

EVEN before the mission of Palladius to Ireland, it is probable that Christian communities had been founded

---

* S. Patricii, Opuscula, ed. Jac. Waræus, Lond. 1658.—Confession of S. Patrick in Actis SS. Mart. ii. 517; and in a shorter form in W. Betham's Irish Antiquarian Researches, Dublin, 1826.—Probi (an Irishman of the 10th century) Vita S. Patricii, in Bedæ opp. ed. Basil. 1563, and in Colgan's Tria Thaumaturga (Patricius, Brigida, Columba) Lovan 1647. The Tripartita (a Life of St. Patrick translated from Irish into Latin, also of the 10th century) in Colgan's Tria Thaum. Of less value, and of a later period, are the Lives II. III. IV. in Colgan's

on the island: for between Ireland and Gaul there existed a considerable commerce; and we know from Tacitus, that the ports of Ireland were better known, and more frequented by merchants, than those of Britain. We may suppose also that the Irish may have become acquainted with the doctrines of the Christian religion by means of the many captives, whom, in their expeditions of plunder, they bore away from the British and Gallic shores. Cœlestius, the companion of the heretic Pelagius, was, as we learn from St. Jerome, an Irishman (Scotus). This beginning of Christianity in Ireland attracted the attention of Pope Celestine, who consecrated the Roman deacon Palladius, and sent him from Rome in 431, as first bishop of the Irish.* So great was the success that attended the new bishop, that Prosper could venture to say, that by the care of Celestine, Ireland had become a Christian country.† Intimidated, however, by threats of the infidels, Palladius left the island and died in Britain. The entire conversion of Ireland was reserved for St. Patrick, for, according to the ancient Irish proverb, "Not to Palladius but to Patrick did God give the Irish."

St. Patrick was born in the year 387, and, according to his own account, at Bonavem Tavernirae, that is, at Boulogne, on the coast of Picardy,‡ which was then

---

and Jocelin's Vita S. Patricii.—Cuminei Vita S. Columbæ in Mabillon; Acta SS. Bened. Adamnani, Vita S. Columbæ in Messingham's Florileg. Insulæ Sanctorum. Jac. Usseri, Britannicarum Ecclesiarum Antiquitates, Dublin, 1639, Lond. 1687; John Lanigan, Ecclesiastical History of Ireland, 2nd edit. Dublin, 1829, 4 vols.

* "Ad Scotos in Christum credentes ordinatus a Papa Cælestino Palladius primus episcopus mittitur."—Prosperi Chron. ad annum 431.

† "Ordinato Scotis episcopo, dum Romanam insulam (Britanniam) studet servare catholicam, fecit etiam Barbaram Christianam," says Prosper, de Gratia Christi, speaking of Pope Celestine, c. 41.

‡ Not at Kilpatrick in North Britain, as it has been generally supposed since the time of Usher. Bonavem, in the Celtic language, is the Latin Bononia, and the adjunct Taverniæ designates the *regio Tai bannensis* (Tarabanna, or Tarvenna, the same as Terouanne) where Bononia was situated. See Lanigan, i. 93. If St. Patrick is frequently called a Briton, (Britannus) we are not to suppose that it is

named Armorica. His father, Calpurnius, was a deacon, his grandfather, Potitus, a priest. At the age of sixteen, he was seized by an Irish chieftain, who had made a descent upon the coast, and by him was taken away captive to Ireland. There he was doomed to tend the flocks and herds of his master. In his solitude, sentiments of repentance for the offences of his youth, and deep feelings of devotion, were awakened within him. After six years of bondage, he found the means of escape, and returned to his native Gaul. He retired to Tours, and in the school and cloister of the holy bishop, St. Martin, he applied himself during four years to acquire true Christian knowledge and perfection. From Tours he went back to his parents, and whilst in the house of his father received, in a vision of the night, the first call to his mission in Ireland. He did not, however, immediately follow this call, but visited, in the year 418, the newly ordained bishop of Auxerre, St. Germanus, who sent him, for his further improvement, to a cloister-school, probably to that on the island of Lerins. Thence he returned to St. Germanus; and in the year 431, by his command, and in company of a priest, whom the bishop sent to bear witness to his great merit, he travelled to Rome.* There he received the benediction of Pope Celestine, and full powers to preach the gospel in Ireland. On his journey from Rome, he heard of the death of Palladius; and as the Irish mission was now in need of a bishop, he received the episcopal consecration at Eboria, the ancient name of Evreux.

---

intended to signify that he was a native of the British island, for the inhabitants of the country round Boulogne, were called Britanni as early as the days of Pliny.

* The journey of St. Patrick to Rome is mentioned not only by Probus and other biographers, but also by Hericus, Vita S. Germ. i 12. (in Actis Sanctorum, Julii, t. vii.) Hericus however wrote about the year 860. But as the Book of Armagh, and the Life of St. Patrick, contained therein, were written by the blessed Aidus, of Sletty, who died in 698, we have an authority for this journey in the seventh century. The silence of the Confession, in which St. Patrick relates only those circumstances in which he beheld an especial Divine Providence, cannot be adduced as an authority against this journey.

With a few companions, amongst whom Auxilius and Isserinus are particularly named, he landed in Ireland in the year 431.

He found the heathen inhabitants of the island addicted to the worship of the stars : fountains also were objects of their adoration, and as they honoured water as a beneficent deity, they considered fire as a principle of evil. The use of idols of their gods was not general; they are indeed sometimes mentioned, but they were no more than rude figures of stone. Mountains and hills were their ordinary scenes of worship. The chiefs of the religion, who in the history of St. Patrick are called Magi, appear to have practised magic and soothsaying. They were as distinct from the Druids as the religion of Ireland was different from the religion of Britain and of Gaul. The people formed two separate classes ; the ancient aborigines, who, according to the traditions of the country, were Milesians that had come from Gallicia, and the more recently arrived Scots. The former were held in subjection by the superior power of the invaders.*

St. Patrick preached before the chief king of the island, Leogaire, and the princes who were assembled around him. The first fruit of his preaching was the conversion of a famed poet, named Dubtach. The most powerful princes of the land soon listened to his words, and Corrall, a brother of the chief king, was amongst the earliest of his disciples. Many sons of chieftains, whose good will he had won by presents, followed him and shared in his apostolical labours : virgins, whom he had converted, embraced an ascetic state of life, and the number of these nuns seemed to encrease in proportion as they were persecuted by their parents.†

---

* St Patrick calls the great body of the original natives Hibenonaces, for Ireland in his writings is named Hiberione. Not only numbers of these, but many also of the ruling class, had, he says, in his Confessions, become Christians.

† " Filii Scottorum et filiæ regulorum monachi et virgines Christi esse videntur." In the letter against Coroticus, written before the

But the most celebrated and the most numerous conversion was in Connaught, where St. Patrick arrived when the seven sons of a king and a large body of people had met there in assembly: he baptized the young princes and one hundred and twenty thousand of the people in the fountain of Enardhac.* From the year 439, he was aided by the co-operation of three bishops, Secundinus, Auxilius and Isserinus, whom he had before sent to Britain or to Gaul to receive consecration. The only one of the letters of St. Patrick, which has been preserved, appears to have been written in the earlier part of his labours: it is a circular epistle against Coroticus, a British chief, and his followers, who had made a predatory descent upon the Irish coast, and had violently borne away as captives many of the natives whom St Patrick had baptized.† In this letter, he pronounces excommunication against the chief and his companions; and requests the faithful into whose hands the letter may fall, to read it in the presence of the people and even of Coroticus himself. He remarks that the Roman and Gallic Christians sent large sums of money to redeem Christian captives from the power of the Franks, whilst he, Coroticus, carried on a detestable commerce with the members of Christ, that he might sell them to heathens.

About the year 455, he erected a church upon land that had been presented to him in the district of Macha. Around this church arose the city of Ardmacha or Armagh, and as St. Patrick had there placed his see, this city became the ecclesiastical metropolis of all Ireland. Between Armagh and his beloved retreat at Saul, the holy bishop passed the remaining days of his

---

Confessions, these Scots are spoken of as persecutors of the Christians. It was not until about eighty or ninety years from this period that the appellation of Scots was given in common to all the Irish, and that the island was known by the name of Scotia. The present Scotland was not so called before the eleventh century.

* See Usseri Antiquit. ed. Dublin, p. 865.

† " De sanguine innocentium Christianorum, quos ego innumeros in Deo genui atque in Christo confirmavi, postera die qua Chrisma, neophyti in veste candida flagrabat in fronte ipsorum."

life. Never again did he think of a return to the land of his fathers, nor was he ever from Ireland for any length of time sufficient to visit his relatives. Such an absence he would have considered as a disobedience to Christ, who had commanded him to go to the Irish and to remain with them during the whole of his life.* Soon after the erection of his church, he held a synod with Auxilius and Isserinus, in which a series of canons for the regulation of the infant Church was formed. Of the bishops whom St. Patrick consecrated, some were converted natives, others were Romans, that is, foreigners from the continent, many of whom were compelled to seek an asylum in Ireland from the persecutions of the Franks, who had not yet received the faith. In the last years of his life, St. Patrick wrote his *Confessions*, in which he declares that he had visited every part of the island; that he had every where ordained priests, and tells us, that Christianity reigned amidst the greater number of the people. He died at Saul, about the year 465. His successor in the see of Armagh was his favourite disciple, Benignus, who with his whole family had been baptized by St. Patrick.†

By the prudent ordinances of St. Patrick, ecclesiastical schools and seminaries, which were named cloisters, and were under the guidance of the bishops, were established in Ireland. Some of these were founded during his life, and many more after his death. One

---

* Confess. p. 17.

† The so-called purgatory of St. Patrick does not appear to have been known before the eleventh century. Jocelin is the first who speaks of such a place of purgation, which was on the summit of the mountain Eroagh-Patrick, where the penitent fasted and watched in the hope that he should there be freed from his sins, and delivered from the pains of hell. Henry, of Saltery, an English monk of the 12th century, gives an account of another purgatory, a cave at Loughdeargh, which St Patrick placed under the care of the Canons of St. Augustin. He, it was said, who being truly sorry for his sins, should pass a day and a night in this cave, should be freed from his sins, and should behold in a vision the sufferings of the condemned and the joys of the blessed. This purgatory, which, it will be seen, had reference to the living and not to the dead, was destroyed in 1497, by order of the Pope.

of the first of these institutions was the school of the bishop Fiech of Sletty: others were formed by bishop Ailbe, by Ibar of Beg-Erin* and by Olcan at Dercan. St. Patrick had previously erected one at Armagh. Abodes of piety for females were provided by St. Briget, who towards the close of the fifth century introduced into Ireland rules for nuns, and established several nunneries in different parts of the island. Of these the largest and the most celebrated was that founded in 490, at Kildare. At the instance of St. Briget an episcopal see was formed also at the same place. The Christian religion was not yet universally established. Lugdach, who had been chief king of Ireland since 483, lived and died in idolatry. In the sixth century Christianity reigned triumphant and alone. Muchertach, who was chief king from 513 to 533 publicly professed himself a Christian.

North Britain, or, as it was named in the eleventh century, Scotland, was inhabited by the Caledonians or Picts, a people who had emigrated from Scandinavia. The southern Picts, who dwelt between the Forth and the Grampian Hills, were converted to the faith in 412, by the British bishop Ninian, who had been educated in Rome, and who on his return to North Britain remained for some time with St. Martin at Tours.† The apostle of the Northern Picts was the great St. Columba, who began to preach about 150 years later.‡ St. Columba was born in Ireland in 521. He studied in the famed school of St. Finnian of Maghbile, and founded in 546 a cloister at Tirconnel, where the city of Derry, now Londonderry, was afterwards built. In

---

* In the life of Ibar, (in Usher's Antiq. p. 1061), it is said of him, " Ad fines Langeniensium venit et australem ejus partem, ubi est litoralis parva insula, Beg-Erin, id est, parva Hibernia dicta, ubi celebre condidit cœnobium, et sacras ibidem literas, aliasque artes optimas docuit maximam multitudinem Hibernorum et aliorum.

† Beda, Hist Eccl. iii. 4. Usserii Antiquit p. 681.

‡ His first name was Crimthan, which, on account of the dove-like purity and innocence of his life, was changed into Columba He was also called Columbkill, from the number of the cloisters, *cells*, which he founded. See Bede, Eccl. Hist v. 10

550, he was ordained priest; his humility would not permit him to be raised to the episcopal dignity. Soon after his ordination he left the island, to labour in the conversion of the Northern Picts, who were still immersed in infidelity, and to reform his own countrymen, who had settled in Argyle and in the neighbouring districts. These were Christian Irish or Scots, who had emigrated into North Britain, under Loarn, the son of Erk.* St. Columba received from his relative, Corrall, King of the Alban Scots, the island of Hy, or Iona, (afterwards named Hy-Columbkill), one of the smallest of the Hebrides. He sailed thither, in 563, with twelve disciples: he built a church and a cloister, and in 565 began, with the most happy success, to announce the word of God. God confirmed his mission by miracles. He raised to life a youth, who died a few days after he and his parents had been baptized, and whose death had given to the heathen priests occasion to glory in the power of their gods over the God of the Christians.†
St. Columba did not remain always on the continent of Scotland: he frequently revisited the Hebrides, preaching to the inhabitants, particularly at Hymba, where he founded a cloister, and at Ethica, or Eig, where he or his disciples established many religious communities: he also visited these islands to defend them against the British Scots, whom he had excommunicated in punishment of their frequent incursions of plunder and devastation. Whilst he thus gave his attention to the Church of the British Scots, and erected many monasteries amongst them, he did not withdraw his zeal from those communities which he had previously established in Ireland: he from time to time sent messengers to inquire into their state, and received visits from Irish ecclesiastics and religious who came to seek his coun-

---

* These Scots possessed the country between the mouth of the Clyde and the west of the Grampian Hills. the Picts, whom St. Ninian had converted, possessed, after the arrival of these Scots, only the eastern part of Scotland, between the Frith of Forth and the Grampians.

† Adamnan. ii. 32   Cumin c. 22.

sel.* The Picts as well as the Scots held St. Columba in the highest veneration. In 590, he returned to Ire-

* Adamnan, a successor of St. Columba in the abbey of Hy, which he governed from 679 to 704, relates the following anecdote in his life of the saint "Cronan, a bishop from the Irish province of Munster, once visited St. Columba, and through humility concealed his real dignity On Sunday, St. Columba requested him to celebrate mass (*Christi Corpus ex more conficere*) He did so, and when he came to the breaking of the host, he called St. Columba to him, to perform, as a priest, that rite with him (*ut simul quasi duo presbyteri Dominicum panem frangerent*). St. Columba approached the altar, and looking upon Cronan in the face, said to him, 'Christ bless thee, my brother, do thou perform this alone, according *to the episcopal rite:* for now we know that thou art a bishop. Wherefore hast thou endeavoured to conceal thyself from us, and to prevent us from paying to thee the honour that is due to thy rank'" By *the episcopal rite* was understood the blessing which bishops gave to those who assisted at the sacrifice immediately after the breaking of the host, and before the separated particle was let to fall into the chalice From this short narration, it will appear how unfounded is the assertion that St Columba and his monks acknowledged no superiority of bishops over priests. Blumhardt, in his "History of Missions," and Munter, in his "Dissertation on the Ancient British Church" (in the Theological Studies, for 1833, p. 750), have copied this from Ledwich, Smith, and Jamieson, and what is more, they have made the monks of St. Columba to have been Culdees. Here is a manifest anachronism, for the Culdees were not known in Scotland before the ninth, nor in Ireland before the tenth, century, nor were they ever in the most distant connexion with these or with any other monks. Munter adds, that Bede speaks of bishops who were ordained by the monks of Hy, and concludes (p. 749) "The abbots themselves were only priests, and the monks could not be of a higher rank The priests therefore of Hy consecrated bishops whom they sent from their abbey." A most erroneous conclusion, for there could have been, as indeed there were, bishops amongst the monks, and that it was so at Hy, Usher has shewn (in his Antiquit p. 701) from the annals of Ulster. Bishop Aidan, whom the monks of Hy sent from their monastery to convert the pagan Saxons, after he had been consecrated amongst them, founded the abbey of Lindisfarne, on the coast of Northumberland, after the model of the abbey of Hy. Of this abbey, Bede, in his Life of St. Cuthbert, says: "Regente monasterium abbate, quem ipsi episcopi cum consilio fratrum elegerint, omnes presbyteri, diaconi, cantores, lectores, cæterique gradus ecclesiastici monachicam per omnia, *cum ipso episcopo* regulam servant." The consecration of bishops among the Scots and Britons was remarkable for this, that it was generally performed (not in accordance with the canons) by one bishop. Thus it is said in the Life of St. Kentigern, of Glasgow, "Accito de Hibernia uno episcopo, more Britonum et Scotorum in episcopum ipsum consecrari fecerunt. Mos enim in Britannia inoleverat in consecratione Pontificum, tantummodo capita

land, and assisted with Aidan, the king of the British Scots at the great council of Drumceat, which had been called by Aid, the chief king of Ireland. In this assembly it was resolved to suppress and banish the numerous order of the Irish bards, whose avarice and corruption had long been subjects of complaint. But the intercession of St. Columba in their favour was heard by the council. The bards were spared, but subjected to severe regulations, and their numbers were diminished.* The holy abbot returned to Hy, whence he directed his attention to his cloisters and churches.

---

corum sacri chrismatis infusione perungere cum invocatione S. Spiritus et benedictione et manus impositione. Insulani enim quasi extra orbem positi, emergentibus paganorum infestationibus, canonum erant ignari." See Usserii Antiq. 684. It is also related that Kentigern afterwards visited Rome; that the Pope, St. Gregory I, ratified his consecration; and was induced, though with reluctance, to supply the ceremonies that had been omitted. Giesler (Eccl. Hist. i. p.716) says that the conviction of the perfect equality of bishops and priests was general in Ireland in the twelfth century. Of this assertion, however, he brings no other proof than the words taken from a manuscript of Ecchehard, a monk of St. Gall, contained in the History of St. Gall, by Arx (i 267): " In Hibernia episcopi et presbyteri unum sunt." In the whole Irish history, from the fifth to the eleventh century, not a trace of this belief, but in every page the contrary, is to be found. It is easy to divine the cause of the monk's mistake;—it arose evidently from the great number of *chorepiscopi* in Ireland, an order which continued to exist there long after it had been abolished in every other part of the western Church. Of this, St. Bernard, in his Life of St. Malachy, complains, saying, " that in Ireland almost every Church had its bishop,"— not that the Irish considered bishops and priests to be equal in rank, which would have been more offensive to him. Lanfranc, in his account of the abuses existing in Ireland in his time (the eleventh century), speaks not of this idea of the equality of bishops and priests, but complains that bishops, chiefly chorepiscopi, were ordained by only one other bishop (see Usher, Sylloge epp. Hib. p. 50). It was therefore decreed at the Synod of Kello, in 1152, that as the chorepiscopi and the bishops of smaller places died, archpriests should be appointed to succeed them. As those chorepiscopi, who were not bishops by consecration, belonged to the order of the priests, and in name and in some of their privileges were associated with the bishops, they might thus appear to stand between the two orders. Ecchehard, who was ignorant of this class of ecclesiastics and of their station, might easily be led, by what he had heard of Ireland, into the belief, that in that country no distinction was made between bishops and priests.

* Pinkerton's " Enquiry into the History of Scotland," London, 1794; ii 114

He died in 597, at the age of seventy-six years. He expired in the church, praying with his brethren, and pronouncing over them his last and solemn benediction.

As apostle of the Northern Picts, and as founder of many Churches amongst the British Scots and on the Hebrides, St. Columba enjoyed an ecclesiastical jurisdiction which extended through these countries, and even over the bishops of the different sees within them. In respect to his memory, the same distinction was conceded to a long succession of the abbots of Hy, although they, as St. Columba had been, were only priests.* The venerable Bede names the district, which was comprehended within the jurisdiction of the abbot, a province: it included the country of the British Scots, North Pictland, the island of Hy, and the other Hebrides. In this province there were, as the words of Bede declare, several bishops: one of these was always in the island and in the cloister of Hy; the island and the nearest of the surrounding Hebrides formed his diocese. He was a monk, and as such was subject to the abbot: the other bishops, although not resident in the monastery, were likewise under his jurisdiction; a circumstance which Bede mentions as extraordinary and irregular. In the time of Bede it was a case of rare occurrence that a priest should possess jurisdiction over a bishop; in a later age examples were numerous. The successors of St. Columba exercised this power, however, not as priests but as abbots or as generals of their order.† St. Columba had given to his disciples a body of monastic laws which was numbered amongst the eight celebrated rules then followed by the religious of Ireland.

---

* "Habere autem solet ipsa insula (Hy) rectorem semper abbatem presbyterum, cujus juri et *omnis provincia* et ipsi etiam episcopi, ordine inusitato, debeant esse subjecti, juxta exemplum primi doctoris illius (Columbæ) qui non episcopus, sed presbyter extitit et monachus." Beda, Hist. Eccl. iii. 4.

† Bede, (iii. 4) after making mention of several monasteries founded by St. Columba, or which followed his rule, says; "In quibus omnibus idem monasterium Insulanum (Hy) in quo ipse requiescit corpore principatum tenet."

During the sixth and seventh centuries, the Church of Ireland stood in the full beauty of its bloom. The spirit of the gospel operated amongst the people with a vigorous and vivifying power: troops of holy men, from the highest as from the lowest ranks of society, obeyed the counsel of Christ, and forsook all things, that they might follow him. There was not a country in the world, during this period, which could boast of pious foundations or of religious communities equal to those that adorned this far-distant island. Amongst the Irish, the doctrines of the Christian religion were preserved pure and entire : the names of heresy or of schism were not known to them, and in the bishop of Rome, they acknowledged and reverenced the supreme head of the Church on earth,* and continued with him,

---

* St Columba thus describes the Irish Church in his Epistle to Pope Boniface IV. in 613. (Biblioth. PP. Max. xii. 28.) "Nos enim SS. Petri et Pauli et omnium discipulorum divinum canonem (dictante) Spiritu S. scribentium discipuli sumus, toti Heberi, ultimi habitatores mundi, nihil extra Evangelicam et apostolicam doctrinam recipientes: nullus hæreticus, nullus Judæus, nullus schismaticus fuit : sed fides Catholica, sicut a vobis primum, SS. scilicet apostolorum successoribus, tradita est, inconcussa tenetur"—(an evident proof that the mission of St. Patrick proceeded from Rome. In like manner Cummian says, in reference to the Roman rite of celebrating Easter : "Decessores nostri mandaverunt per idoneos testes, alios viventes, alios in pace dormientes, ut meliora et potiora probata a fonte baptismi nostri et sapientiæ et successoribus apostolorum Domini delata sine scrupulo humiliter sumeremus.")—"Nos enim, ut ante dixi, derincti sumus cathedræ S. Petri. Licet enim Roma magna est et vulgata, per istam cathedram tantum apud nos est magna et clara....Propter Christi geminos apostolos vos prope cælestes estis, et Roma orbis terrarum caput est ecclesiarum, salva loci Dominicæ resurrectionis singulari præerogativa." This testimony is the more remarkable as St. Columba in the same letter speaks with great freedom, or rather with great severity, of Pope Vigilius, who, as he thought, had in the fifth general Council, absolved Eutyches, Nestorius and Dioscorus. When he speaks of the particular authority of the Church of Jerusalem, he confounds the veneration which was due to that Church on account of possessing the holy scenes of our redemption, and of being the place of pilgrimage for the whole world, with its ecclesiastical authority. This was not essentially attached to the Church of Jerusalem, but only as it was one of the apostolical, patriarchal Churches of the East. Cummian, a countryman and contemporary of St. Columba, appealing to the authority of the apostolic Churches, names the Church of Jerusalem immediately after the Church Rome, and then those of Antioch and Alexandria, (Usseri. Vet. Epis-

and through him with the whole Church, in a never interrupted communion. The schools in the Irish cloisters were at this time the most celebrated in all the West; and in addition to those which have been already mentioned, there flourished the schools of St. Finian of Clonard, founded in 530, and those of St. Cataldus, founded in 640. Whilst almost the whole of Europe was desolated by war, peaceful Ireland, free from the invasions of external foes, opened to the lovers of learning and piety a welcome asylum. The strangers, who visited Ireland, not only from the neighbouring shores of Britain, but also from the most remote nations of the continent, received from the Irish people the most hospitable reception, a gratuitous entertainment, free instruction, and even the books that were necessary for

---

tolam. Hib. Sylloge, Paris, 1669.) The primacy of the Church of Rome is sufficiently designated by those words of St. Columba:— " Caput orbis terrarum Ecclesiarum." Soon after this was written, in 630, the Irish bishops sent a deputation to Rome, on occasion of the controversies relative to the celebration of Easter; for, as Cummian writes, " causæ majores *juxta decretum synodicum* ad caput urbium sint referendæ." This synodical decree to which he alludes, is the canon ascribed to St Patrick, " Si quæ quæstiones in hac insula oriantur, ad sedem apostolicam referantur." (*Patricii opuscula*). Usher, in his " Discourse on the Religion anciently professed by the Irish," gives this canon more at large, from the ancient codex of the church of Armagh. " Quæcunque causa valde difficilis exorta fuerit, atque ignota cunctis Scotorum gentium judiciis ad Cathedram archiepiscopi Hiberniensium (id est Patricii) atque hujus antistetis examinationem recte referenda. Si vero in illo cum suis sapientibus facile sanari non poterit, talis causa prædictæ negotiationis ad sedem apostolicam decrevimus esse mittendam, id est ad Petri Apostoli cathedram auctoritatem Romæ urbis habentem. Ili sunt qui de hoc decreverunt, id est, Auxilius, Patricius, Secundinus, Benignus." But, as Lanigan remarks, the canon in this form must have been drawn up after the time of St. Patrick, for the expression, "*cuncta Scotorum gentium judicia*," refers to Scottish Churches out of Ireland, which Churches did not exist until after the death of St. Patrick Irish ecclesiastics frequently in this age travelled to Rome, notwithstanding the length and the dangers of the journey: many instances may be found in Usher, as that (p. 920) of the abbot Dagan, who took to Rome the rule of St. Molua, to submit it to the pope, St Gregory the Great. Giraldus Cambrensis also, in his Life of St. David (in Wharton's Anglia Sacra, ii. 365), says: " Mos erat illis diebus Hybernensibus Romam peregre proficiscendo, apostolorum limina præ locis omnibus magis frequenta devoto labore visitare."

their studies.* Thus in the year 536, in the time of St. Senanus, there arrived at Cork from the continent, fifteen monks, who were led thither by their desire to perfect themselves in the practices of an ascetic life under Irish directors, and to study the sacred Scriptures in the school established near Cork † At a later period, after the year 650, the Anglo-Saxons in particular passed over to Ireland in great numbers for the same laudable purposes. On the other hand, many holy and learned Irishmen left their own country to proclaim the faith, to establish or to reform monasteries in distant lands, and thus to become the benefactors of almost every nation of Europe.

Of the greatest utility in acquiring a true knowledge of the ancient Irish Church is the catalogue published by Usher,‡ of the Irish saints. This catalogue was probably not fully compiled at the time of the controversies respecting the Easter cycle and the form of the ecclesiastical tonsure, perhaps not before the end of the seventh, or the beginning of the eighth century. In it the Irish saints are ranged in three classes, according to the ages in which they lived. The first class is of those who lived from the coming of St. Patrick in 432, to the year 542, and to it belong 350 bishops or founders of Churches, " for all the Irish bishops were then holy and filled with the spirit of God."§ Being united under their one head, Jesus Christ, they all observed the discipline which had been introduced by St. Patrick; they all used the same liturgy, one form of the tonsure, and one Easter cycle. They did not en-

---

* " Quos omnes Scoti libentissime suscipientes, victum eis quotidianum sine pretio, libros quoque ad legendum et magisterium gratuitum præbere curabant." Beda, Hist Eccl. iii. 27. Bede mentions, amongst others, Agilbert, a Frank, who dwelt for a long time in Ireland, " to study the holy Scriptures."—iii. 7.

† Vita S. Senani, c. 20, in Actis SS. Bolland. 8 Martii. They are designated as "monachi patria Romani."

‡ Antiquit p. 913, et seq, with an explanation of the catalogue, extending through fifty-seven pages.

§ If this number appear too great, we must include the chorepiscopi, of whom there were so many in Ireland.

tirely separate themselves from society with females, but as they confided in the grace of Christ for strength to withstand temptation, they permitted the services of women in their household.* They were all Romans, (that is, descendants from the inhabitants of the former Roman provinces, as were St. Patrick and those companions of Palladius who remained in Ireland), or Franks, Britons or Scots. Of the second class of saints, which comprehends those who lived from 540 to 598, and which comprises three hundred persons, the smaller number is of bishops, the greater of priests, probably abbots and monks, as during this period the monasteries of Ireland flourished in all their splendour. They all observed the same time in the celebration of Easter, and bore tonsures of the same form: but the liturgies

---

* We may here shew the falsity of the assertions recently made, that in Ireland both bishops and priests were married. An example of a married priest or bishop in Ireland, down to the time of the English invasion, cannot be shewn. The allusion to the grandfather of St. Patrick, who was a priest (Giesler, Eccl. Hist. i. 715), cannot have been seriously intended; for there have been thousands of priests and bishops in the church, who have had sons before their ordination. To learn how severely celibacy was enforced among the Irish clergy, see the *Pœnitentiale* of the Irish abbot Cummian, in the Bibliot. Max PP. xii. 42: " Si clericus aut monachus postquam se Deo voverit ad sæcularem habitum reversus fuerit, aut uxorem duxerit, decem annis pœniteat, tribus ex his in pane et aqua et nunquam postea in conjugio copuletur. Quod si noluerit, S. Synodus vel sedes apostolica separavit eos a communione et convocationibus Catholicorum." Persons who were married before their ordination, were bound to live a life of chastity. See the 20th canon in the " liber de pœnitentiarum mensura taxanda" of St Columba, in the Bibliot. Max. PP. xii. 21. To the same intent is the 12th canon of the *Pœnitentiale*, which was found with a missal at Bobbio (Mabillon, Museum Italicum, tom. i.), and which most probably came from Ireland. When, therefore, in the 6th canon of the so-called Synod of Patrick, Auxilius and Isserinus, mention is made of the wives of clerics, we are to understand only the inferior clerics ("quicunque clericus ab ostiario ad sacerdotem sine tunica visus fuerit, &c., et uxor ejus, si non velato capite ambulaverit, pariter," &c.) Lanfranc knew nothing of married priests in Ireland, or certainly he would not have omitted them in his account of abuses prevalent in that country. The married bishops of the twelfth century, to whom Giesler alludes, were laymen without any orders, who, being descended from noble and powerful families, had, contrary to all law and right, intruded themselves into the see of Armagh. St Bernard, in his Life of St Malachy, calls them, *uni uxorati et absque ordinibus, literati tamen*

and the rules of their monasteries were different. They adopted liturgies from the Britons, David and Cadoc. Entrance into their cloisters was strictly prohibited to all females.* To them belonged, among other great saints, Finnian, the chief of the school at Clonard; Finnian, bishop and abbot of Maghbile; Brendan, founder of the great abbey of Clonfert; Jarlarth, first bishop of Tuam; and Kieran, founder of the cloister of Clonmacnois, who is numbered amongst the fathers of the Irish Church,† and whose rule was introduced into many communities; and Cirngall, who in 559 erected the famed abbey of Banchor, near the Bay of Carrickfergus, and under whose guidance three thousand monks lived in different monasteries. Amongst these was Connar, king of South Leinster, who passed the last years of his life in the abbey of Banchor.

The third class of saints consisted of priests and of a few bishops, in number about one hundred persons. They dwelt in solitudes and lived upon herbs and water, or upon what they received in charity. They possessed nothing in private; they followed different rules and liturgies: their tonsures were of different forms, some having them in the form of a *crown*, whilst others were unshorn. In the celebration of Easter, also, they varied from each other; for while one party solemnized the festival on the fourteenth day of the moon, the other adhered to the sixteenth day. They lived during the reigns of four dynasties, down to the period of the great mortality, (from 605 to 665). Amongst the bishops was the celebrated Ædan or Maidoc, who built a monastery on land which had been given to him by King Brandubh at Ferns, and finally became bishop of the small town which rose around the monastery. Here, in 599, a synod was called by the influence of the king, and Ferns was raised by it to the rank of the archiepiscopal see of Leinster. But in Ireland, the archbishops, with the exception of the primate of

---

* This prohibition was enforced by St. Senan in the cloister at Inniscatty, by Carthag in Lismore, by Molua, Fechin, and others

† Alcuin ranks him with St. Patrick as " Scottorum gloria gentis."

Armagh, possessed no jurisdiction over their suffragan prelates: theirs was no more than a distinction of honour. Until the commencement of the twelfth century, Armagh was the only real metropolitan Church in Ireland.

SECTION III.

THE BRITISH CHURCH.—CONVERSION OF THE ANGLO-SAXONS.—THE FIRST AGES OF THE ANGLO-SAXON CHURCH.*

MELANCHOLY is the contrast with the flourishing condition of the Irish Church that is presented to us by the state of decay and oppression, in which at this period we find the Church of Britain. The devout Gildas has left to us a strongly coloured picture of the degeneracy and corruption of the people, and of the disgraceful lives of the clergy in the first half of the sixth century: he tells us that amongst the latter there were many avaricious and wicked men, priests, who seldom offered the adorable sacrifice; who seldom stood before the holy altars with pure hearts; who visited their churches only for the sake of lucre; and who, by the viciousness of their lives, gave to the people the worst of examples: that amongst the bishops there were many worldly-minded men, who disgraced and disturbed the Churches which they were appointed to rule. Severe, but not unmerited, was the judgment that was inflicted upon the Britons and their Church, first by the swords of the Picts and Scots, and later by

---

* Gildæ Sapientis Epistola, in Gale's Scriptores Histor Britann Oxon 1691, tom 1.; Bedæ Vener. Eccl. Hist. Gentis Anglorum, ed. J. Smith, Cantab. 1722; The Saxon Chronicle, with a translation, by J. Ingram, London, 1823-4; Eddii Vita S. Wilfridi, Ep Eborac. in Gale's Scriptores, i 40 et seqq

J. Lingard, Antiquities of the Anglo-Saxon Church, Newcastle, 1806, 2 vols

the desolating incursions and heavy yoke of the pagan Saxons and Angles. There were, however, amongst them virtuous men who endeavoured to stem this torrent of corruption. In this number was the holy David, who about the year 540, was bishop of Menevia and metropolitan of the Cambrian Church. The dignity of metropolitan had been hitherto attached to the see of Caerleon (Legio), but had been transferred to Menevia by the synod of Brevy.* Menevia was afterwards named St. David's, in honour of the saint. The see of Landaff, however, never acknowledged the superiority of the new metropolitan Church: its bishops resisted its authority, and one of them, Oudoceus, was consecrated with the consent of king Mouric of Glamorgan, by St. Augustin, archbishop of Canterbury. His successors continued to follow his example,† by being consecrated by the English metropolitan.

Contemporary with St. David was Gildas,‡ the severe censurer of his countrymen, and of his brother priests. He visited many of the schools of Ireland, and in 517 returned to Britain, where he composed in solitude the few short writings which have come down to our times. His friend Cadoc, a relative of St. David, founded a monastery and school, at which Gildas for a long time taught, at Lancarvan.§

---

* Giraldus, in his Life of St David (Usserii Antiq. p. 475), mentions two synods of the British clergy at which St. David assisted, that of Brevy, and another which he calls Victoria; and adds: "Ex his duobus synodis omnes Cambriæ totius ecclesiæ modum et regulam, ecclesia quoque Romana authoritatem adhibente et confirmante, susceperunt."

† Wilkins, Concilia Brit. i. 17. Usserii Antiq. p. 85.

‡ Usher, and many others after him, have erroneously supposed that there were two writers at this period of the name of Gildas, one named Albanius, the other Badonicus. Of these, one is placed at too early, the other at too late, a period. Gildas, according to his own account, was born in the year of the great massacre, at Bath; that is, as Bede assures us, in the year 493. See Lanigan, i. 477, et seq.

§ To the few monuments that have remained to us of the ancient British Church, belongs an account of three synods (Wilkins, Conc. Brit. i. 17) which were held at Landaff. This account confirms the description given by Gildas of the awful corruption of the Britons These synods were held by the bishop Oudoceus, the same that was

PERIOD THE SECOND

Whilst the Britons, occupied by internal dissensions and wars, opposed only a feeble resistance to the destructive invasions of the Northern Picts and Scots, two Jutish chieftains with their followers, invited by the British king Vortigern, landed in Britain, in the year 450. They encountered and defeated the northern invaders, and returned to the Isle of Thanet, which had been allotted to them as a residence. They soon, however, passed from their narrow abode; and being enforced by new comers from Holstein, Schleswig, Jutland and Friesland, these German plunderers, in the course of 150 years, made themselves masters of the largest and best portion of Britain. They drove and confined the natives who would not submit to their sway, to the mountains of the west. The long and bloody wars which now arose between the Christian

---

consecrated by St. Augustin, and was composed of the clergy and the three abbots of his diocese. They were for a time interrupted by the confusion occasioned by a murder committed by the king of Glamorgan, on the person of a relative or rival. The bishop and the synod excommunicated the murderer, and placed his kingdom under a kind of interdict (" depositis crucibus ad terram et cymbalis versis") until he should subject himself to penance. Another remarkable monument of the same church is a Litany of Saints, which Mabillon, who published it in Vet Analecta, p. 168, rightly conjectures to belong to the seventh century, as the last of the saints therein named died before the year 650. He supposes it to have belonged to an Anglo-Saxon church, as one of its petitions runs thus, " Ut clerum et plebem Anglorum conservare digneris, Te rogamus," &c. But in this he is wrong: the litany more probably belonged to a British church which was subject to the Anglo-Saxons, as Dr. Lingard, Antiquities, &c. ii. 362, suggests. An Anglo Saxon saint is not named in the whole litany, for the *Augustinus* is proved, from the place which the name occupies, to be the great bishop of Hippo. Besides the saints who are honoured throughout the whole Church, we here find saints of Ireland, Britain, and Bretagne: amongst the Irish are, Patrick, Carnech, Brendan, Petranus, Columkille, and Briget: amongst those of Bretagne, Samson, Briocus, Judicael and others, of those of Britain are, Gildas, Paternus, and many others less known Amongst the confessors are the Popes Leo and Silvester, and in the number of the martyrs, the Roman immediately follow those of the apostolic age. The Roman saints occur in great numbers. Of the saints of Gaul only Hilary and Martin are mentioned. St. Germanus of Auxerre occurs amongst the saints of Britain, on account of his great labours in the British Church Only two oriental saints two martyrs are named in the litany

Britons and the idolatrous Saxons, was destructive of the Church, wherever the swords of the latter could reach. The priests were oftentimes slain at the altar,—the churches were burnt and razed to the ground or converted into heathen temples. Upon the ruins of the British Church a new idolatry rose up triumphant, more rude than the ancient religion of the Celts, and more hostile to Christianity, as long as this continued to be the distinctive profession of their enemies. The Britons were filled with so bitter a hatred against their barbarian oppressors, and the spirit of the Gospel, too, had grown so cold amongst them, that they never once attempted to conquer their Saxon foes by converting them to the religion of Christ.

The conquerors formed in Britain an heptarchy, that is a number of unequal independant kingdoms; which were not always seven in number, as the term heptarchy would seem to imply, but were sometimes more and sometimes less. At the head of these states was the sovereign Bretwalda, who possessed a nominal rather than a real superiority. The Angles founded the kingdoms of Mercia and Northumberland: the Jutes settled in Kent, the Isle of Wight and a part of Wessex: the more numerous bodies of the Saxons ruled in the remaining part of Wessex, in Sussex and in Essex. The Anglo-Saxons—this was the collective name given to the several tribes—had not terminated their wars with the Britons, before they entered into conflict with each other. Endless barbarism and heavy mental darkness would have been the lot of Britain, had not God awakened in the mind of a great and holy Pope the resolution to undertake the conversion of the pagan islanders.

St. Gregory the Great was yet a monk in a monastery at Rome, when the sight of some Anglo-Saxon youths, who were exposed in the city, as slaves for sale, inspired him with the desire to travel to the nation from which they had come, and in the capacity of a missioner to announce to it the Gospel of Christ. But the Roman people would not permit his departure.

He lost not, however, his object from view; and when raised to the chair of St. Peter, he purchased several captive Anglo-Saxon youths, whom he placed in monasteries, where they were instructed in the doctrines of Christianity. In the year 595, he sent the abbot Augustin with fourteen Roman religious as missionaries to Britain. But the difficulty of acquiring the language, and the description which had been presented to them of the ferocity and cruelty of the Anglo-Saxons, shook the resolution of the missionaries. St. Augustin returned from Lerins in Gaul to Rome, to represent to the pontiff the hopelessness of their undertaking. Happily for England, the holy Pope remained unmoved: he exhorted, conjured St. Augustin and his companions to continue their journey; he recommended them to the protection of the king and bishops of France, and requested the latter to provide them with interpreters. St. Augustin and his monks landed in 597 on the Isle of Thanet, at the same place where, a century and a half before, the two brother chieftains, Hengist and Horsa, first touched the British shores. Ethelbert, the king of Kent, who was then recognized as Bretwalda by the other Saxon kings, had married Bertha, the daughter of the French monarch. She had brought with her from her native country, Luidhard, a Christian bishop, who practised the rites of his religion in a church which had been preserved near Canterbury, since the time of the Romans. Although the king was not ignorant of the Christian religion, he received the messengers of the Gospel in the open air, as he had been taught to apprehend in any other place the magic spells of the Roman priests. These appeared before him in solemn procession, bearing a silver cross and an image of Christ, in whose honour they sung hymns in alternate choirs as they approached the king. To the exposition of the object of his coming made by St. Augustin, Ethelbert replied, that on account of their alluring, but to him new and insecure, promises, he would not forbid his people to embrace the faith, and promised him, moreover, freedom and protection as long as the missionaries should preach in his kingdom.

St. Augustin and his companions now commenced their apostolic labours at Canterbury. The austerity and purity of their lives, and their disinterested zeal, won for them first the attention, then the respect and veneration, of the people. The ancient idolatry was not more firmly fixed in the minds of the Anglo-Saxons, than in the minds of any other German tribe, that had passed from its native abode: many of them were therefore soon baptized, nor did the Bretwalda himself long delay to receive the faith and baptism. The example of the king was a powerful incentive to his people. The gratified and delighted pontiff, St. Gregory, in writing to Eulogius, patriarch of Alexandria, could declare, that during the festival of the Nativity of our Lord, St. Augustin had baptized ten thousand of the converted Anglo-Saxons.

At the command of the pope, St. Augustin passed over to Arles, where he was consecrated first bishop and metropolitan of the Anglo-Saxon Church. In the confidence that the conversion of England would continue to advance in an uninterrupted progress, St. Gregory directed the new metropolitan to ordain twelve suffragan bishops in the south; and when the gospel had reached the north, to appoint a bishop at Eboracum (York), as metropolitan of the northern provinces, also with twelve suffragans. At the same time, he sent new labourers to assist in the holy work, amongst whom were Mellitus, Paulinus, Justus and Rufinian: he sent also books, sacred vessels, vestments, church ornaments, and relics of saints, which were to be placed in the churches to be erected in different parts of the country. When St. Augustin narrated to him the wonders which God had been pleased to work by his means, he exhorted him to humility, and to a continual severe self-probation, and reminded him that the miracles of which God had made him the instrument, were not given to his merit, but for the conviction and enlightening of the heathens. Ethelbert gave to the missionaries the city of Canterbury with the surrounding country: he caused an ancient British church to be restored and enlarged for the bishop and his clergy, and a cloister to be erected out of the city for the Roman monks. According to the prudent counsel of the pope, the pagan temples were not destroyed; but as soon as the natives had embraced Christianity they were converted into churches, by being sprinkled with holy water, and by the erection of altars in which the relics of martyrs were deposited. The feasts with which the pagan Anglo-Saxons had been wont to commence their festivals and sports were not abolished or prohibited, but were changed into feasts of thanksgiving, which were celebrated in honour of the true God, on the days of the dedication of their churches, or on the festivals of the saints whose relics were preserved within them. For the more distant parts of Kent, the metropolitan consecrated his disciple Justus, who placed his episcopal see at Rochester.

Into the neighbouring kingdom of Essex, of which the king, Sabercth, was a nephew of Ethelbert, the missionaries found an easy entrance. Mellitus baptized the king in 604, and was consecrated the first bishop of London, which was at that early age a populous and flourishing city. But when in 616, Ethelbert and Sabercth both passed after a short interval to the grave, the prospects of Christianity in both kingdoms became lowering and gloomy. Eadbald, the son of Ethelbert, who had continued in idolatry, took the widow of his father for his wife,* and his wicked example was the occasion of fall to many of his subjects. The three sons of Sabercth had contemned the Christian faith, and had continued in the ancient idolatry, but required of the bishop Mellitus that he would permit them to approach to the holy table. He of course indignantly refused, whereupon they banished him from their territories. In company with Justus, he withdrew to Gaul; and even Laurence, archbishop of Canterbury, whom St. Augustin had ordained as his successor, entertained serious thoughts of leaving the island. But on the morning after he had formed his resolution, he

---

* Not Bertha, but a second wife of Ethelbert.

entered boldly into the presence of the sovereign, and announced to him that during the night, the apostle St. Peter had appeared to him in a vision, and had severely rebuked him for the cowardice which would persuade him to forsake the flock that had been entrusted to him. Eadbald entered into himself: he now considered the attacks of delirium with which he had been tormented, as admonitory judgments of God : he dissolved his incestuous marriage, received baptism, and recalled Mellitus and Justus from Gaul. But the pagan inhabitants of London would not receive again the bishop of their city, and Mellitus therefore, after the death of Laurence in 619, succeeded him in the archbishopric of Canterbury.

Northumberland was the next kingdom that received the faith. Edwin, the king, had espoused Edilberga, the daughter of Ethelbert, and had pledged his honour that she should enjoy unmolested the free exercise of her religion. With the queen went the bishop Paulinus, who was not without hopes of converting the king to Christianity : but the exhortations of Paulinus, the prayers of Edilberga, and the letters and presents of Boniface, the Roman pontiff, were for a time alike unavailing. His escape from the dagger of an assassin, and the happy delivery of his queen, worked a favourable impression upon his mind, and in proof thereof he permitted the bishop to baptize his new-born daughter. A sign that was now given to him completed his conversion. Once, in his youth, being a homeless wanderer, he saw himself in the danger of instant death ; when a stranger appeared to him in the night, and promised to him present deliverance and future happiness and power, but exacted from him a promise that he would listen to the words of him who should present himself to him with a certain sign (of placing the right hand upon his head), and receive from him the tidings of eternal salvation Now, when a complete victory over his enemies, the West-Saxons, recalled this prophecy again to his memory. Paulinus appeared suddenly before him, and laying his right hand upon his head, asked of him, if he could remember that sign. The astonished king wished to cast himself at the feet of the bishop, but Paulinus prevented him with words of friendship, and conjured him, as God had thus visibly conducted him to the means of salvation, to hearken to the voice of heaven, and no longer to defer his conversion. But Edwin would not take so important a step before he had consulted with the nobles of the land. He therefore called them together, and required them to express their sentiments on the great question of religion. Coifi, the chief priest of the idols, first addressed him. He declared, that he was of opinion, that their ancient religion was in itself nothing: he had been one of the most zealous of the worshippers of his country's Gods, but he had never yet received a benefit from them, whilst others, who neglected their service, were more fortunate than he had been: if, therefore, the new religion could make better offers to its followers, the king should without hesitation embrace it. After the priest, a thane arose, and speaking said, that the life of man might be compared to the flight of a sparrow, which enters the hall at night and of which no one can tell whence it comes or whither it goes: no one can tell what has preceded the short existence of man, nor what shall thereafter follow: if the new religion can teach us these things, we ought at once to receive it. This declaration was followed by the assent of the whole assembly. Paulinus was called in, and was asked to explain the chief doctrines of Christianity. Coifi was the first to declare himself convinced of their truth, and immediately proposed the demolition of the temples and altars of the Gods. Assuming the arms of a warrior, he mounted a horse, an action which, as it was forbidden to the priests, was attributed to insanity. He proceeded on his charger to the neighbouring temple of Godmundingham, against the walls of which he hurled the lance which he bore in his hand, and then caused the edifice to be consumed by fire. The king, his sons, and many both of the nobles and people, now (in 627) received baptism, and so great was the concourse of the

Northumbrians who crowded around Paulinus, that for thirty-six days he was incessantly employed, from the morning until evening, in instructing them in the faith of Christ, and in baptizing them in the river that was near. A cathedral was erected at York; pope Honorius sent to Paulinus, as archbishop of York, the archiepiscopal pallium, as it had before been granted to the archbishop of Canterbury, and permitted at the same time, that whenever either of the English metropolitans should die, the survivor should consecrate his successor without having previously consulted the apostolic see.

In East-Anglia, the king Redwald had been baptized by a disciple of St. Augustin: he did not, however entirely renounce idolatry, and erected a Christian altar at the side of an altar of sacrifice in a heathen temple. More sincere was the conversion, effected by king Edwin, of Eorpwald, the son of Redwald. But a violent death, inflicted by the hand of a pagan assassin, impeded the fruits of his example amongst his people. His brother Sigebert, who had embraced Christianity in Gaul, effectually cooperated with the Burgundian bishop Felix, who had received his mission from Honorius, archbishop of Canterbury, to introduce the Gospel into his kingdom. An episcopal see was established at Dunwich, and a school was formed on the model of that which had a short time before been opened at Canterbury. Sigebert was the first of the Anglo-Saxon princes that assumed the monastic habit; he was, however, soon compelled to forsake it, to lead his people against the pagan Mercians, who had invaded their lands, and was slain in the battle. Christianity continued to proceed notwithstanding the evils which afflicted East-Anglia; and after seventeen years of labour, Felix had completed the conversion of the entire nation.

In Northumbria, which then comprised a considerable part of the south of Scotland, Christianity met with many obstacles. The excellent king Edwin and his son perished, in 633, in a battle with the Mercian king Penda and the British Ceadwalla. The country was made a scene of devastation by the conquerors.

Edilberga, her children, and the bishop, sought a retreat in Kent, where Paulinus succeeded to the see of Rochester, and the newly-converted Northumbrians, being deprived of all spiritual assistance, fell back into paganism. In the mean time, Oswald, the son of Adelfried, the brother and predecessor of Edwin, had, during his exile in Ireland, professed himself a Christian. At the head of a small band of Saxons who had collected around him, he marched against Ceadwalla. Before the battle, he and his followers prostrated themselves before a cross of wood, that had been hastily erected, to implore the aid of the God of the Christians. He attacked and defeated Ceadwalla, and placed himself in undisputed possession of the kingdom of Northumbria. He immediately applied to the Irish prelates with whom he had been acquainted, and requested them to send to him a bishop for the conversion of his subjects. They consecrated and sent to him Aidan, an Irish monk of the abbey of Hy,* to whom Oswald assigned the isle of Lindisfarne, on the coast of Bernicia, as the seat of his bishopric. The diocese of Aidan extended as far as Scotland, and embraced the diocese of York, which Paulinus had abandoned, and which Aidan and his successors continued to govern for thirty years, but without the name of metropolitans.† As he was, at the beginning of his mission,

---

* Aidan was not, as Lingard and Lappenberg (Hist. of England, i. 154) suppose, a Scotchman, but an Irishman, and as such he is named in the Irish annals and calendaries. The great majority of the monks of Hy were at this period Irishmen. Oswald did not find an asylum amongst the Scotch, who were so hostile to his nation and family, but amongst the friendly Irish, and the *majores natu Scotorum*, to whom, as Bede says, Oswald applied, were consequently Irish bishops and abbots. The assembly in which the mission of Aidan was determined, as well as his consecration, which could not have been performed without the consent of his abbot Segenius, may have well taken place in the abbey of Hy

† " Recedente Paulino, Eboracensis ecclesia per xxx. annos proprium non habuit episcopum, sed Lindisfarnensis ecclesia præsules, Aidanus Finanus, Colmanus et Tuda, Nordanhembrorum provinciæ administrarunt Pontificatum." Simeon Dunelmensis, epist. ad Hug. de Archiep. Eboracen. in Twysden, Scriptores x.

ignorant of the Saxon tongue, the pious king, who had learnt the Irish language during his abode in Ireland, served him as interpreter. He was in a short time assisted by the arrival of fellow-labourers, chiefly Irish monks, who passed over to him from Ireland; and according to the custom of Ireland, he built on the isle of Lindisfarne a monastery, in which he resided as a monk, with the clergy of his church. He was in truth the model of a perfect bishop, and the blessing of the nation whose salvation was entrusted to his zeal. Severe and fearless towards powerful sinners, he was the constant and bountiful benefactor of the poor, upon whom he bestowed all that he possessed. In the visitations of his vast diocese, he journeyed always on foot, that he might be able to announce the gospel to all whom he should meet: wherever he might be, it was his daily practice to read the sacred Scriptures with his companions, priests and laics, to repeat the Psalter and to pray with them. He redeemed many captives, of whom he educated some and ordained them priests. Such is the portraiture of this holy man, that has been left to us by the venerable Bede, who has no fault to lay to his charge, except that he introduced the Easter cycle which was observed in the north of Ireland, whilst the southern Irish had adopted the Roman calculation.* So general, however, was the veneration in which the sainted bishop was held, that no one molested him on this account; and Honorius of Canterbury, and Felix, bishop of the East-Angles, exhibited towards him every demonstration of respect. He died in 651, in the seventeenth year of his episco-

---

* "Hæc dissonantia Paschalis observantiæ vivente Aidano patienter ab omnibus tolerabatur, qui patenter intellexerant, quia etsi Pascha, contra morem eorum qui ipsum miserant, facere non potuit, opera tamen fidei, pietatis et delectionis juxta morem omnibus sanctis consuetum diligenter exequi curavit." Beda, Histor Eccl. iii. 25.— This, and similar passages which immediately follow, and from which it is evidently proved that St. Aidan was in communion with the bishops who had come from Rome, have been overlooked by those who extend the difference which existed concerning Easter, to other more essential points.

pacy. To the sanctity of the bishop corresponded the piety of the sovereign. He, who was acknowledged as Bretwalda, not only by the Saxons, but by the Picts and Scots, was humble and gentle to strangers and to the poor; and when, like his predecessors, he fell in battle against the infidel Mercians, his last words were a prayer for the spiritual happiness of his people. Immediately after his death, he was honoured as a saint by his subjects; and soon the fame was spread, that on the place where his blood had flowed, wonderful miracles were wrought. The successor of Aidan in the see of Lindisfarne was Finan, also a monk of Hy.

To Finan was reserved the happiness of leading to the waters of baptism the prince of the Middle-Angles, Peada, the son of Penda, the pagan king of Mercia. Peada had come to the court of the Northumbrian king Oswio, to ask his daughter, Alchfleda, in marriage. There he learned to know and to prize the Christian faith, and returned a Christian to his native land, with four priests, three Anglo-Saxons and one Irish, named Diuma. The aged father of the young convert remained in his idolatry, but granted religious freedom to his Christian subjects, and shewed his displeasure against those who by baptism had become Christians in name, but continued in morals idolaters. As soon as the converts amongst the Middle-Angles had been greatly increased, Diuma was consecrated their bishop. His district included not only the country of the Middle-Angles, but Mercia also, when it passed under the dominion of the Christian king, Oswio. Diuma was succeeded by Kellach, a monk of Hy: he soon, however, returned to his monastery, and was followed in his see by Trumheri, an Englishman, who had been educated and ordained amongst the Irish.

Finan baptized also Siegbert, king of the East-Saxons, who had been converted by the exhortations and persuasions of his friend, the Northumbrian king, Oswio. The East-Saxons had fallen away from their faith after the expulsion of their bishop, Mellitus; but the English priest, Cedd, whom Oswio had brought with him from Northumbria, found them constant and attentive hearers to his preaching. When in a short time he was able to inform Finan of the rapid progress of the gospel in Essex, the bishop of Lindisfarne, having brought with him two other prelates, consecrated him bishop of the East-Saxon Church. The new bishop placed his see in London.

The Christian religion, in the meantime, had made its way amongst the south-western Britons in the Saxon kingdom of Wessex. Birinus, whose native country is unknown, had obtained from Pope Honorius a mission to announce the gospel in the still pagan parts of Britain. He received episcopal consecration from Artorius, bishop of Genoa. It was by an especial providence, that when, in 635, he landed in Wessex, Oswald, the virtuous and powerful king of Northumberland, was at the court of Kinegils, the West-Saxon king. His words and example were a strong support to the preaching of the bishop. Kinegils was baptized and was received from the font by Oswio. Birinus selected Dorchester, in the neighbourhood of Oxford, as the seat of his bishopric. Kennewalc, the son of Kinegils, who died in 643, was not converted with his father: but being defeated in battle and dethroned by the Mercian Penda, he fled for refuge to the court of Anna, the Christian king of the East-Angles. There he became a Christian. In a short time he recovered his kingdom; and upon his return, completed the great cathedral at Winchester, which his father had begun. Birinus died, in 650, at Dorchester, and was succeeded by Agibert, who was a native of Gaul, and had long studied in the schools of Ireland. But his defective utterance of the English language displeased the monarch, who therefore procured the consecration of Wina, an Anglo-Saxon, and divided the diocese into two parts, of which Agilbert was to retain the northern with Rochester, and Wina received the southern with Winchester, the capital of Wessex, as his episcopal see. The former preferred to resign his bishopric and to return to France, where he was soon after appointed bishop of Paris. Kenewalc however, soon learnt that Wina was unworthy of his high station: after three years, he expelled him from his diocese, and by an embassy to Paris, invited Agilbert to return. Agilbert could not forsake the church to which he had bound himself, but he sent his nephew, Eleutherius, who was received with joy by the king and the people, and, in 670, was consecrated by the archbishop of Canterbury, bishop of the West-Saxons. Ceadwalla, one of the successors of Kenewalc, continued for many years a pagan, but such was his respect for the Christian religion, that he dedicated to the God of the Christians a tenth part of the spoils taken in war. He was at length instructed by the bishop, St. Wilfrid, and became truly a new man. Ferocious before, cruel and blood-thirsty, he was now mild, meek and humble; he resigned his royal dignity and went as a penitent pilgrim to Rome, where he was baptized. He died there, whilst he yet had on the white robes of a neophyte. His successor Ina, after a reign of thirty-seven years, journeyed also to Rome, where as a sign of his renunciation of all worldly distinction he cut off his long-flowing hair, which amongst the Saxons and Franks was a sign of high rank. He did not long survive this act of humility and virtue.

The inhabitants of Sussex were the last of the Anglo-Saxons who entered the Christian Church. Their king, Edilwalch, had given his name to the faith, but they resisted the efforts of every missionary that had been sent to them; until the Northumbrian bishop, Wilfrid, who had been driven from his own diocese, appeared amongst them. His first converts were two hundred and fifty slaves, whom Edilwalch gave to him, in 678, together with the island of Selsey. On the day of their baptism, they heard with wonder the declaration made by their holy teacher, that then, as children of Christ, they ceased to be slaves of men. This magnanimous act made so favourable an impression on the minds of the West-Saxons, that they came in crowds to hear the instructions of the bishop, and the decided will of the king operated here, as in all the Anglo-Saxon States; so that many who were not inwardly convinced, outwardly professed Christianity. After five years, Wilfrid had firmly established the faith in Sussex. The kingdom was at first under the spiritual jurisdiction of the see of Winchester, but in a synod it was decreed to give to it a bishop: the first that was chosen was Edbert, abbot of the monastery founded by Wilfrid on the isle of Selsey.

The pope St. Gregory the Great, had formed the plan of the constitution and division of the rising Church of the Anglo-Saxons. His design was not, however, immediately carried into effect. He intended that London and York should form two metropolitan sees, each having attached to it twelve suffragan bishoprics. But St. Augustin gave the preference to Canterbury before London, and succeeding pontiffs sanctioned his choice: in York, as we have seen above, the succession of metropolitans was for a long time interrupted. For many years, therefore, the Anglo-Saxon Church had only one metropolitan; and until the time of archbishop Theodore (699), his power did not extend over all the bishoprics of the island. When, during a great pestilence, Deusdedit, the sixth archbishop of Canterbury, and several of the bishops, had been carried off by the infection, the kings of Northumberland and of Kent selected the priest Wighard as the successor of the deceased metropolitan, and sent him to Rome, that he might be consecrated by the pope, and that by him the bond of union between the Roman and the Anglo-Saxon Church might be more closely drawn. But Wighard died soon after his arrival in Rome, and the pope, Vitalian, seized with joy the opportunity of placing in the metropolitan Church of the British islands a priest of extensive learning and of great energy of mind. His choice fell upon Theodore, a Greek monk, of Tarsus in Cilicia. Theodore arrived in England in 699, in company with the abbot Hadrian, an African, and was received without opposition by the English kings and prelates' He assumed the title of archbishop of Britain, and asserted the jurisdiction of his Church over all the Anglo-Saxon bishops to the full extent that it had been conferred by St. Gregory upon the apostle of the nation. The dioceses of the country, especially those of York or Lindisfarne, and of Winchester, were so vast in extent, that it was impossible for the bishops of them to fulfil their duty or satisfy the wants of their people. Theodore therefore determined to divide them into districts of less extent, and he executed his difficult undertaking with a courage and with an energy, which bordered almost upon violence. Thus, after he had deposed Winfrid, the opposing bishop of Mercia, he formed of his diocese five bishoprics. By these means, the number of the Anglo-Saxon sees had, at the close of the century, increased from seven to seventeen.* The endeavour fully to effect his plan of the division of the dioceses, intangled Theodore in a contest with a great and virtuous prelate. In this controversy, Theodore's proceedings were contrary to all right. Bishop Wilfrid had earned for himself the indignation of his king, Egfrid of Northumbria, by presuming to reprove the queen for her light and scandalous conduct. At the invitation of the king, Theodore visited the court of Northumbria, and seized the welcome opportunity to further his design of increasing the number of bishoprics. Without the co-operation, even without the knowledge of Wilfrid, he divided the large diocese of York into three districts, in each of which he placed a bishop consecrated by himself. Wilfrid appealed to the canons; and when he saw that that was in vain, he had recourse to the only means now left to him, which he adopted by the advice of several of his episcopal brethren,—he appealed to the see of Rome. He at once commenced his journey; but as he delayed during the winter in

---

* They were: in Kent, Canterbury and Rochester, in Essex, London; in East-Anglia, Dunwich and Helmham; in Sussex, Selsey; in Wessex, Winchester and Sherburne; in Mercia, Litchfield, Leicester, Hereford, Worcester and Sydnacester; in Northumbria, York, Hexham, Lindisfarne, and Whithern (*Candida Casa*, the ancient see of Ninian, the apostle of the Southern Picts).

Friesland, preaching the gospel to the pagan inhabitants, the monk Coenwald, the ambassador of Theodore, reached Rome before him. When at length he arrived, Pope Agatho summoned a synod of the Roman clergy, in which it was determined, that the bishops, who had been appointed in the absence of Wilfrid, and contrary to all right, should be deposed, but that Wilfrid, with the aid of a council which he should assemble, should elect three of his clergy, whom the archbishop should consecrate, and whom he should associate with himself in the government of his extensive dioceses. Should any person presume to oppose this decision, he should be punished,—if an ecclesiastic with suspension, if a laic with excommunication. But when Wilfrid returned to Britain with the decree of the synod, he was seized by order of Egfrid and of his revengeful queen, and cast into prison. He was liberated at the intercession of the abbess Edda, but was compelled to sign a declaration, that he would never again enter the dominions of Egfrid. During his exile, he became the apostle of the South-Saxons.* At the close of his life, Theodore saw the full extent of his injustice to Wilfrid. He sent for the injured prelate to London; reconciled himself with him and wished to appoint him his successor in the see of Canterbury. To this Wilfrid would not consent. His persecutor, king Egfrid, had in the meantime been slain in battle. Theodore wrote to his successor Aldfrid, and to Ethelred king of Mercia, imploring them, (at the same time referring them to the papal decree), to receive Wilfrid in peace, and to reinstate him in the possession of all his rights. His prayer was heard. Aldfrid resigned to the bishop the see of Hexham, and, in a short time, Lindisfarne and York. The holy Cuthbert had,

---

* When Wilfrid arrived in Sussex, so great was the famine that reigned there, that the inhabitants, in companies of forty and fifty persons, would ascend the highest points of the rocks, and, clasping each other in their arms, cast themselves from the precipice into the sea. The holy bishop ministered first to their corporal wants, by teaching them the art of making fishing nets, and next to their spiritual necessities, by preaching to them the gospel. Bede, iv. 13.

in 685, been placed against his will in the see of Lindisfarne, but retired from it after the expiration of two years. For five years, from 692 to 697, Wilfrid governed these three sees, or the ancient extensive diocese of York, but in continued conflicts with a powerful party, whose private interests had been injured by his restoration. The king, also, displeased with the inflexible character of the prelate, passed over to his enemies. Wilfrid was required to surrender his abbey of Rippon, which he had enriched and beautified, to the king, whose intention it was to convert it into an episcopal see and to place in it a bishop. He resisted and fled from his enemies to the court of Ethelred, king of Mercia, who bestowed upon him the vacant bishopric of Lichfield. But archbishop Brithwald, who had now united himself with the numberless enemies of Wilfrid, assembled a great council at Nesterfield in Northumbria. Wilfrid appeared before it, but experienced not that kind and impartial treatment to which he was entitled. He was asked to promise beforehand an unconditional submission to the decision of the council and to acknowledge the validity of the ordinance (respecting the division of the diocese of York and of his ecclesiastical possessions) drawn up by Theodore, during his controversy with him. The bishop rejected the proposal as unjust, and appealed in his defence to the decrees of the popes Agatho and Sergius. Finally, the abbey of Rippon was promised to him, if he would renounce all further pretensions and abstain from all exercise of his episcopal power. With a feeling of indignation, he replied that he protested against a proposal, by the adoption of which, he should subscribe his own deposition and confess himself a culprit : let those, who sought to deprive him of his authority and rights follow him to Rome and lay their accusations before the pontiff. To Rome, whither Wilfrid again went, Brithwald sent a deputation of monks, in the name of the council. The controversy was laid before the pope, John, and was examined, in seventy sessions, in a council called by him. Wilfrid required the full execution of the decrees issued in his favour by the popes Agatho, Benedict, and Sergius, and which commanded the restoration to him of his diocese of York, and of his monasteries, with all their possessions, in Northumbria and Mercia. As, however, it was probable that king Alfrid would resist the restitution, through motives of personal animosity, he was willing to cede the bishopric of York to any prelate whom the pope might nominate to it, provided that he might enjoy undisturbed his two beloved monasteries of Rippon and Hexham. His adversaries grounded their accusation against him, on his presumed contempt in open synod of the archbishop of Canterbury, whom the pope had placed over all the Churches of Britain. The pontiff declared Wilfrid innocent, and directed Brithwald to assemble a synod, in which he might effect a reconciliation between him and the bishops Boza and John, who had been appointed to the sees of York and Hexham. Brithwald evinced his readiness to obey the papal mandate, but Aldfrid declared that he would never recede from the resolution which he had formed with the archbishop, (who was moreover the legate of the apostolic see), and with almost all the bishops of Britain.* Aldfrid did not long survive this declaration. Brithwald, soon after the death of the king, presided at a synod, at which three bishops and the thanes, who during the minority of Osred held the supreme power, were present. The abbess Ælfleda, the sister of Aldfrid, appeared before them, and declared that the last wish, and the last command of her brother upon his death-bed, had been that Wilfrid should be restored to his former dignity and authority.

---

* " Quod nos cum archiepiscopo *ab apostolica sede emisso* judicavimus.—"Edd. c. 61. He is named by his delegates " Brithwaldi Cantuariorum ecclesiæ et totius Britanniæ archiepiscopi, ab hac apostolica sede emissi.—"c. 51. Brithwald was, however, an Anglo-Saxon, and elected by the clergy of Canterbury. This appellation of apostolical legate was derived fram his receiving the pallium, and the accompanying authority of metropolitan, or primate over all the bishops of Britain. Hence the pontiff John says, " Ammonemus Brithwaldum, præsulem S. Cantaur. ecclesiæ, quem auctoritate Principis Apostolorum, archiepiscopum ibidem confirmavimus."- -Edd c. 52.

The thanes willingly accepted the papal decree, and the Northumbrian bishops, after some opposition, found themselves compelled to accede to the compromise proposed by Wilfrid, which secured to him the monasteries of Rippon and Hexham, with all their possessions.

From the earliest ages of the Anglo-Saxon Church, there had existed between it and the Church of Rome the closest connexion. The devotion of many, ecclesiastics and laymen, and even kings, conducted them to Rome, that they might there visit the holy places and adore God at the tombs of his apostles. These journeys, and the consequent intercourse with foreign nations and Churches, particularly with France, produced this most beneficial result, that the Anglo-Saxons, who in their insular separation from the other nations of Europe, had had but few opportunities of intellectual improvement, became observant of the superiority of their neighbours, and eager to transplant into their own Church whatever they saw worthy of imitation in the Churches of Rome and of France; they were taught by what they beheld in the government of these Churches, the defects or the abuses that existed in their own. When Pope Vitalian sent Theodore and Hadrian to Britain, he laid the foundation of a more extensive knowledge of the sciences than at that period anywhere existed in the more distant nations of the west. These ecclesiastics brought with them books, amongst which were the Greek classics; they opened schools, in which, besides theology, astronomy, arithmetic, and prosody were taught; and Bede relates, that in his days there lived many of the scholars of these accomplished masters, who were as well acquainted with the Latin and Greek languages as with their own vernacular tongue. Contemporary with Theodore, and of a like spirit for learning, lived the holy Bennet (Benedict) Biscop, who, having applied himself to study at Rome and in the abbey of Lerins, in Provence, visited the continent five times in pursuit of knowledge, and placed, as the fruits of his travels, a valuable library, which he had collected in foreign nations, in his abbey of Wearmouth.

No less advantageous to the Anglo-Saxon Church was its constant intercourse with the then flourishing Church of Ireland. As we have already seen, the foundation of many of the English sees is due to Irishmen: the Northumbrian diocese was for many years governed by them, and the abbey of Lindisfarne, which was peopled by Irish monks and their Saxon disciples, spread far around it its all-blessing influence. These holy men served God and not the world; they possessed neither gold nor silver, and all that they received from the rich passed through their hands into the hands of the poor. Kings and nobles visited them from time to time, but only to pray in their churches or to listen to their sermons; and as long as they remained in the cloisters they were content with the humble food of the brethren. Wherever one of these ecclesiastics or monks came, he was received by all with joy; and whenever he was seen journeying across the country, the people streamed around him to implore his benediction and to hearken to his words. The priests entered the villages only to preach or to administer the sacraments, and so free were they from avarice, that it was only when compelled by the rich and noble that they would accept lands for the erection of monasteries. Thus has Bede described the Irish bishops, priests, and monks of Northumbria, although so displeased with their custom of celebrating Easter. Many Anglo-Saxons passed over to Ireland, where they received a most hospitable reception in the monasteries and schools. In crowds, numerous as bees, as Aldhelm, a contemporary of Theodore and Wilfrid, writes,* the English went to Ireland, or the Irish visited England, where the archbishop Theodore was surrounded by Irish scholars. Of the most celebrated Anglo-Saxon scholars and saints, many had studied in Ireland: among these were St. Egbert, the author of the first Anglo-Saxon mission to

---

* " Epistola ad Eahfridum ex Hibernia in patriam reversum," in Usserii Sylloge, p. 27. " Hibernia quo catervatim istinc lectores classibus adverti confluunt."

the pagan continent, and the blessed Willebrod, the apostle of the Frieslanders, who had resided twelve years in Ireland.* From the same abode of virtue and of learning, came forth two English priests, both named Hewald; who, in 690, went as messengers of the gospel to the German-Saxons, and received from them the crown of martyrdom. An Irishman, Mailduf, founded, in the year 670, a school, which afterwards grew into the famed abbey of Malmsbury (originally Maildufsbury): amongst his scholars was St. Aldhelm, afterwards abbot of Malmsbury, and first bishop of Sherburne, or Salisbury; and whom, after two centuries, Alfred pronounced to be the best of the Anglo-Saxon poets. Happily this friendly and sacred relation of the two Churches was not entirely broken by the disputes concerning the celebration of Easter; although in particular cases, as in Northumbria, after the conference at Whitby, separations took place.

If we compare the manners and social life of the Anglo-Saxons before and after their conversion to Christianity, we shall be convinced that this divine religion quickly exerted amongst them the full power of its penetrating and purifying spirit. The condition of the numerous slaves was in many ways mitigated: on Sundays and festivals they were freed from their bondage, and the slave who should be compelled by his master to labour on those days, was liberated by the laws, for ever. Even to those who were before outlawed slaves, the law of the land extended its protection; and the way for the entire abolition of slavery was prepared, as the Christian Anglo-Saxons no longer reduced their prisoners taken in war to a state of bondage, and had now learnt that by baptism all men become brethren. So deep in barbarism had the Anglo-Saxons been sunk, that it was a common practice amongst them, to sell not only the peasants but even their own children, as slaves to the merchants of the

---

* ' Quem tibi jam genuit fœcunda Britannia mater,
Doctaque nutrivit studiis sed Hibernia sacris,
Nomine Willbrordus."—Alcuin, Vit Willibr. l. 2.

continent.* This was now forbidden by the severest prohibitions of the law. If plunder and rapine had before formed the chief and favourite occupation of their lives, many of them now parted with their lawful possessions to assist the poor, to build churches, hospitals, and cloisters, or to free themselves from the temptation to avarice and the distracting cares of the world. It was a pure, animating, and persevering spirit of faith and piety, which induced so many kings, queens, and children of kings and queens, to lay aside unreservedly their authority and possessions, to renounce all earthly pleasures, and to dedicate themselves to the severe life of a cloister. Amongst the Anglo-Saxon kings, who about the time of Theodore and Wilfrid resigned, that they might live to God in solitude and silence, there were, besides the above-named, Ceadwalla and Ina, kings of Wessex; Seigbert, king of the East-Angles; Ethelred and his successor Kenrid, kings of Mercia; Sebba and Offa, kings of the East-Saxons; and Ceolwulph and Eghbright, kings of Northumbria. There are numbered more than thirty English kings and queens, who, in the seventh and eighth centuries, offered the same pleasing sacrifice to God.†

SECTION IV.

CONTROVERSIES IN BRITAIN AND IRELAND CONCERNING THE TIME OF THE CELEBRATION OF EASTER, AND THE FORM OF THE TONSURE.‡

The council of Nice had terminated the paschal controversy, by its decree, that the festival of Easter should

---

* " Hujus tempore venales ex Northumbria pueri, familiari et penè ingenita illi nationi consuetudine, adeo ut non dubitarent arctissimas necessitudines sub prætextu minimorum commodorum distrahere." Guill. Malmesbur. de reg l. 3.

† From the seventh to the eleventh century there lived twenty-three Anglo-Saxon kings, sixty queens and children of royal parents, who are honoured amongst the saints.

‡ Beda, Hist. Eccl. ii. 2, 4, 19; iii. 25, 26, v. 16.—Cummiani Hiberni Epistola de Controversia Paschali, in Usseri Sylloge, p. 17.

be celebrated throughout the whole Church on the same day,—the Sunday after the fourteenth day of the moon of March. But a new difficulty arose. How was the beginning of the lunar or Easter month to be determined? The ancient Christians had followed the Jewish cycle of eighty-four years: but as since the Nicene council, it had been the duty of the patriarch of Alexandria to learn from the philosophers of Egypt the time of the due celebration of Easter and to make it known to the pope, who would notify it to the distant churches, the cycle of nineteen years which was first used by Anatolius and improved by Eusebius, was now adopted at Alexandria. But in Rome and consequently in the whole Western Church, the old cycle of eighty-four years was still preserved. By this the course of the moon was shortened by two minutes and some seconds. The days of the solar month on which the first day, or the new moon, of the Easter course, might fall, extended among the Latins from the 5th of March to the 2nd of April, amongst the Alexandrines from the 8th of March to the 5th of April; so that the fourteenth day, in the Latin Church, could not occur before the 18th of March, nor after the 15th of April; in the Alexandrian Church not earlier than the 21st of March, nor later than the 18th of April. The Roman computation would not admit of Easter Sunday before the 16th day of the month; according to the Alexandrian it might fall on the fifteenth. Hence it happened that at Rome, in 387, Easter was celebrated on the 18th of April; but at Alexandria and also at Milan not before the 25th of the same month. In the year 444, the difference of calculation had reached almost to a month: the pope, Leo, therefore commanded that the festival should be solemnized on the 23rd of April, the day appointed according to the calculation of Alexandria. After the death of Leo, the cycle of Victorinus Aquitanus, which contained 532 years, and which came nearer to the Alexandrian, was adopted. Finally the cycle of Dionysius Exiguus succeeded, towards the middle of the sixth century, to that of Victorinus. The cycle of Dionysius coincided in every respect with the cycle of Alexandria, and thus an uniformity in the celebration of Easter was established in the two Churches.

The British Churches had, from their first foundation, celebrated Easter according to the Roman calculation.* When St. Augustin and his companions arrived in Britain, they found the ancient cycle of eighty-four years, and the ancient method of calculation, in use, as they had been in Rome before the adoption of the cycle of Dionysius Exiguus; with this one exception, that the Britons celebrated Easter on the 14th day of the lunar month, if that day fell on a Sunday; whereas, in the ancient practice of Rome, Easter day could not occur before the sixteenth day.

The pope, St. Gregory, had invested St. Augustin with jurisdiction over all the bishops of Britain, and St. Augustin endeavoured to exercise this authority in regenerating the British Church and in reforming the many abuses by which it had been disfigured. To establish an uniformity with the whole Catholic Church in the solemnization of Easter formed one object of his desires. But the consciousness of the defects in their ecclesiastical discipline, and their implacable hatred of the Saxons, whose bishop St. Augustin was, determined them not to subject themselves to his authority. Through the influence of king Ethelbert, he induced them to meet him in conference on the borders of their country, but neither by his prayers nor by his exhortations could he persuade them to discontinue practices which distinguished them from all other Christians, but which they revered as an inheritance descending to them from their sainted ancestors. At length he proposed, that the question on whose side right and the truth lay should be determined by Divine interposition, that a miracle should decide their cause. To this the British bishops consented with reluctance. A blind man was placed before them, and to him St. Augustin restored

---

* Of this the Emperor Constantine speaks in his letter, preserved by Eusebius, in Vita Constantini, iii. 19.

his sight by his prayers, after the British had in vain attempted the cure. They, however, required that another and more numerous assembly should be convoked to decide upon an affair of so great importance: for without the consent of their countrymen they dared not to abandon their ancient rites.* At this second

---

* What were these ancient and peculiar rites? Bede, ii. 2, after mentioning their custom of celebrating Easter, says, in general terms, "sed et alia plurima ecclesiæ contraria faciebant" He afterwards, v. 19, says more precisely, " Britones .... alia plura ecclesiasticæ *castitati et paci* contraria gerunt." Gildas also speaks in similar terms. It is probable that the degenerate priests of Britain frequently married, or that married men, continuing in the married state, occupied places in the Church, and clerogamy has been in every age and in every part of the Church a symptom indicative of ecclesiastical decay. The reproach of Bede refers only to the British, not to the Irish. The other differences were the omission of the anointing in baptism, the form of the tonsure, their manner of consecrating bishops, who were often consecrated by only one other bishop, and the use of unleavened bread in the Eucharist, for at that period leavened bread was employed at the altar in Rome, and generally in the west. That the use of azym, or unleavened bread, was peculiar to the Britons, we learn from a passage in the *Capitula selecta canonum Hibern.* in D'Archery, Spicileg. i. 505. "Gildas ait. Britones toto mundo contrarii, moribus Romanis inimici, *non solum in missa* sed etiam in tonsura cum Judeis umbræ futurorum servientes." Thus also Nicetas expresses himself, (Contra Latinos, Bibl. PP. Max xviii. 405): "Qui azymorum adhuc participant, sub umbra legis sunt et Hebræorum mensam comedunt." It is however clear, from the whole course of the controversy, and from all that has been written by Bede on the subject, that there was not the slightest difference between the Britons and the Romans in points of faith. If there had been, how could St Augustin have conjured the Britons so earnestly to labour with him in the conversion of the Saxons? Had there existed between them a difference of faith, their co-operation would have sown in the then recently formed English Church the seeds of schism and of endless confusion, and St. Augustin would have prepared for himself and his successors difficulties from which they would have found it impossible to extricate themselves. This improved method of conversion was reserved for more modern ages. See Medhurst's China (Introduction, p 11). "Episcopalians, Presbyterians, Baptists, and Independents, alternated with each other in the performance of religious services and the *celebration of the holy sacraments*" No allusion was made to any difference of this kind, and it is inexplicable how subjects of minor importance should have been discussed by both parties, and that this chief point of all should not have been mentioned. Gieseler indeed (Eccl. Hist i. 717), and many others both before and after him, have found out one subject of the greatest moment, which was omitted by Bede, and at the same time discovered that this was

conference, there appeared seven British bishops, and many of the monks from the great abbey of Bangor.

the principal point of controversy between St. Augustin and the British bishops—the Britons did not acknowledge the supremacy of the Roman pontiff. As a proof of this, the declaration supposed to have been made by Dinoth, abbot of Bangor, to St Augustin, is adduced. Spelman and Wilkins have given this declaration in their Collection of Councils, in the ancient British original, and in a Latin translation. The translation runs thus : " Notum sit et absque dubitatione vobis, quod nos omnes sumus, et quilibet nostrum obedientes et subditi ecclesiæ Dei et papæ Romæ et unicuique vero Christiano et pio, ad amandum unumquemque in suo gradu in perfecta charitate, et adjuvandum unumquemque corum verbo et facto fore filios Dei. Et aliam obedientiam quam istam, non scio debitam ei, quem vos nominatis esse papam, nec esse patrem patrum vindicari et postulari : et istam obedientiam nos sumus parati dare et solvere ei et cuique Christiano continuo. Præterea nos sumus sub gubernatione episcopi Caerlionis super Osca, qui est ad supervidendum sub Deo super nobis ad faciendum nos servare vitam spiritualem." In its remarks upon this passage, the criticism of Protestants, which is generally so vigilant, has for once slumbered, for the piece bears upon itself every mark of forgery. 1. How came the abbot of Bangor to make this declaration to St. Augustin in a language unknown to him? For it is evident that to him who had lately experienced great difficulty in acquiring a knowledge of the Anglo-Saxon tongue, the language of the Britons, with whom he had had but little intercourse, must have been at the time of the conference an unknown language, and it is evident that the *most learned men* (viri doctissimi) of Bangor, as Bede calls them, were sufficiently acquainted with Latin to confer with St. Augustin in that language; particularly as Lappenberg (Hist. of England, 1. 124) remarks, that a Roman education was given to those who frequented the schools of Wales. 2. The language of this pretended ancient British monument, which, if it were genuine, would be the oldest of its kind, is modern; and the whole, therefore, the fiction of a later age. This has been confessed by English authors. See Tuberville's " Manuale Controvers." p. 460. Thus we find in it the *Anglo-Saxon word* HELPIO, *to help, adjuvandum.* 3. There occurs in it also an evident anachronism, for Dinoth is made to represent the bishop of Caerleon on the Osca, as metropolitan of the British Church; and it is well known, as we have seen above, that the bishop of Menevia had long before been raised to that dignity. Spelman, who first made the discovery of this declaration known, confesses that the manuscript on which it was found was not ancient, but supposes that it might have been copied from another of a more early age. That the Britons in the time of Gildas acknowledged the supremacy of the bishop of Rome is clear, from a passage in which that writer objects to the British ecclesiastics, that many amongst them who could not obtain lucrative benefices, went to Rome to urge their complaints against their competitors. " Etenim eos, si in parochia, nonnullis resistentibus sibi et tam pretiosum quæstum severe denegantibus commessoribus, hujusmodi margaritam invenire non possint, præ-

Before assembling at the conference they consulted a hermit, who was famed and revered for his sanctity. By him they were counselled to accede to all the requests of St. Augustin if he should advance to meet them with humility and without haughtiness; but if such should not be his conduct to dismiss him and to contemn him: if at their approach he should arise to receive them, they should consider him as meek and humble, if not, as proud and unworthy of their attention. It happened that at their coming he was seated, and rose not to greet them, and by this trivial accident were the Britons determined to withhold their approbation from all his proposals. These were three: that they would adopt the Roman computation of Easter, that they would administer the sacrament of baptism according to the Roman rite, and that they would unite with him in preaching the gospel to the Anglo-Saxons. These they rejected, and declared that they would never recognize him as their archbishop; for, said they amongst themselves, if once he acquire a superiority over us, he will humble us and treat us with contempt. The holy bishop, in anguish at their hard-heartedness, exclaimed, that they who would do nothing towards the conversion of the pagan Anglo-Saxons, should receive from them the severest of punishments. This prophecy, as Bede narrates, was soon fulfilled: eight years after the death of St. Augustin, Edilfrid, the pagan king of Northumbria, entered the territories of the Britons. In the army that opposed him there were numbers of ecclesiastics, and particularly of the monks of Bangor, who were destined to pray whilst their countrymen met their foes in the field. When Edilfrid perceived them, he exclaimed, "if these men invoke their God, although unarmed, they fight against us," and ordered the first attack of his troops to be made upon them. Of their number twelve hundred were slain, and only fifty escaped.

---

missis ante sollicitè nuncius, transnavigare maria, terrasque spatiosas transmeare non tam piget quam delectat, ut omnino talis species... comparetur. Deinde, cum magno apparatu magnaque phantasia, vel potius insania, repedantes ad patriam... violenter manus... sacrosanctis Christi sacrificiis extensuri."—Gildæ Epis. p. 24.

The Irish Church had, from the time of its first foundation by St. Patrick, employed the cycle of eighty-four years, but with the improvements which had been added to it in Gaul by Sulpicius Severus. According to this computation, Easter-day might fall on the 14th day of the moon; whilst the 16th day, the earliest on which, according to the Roman calculation, Easter Sunday could be, was, on account of the defects of the old cycle, in reality the fourteenth. St. Patrick introduced this improved cycle into Ireland; thence it was extended to the British Churches, and was given to the north by St. Columba and his disciples. The Roman missionaries, as their Church had in the meantime received the Alexandrian cycle, imagined that they saw in the British calculation, in which Easter-day might fall on the fourteenth day of the lunation, the ancient error of the Quartodecimans; not reflecting that the fourteenth day was that which they would have named the sixteenth, and that the Irish and British commemorated the resurrection of our Lord on that day, only when it coincided with the Sunday. The Irish were first informed of their variation from the Church of Rome, in 609, by a letter from Laurence, archbishop of Canterbury, and the bishops Mellitus and Justus: they, however, adhered to their ancient system, until the year 630, when a letter on this subject was addressed to them by Pope Honorius I. Upon the receipt of this letter, the bishops and the abbots of the south of Ireland assembled at Old-Leighlin, when the most distinguished of the prelates declared, that, as according to the tradition of their ancestors, it was their duty to receive with respect the decrees of the successors of the apostles, they, therefore, resolved that they would celebrate Easter in unison with the universal Church. But the execution of their resolution met with opposition: deputies were, therefore, sent to Rome, as " children to their parent,"[*] who, at their return, re-

---

[*] Thus speaks Cummian, Epist. p. 23. Bede also relates the effect of their journey, ii. 3: " Porro gentes Scotorum quæ in australibus Hiberniæ insulæ partibus morabantur, jamdudum ad admonitionem apostolicæ sedis antistitis Pascha canonico ritu observare didicerunt."

lated how they had seen in Rome, Christians from the most distant and different countries, solemnizing the feast of Easter together, and at the same time. Thenceforward, from the year 633, the new Roman cycle was introduced into the south of Ireland, that is, into Munster, the greater part of Leinster, and a part of Connaught. At the same time, Cummian,* a Columbian monk, addressed his letter on the paschal solemnity to Segienus, abbot of Hy. The monks of Hy were zealous adherents to the Irish computation, and loudly expressed their dissatisfaction with Cummian for his adoption of the Roman. In his defence, amongst other things, he enquired, " Can any thing be imagined more perverse than to say: Rome is in error, Jerusalem, Alexandria, Antioch, the whole world is in error ; only the Scots and Britons are right!"

In the north of Ireland an excitement arose on the same subject. Thomian, archbishop of Armagh, with many other bishops and ecclesiastics, addressed the pontiff, but as their letter arrived only a short time before the death of Severinus, it remained a long while unopened, and was at length answered, in 640, by the Roman clergy, during the vacancy of the Holy See From their reply we learn that in Rome also a false idea of the cause, and peculiar circumstances of their variation in the cycle, was entertained : it is therein objected to the adherents of the Irish computation, that they renewed the heresy of the Quartodecimans, and solemnized the pasch with the Jews. This misunderstanding, and the great influence which was exercised by the monks of Hy in the north of Ireland, caused the bishops in that part of the island to retain their ancient calculation. This calculation was introduced into Northumbria by St. Aidan, bishop of Lindisfarne, and

---

* He has been erroneously confounded with *Cumineus Albus*, his contemporary, abbot of Hy, and biographer of St Columba. Cummian was author of the work cited, " De Pœnitentiarum mensura." Both that work and his " Epistolis Paschalis " exhibit to us a profound learning for his age, and the riches of the Irish libraries. See Lanigan, ii 30C.

as, during the time of his successor Finan, who was also a monk of Hy, other ecclesiastics from France and Kent laboured in the conversion of the Anglo-Saxons, North Britain, the present Northumberland and the south of Scotland, became the battle-field of the paschal controversy. An Irishman, named Nonan, who had learned the true mode of calculation on the continent, and the deacon James, whom St. Paulinus had left at York, were at the head of those Northumbrians, who celebrated Easter in the manner of Rome; to them was joined the queen Eanfleda; whilst the king, Oswio, and the bishop Finan, followed the computation of the Irish. Thus it happened that when one party was solemnizing the feast of Easter, the other had not yet completed the preparatory fast of Lent; and, what was perhaps of greater importance, this discrepancy threw confusion into almost the entire ecclesiastical year, as all the moveable feasts were dependant on the time of Easter.

When, in 661, Colman, an Irish monk of the order of St. Columba, succeeded Finan in the bishopric of Lindisfarne, the contest was renewed, but another, though less important, ingredient of dissension, the form of the ecclesiastical tonsure, had now been added to the former subjects of dispute. It appears that in Rome no notice had been taken of this latter point, but the newly converted Anglo-Saxons, of whom many, such as St. Wilfrid, and the favourers of his cause, were more attached to Roman customs than even the Romans themselves, would admit of nothing in their Church which was not Roman, and which was not performed as performed in Rome.* In Rome it was the custom to shave the upper part of the head, and to leave

---

* That the pontiff, St. Gregory the Great, did not consider an entire conformity in all ecclesiastical rites as absolutely necessary, but only desirable, may be shewn from the instruction sent by him to St. Augustin: "Novit fraternitas tua Romanæ ecclesiæ consuetudinem, in qua se meminit nutritam. Sed mihi placet, sive in Romana, sive in Galliarum, seu in qualibet ecclesia aliquid invenisti quod plus omnipotenti Deo possit placere, sollicite eligas, et in Anglorum ecclesia institutione præcipua, quæ de multis ecclesiis colligere potuisti infundas."— Bede, interrog. ii.

around the lower part a circle of hair, in the form of a crown: the Irish and the Britons, on the contrary, shaved only the front of the head, in the shape of a semicircle, and suffered the hair to flow down on the back; a form of tonsure worn by many monks, at least in the earlier ages of the Church, also on the continent.*
St. Wilfrid, and those who followed him, now maintained that the Roman form was that instituted by St. Peter, whilst the Irish form drew its origin from Simon Magus. It is impossible to determine what could have given rise to this idea, but it is certain that the imaginary descent of the Irish tonsure from the protoparent of all heretics, was the chief motive urged for its abolition.

St. Wilfrid, after having spent the years of his youth with the Irish monks in the Abbey of Lindisfarne, travelled to Rome, where he learned from the archdeacon Boniface the Roman method of computing the time of Easter. After his return, he acquired the confidence and friendship of his scholar Alchfrid, who reigned, together with his father Oswio, in Northumbria. Oswio bestowed upon him the abbey of Rippon, as its former possessors chose rather to resign it than to forsake their own Easter cycle and form of tonsure. At this time, 664, the evils of the variation had become so manifest, that, to establish uniformity, a synod or conference was assembled in the nunnery of Strenæshalch (Whitby), at which the two kings, Oswio and Alchfrid, were present. The bishop Colman and his Irish clergy, the bishop Cedd, and the abbess Hilda, appeared as the adherents and defenders of the Irish practice. St. Wilfrid, and the bishop Agilbert, (by whom he had been lately ordained priest), the priest Agatho, Nonan, and James, appeared as the supporters of the rite followed by Rome. Colman first arose and addressed the assembly: he appealed to the tradition of his predecessors, and to the authority of the apostle St. John, who, with the Churches which he founded, celebrated Easter in the

---

* This we learn from St. Paulinus of Nola, who (Epist vii.), about the year 420, speaks of monks who were " inæqualiter semitonsi et destituta fronte prorasi."

same manner in which the Irish continued to celebrate it. St. Wilfrid, in his reply, correctly stated that St. John solemnized Easter as did the Jews, on the fourteenth day of the moon, without regard to the day of the week, whilst the Irish always observed the Sunday, and could not, therefore, lay claim to an uniformity with the practice of the apostle. No less faulty, however, than the assertion of Colman was the declaration of St. Wilfrid, that the Roman calculation was introduced by St. Peter, and had never been changed. The true cause of the attachment of the Irish to their practice was made known by Colman when he asked— "Is it then to be supposed that their venerable father, Columba, and his holy successors, men whose sanctity had been proved by miracles, could have had false ideas on this subject, or have acted contrary to precept?" To this St. Wilfrid answered, that to suppose that these holy men might have been led by ignorance into an erroneous calculation, did not derogate from the honour which was due to their memory, but that they, their successors, sinned by acting against the decree of the apostolic see, of the universal Church, and against the spirit of the holy Scriptures. Here St. Wilfrid went too far: he had as little authority to cite the sacred Scriptures for or against a practice which depended entirely upon astronomical observations, as he had to mention a decree of the universal Church in favour of any particular paschal computation; only the Judaizing Quartodecimans had been cast out of the Church; and only his ignorance of the true state of the points of difference could class the Irish with them.

A deep impression was made upon the assembly, and particularly upon Oswio, who had espoused and hitherto defended the cause of the Irish, when to the authority of St. Columba, to which Colman had appealed, St. Wilfrid opposed the authority of the prince of the apostles. Interrogated by the king, Colman confessed that to St. Peter, not to St. Columba, were the great promises made and authority given by our Lord Jesus Christ. Oswio then declared in favour of Rome.

The form of the tonsure was not brought into discussion : it was dependent on the computation of Easter ; and those who adopted the Roman calculation abandoned the crescent form of the Irish tonsure and received the Roman *crown*.

Determined, however, not to forsake his ancient usages, Colman in 664 resigned his diocese of Lindisfarne, and, with the Irish, and part of the English monks, left the country. He was succeeded in his see by Tuda, who, having been educated and ordained in the south of Ireland, was accustomed to the Roman rite. After his death, which followed quickly upon his consecration, Ceadda, a disciple of St. Aidan, was appointed to York; but Lindisfarne still retained its rank as an episcopal see, and Eata, another disciple of St. Aidan, who had acted as abbot over the English monks who remained in the island, was consecrated to succeed Tuda. Colman erected, for the Irish and English monks who had followed him, a monastery on the island of Innisboffin, on the western coast of Ireland ; but as the monks of the two nations were continually engaged in disputes, he removed the English to Mayo, where they founded a large monastery, which in the eighth century was still peopled by English. They soon received the Roman cycle, and Bede testifies of them that they strictly followed a severe rule, lived under the guidance of an abbot in great purity of life, and gained their subsistence by the labour of their hands.

Adamnan, who in 679 was made abbot of Hy, and consequently superior of the whole Columbian order, manifested a strong inclination, while he was at the court of Alfrid of Northumbria, as representative of the Irish, in 701, to receive the Roman rites, and to establish an entire uniformity. At his return he endeavoured to infuse a like disposition into the minds of the monks of Hy and of all its dependent monasteries. His attempt failed ; but in 703 he passed over to Ireland, where he prevailed upon all the monasteries in the north, with the exception of those that were immediately connected with Hy, to adopt the Roman cycle. He died at Hy in the course of the following year. That which he had been unable to accomplish was effected by the holy Egbert, an English priest After a residence of many years in Ireland, he went to the abbey of Hy, and by his persuasions led the monks to follow the Roman cycle in the calculation of Easter, and to wear the Roman tonsure. Thus was this long controversy finally terminated, and an uniformity of practice, even to the most remote of the western British Churches, firmly established.

It is impossible not to have remarked, in the history of this dispute, how greatly the importance of their differences was exaggerated by both parties, and how unjust were the consequences which they deduced from the practice of each other. The Roman See displayed throughout that prudent wisdom and liberality which is peculiar to itself: so far was it from considering the attachment of the Irish to their own cycle as any thing schismatical or heretical, that it placed in its martyrology, and honoured as saints, two ecclesiastics, Colman of Luxeu, and Aidan, who were among the most zealous defenders of the usages of their country. But Wilfrid, and even Bede, viewed this question as a subject of great, almost of dogmatical, importance. The former estimated the bishops of the opposite party as no better than the Quartodecimans, as schismatical, and out of the communion of the Church; nor would he receive the episcopal consecration from them, or from those who had been consecrated by them. And yet so convinced was he of the orthodox faith of all the British, Irish, and Pict Churches, that, when at Rome, he bore solemn testimony to the same, before a synod of one hundred and twenty-five bishops.*

But on the other hand the Britons manifested a spirit of enmity, and bitter hate, towards the Anglo-Saxons

---

* " Wilfridus . . . . cum aliis cxxv. coepiscopis in synodo judicii sede constitutus pro omni aquilonali parte, Britanniæ et Hiberniæ insulis, quæ ab Anglorum et Britonum, nec non Scotorum et Pictorum gentibus incoluntur veram et Catholicam fidem confessus est et conscriptione s ... ... Al ... ...

as a nation, and which they endeavoured to conceal beneath a pretended spirit of zeal for the due celebration of Easter. When the Irish Churches on both islands united with the Church of Rome in this observance, the Britons treated the Anglo-Saxons as if still they were pagans, and the clergy of Demetia proceeded so far in their abhorrence, that they accounted all vessels which had been used by an English priest as defiled, and would carefully purify it with ashes or sand.* If it happened that an Anglo-Saxon fixed his abode amongst them, he was subjected to a penance of forty days before he could be admitted to ecclesiastical communion, or to the reception of the sacraments.†

SECTION V.

CHRISTIANITY IN GERMANY AND IN THE ADJACENT COUNTRIES.‡

During the period of the Roman dominion in Germany, the Christian religion had accompanied the progress of

---

* The slightest causes were sufficient to provoke such conduct of the one party against the other. Thus, Eddius relates of the adversaries of St. Wilfrid, against whom their enmity rested on purely personal grounds: "Inimici vero qui hæreditatem S. pontificis nostri sibi usurpabant, annunciantes nos esse a sorte fidelium segregatos et eos qui nobiscum participarent in tantum communionem nostram exsecraverunt ut si quispiam vel presbyterorum nostrorum, a fideli de plebe rogatus refectionem suam ante se positam signo crucis Dei benediceret, foras projiciendam et effundendam, quasi idolothytum, judicabant et vasa Dei, quibus nostri vescebantur, lavari prius, quasi sorte polluta jubebant, antequam ab aliis contingerentur."—c. xlvii.

† Aldhelmi, Epist. ad Geruntium Regem in epp. S. Bonifacii, ed. Serar. p. 59. Far more temperate and more Christian was the conduct of the Irish during the course of this controversy. The bishop Dagan was the only one who seemed to have imbibed a portion of the spirit of the Britons, and this in the beginning of the contest. After a conference with the Roman prelates, who had come from Rome, Mellitus, Laurence, and Justus, he refused to eat at the same table or even in the same house with them. But as he visited them of his own accord, his refusal was not the consequence of any previous resolution, but only of some degree of animosity caused by the interview.

‡ Jonæ Vita S. Columbani in Mabillon sæc ii. Benedict.—Walafridi

the Roman power, and of Roman colonization. Christian communities formed themselves in the higher and lower Germany, on the banks of the Rhine, in Helvetia, Rhætia, Vindelicia, and Noricum. But during the emigrations of the inhabitants, and the wars of destruction which desolated these countries towards the end of the fourth century, many of these Churches disappeared, as did the cities and the people; and if, indeed, a few of the Churches outlived the miseries and the evils of the times, and could preserve unbroken the succession of their bishops, we are without a narration of facts connected with them; and the early history of Christianity in Germany must be gathered from scattered accounts in the lives of saints, or in the subscriptions to the acts of councils. It is not before the seventh century that these accounts become more abundant, and more full, and narrate to us more precisely the history of the conversion of the German population.

In Helvetia, at Vindonissa, there was an episcopal Church, of which the district extended over the greater part of the then pagan Alemannia. The boundaries of this vast diocese, towards Augsburg, Basil or Augst, Strasburg, Lausanne and Chur, were defined, in 630, by king Dagobert I, whose diploma, which is now lost, was cited at a later period by the emperor Frederick I. Bubulcus, who, in 517, was present at the synod of Epaona, is the first known bishop of Vindonissa: his successor, Maximus, between the years 553 and 561, transferred his see to Constance, either on account of the great increase of the Alemannian Christians, or of the destruction of Vindonissa. The bishopric of Aventicum

---

Vita S. Galli, ibid.—Eugippii, Vita S. Severini, in Pezii Scriptor. rerum Austr t. i.—Meginfredi Vita S. Emmerami in Canis Lect. antiq. ed Basnage, t. iii.—Baudemundi, Vita S. Amandi in Mabillon, l. c.—Audoeni Vita S. Eligi, ibid.—Vita antiquissima S. Ruperti in (Kleinmayrn) Nachrichten von Juvavia, Salzburg, 1784.—Altera Vita S. Rup. in Actis SS. Martyrum, iii. 702.—Tertia Vita, ibid. p. 704.

Sig. Calles. Annales Ecclesiæ Germ. tom. i. ii.—V. A. Winter, Alteste Kirchengeschichte von Altbaiern, Oestreich und Tyrol. Landshut, 1813.—Alb. Muchar Romisches Norikum ii. Theil. Alteste Kirchengeschichte [illegible] 1826

(Avenche, near Bern), appears to have been founded somewhat later. Superius, bishop of this see, assisted in 535 at the synod of Clermont, and the bishop Marius, author of a chronicle of that age, was present in 584 at the second council of Macon. He is probably the same who removed from Aventicum to Lausanne; for in ancient records he is named bishop of Aventicum and Lausanne. That an episcopal Church existed at this time also at Geneva, (then called Genava or Gebenna), we know only from the subscriptions to the council of Epona, in 517, among which there is the name of Maximus, bishop of Geneva. But one of the most ancient of these Churches was that of Octodurum in the Valais; for, as early as the year 381, Theodore, the bishop of this city, was present at the synod of Aquileia. After the year 584, the bishops were not styled bishops of Octodurum, but of Sitten. Rhætia had a bishop at Chur in the middle of the fifth century; for we know that Abundantius, bishop of Como, subscribed the decree of the council of Chalcedon, in the name of Asimon, bishop of Chur.

Under the dominion of the Franks, the paganism of the Alemanni gradually retired before the faith of Christ, and much is due here also to the zeal of apostolic men from Ireland. As early as the year 511, Fridolin, an Irishman, after many long labours in France, founded the nunnery of Seckingen, on an island of the Rhine above Basle, and preached the gospel on both banks of the river. About a century later, the holy Columba and his disciples preached to the pagan Alemanni on the borders of the lake of Constance.

This great man had lived, as a religious, for many years in the celebrated Irish abbey of Bangor under the holy abbot Cungall, and was sent, about the year 590, with twelve brethren, into Gaul, where there was then great need of energetic and enlightened missionaries, to arrest the frightful and increasing barbarism of the people, and to awaken the clergy from their lethargy and indifference. As many persons soon placed themselves under the guidance of St. Columba, he founded the monastery of Luxeu in a desert of the Vogese; and as the numbers of those who gathered around him rapidly increased, he was compelled in a short time to erect another, at Fontaines, not far from Luxeu. Although living in Gaul, he observed the Irish rite in the solemnity of Easter; and as a difference arose on that account between him and the native bishops, he defended himself and his system in a letter to pope Gregory the Great. In the year 602, he wrote to a synod of Gaulish bishops, who had assembled to deliberate on this affair, and his letter declared his resolution of adhering to the Easter calculation of his Irish ancestors. He travelled to Rome, and supplicated the successor of St. Gregory, that he might be allowed to follow the practice of his native land in this point, since it did not oppose the faith of the Church, and as he did not disturb others in their peculiar customs. "We desire," he said, "peace and ecclesiastical unity, as did Polycarp with the pontiff Anicetus."

At his return, he saw himself exposed to the persecution of Brunhilden, the grandmother of the young Burgundian king Theoderic. This woman had led her grandson into early follies, that she might the more easily guide him, and rule his kingdom in his name. The young king, who honoured Columba, promised to repair the scandals which he had given, but violated his word; and having been therefore more severely reproved by Columba, Brunhilden sent soldiers to Luxeu, to expel him from his monastery, and to drive him, and the Irish and Britons who were with him, into banishment. The holy men were conducted to the western coast, and there placed on board a ship: the vessel was, however, driven back by the waves; the pilot allowed them to disembark, and they remained for some time at Nantes. After a short delay in the territories of Clothaire, Columba visited Theodebert, king of Austrasia, who had invited him to select a residence in his dominions. He passed the Rhine, the Limat, and the lake of Zurich, and settled with his disciples at Wangen, near the mouth of the Limat, in the midst of a pagan people. But it happened that Gall, one of his companions, in the ardour of his zeal, cast the victim which was destined for sacrifice to Wodan into the lake, and set fire to the temple of the idol: the infuriated people thereupon sought to kill him, and to scourge Columba. They then retired to Arbon on the lake of Constance, where they were kindly received by a priest named Willimar, who recommended to them the neighbourhood of the destroyed city of Bregenz as a fit place of abode. Here they laboured to convert the pagan inhabitants, and in a short time after their coming, Columba ordered Gall to break in pieces three bronze idols which the people had assembled to adore, and to dedicate the temple in which they had stood to the honour of God. A monastery was soon raised in the same place, where Columba and his companions lived by the labour of their hands. But as now Brunhilden and Theoderic had extended their power into Alemannia, by a victory over Theodebert in 612, and as the pagans had murdered two of his disciples, Columba left the country and went into Italy. From Milan he wrote to Pope Boniface IV a letter on the *Tria Capitula*, and in 613 founded a monastery at Bobbio, where he died aged seventy-two years.

His disciple Gall was left behind on account of illness. He chose for his abode a small and retired valley near the stream Steinach. He restored to health the daughter of the Alemannian duke, Genzo, and at his invitation was present at the election of a bishop for Constance, where he met Flavian, bishop of Autun, Hermaufried of Verdun, and Athanasius of Spiers. All turned their eyes towards him as the most worthy to fill the vacant see, but he refused, urging that he was a stranger, and recommended to their choice his scholar, John, a deacon, who was a native of that country. John endeavoured to conceal himself, but was discovered and consecrated. On this occasion Gall delivered to the assembly the discourse which is still extant. He then returned to his solitude, and when in 625 the monks of Luxeu wished to possess him as their abbot, and sent six Irish monks to solicit his consent, he refused this dignity also, that he might not be compelled to forsake his Alemanni, who were yet pagans or only in part converted. He died at Arbon in 645, in the ninety-fifth year of his age. His tomb soon became a favourite place of pilgrimage. After his death, his disciples continued the severe mode of life which he had taught them from the rule of St. Columba, in the monastery, which is to this day called the Cell of St. Gall. Two of these religious left their monastery to preach to the pagans: one, named Theodore, founded a new monastery at Kempten; the other, named Mang, laboured in the country near the river Lech, where he died in 666.

In that part of Pannonia which is now called Steyermark, the bishopric of Petau (Petovio) was founded before the end of the third century. Marcus, the Catholic bishop, was driven from his see, in 380, by the Arian Julianus Valens, who was favoured by the Goths; but as the Catholic population would not receive him, the intruder was obliged to retire to Milan. We are unacquainted with the origin of the bishopric of Cilly (Celjia); but we find a bishop of this see, named John, in 558, at the council of Aquileia. At Tiburnia in Carinthia (some have supposed this to be Ratisbon), Paulinus was bishop in the second half of the fifth century. Several bishops of these countries, by their connexion with the metropolitan of Aquileia, were involved in the schism which arose from the disputes on the Tria Capitula; and when the kings of Austrasia made themselves masters of a part of the neighbouring Italy and Norgaw, the Gallic prelates broke off this schismatical union, by placing other bishops in three of these sees. The bishops of the metropolitan diocese complained against this proceeding, in 590, to the Greek emperor Mauritius, They call the three bishoprics which the Gallic prelates had taken to themselves, *Beconensis*, *Tiburniensis* and *Augustana*. What place can have been meant by the first name, we can only conjecture: by the Church at Augusta, can be understood Cilly or perhaps Augsburg, although it is uncertain whether Augsburg possessed an episcopal Church at this time; and as late as the eighth century there is a mere list of the names of the Augsburg bishops, unconnected with any certain facts. Together with Aquileia, the ancient Church of Laureacum (Lorch) also enjoyed metropolitan rank, and from it, as the popes Symmachus and Agapitus II testify in their bulls, Upper and Lower Pannonia received the Christian faith. Petau in Steyermark, and Seiseia (Sissec) in Croatia, were probably suffragans of Lorch. Of the bishops of Lorch only two are known, Constantius, who is named in the life of St. Severinus, and Theodore, to whom pope Symmachus, about the year 500, sent the pallium, with a letter that implies that several of his predecessors had worn that emblem of the metropolitan dignity.

In that part of Rhætia which forms the Tyrol, Trent and Brixen were bishoprics in the fourth century. The names of Abundantius and Vigilius, bishops of Trent in that age, have been preserved, as also the names of Philastrius and Gaudentius, bishops of Brixen. The bishopric of Sabiona or Seben, in the Tyrol, arose at a later period: the first bishop of this see whose name is known, is Ingenuinus, who lived towards the end of the sixth century, and who, with his contemporary, Agnellus of Trent, took part in the schism of Aquileia More ancient is the Church of Amona, (Laibach), of which the bishop, Maximus, was at Aquileia in 381.

To the Roman castle, Castra Batava, now called Passau, situated at the confluence of the Inn and the Danube, came in the year 440 the holy man St. Valentine. He was born on the Belgic sea coast, and now left his home to preach to pagans, and to Christians who had been tainted by Arianism. But he soon bethought him that for this purpose he required a mission from the Holy See; he therefore journeyed to Rome, received from pope Leo the necessary powers, and returned to Castra Batava. The hatred of the pagans and Arians soon compelled him to retire. He again went to Rome, where he was consecrated bishop by the pope, and obtained a commission, if he should be unable again to return to the place which he had left, to preach in any other province. When he presented himself to the people of Castra Batava, he was treated by them with great cruelty, and was driven from their city; he therefore turned himself to the highlands of the Rhætian Alps, the Tyrol, where he converted many to Christianity, and died the death of the saints.*

Soon after St. Valentine, the holy Severinus, probably an African by birth, appeared in Pannonia and Noricum. To the scattered and oppressed Christians of those countries he afforded both corporal and spiritual relief; even the chiefs of German barbarians respected and revered him, and he employed the authority which he had acquired amongst them, in favour of the enslaved Christians. He sojourned generally in the country around Fabiana (Vienna), and in the neighbourhood of Passau. Near Vienna he built for himself a cell; and not far distant he founded a monastery, from which many holy men and preachers of the faith went forth into Pannonia and Noricum. Near Passau, also, he erected a small cloister; but after a short time he persuaded the greater part of the inhabitants of that city, (the fate of which he foresaw), to accompany him to Lorch. Not long after their departure, those who remained behind were attacked by the Thuringians, and either slain or carried away captives.

At his death, which was at his monastery near Vienna, in 482, St. Severinus foretold the emigration of the Christians of Roman origin from Noricum, and the total desolation of the country. Six years afterwards the expedition to Italy commenced. Juvavia (Salzburg), Reginum (Ratisbon), and Quintana (Osterhaufen?), were

---

* These circumstances are contained in an inscription engraved in lead, which was found in the tomb of St. Valentine. See Resch Annal. Sabion, 1 281-91; and Winter, Vorarbeiten, b. 11. In the biography of St. Severinus, by Eugippius, it is related that the priest Lucillus observed the anniversary of St. Valentine, who was his abbot, and bishop (Regionarius) of the two Rhætias Venantius Fortunatus speaks of a church dedicated to St. Val ntine, at ?n.

converted into heaps of ruins by the Alemanni, the Herulians, and the Thuringians. The fugitive Christians from the Upper Danube sought for safety in Lorch, and they also after a short time fled into Italy under the guidance of Odoacher. About the year 526, after the destruction of the Roman cities and castles, Lorch was destroyed by the Sclavi: the whole country presented the appearance of one vast wilderness, and from that time Christianity disappeared from the land. Three German tribes, the Alemanni, the Bojoari, and the Thuringians, took possession of southern Germany. We are unacquainted with the origin of Christianity among the Bojoari, or Bavarians, who had now settled in Noricum and Vindelicia. Their connexion with the Franks, whose superiority they acknowledged, may have first opened a way for the faith; and towards the end of the sixth century, one of their dukes, Garibald, the father of Theodelinda, was a Christian. His relative Theodo, another duke, although he and his people were yet pagans, called to his court St. Rupert, bishop of Worms: he probably foresaw that the propagation of Christianity in his dominions would be the means of his forming an union with the Austrasian kings, as it had enabled Garibald to connect himself with the Lombards. St. Rupert arrived at Ratisbon about the year 580: he preached; and soon after baptized the duke, with many of his nobles and people, and continued his labours along the banks of the Danube as far as the confines of the Lower Pannonia. At the Wallersee, in Salzburgau, he built a church, afterwards called the Seekirchen, but chose the place where Juvavia had before stood for his residence. Theodo bestowed upon him this place, with the surrounding district, and Rupert built there, first a church in honour of St. Peter, and afterwards a monastery The monastery was soon peopled by solitaries, who came in numbers to the holy founder, and Juvavia arose again from its ruins under the name of Salzburg. St. Rupert now brought fresh labourers into the field, twelve priests and monks, and his nephew Ehrentrud, from Gaul, whither he had gone to seek them. The

Church of Salzburg was the parent Church of many others in Bavaria, Austria, Steyermark, and Carinthia. In the school of the cloister priests were educated; and in the house of nuns, which was under the guidance of Ehrentrud, a school was opened for females. St. Rupert died in 623, after forty years of blessed labours, and was honoured as the father of the Bavarian Church.* A short time before his death, Eustasius, a scholar of St. Columba, being invited by the king of the Franks, Clothaire II, went with his friend Agilis to assist in the conversion of the Bavarians; but he found so many difficulties to encounter, that he returned intimidated, and died at Luxeu in 625.

In the year 652, Emeran, a bishop of the Franks, left his home, with the intention of preaching to the pagan Avari in Pannonia. On his journey he arrived at Ratisbon, where duke Theodo then resided. The duke would not permit him to proceed further, but obliged him to remain in Bavaria to instruct the inhabitants, who had been only recently converted, and to preach the faith to those who still continued in paganism. For three years he laboured, and blessings crowned his toils. He then wished to travel to Rome; but before his departure he endeavoured, by an act of self-sacrifice, to reclaim the daughter of the duke from crimes of which she had been guilty; the consequence, however, of his attempt was, that he was followed by Landpert, the brother of the princess, and by him was barbarously murdered.

If we turn now to the countries on the banks of the Rhine, we find that in the fourth century there was an episcopal see at Argentoratum, now called Strasburg, the first bishop of which, Amandus, was present at the council of Sardica. In the following century the succession of the bishops was interrupted here also, and

---

* Mich Filz, in his Historico-Critical Dissertation on the Times and Labours of St. Rupert in Bavaria, and on the foundation of the see of Salzburg (Salzburg. 1831), has proved against Mabillon, Hansiz, Resch, and others, who maintained that the saint died in 718 or 723, that he must only died a full century before that period

from the sixth century, when the succession was restored, to the year 646, when St. Amandus II removed from Strasburg to Maestricht, we know the names of only two bishops. After Rothar, who succeeded St. Amandus at Strasburg, there followed two Irish prelates, Arbogast and Florentius. They seem to have come from Ireland with king Dagobert, who in his youth had fled to Ireland to seek an asylum from his enemies.

At Spiers, formerly called Augusta Nemetum, a bishopric was founded by Jesse, who had been sent there by the Roman see, and whose name is found among the subscriptions to the council of Sardica. The province of Germania Prima comprised the bishoprics of Strasburg, Spiers, and Worms (Civitas Vangionum), under the metropolitan of Mentz or Mayence. The bishops of Germania Prima are first mentioned by St. Hilary of Poitiers, when in 358 he addressed to them his work *On Synods*. The Church of Spiers, like so many others of its contemporaries, was swept away by the whirlwind of emigration; for between Jesse and Athanasius, who lived in the seventh century, we hear of no bishop of Spiers. The beginnings of the Church of Mentz are uncertain, and until the year 546 nothing is known of its bishops but a doubtful series of names. St. Aureus, indeed, who according to the Roman martyrology was burnt, together with his sister Justina, and many other Christians, in the church at Mentz, in 451, is supposed to have been bishop of that city. The memory of the bishop Sidonius, who lived about the year 547, has been preserved in the panegyric composed in his honour by the poet Venantius Fortunatus.

The Church of Triers, or Treves, was founded at the end of the third, or in the beginning of the fourth, century, by Maternus, Eucharius, and Valerius. It appears that these three missionaries were sent from Rome, whence arose the saying that they had been sent by the apostle St. Peter. Maternus left Triers to preach to the Ubieri and the Eburoni: he was the founder of the see at Tongres, and, lastly, bishop of Cologne, where he died.

The first bishop of Triers was probably Agrotius, who was at the council of Arles in 314. To him succeeded Maximin, who is known by being present at the council of Sardica. Maximin was succeeded by Paulinus, who was banished by Constantius on account of his persevering opposition to Arianism. The bishop Felix, in 386, received ordination from the Ithacianians, who, on account of the affairs of the Priscilians, were then at Triers: he was, therefore, considered by the synod of Turin, in 398, as excommunicated: In the emigrations towards the south, Triers was four times depopulated; and, although the names of thirteen bishops of Triers in the fifth century have been handed down to us, it is very doubtful whether the existence of the Church, and the successions of its bishops, were then preserved. After the conversion of Clovis, the Church of Triers was raised to its primitive splendour, particularly by the virtues of many of its bishops. Amongst these stands conspicuous St. Nicetus, who, when yet only abbot, reproved king Theoderic for his crimes so freely, and with such success, that, at the death of St. Aprunculus, in 527, the king caused him to be chosen bishop of Triers.

The bishopric of Metz acknowledges, according to an ancient tradition, for its founder, Clement, who had been sent thither from Rome in the beginning of the fourth century. In the succession of bishops, who followed him, the first whom we can name with certainty, is Sperus or Hesperius, who in 535 assisted at the council of Clermont. But the glory of this Church was the blessed Arnulf, the ancestor of Charlemagne. When in the service of the Austrasian king, Theodebert II, he had been married, and was the father of two sons, but, with the consent of his wife, he forsook the world, and dedicated himself to a life of solitude. In the year 611, the people and clergy of Metz, after the death of their bishop, Pappolus, demanded Arnulf for his successor; and, although he was only a layman, so great was the fame of his virtues, that the laws of the Church were dispensed with, and he was consecrated bishop. In 623, he was chief minister of Dagobert, the young king of Austrasia; but three years later, despite all the opposition and threats of the king, he executed his design of withdrawing himself at once and entirely from the world. He chose his residence first in the Voge, where he consecrated himself to the service of lepers, but afterwards enclosed himself within a cell, in which he died in 640.* One of his sons, in 650, became also bishop of Metz. The Church of Verdun was founded by the holy Sanctius, a disciple of St. Dionysius, the first bishop of Paris. He had been consecrated by St. Dionysius, bishop of Meaux, after which, in 332, he established the see of Verdun, and governed it twenty-one years.

Of the following bishops only the names, or some uncertain sayings, are preserved; and it is only in the sixth and seventh centuries that the bishops stand on sure historical grounds. In Toul, the city of the Leucii, St. Mansuetus, (who was not, as it has been said, a disciple of St. Peter, for he did not live before the fourth century), founded the first Christian community. Auspicius, bishop of Toul, who died in 478, is known by a panegyric composed by Sidonius Apollinaris, and by his poem to the Count Arbogastes. In the year 680, Adeodatus, bishop of Verdun, assisted at a council held at Rome against the Monothelites, as the representative of the bishops of the Franks.†

The first bishop of Cologne, or at least the first with whom we are acquainted, was St. Maternus, whose name we find at the council of Arles. His successor, Euphratas, was a distinguished prelate, and an undaunted champion of the Catholic faith against Arianism, for which cause he was sent by the council of Sardica as its ambassador to the emperor. We are, however, told that he unhappily fell from the faith himself, and was, therefore, deposed by a synod held at Cologne in 346:

---

* Vita S. Arnulfi, by a contemporary, in Mabillon, Act. SS. O. S. Bened. sæc. ii. p. 140, et seq.

† He subscribed himself, "Adeodatus, humilis Episcopus S. Ecclesiæ Leucorum, legatus venerabilis synodi per Galliarum provincias constitutæ."

but the acts of this synod are at the least very doubtful.* The bishop Evergistus was murdered in 439, whilst preaching to the infidels of Tongres. Of the bishops who governed the Church of Cologne, under the dominion of the Franks, the first that is known, except Domitian, who subscribed to the council of Clermont in 535, is Charentinus, who was celebrated in a eulogy by Venantius Fortunatus, about the year 570. St. Cunibert, who was first archdeacon of Triers, and, in 623, bishop of Cologne, was appointed by king Dagobert preceptor to his son Siegbert, and after the death of Dagobert governed the Austrasian kingdom until 656, with his friend Pepin, the mayor of the palace. Whether Cologne were then a metropolitan Church, and Cunibert its first archbishop, is now uncertain.

That there existed in Belgium, in the beginning of the fourth century, many episcopal Churches, we learn from the book of St. Hilary *On Synods*, which was addressed to the bishops of the first and second province of Germany, and of the first and second province of Belgium. The most ancient of these Churches appears to have been that of Tongres, of which the bishop Servatius was at the councils of Sardica and Rimini. Some years later, St. Victricius of Rouen, preached the faith in the countries of the Nervii and Morini, the present Flanders. But the desolating inundations of the Huns, Vandals, Alani, and lastly of the Franks, swept Christianity from the land, and paganism held the sway for one hundred and fifty years after the conversion of Clovis. But bishops still continued to labour during the fifth and sixth centuries. The blessed Arvatius of Tongres founded in 452 the episcopal see of Maestricht, and his successors were for a time called bishops of Tongres. Theodore was the first bishop of the Christians, who, in 487, were driven by the pagans from

---

* Their genuineness is surrendered by almost all modern writers, and the proofs that they are not genuine have been collected by Harzheim. (Concil. Germ. i. 22, et seqq.) Grandidier, however, in his Hist. de l'Eglise de Strasburg, i. 132, has again undertaken the defence of this council.

Tournay: he was followed by Eleutherius, who, after the baptism of Clovis, returned with his community to Tournay, and converted a great number of the pagans. The successor of Eleutherius was St. Medardus, who had before been bishop of Noyon: from his time to the year 1146, the two Churches continued united. At Arras, St. Remigius, in 500, placed St. Vedastus as the first bishop of that see. St. Vedastus joined with Arras the see of Cambray, and the two Churches formed but one see until the year 1093; but, about the year 545, St. Vedulf left Arras to reside at Cambray, from which city the bishops thenceforth took their title.

St. Amandus, who has been mentioned above as bishop of Strasburg, undertook, in the year 630, to convert the pagan populations of Belgium; but as he soon remarked that he could make but little impression on these rude and wild adorers of idols, he obtained from king Dagobert a decree, in virtue of which, all, without distinction, were to be baptized. Amandus employed this command of the king only to gain a hearing amongst the infidels, for he possessed too much of the true spirit of the gospel, not to despise force or coercion in the labours of his mission, and he had to thank not this royal decree, but the patience and heroic perseverance with which he encountered the most obstinate opposition and cruelties, even after his own companions had forsaken him, for the blessing that attended his preaching in the conversion of the countries around Tournay and Ghent. He founded a monastery at Ghent, built a church at Antwerp, and in obedience to the will of king Siegbert II, undertook, in 646, the government of the diocese of Maestricht. Dispirited by the opposition of some of his clergy, who refused to practise the discipline which he had introduced, he, three years later, implored permission from Pope Martin to resign his bishopric. The pope's reply was an exhortation to him not to think of abandoning his Church; whereupon he went to Rome and obtained in person his request from the pope. He died in 684 at the abbey of Elnones.

Contemporary with Amandus, the holy Audomar or

Omer, who was by birth an Alemann, and a scholar of the monastery of Luxeu, preached to the idolatrous Morini, who inhabited the coast from Boulogne to the mouth of the Scheld. He destroyed their idols and sacred groves, baptized many, and, by founding the abbey of St. Bertin, provided a seminary of learning for the education of priests. At the same time came St. Livin, an Irishman, to announce the faith to the Brabantans, but he was received by them with contempt and cruelty, as he relates in his poetical epistle to St. Floribert, abbot of Ghent.* The expectation which he expresses in this work of his approaching martyrdom, was soon accomplished: he was slain by the pagans in 656, in the neighbourhood of Hauthem. With greater success did St. Eligius labour in the extirpation of idolatry in western Flanders. He had been by profession a worker in gold, but had so distinguished himself by his piety and humility, that, although a layman, he was chosen and consecrated bishop of Noyon and Tournay. His biographer relates, particularly, that he preached with great success at Antwerp, and that he converted the Suevi, who remained in that country at the time of the general emigration.†

---

* This epistle, and his epitaph on St. Bavo, are perhaps the best poetical specimens of the time, and awaken within us an idea of the high state of mental cultivation which then existed in Ireland. Let us take the beautiful passage (Usser. Epist. Hibern. Sylloge, No. 8):
"Hos postquam populos conspexi luce serena,
  Sol mihi non luxit, nox fuit una mihi,
Impia barbarico gens exagitata tumultu,
  Hic Brabanta furit, meque cruenta petit.
Quid tibi peccavi, qui pacis nuncia porto?
  Pax est quod porto: cur mihi bella moves?
Sed qua tu spiras feritas sors læta triumphi
  Atque dabit palmam gloria martyrii.
Cui credam novi, nec spe frustrabor inani
  Qui spondet Deus est, quis dubitare potest?"

† That a true estimation of the great services and influence of Irish ecclesiastics, in the Churches of Gaul, Belgium, and Germany, may be formed, we will speak briefly of those who assisted in the propagation of Christianity in those countries, during the seventh century, and whom we have not yet mentioned. About the year 622, two Irish priests Cadoc and Fricor laboured at Pouthieu, in Picardy. A noble-

PERIOD THE SECOND.

SECTION VI.

MUHAMMEDISM AND ITS FOUNDER.*

WHILST thus in the most distant West the Christian religion displayed its victorious power, whilst flourishing Churches arose where a short time before all things lay buried in the confused and dark night of paganism, counsels of God of another kind were fulfilling in the East. A more powerful rival of Christianity, and one prepared for the conflict, now arose in the Arabian peninsula, and went irresistably onwards to the twofold destiny which God had marked out for it—the chastisement of the degenerate and corrupted Christians of the

---

man of the country, named Fricarius, who had been instructed by them, built for them a monastery, in which they all three passed the remainder of their lives. Rantic, Kilian, and Bolcan (Vulganius), a bishop, preached in Belgic Gaul about the year 650. Another Kilian, or Chillen, taught, in 628, in Artois, and a few years later, Fiacre founded a monastery at Breuil, in the diocese of Meaux; and in 644, the famed St. Fursey built an abbey at Lagny, near Paris. His brothers, Foillan and Ultan, being invited by St Gertrude, abbess of Neville, into Brabant, built there a monastery for their countrymen, at Fosse, in the neighbourhood of Neville. Towards the end of the century, an Irishman, St. Erhard, who had been bishop of Ardagh, in his own country, penetrated as far as Bavaria: he preached chiefly at Ratisbon, where he died. Another, named Wiro, who had been consecrated bishop in Rome, went in the time of Pepin from Heristal, and obtained from him a residence at Odilienburg, in the territory of Luttich His countryman, Dysibod, erected, about the same time, a Benedictine abbey, not far from Creuznach.

* Alcorani Textus universus, edidit Lud. Marraccius, Patav. 1698, fol —Albulfeda, De Vita et Rebus gestis Mahomedis, ed. Jo. Gagnier, Oxon. 1723 —Abu Zacarja Jahja En-Navavi, Vitæ illustrium Virorum, ed. H. F. Wustenfeld, Gotting. 1832.—La Vie de Mahomet, par J. Gagnier, Amsterdam, 1732, 2 vols.

C. Forster, Mahometanism Unveiled, Lond. 1829, 2 vols.—Reinaud, Description des Monumens Musulmans du Cabinet de M Le Duc de Blacas, Paris, 1828, 2 vols —G. Sale, Preliminary Discourse, prefixed to his English translation of the Koran, London, 1764, vol. 1.

Since the publication of this history, Professor Dollinger has written a masterly work on the "Religion of Muhammed.' See the Dublin Review, No XIII. August, 1839

east, and the preparation of the nations yet unripe for the doctrines of the Christian faith, in other regions of the east and south.*

Until the commencement of the seventh century, the Arabians, far removed from the theatre on which the great scenes of the world had hitherto been enacted, were a people almost unknown, and apparently insignificant, which had indeed preserved its own independance, but was without any influence beyond its own territories. Enclosed within the almost impenetrable fastnesses of its peninsula, it exhausted its best strength in perpetual feuds and petty wars amongst its own tribes. But on a sudden this hitherto almost unobserved people came forth from its sandy wastes, frightfully strengthened, and united by a new faith, proclaiming an exterminating war to all who would not embrace this faith; and founded an empire which in extent would compete with the empire of Rome, and which yields to it alone in power and duration. The religion, which thus almost instantaneously imparted such energy and enthusiasm to the people of Arabia, remained for a time concealed. Its founder was an uneducated Arab, who, although a member of a powerful tribe, was so far from finding a support to his attempt in this connexion, that he was for a long time despised and persecuted by his own relatives, as a deluded and deluding man. And this religion, which had no forerunner, the author of which aspired not to the power of working miracles, but rested his mission on the bare assertion that God had revealed himself to him, connected together, in the short space of twenty years, tribes that had been split asunder by enmities and inherited hatred, as into one family, as into a nation animated by one spirit; and displaced a deeply rooted and zealously defended idolatry by the worship of the true God. To this first victory, others and not less wonderful succeeded. Islam subdued and annihilated the ancient religion of Persia, and trampled upon Christianity in

---

* See this idea developed in the author's "Religion of Muhammed."

those countries where it was first spread and flourished the earliest—in Syria, Mesopotamia, Palestine, and the north of Africa.

The Sacred Scriptures contain strikingly prophetic declarations of the great and world-involving destinies which were reserved for the Arabian nation, on account of its descent from Ismael, the son of Abraham. These declarations are contained in the promises made to the patriarch Abraham and to Agar, respecting their son, Ismael. It was foretold to Abraham, that from him a mighty people should arise, and that in him all the nations of the earth should be blessed. This prophecy divided itself into two parts, or into two classes of promises to the two sons of the patriarch; of these promises, the one class, the higher and the spiritual, fell to the true son, Isaac the son of promise,—and were the ground of the never-ending covenant that was made with him: the other class of lower, temporal, earthly promises, (which, however, were the effects of a covenant), was the lot of Ismael, the son of the hand-maid, —that from him a great nation should spring. The promises made to the two brothers, were, until the particular inheritance of Isaac came to him, concurrent; and, in the parallel histories of the Jewish and Arabian people, were fulfilled, in a manner that must appear extraordinary. As from Isaac, through Jacob, sprung the twelve patriarchs, the fathers of the twelve tribes of Israel, so from Ismael, according to the Divine promise (Genesis xxv. 16), were born the princes of twelve tribes or nations. As the twelve tribes of Ismael possessed the land of Canaan, in virtue of the promises to Isaac, so the dwelling place of the twelve tribes of the Ismaelite Arabians, according to the prophecy respecting Ismael, (Genesis xvi. 12), "that he should pitch his tents over against all his brethren," extended along the confines of Canaan, from the Euphrates to the Red Sea. In both nations, notwithstanding their frequent turnings to idols, the patriarchal belief in the One God of Abraham was preserved. Both nations preserved the seal of the covenant made by the Almighty with their common father—circumcision: and as the Jews, who were descended from Isaac, practised this rite, as it was practised on him, on the eighth day after birth, so the Ismaelite Arabs circumcised their sons in their thirteenth year, the age at which their progenitor Ismael was circumcised.*

Muhammed was born in the year 590, after the death of his father: he was of the tribe of the Koreichites, and of the family of the Haschemites. At the age of six years, he lost his mother; he was then taken into the house of his grandfather Abdelmutalleb, the most powerful man in Mecca, the chief of the Kaaba or Sanctuary, and the head of his tribe. After two years Abdelmutalleb entrusted the education of the youth to his son, Abu Taleb, the uncle of Muhammed. He formed his nephew to the then highly-honoured profession of a merchant, took him with himself in his commercial travels into Syria, and recommended him, after he had acquired the appellation of the Faithful in a war with hostile tribes, to the rich widow Khadidscha, as the conductor of her affairs. After his return from another journey into Syria, he became, at the age of twenty-five, the husband of the widow, and thereby one of the richest of the merchants of Mecca. Repeated journeys enlarged his views, increased his knowledge of mankind, and made him acquainted with the different religions of Arabia, and of the neighbouring countries. He had ever shown a love of solitude; it was his custom to withdraw himself from his mercantile avocations, and to retire for a month in every year into a cavern in a mountain near Mecca. In his fortieth year, in 609, he commenced his career of prophet. In the night of the 24th and 25th Ramadhan, (called Elkadar, "the night of the Divine counsels"), whilst he was in his cavern— these are his own words—the archangel Gabriel approached to him, and announced to him his vocation, as apostle of God, to extirpate idolatry, to reform Juda-

---

* As we learn from Josephus, Antiq Jud. 1. 10, and from Origen in Genes. opp. ii. 16, ed. De la Rue.

ism and Christianity, and to reduce both according to the model of Islam,—the true, the ancient religion of Abraham, and of all the prophets who had been sent by God. At the same time, the archangel showed to him the whole Koran, which was afterwards made known only by degrees, during the space of twenty-three years, and, commanding him to read, imparted to him who could not read before, the faculty of doing so, merely by a touch. Muhammed related the pretended vision, at first, only to his most confidential friends and relatives. Khadidscha was the first who declared her belief in his mission: she was followed by his cousin, the youth Ali, his slave Zeid, Abu Beker, Othman, and a few others, amongst whom were some of the most considerable men of Mecca. After three years Muhammed came before the world with his doctrines and his high pretensions. At a banquet, prepared by Ali, he announced himself to his tribe as a messenger sent by God to men. But his declaration was coldly received. He then preached to the people; and when he saw the slight impression produced by his discourses, he proceeded to threaten with the torments of hell the idolatry and infidelity of his countrymen. The enraged Meccanians declared themselves his enemies, and he was compelled to flee for refuge to his uncle, the powerful Abu Taleb, who protected him, but would not embrace his doctrines. The disciples of the new prophet were so severely persecuted at Mecca, that sixteen of them fled, with his consent, into Abyssinia. As they were there kindly received by the Christian king, Negusch, they were followed by others, until their number amounted to eighty-three men and eighteen women. Muhammed continued in the mean time with those adherents who had remained in Mecca, in the house of Orkham. His party was soon strengthened by the conversion of his uncle Hamsa, and of Omar, who, from a deadly persecutor of the prophet, became, on hearing him recite a part of the Koran, one of his most enthusiastic followers. Rejected and persecuted by his own tribe, Muhammed retired, in 622, to Medina, which was thence named Medinat al Nabi, "the city of the prophet." Here he began his wars against the Koreischites, by plundering their caravans; and in the year 629 attacked and took Mecca, where the ancient national sanctuary, the Kaaba, became thenceforth the centre of his religion. At the time of his death, in 632, the whole of Arabia was subjected to his doctrine, and to his dominion. Many willingly, many compelled by force after strong opposition, had embraced the new faith. The Koran, or revelations which Muhammed had made known to his followers at different times, was collected after his death, by Abu Beker, the first Muhammedan caliph or spiritual and civil prince.*

Warned by his first failure, Muhammed announced to his countrymen, that the religion which he was to give to them, should rise upon the ruins of all others that had preceded it, even of the Christian and Jewish; that it should reign as the only true universal religion, in its last and most perfect form. The unity of God, in

---

* The following anecdote will give an insight into the character of Muhammed, and an idea of the mixture of self-delusion and deceit which distinguished him. After the battle of Beder, he enquired of his friends what should be done with the prisoners, amongst whom were several of their own relatives. Abu Beker advised that they should be liberated for a ransom of gold, but Omar would condemn them, as stiff-necked infidels, to death. Muhammed adopted the advice of Abu Beker. Soon after, Omar entering the tent of the prophet, found him and Abu Beker in tears. On enquiring the cause, Muhammed related to him that the 70th verse of the 8th Sure had just been revealed to him: "It is not permitted to any prophet to take prisoners into his possession, until he has formed a bath of blood amongst the infidels." He added, that if God had not been merciful they should have all been destroyed; even Omar and Saad Ebu Moadh, who had advised the death of the captives. But their clemency did not pass wholly unpunished, for in the battle of Ohed the Moslems lost as many of their men as they had made prisoners at Beder. When some years after, the Jews of the tribe of Koraida surrendered to Muhammed, they appealed to the mediation of their ancient friend Moadh: but he, who had that day finished his evening prayers with these words, "Grant, O God! that before my death, I may feed my eyes with the blood of the Koraidites," condemned all the men to death, and their wives and children to slavery. Enraptured with his reply, Muhammed exclaimed, "This was a heavenly sentence, a sentence which came from the seventh heaven." Abi fela Annal i. 112.

opposition to the polytheism of idolaters and the Trinity of the Christians, was its fundamental doctrine. The greatest influence was produced upon the Moslem mind by the doctrine of the unconditional decree by which God has unalterably preordained all the actions and destinies of men, and of the sensual paradise which, they were told, should receive the faithful after death. The most remarkable of the acts of the Muhammedans were, their daily prayer, their alms, their fasts, and their pilgrimages to Mecca: but the most meritorious of all was declared by the prophet to be co-operation with the saints in extending the new religion by force of arms. A plurality of wives was permitted, but the use of wine was forbidden. In its essence, Islam was a species of Judaism extended beyond the limits of the religion of a single people; but Judaism stripped of its typical and symbolical character,—Judaism debased and corrupted.

Although Muhammed declared our Saviour Christ to be no more than man, and only one of the many teachers whom heaven had sent to men, he ever spoke with the greatest reverence of him, and of his gospel: he named him the Word of God, whom God had formed in Mary, the word of truth, the spirit of God. He did not, however, imagine to himself any thing like to the Word, the Logos, of which St. John writes; but borrowing his expression from a form of speech then in use amongst Christians, he intended to signify no more than a highly gifted prophet and preacher of the Divine word. His supernatural resurrection he ascribed to the omnipotent will and word of God. That God had empowered Jesus to work miracles is particularly declared in the Koran: even miracles contained in apocryphal gospels are produced; such as that Jesus spoke when a child in the arms of his mother, and in the cradle; that he formed birds of clay and gifted them with life; also that he imparted sight to those who had been born blind; that he cleansed lepers, and raised the dead to life. The most extraordinary is perhaps the narration contained in the 5th Sure, that God, at the prayer of Christ, and to prove his mission, sent down food from heaven to feed his disciples. This is without doubt a designed or accidental deformation of the history of the institution of the Holy Eucharist, blended perhaps with the miraculous feeding of the five thousand men. The Eucharist could have no signification for Muhammed, as he denied the redemption of man by Jesus Christ, and in particular his death on the cross. Although the Jews, he says in the 4th Sure, boast that they crucified Jesus, this is not true: another man, like to him, put himself in his place and was crucified; he was taken up by God and raised to a state of sublime blessedness in heaven, in the immediate presence of God. The Koran does not determine whether Jesus died on this earth or was borne corporally into heaven. The supposition regarding the crucifixion, though not entirely docetic, (for Muhammed confessed the reality of Christ's body) makes it probable that he had had some communication with the remains of the Gnostic sects in Arabia, or that he or his companions had consulted Gnostic writings. If he gave the preference to the Gnostic doctrines before those of all other Christians, this was occasioned by his determination not to acknowledge that Christ had effected the redemption of man, for this would have made it impossible for him to declare himself as the last and the greatest of the prophets.* The Koran speaks often, and with the greatest praise, of the virgin mother of Christ. She was chosen, it says, before all other women, by the Almighty: she is the wonder of all ages, is honoured even by angels, and raised by God

---

* The Koran speaks in brief and obscure terms of the return of Christ at the end of the world. "He (Jesus) is the knowledge of the hour:" that is, according to the Moslem explanation, his reappearance shall be the sign of the coming judgment of the world. According to the Moslem traditions, Jesus shall come at the end of time as the successor of Muhammed, and as the last of the universal caliphs; he shall reign over all nations, and bring all to a knowledge of Islamism. When the caliphat passed from the Ommiades to the Abbassides, Abdallah was proclaimed by his uncle Dawud in these words: "The caliphat has been given to our house by a Divine ordinance, and shall be preserved by the same, until the time when we shall resign it into the hands of Jesus Christ, the son of Mary."

with her son to the glories of paradise. By a strange anachronism, Muhammed appears to have confounded her with Miriam, the sister of Moses and of Aaron, as he on one occasion calls her the sister of Aaron.

After the death of Muhammed, many of the Arabian tribes fell from the religion of this dreaded prophet. But their desertion was soon chastised, and the return of these faithless men to Islam, and obedience to the successor of Muhammed, was forced by many a bloody combat. Then commenced external conquests. Syria and Palestine were subdued, and compelled to receive the religion, and obey the power, of the Moslems, in 639, Egypt in 640, and Persia in 651. All those who embraced Islam were admitted to the rights and privileges of the victors.

Of the condition of the Christians under their Muhammedan rulers, we have scarcely any information: the Moslem historians, in their haughty contempt of all unbelievers, are almost silent on this subject; and it is well known how barren are all the sources of the Christian history of the east during the seventh century. According to Elmakyn, Muhammed gave letters of peace and security to Christians even of Arabia; but this is to be understood only of the Nestorians of Negran, for whom the Nestorian patriarch, Jesuiab II, purchased this favour by a present of two thousand garments. In this letter they were promised a free exercise of their religion, exemption from military service, and the permission to restore their churches, even with the assistance of the Moslems. A tribute, of which priests and monks were free, of four drachmas on the poor and twelve on the rich, was levied on the laity.*

---

* The so-called will of Muhammed, which the capuchin missionary, Pacificus Scaliger, received from the Carmelites in Palestine, and which was printed at Paris in 1630, and several times later, as well as another document which Muhammed is said to have given to the monks and other Christians of Mount Sina, bear upon them every sign of invention. In the chief points they agree with the letter given to the Christians of Negran, but they contain so many more and such greater privileges, that, as Tychsen remarks, the condition of the Christians would have been better than that of the Muhammedans.

Other Christians of Arabia also obtained an assurance of protection from Muhammed by the payment of a yearly tribute. But at his death, he left to his successors the injunction not to tolerate two religions in Arabia. The caliph Omar, therefore, expelled the Christians from Dumeh, and probably also from Negran: those from the latter place appear to have passed into Persia. Christianity disappeared, it is uncertain for how long, entirely from Arabia. In the conquered countries the lot of the Christians was unequal: in many places they were obliged to surrender their churches; at Damascus they were permitted to retain only seven. The erection of new churches and cloisters was prohibited, that the service of God might cease with his temples. The condition of the Nestorians in Persia, and of the Jacobites in Egypt, appears to have been the most favoured.

CHAPTER THE THIRD.

THE SCHISMS AND HERESIES TO THE END OF THE FOURTH CENTURY.

SECTION I.—THE SCHISM OF THE DONATISTS.*

THIS schism, which in its consequences and duration surpassed most others, sprung in its origin from personal animosity. Two Numidian bishops, Secundus of Tigisis, and Donatus of Casa Nigra, uniting with some discontented persons at Carthage, formed a party against Mensurius, the bishop of that city, and his deacon Cecilian. By their accusations, that Mensurius had delivered up the sacred volumes to the idolaters, in the persecution of Diocletian, and that he had, through his deacon, denied all succour to the Christians, who were languishing in prison, they caused a schism in the Carthaginian Church, about the year 306. But when, after the death of Mensurius, Cecilian was chosen to succeed him, their separation came to an open rupture. Cecilian was consecrated before the arrival, and without the cooperation (which was not at all required by the canons). of the Numidian bishops, by Felix of Aptunga. The seventy Numidian bishops, when they arrived at Carthage, found there a small party who were hostile to

---

* S. Optati Milevetensis, De Schismate Donatistarum, lib. vii ed. L E Dupin, Paris, 1700 —Monumenta Vetera ad Donatist Hist pertinentia, in Dupin, edition of S. Optatus —The writings of St. Augustin against Parmenius, Cresconius, Petilianus, Gaudentius: also his books, De Baptismo; Ad Catholicos Epistola contra Donatistas; Breviculus Collationum contra Donatistas, Ad Donatistas post collationem Carthag.; De gestis cum Emerito Donatista, collected in the ninth volume of the Benedictine edition of his works.
Historia Donatistarum ex Norisianis Schedis excerpta, in H. Norisii Opp. ed. a P. et H. Ballerinis, Veron. 1752, tom. iv.

Cecilian: this party consisted of two priests, who had been disappointed in their hopes of obtaining the bishopric, and a lady, named Lucilla, whose riches gave her power. In 312, a synod was held, at which Secundus of Tigisis presided, and in which the Lector Majorinus, one of the household of Lucilla, was elected bishop of Carthage, in opposition to Cecilian. The close connexion in which Carthage stood with the whole of the African province, accelerated the progress of the schism through the Roman Northern Africa. The Donatists (this was the name given to the abettors of the schism, of which Donatus, of Casa Nigra, was the chief author, and who had consecrated Majorinus), appealed, in the year 313, to the emperor Constantine, and prayed that their cause might be submitted to the arbitration of a number of Gallic bishops. Accordingly, at the request of the emperor, a synod was assembled, at which there were present nineteen Gallic and Italian bishops, and the pope Melchiades. The accusations of the Donatists against Cecilian were heard with attention, and the persecuted bishop was declared innocent. The accusers now rested their objections to Cecilian on the pretended fact, that Felix, who had ordained him, had been a *traditor*.* Constantine, therefore, commanded that this charge should be examined by Ælian, the proconsul of Africa, and the result of the trial was the unconditional acquittal of the holy bishop. But the Donatists did not cease to molest the emperor until he caused to be assembled, in 314, the great western synod at Arles; and, when the council declared in favour of Cecilian, they appealed again to the judgment of Constantine. Against his will, he heard both parties at Milan, and he also could discover no cause of accusation against Cecilian. He, therefore, ordered that the obstinate schismatics should be deprived of their Churches, and suffer the confiscation of their property. A fanatical fury now took possession of the party, and produced the *Circumcelliones*,—who were called *Agonistics* by

---

* One who had given up the Scriptures to the idolaters.

their friends,—wild troops of peasants and of emancipated slaves, who were enthusiastic to a degree of frenzy for the cause of the Donatists, and who served them as body-guards. The desire of martyrdom in this sect was nothing less than madness: to be slain by pagans or Catholics was to be crowned as martyrs. They provoked the former and conjured the latter to slay them; and, when they could find none to confer this favour upon them, they would cast themselves down precipices, into fire or into torrents. They naturally would not spare the lives of others more than their own; and with the cry, "For the honour of God," they would attack during the night and burn the houses of the Catholic priests, and wound and murder the inmates.

To possess, like the Catholic Church, a centre of unity, and an imaginary successor of St. Peter, the bishops of the schism sent an African, named Victor, to Rome, as the chief bishop of the Donatists. But their attempts to establish themselves abroad all proved abortive In the north of Africa, they were numerous and powerful, especially after the permission granted by Constantine, in 321, to the exiled bishops to return, and his command to the Catholics to treat their adversaries with patience and forbearance. The chief of the sect, after the premature death of Majorinus, their bishop of Carthage, was Donatus the Great, a man of high talent, and to whom his adherents were so attached, that they openly called themselves the party of Donatus, and were accustomed to swear by his name. Under the sons of Constantine the extravagances of the Circumcelliones, who had become intolerable to their own bishops, called for severe measures from the civil power: the count Taurinus, who was sent against them, in 346, brought many of them to execution. Paullus and Macarius were then commissioned by Constans to go amongst them, and to endeavour to allure the poorer of them by gifts of money. When Donatus, the bishop of Bagajæ, collected his Agonistics against Macarius, the soldiers, who had been given as a guard to the latter, proceeded to acts of violence: many Donatists were slain; two bishops were condemned and punished as authors of the insurrection, and were honoured by their partners as martyrs. Many of the schismatical bishops now fled from their Churches, others were banished, and an union effected by Macarius. The apparent peace continued unto the year 362. But when, with the permission of the apostate Julian, the banished Donatists returned to their homes, they drove with violence, and not without the effusion of blood, the Catholics from many of their Churches, and took a deep revenge for the severities which they had before endured.

The Donatists endeavoured to justify their schism dogmatically, by asserting that only that Church, which would not tolerate a known sinner within itself, could be the true Church; that, except their own, all other Churches, (as they admitted the traditors Cecilian and Felix of Aptunga into their religious communion), had been corrupted and separated from the true Church, of which they ceased to form a part. They imagined, therefore, that they could persuade men, that the Catholic Church in all other parts of the world had fallen, and was centred only with them in Africa. As, moreover, they asserted that the effects of the sacraments depended on the merit and sanctity of the minister, they concluded that all sacraments conferred out of their Church were thereby invalid; they, therefore, rebaptized all those who went over to their party, and even hesitated not to call the holy sacrifice of the Catholics an act of idolatry. Like to the Novatians, they considered themselves the only pure and holy of men, they boasted of their martyrs, and carried their horror of the Catholics, "the sons of the traditors," so far, as to avoid every kind of intercourse with them.

Imperial laws, especially from the time of Gratian, prohibited the assemblies of the Donatists, and commanded that their churches should be closed or restored to the Catholics; but by its own internal disputes and schisms, more than by these laws, was this sect destroyed. Primianists, Maxianianists, Rogatists, Claudianists, and others, conflicted with each other in mutual hate, and each claimed to be the only true Catholic Church The spirit of schism, which had called the sect into existence, grew so powerfully with it as it advanced, that, according to the testimony of St. Augustine, in Numidia alone, where the Donatists were indeed the most numerous, and where they formed the great majority of the inhabitants, their different parties could not be enumerated. Towards the close of the fourth century, they had four hundred bishops in Africa. A law of the Emperor Honorius, in 405, occasioned by the renewed violences of the Circumcelliones, commanded these men, under the severest penalties, to reunite themselves with the Catholic Church; and as, at the same time, St. Augustin wearied not in combating against the Donatists with all the power of his mighty mind, and had brought into the clearest light their subterfuges and sophisms, many of them returned to the Church. In the year 411, a conference, at which there were present two hundred and eighty-six Catholic, and two hundred and seventy-nine Donatist, bishops, was held at Carthage, at the command of the emperor, and under the superintendence of the prætor, Marcellinus. The Catholic bishops pledged themselves, in the event of reunion, to receive the Donatist bishops with all their ecclesiastical dignities,—an act of self-denial which was met with pride and contempt. "The sons of the martyrs can have nothing to do with the race of traditors," was the scornful reply, that had been before returned to the Catholic offers of peace. By endless evasions, and petty contrivances, the Donatists sought to defer, or entirely to avoid, the principal subjects of controversy. At length St. Augustin was enabled to refute the dogmatical proposition which his adversaries finally advanced: he proved that the Church, by the unavoidable tolerance of wicked men, had not thereby forfeited its character of sanctity, truth, and Catholicity. At the conclusion of the conference, Marcellinus declared that the Donatists had been defeated, and ordered that the laws against them should be put into full execution. Another and a more decisive law of the year 413, produced the effect that many of the Donatist communities passed together with their bishops over to the Church. At the death of St. Augustin, in 430, the schism had generally disappeared. But as late as the time of St. Gregory the Great, there were still remnants of the sect to be found; and the complaints of this pope, as well as of the African bishops, prove how unquiet these few Donatists still were, and how frequently Catholics were rebaptized by them.

In the beginning of the century, and prior to the Donatist, was the Meletian, schism in Egypt. Meletius, bishop of Lycopolis in Thebais, had separated himself from his patriarch, the amiable Peter of Alexandria, on the question concerning the reception of those who had fallen during the persecution. Taking advantage of the imprisonment of the patriarch, Meletius travelled through Egypt, ordaining and deposing bishops, and thus formed to himself his party, which named itself the Church of the Martyrs. The council of Nice retained in their dignity those bishops whom Meletius had ordained, and deprived only him of jurisdiction. The Meletians afterwards made common cause against St. Athanasius, with the Arians, without, however, adopting their heresy. The schism expired in the fifth century.

SECTION II.

THE ARIAN CONTROVERSIES.

1. *Down to the Council of Sardica, in 347.*[*]

THE mighty contest of the fourth century respecting the sacred Trinity, is an event which, being prepared

---

[*] S. Athanasii, Libri et Orationes contra Arium; Epistola de Decretis Synodi Nicænæ; Historia Arianorum, Apologia i.; Opp. ed. Montfaucon, Paris, 1698.—Epiphanii, Hær. 69.—Fragments of the Eccl. History of the Arian Philostorgius, ed. Gothofredus, Genevæ, 1643.— Gelazii Cyzic. Hist. Concilii Nicæni, in Hardvini. Collec. Concil. t. i.—

by antecedent circumstances, requires that we should treat of it with more historical exactness. The circle of errors against this fundamental dogma of Christianity had not yet been run round. With the heresies, which, maintaining the abstract unity of the Divine essence, denied the eternal and immanent self-revelation of God, the self-division into three personalities, we must now associate a new heresy; which, basing itself on the personal distinction of the Son from the Father, endeavoured to establish between them a difference of nature and of essence. Already some persons in the Church, misled either by their Platonizing philosophy, or by their polemical zeal against the impugners of a personal distinction in the Trinity, or, again, by the innocent but imprudent use of too general expressions, had extended the distance between the Father and the Son,—had designated the Son as a creature, and had spoken of his origin as dependant on the will of the Father. As we have already seen, Dionysius of Alexandria retracted his earlier equivocal expressions, and declared his belief to be in perfect unison with the faith of the Church: but soon after him, another teacher, Lucian, a priest of Antioch, appears to have taught to his numerous scholars, doctrines which required only development to present themselves as one of the most dangerous heresies that had yet opposed the dogma of the Church.

One of the scholars of Lucian, the learned and highly gifted, but proud and arrogant, Lybian, Arius, a priest of Alexandria, nurtured this germ into maturity. His doctrine was this: the Son sprung not from the nature of the Father, but was created from nothing: he had, indeed, an existence before the world,

---

Fragments of the writings of Arius, in the works of Theodoret, SS. Athanasius and Epiphanius.

Travasa, Storia Critica della Vita di Arrio, Venezia, 1746.—Möhler, Athanasius der Gr. und die Kirche seiner Zeit, besonder im Kampfe mit dem Arianismus (Athanasius the Great, and the Church in his Times, more especially in the contest with Arianism), 2 parts, Mayence, 1827.—Hermant, Vie de S. Athanase, Paris, 1671, 2 vols. 4to.—Maimbourg, Histoire de l'Arianisme, Paris, 1675.

even before time, but not from eternity. He is, therefore, in essence different from the Father, and is in the order of creatures, whom he, however, precedes in excellence, as God created all things, even time, by his instrumentality; whence he was called the Son of God, the Logos, or Word of God. As a creature the Son is perfect, and as like to the Father as a creature can be to the Creator But as he has received all things, as a gift, from the favour of the Father, as there was a period in which he was not, so there is an infinite distance between him and the nature of the Father; of which nature he cannot even form a perfect idea, but can enjoy only a defective knowledge of the same. His will was originally variable, capable of good and of evil, as is that of all other rational creatures: he is, comparatively at least, free from sin; not by nature, but by his good use of his power of election: the Father, therefore, foreseeing his perseverance in good, imparted to him that dignity and sublimity above all other creatures, which shall continue to be the reward of his virtues. Although he is called God, he is not so in truth, but was deified in that sense in which men, who have attained to a high degree of sanctity, may arrive at a participation of the Divine prerogatives. The idea then of a generation of the Son from the essence of the Father, is to be absolutely rejected.

This doctrine, which must have corresponded to the superficial understandings, and to the yet half-pagan ideas of many who then called themselves Christians, attacked the very soul of the Christian doctrine of the redemption; for according to this doctrine it was not God made man, but a changeable creature, who effected the great work of the redemption of fallen man. The devout Christian, to whom the faith in the God-man, Christ, the only Divine Mediator, opened the way to an intimate union with God, saw by this doctrine that his Redeemer and Mediator was as infinitely removed from the essence of God as himself; he saw himself driven back into the ancient pagan estrangement from God, and removed to an unattainable distance from him.

The opposition of Arius to the faith of the Church, first appeared when he publicly attacked the doctrines of his bishop, Alexander, on the eternal generation of the Son from the essence of the Father, and the perfect equality of his nature with that of the eternal Father. After many fruitless attempts to induce him to retract his errors, he and his already numerous followers were condemned in a synod of one hundred bishops, held at Alexandria, in the year 321: he was, moreover, degraded from his priestly dignity, and excommunicated. Whilst Alexander received from many parts of the Church, the assurance that his proceedings against Arius were in every respect justifiable, and that his faith was the faith of the Church, the heresiarch secured to himself the approbation and protection of many oriental bishops; of Eusebius of Nicomedia, Paulinus of Tyre, Athanasius of Anazarbe, and others. Of these, some partook fully of his opinions, others he gained by presenting to them a modified system of his doctrines. By saying that the Son was created from nothing, he excluded the idea of a pre-existing matter, or of an emanation from the Divine essence: he was brought forth by the will of the Father, before all time, as a perfect God, the only-begotten; unchangeable, not in his nature, but by the good government of his will, which was foreseen by the Father. Even the learned Eusebius of Cæsarea, who was at this time with his friend Eusebius of Nicomedia, wrote his book entitled *Thalia*, and declared for Arius. A synod held in Bythinia favoured the Arian doctrines: the contest now became more vehement, and even the pagans introduced upon their theatres, as fit subjects for ridicule, these disputes of the Christians In the meantime, Constantine became (in 324) lord of the east. At first he imagined that the controversy might be terminated, by sending amongst the disputants Osius, the bishop of Cordova, with an epistle, in which he designated the points of difference as an unnecessary and trivial contest about words. But in vain. Another synod was called at Alexandria, in which, in the presence and with the approbation of Osius, the condemnation of Arius and of his doctrines was confirmed. After this, the emperor, in 325, decreed that a general council of the Church should meet at Nice, in Bythinia.

In this venerable assembly of three hundred and eighteen bishops, of whom the greater part were Orientals, there were only twenty-two who favoured the principles of Arius. In its dealing with Arius and his followers, the council became convinced that it would be necessary, when defining the true doctrines of the Church, to oppose to their sophisms decided and unequivocal formularies of faith. For this purpose, to the symbol which Eusebius of Cæsarea had composed, it was added, that the Son "was true God, born not made, and consubstantial (ὁμοούσιος) to the Father." Some, amongst whom was Eusebius himself, consented to subscribe to the council, adapting to these clear expressions, sophistical and unjustifiable interpretations of their own. At length when the emperor, who was present at the council, threatened all who should refuse to subscribe, with deposition and exile, the seventeen bishops, who at first hesitated, affixed their signatures. Only Arius, and the two Egyptian bishops, Theonas and Secundus, persevered in their obstinate refusal. Constantine banished them to Illyria; and three months later, Eusebius of Nicomedia, and Theognis of Nice, were also sent into exile.

But the evil had penetrated too deeply into the Church; the Arian party had become too powerful for the decree of the council to terminate the controversy. It was represented to the varying emperor, that Arius was an orthodox Catholic, who had been sacrificed to the passions of other men, and to persecute whom, recourse had been to vain and idle distinctions of words. In 327, Constantine recalled Arius from banishment, and received as a proof of the orthodoxy of the heretic, a confession of faith, couched in general terms, which Arius presented to him. Eusebius of Nicomedia and Theognis now presumed to return to their churches: their party acquired every day new support and strength at the imperial courts, and their next steps were to wreak their revenge on the most distinguished of their opponents; to cast off the yoke of the Nicene council; and to restore Arius to the communion of the Church. Many of the most celebrated of the oriental prelates, such as Eustathius of Antioch, were deposed either by synods or by mandates of the emperor, and their sees given to Arian bishops. But against one man all the efforts of the Arians failed,—against the holy Athanasius, who had been bishop of Alexandria since the year 326. To him before all others was the task assigned of defending and preserving the Catholic faith in the east, amidst the storms and the miseries of the times which now followed. Active and powerful in the use of tradition and of Scripture, clear and penetrating, firm as a rock in the defence of truth, untiring in his pursuit of heresy into its most remote recesses, and in breaking through all the webs of its sophisms,—in detecting, and in unmasking this ever-changing Proteus in its every form,— his person was identified with the cause of which he was the champion, and communion with him was to friends and foes a token of Catholic faith.

By his constant refusal to admit Arius into the Church of Alexandria, or to enter into communion with the Arians, Athanasius incurred the displeasure of the emperor. The Eusebians, (Eusebius was the soul of the party which now rose into power) in conjunction with the Meletians, formed a series of accusations against him. He was commanded by the emperor to answer to them before a synod at Cæsarea, and when he neglected to comply, to appear before a more numerous assembly at Tyre, in the year 335. Here the chiefs of his opponents sat in judgment upon him, the two Eusebiuses, Maris, Theognis, Flacillus of Antioch, Patrophilus, Ursacius and Valens. Although of the accusations which were urged against the holy bishop, many were evidently false, and the others could not be proved, he was declared to be deposed, and was banished by the emperor to Triers. Arius was received into communion by a synod held at Jerusalem; and at Constantinople, (although the bishop Alexander resisted), the heresiarch and his adherents were solemnly introduced into the Church. He died in this city soon after this event, in 336.

The sons of Constantine recalled the exiled Catholic bishops. But the Eusebians soon induced the weak and tyrannical Constantius, emperor of the east, to make himself the blind instrument of their wicked designs. Again they accused St. Athanasius of many crimes, not only ecclesiastical, but political also; they drove him from his see, and intruded a priest named Pistus in his place. It was in vain that a numerous assembly of Egyptian bishops, who met at Alexandria, it was in vain that the Roman pontiff Julius, to whom the synod and the Eusebians both appealed, declared the innocence of Athanasius. At the synod of Antioch in 341, he was formally deposed, and Pistus being removed, Gregorius, a Cappadocian, was consecrated bishop of Alexandria. Gregorius forced his way to the episcopal throne over the bodies of those who had been slain, and through blood that had been shed, by his partisans. He compelled the Egyptians to recognize him as their bishop; and passing through the country, he every where treated bishops, monks, and nuns with disrespect and contumely. In the meantime, the Eusebians who had assembled at Antioch, drew up four formularies of faith, to which, in 345, a fifth of great length ($\varepsilon\kappa\theta\varepsilon\sigma\iota\varsigma$ $\mu\alpha\kappa\rho\sigma\tau\iota\chi\sigma\varsigma$) was adjoined. As they did not then dare openly to attack the authority of the Council of Nice, and as many of them were not entire supporters of the Arian errors, these formularies were made to present an almost Catholic appearance: the real and perfect Divine nature of the Son was therein confessed; but the term consubstantial, ($\dot{\omicron}\mu\omicron\omicron\upsilon\sigma\iota\omicron\varsigma$) was omitted, and the generation of the Son defined to be a free act of the will of the Father. St. Athanasius had, on the contrary, and with truth, maintained, that the generation of the son was in the essence of God, and could not be thought an act of the Father's will. Among the bishops at this synod not a few were in heart true Arians, but with the usual tactics of their party, they gave to these Catholic sounding formularies an Arian interpretation: for some time after, when interrogated what they understood by the expression, " the Word is of God," they replied that no more was understood by it, than by the words of the apostle, that " all things are of God."

The bishops, Marcellus of Ancyra, Asclepas of Gaza, Lucius of Adrianople, Paul of Constantinople, and many others who had been again exiled by the Eusebians, now fled with St. Athanasius to the pontiff Julius, and were by him declared innocent and orthodox, in a synod held in Rome, in 343. A second general council, which the two emperors, Constans and Constantius, assembled at Sardica in Illyria, in 347, was intended by them to give peace to the Church. Eusebius of Nicomedia had died bishop of Constantinople: but his party was not weakened by his death. The majority of the seventy oriental bishops who met at Sardica belonged to that party, whilst fear of the emperor Constantius, and the violence of the Eusebians, held the orthodox prelates in awe. The hundred western bishops, at whose head was the venerable Osius, now ninety years of age, the legate of the pope to the council, were united amongst themselves and in their defence of the Nicene doctrines· only five, amongst whom were Ursacius, bishop of Singidunum, and Valens, bishop of Mursa, declared themselves in favour of the Eusebians. When the Eusebians beheld themselves in a minority, and saw that their former violences would be exposed and condemned, they gladly employed the pretext that was afforded them by the admission to the council of St. Athanasius, and of the other banished bishops, to withdraw to the neighbouring city of Philippolis, were they continued their deliberations. Here they compiled an insiduous confession of faith; they condemned all those who had been absolved by the western bishops; and excommunicated Osius, with many other distinguished Catholic prelates, and even the Roman pontiff, Julius. The western bishops, who remained at Sardica, declared on the contrary their adherence to the symbol of Nice, decreed the restoration of the banished bishops, and pronounced sentence of deposition against the chiefs of the Arians. These events produced for the first time a temporary separation between the eastern and western Churches. There still, however, remained many truly orthodox prelates in the east, but they were heavily oppressed by the yoke of the Eusebians, and of those females and eunuchs, whom they had won over to their interests in the court of Constantius. They, therefore, continued quiet, not daring to avoid communion with their enemies.

2. *The Arian Heresy, from the Council of Sardica to the death of Constantius, in* 361.—*Marcellus of Ancyra.—Eunomius and the Anomœans.—The Semi-arians.**

Constantius, yielding to the solicitations of his brother Constans, in 349 granted to St. Athanasius permission to return to his Church. But the death of Constans, who was slain, in 350, by the usurper Magnentius, reopened a free course to the enemies of the Catholic faith. They now directed their attacks against Marcellus, bishop of Ancyra, the steadfast champion of the consubstantiality of the Son, and whom they had before, in 336, deposed on the charge of Sabellianism. They now, in 351, repeated their act in a council at Sirmium, and deposed him, and his scholar Photinus, who had certainly taught erroneous doctrines. In aid of the Eusebian party, Eusebius of Cæsarea wrote two books, one *Against Marcellus*, the other entitled *On Ecclesi-*

---

* S. Athanasii Apologia II III. De Synodis Arimin. et Seleuc.—S. Hilarii, Liber de Synodis; ad Constantium Aug. lib. ii.—Contra Constantium Imp. Lib unus, Fragmenta, Opp. ed. Maffei, Veron 1730.—Luciferi Calaritani, ad Constantium, lib. ii. · De non conveniendo cum Hæreticis, De non parcendo Delinquentibus in Deum, Quod moriendum sit pro Filio Dei, Opp ed. Coleti, Venet. 1778, fol —Eusebii Cæsar. Contra Marcellum, lib ii ; De Ecclesiastica Theologia, lib. iii., ad calcem ejusd Demonstr. Evang. Colon. 1688.—Epiphanius, Hær. 72 —Eunomii, Libellus fidei. Apologeticus, in Basnage.—Canisii, Thesaur. I. 178.

Rettberg, Marcelliana, Gotting. 1798.—Klose, Geschichte und Lehre des Eunomius (History and Doctrine of Eunomius), Kiel, 1833

astical Theology; in which he accused Marcellus of the Sabellian error, that "the Son is only an impersonal power of the Father." A suspicion of this error could indeed be cast upon Marcellus, for although he was himself orthodox, he had employed the Sabellian expression, of an expansion of the Monas for the formation of the Trias, or Trinity, and had referred the appellation of the Son of God only to the man Christ. He was, however, declared free of error by the pope Julius, in the year 341, and by the council of Sardica in 347. New accusations against St. Athanasius, of civil and ecclesiastical crimes, had confirmed Constantius, now sole lord of the empire, in a bitter hatred of this inflexible bishop. At the synod of Arles, in 353, and at the great assembly of three hundred bishops at Milan, in 355, the emperor, who, surrounded by his courtier bishops, presided over the council, endeavoured by bribery, by deception, and by threats, to induce the bishops to abandon Athanasius and to receive the Arians into the communion of the Church. Dionysius, the steadfast bishop of Milan, Eusebius of Vercelli, and Lucifer of Cagliari, the papal legate, who withstood the emperor, were treated with cruel indignities, and banished The same lot was experienced by the pope Liberius, and the aged Osius. At Alexandria, whence St. Athanasius had withdrawn himself into the desert with the threat of death suspended over him, the barbarous Cappadocian, Gregorius, who was tyrannical as he was infamous, was replaced in the episcopal see by force of arms. Many of the Egyptian bishops were sent in chains to work in the mines, or exiled to the sandy wastes of the country: those Catholics who would not enter into communion with the Arians were tortured and so cruelly scourged, that many died under the lash. Violence and persecution were every where triumphant. "Subscribe or leave your Churches," was the alternative proposed to the bishops: even the Novatians were deprived of their Churches, as defenders of the *Homoousion*. The fall of the Nicene faith now appeared inevitable; for the hoary champion of the faith, the bishop Osius, and, according to some accounts, even the pope himself, fell, subdued by the sufferings of their exile. The latter, it is said, in 357, renounced all communion with St. Athanasius, associated himself with the Arians, and subscribed one, probably the first, of the three formulas that had been compiled at Sirmium. This formulary was so drawn up, that in the true signification of the words it was not heretical, but was of such a nature that orthodox Catholics might, without difficulty, subscribe to it. Many modern historians have endeavoured to prove that the fall of Liberius must be considered as no more than a fiction of the Arians, and have maintained that these heretics corrupted those parts of the works of St. Athanasius, and the fragments of St. Hilary, in which the account of it is contained.* It would seem that Sulpicius Severus, Socrates, and Theodoret, knew nothing of any such fall of the pope, for they make no mention of it; and relate that Constantius was compelled by the prayers of the Roman women, and by an insurrection of the people, to permit the return of Liberius to Rome.

A few, but distinguished, men combated by their writings at this time for the cause of the true faith. In the east, the undaunted Athanasius, besides apologies in his own defence, of which the first was written in 350, the second in 356, and the third in 358, published his history of Arianism, and four treatises against its errors. In the west, St. Hilarius wrote his learned and powerful work on the Trinity in twelve books. Happily for the Nicene faith, its opposers divided from each other at the moment when the Catholics appeared to have been overcome, or, we should rather say, that the spirit of internal strife, which had long been suppressed, now burst violently forth. The more moderate party, the party of the Semiarians, had hitherto been, in the east, by the number of bishops attached to it, and by the favour of Constantius, the more powerful: the real Arians, warned by their numerical weakness, and hoping

---

* See Palma's Prælectiones Hist. Eccl.: Romæ 1839, tom. ii.

to attain their secret object, the destruction of the Nicene faith, and the ruin of Athanasius, had hypocritically concealed their intentions, and united themselves with the Semiarians. But when now, with Ursacius and Valens at their head, they had again acquired the ascendancy at the imperial court, they rejected at a synod at Sirmium, in 355, the expressions *homoeusion* and *homoiusion*, as not contained in the Scriptures; and declared that the Father was in power and majesty superior to the Son, and that the latter was like to all other creatures subject to the Father. The Syrian, Aëtius, and his scholar, the proud but learned dialectician, Eunomius, who was for many years bishop of Cyzicum, formed a new sect, named Anomæans or Eunomians, and of which the doctrines were perfect and openly avowed Arianism. Eunomius, who had already endeavoured to establish the heretical principle of the all-sufficient authority of the Scriptures, against the tradition of the Church, destroyed the idea of all mystery in the Deity; he accused the Catholics that they taught faith in an unknown God, and impiously declared that he had as clear a perception of the divine essence as God himself had. His doctrine taught that the Son was a creature, who had a beginning of existence; that he was by nature mutable, capable even of evil, and mortal; and that only by the grace of God had he become immutable and immortal. He was distinguished indeed from other creatures by having been created immediately by God, and by having existed before time, though not from eternity: he had received the name of God and divine honours only on account of his firm perseverance in virtue; and as that which is ungenerated and immutable cannot unite itself with human nature, he took to himself a human body, but not a human soul.

At a synod which assembled at Ancyra in 358, the Semiarians, at whose head were Basilius of Ancyra and George of Laodicea, declared against the Eunomian doctrines, and defined, that the Son was in essence like (ὁμοιουσιον) to the Father. The third formulary of Sirmium, which was drawn up by Semiarian bishops, with the co-operation of Ursacius and Valens, in 358, contained an equivocal mode of expression, and declared that the Son was in all things like to the Father, according to the Scriptures, but forbade the use of the word *substance* (ουσια), as it might be easily misunderstood by laymen. The Eunomians now rose into power in the court of the emperor, through the influence of Eudoxius, bishop of Antioch, who had embraced their doctrines; and it was intended that a new synod should define the third of the Sirmian formularies, or an Arian formulary like to it, to be the faith of the Church. But the Eunomians feared that those bishops of the east, who were known to be inclined to the Nicene faith, encouraged by the presence of the western prelates, might unite with them: they feared also that the Semiarians, who were nearer allied to the Catholics than to the Eunomians, might also coalesce. They determined, therefore, that the council should be divided into two parts. The bishops of the west met at Rimini, in 359, whilst the oriental bishops assembled at the same time at Seleucia, in Isauria. At Rimini, where of four hundred bishops eighty were Arians, the Nicene symbol of faith was confirmed, with the rejection of all later formulas, and four Arian bishops were deposed. But the ten bishops, whom the council sent as deputies to Constantius, were so long harassed by the artful hypocrisy and threats of the emperor, and of the Arians at his court, and exhausted by long and tedious delays, that at length they subscribed to a formulary, similar to the last of Sirmium, in which a mere likeness of the Son to the Father, " according to the Scriptures," was expressed. After this subscription, they entered into communion with the Arians. By the same acts of fraud, the bishops who had continued at Rimini were induced to take a step similar to that of their deputies. Fatigued by a seven months' confinement, fearing for the consequences of their long absence from their Churches, suffering even from want, and incessantly assailed by the prefect Taurus and by the Arians, who represented to them the responsibility of preventing an union between the Churches of the east and west, for the sake of a word (ουσια, *substance*), which was not to be found in the Scriptures, and was offensive by its novelty—they yielded at length, and calmed their consciences with the Catholic signification of a profession of faith, in which the eternal generation and divinity of the Son of God were expressed. Twenty of the bishops, who refused for a time to sign this profession, finally surrendered; and the more readily, as they saw that the Arians admitted the anathemas, which condemned the grosser errors of Arius. Valens contrived also to insert, in the formula, this insidious proposition, that the Son is not a creature like to other creatures. In reference to the unhappy termination of this synod, St. Jerome, some years later, exclaimed, " that the whole earth mourned, wondering that it had become Arian."*

In the meantime there reigned in the council of Seleucia a spirit of irremediable discord, occasioned by the differences of the Anomæan and Semiarian views, and by the serious complaints against many of the bishops. The greater part were Semiarian, in so far as they censured nothing that was contained in the Nicene symbol, except the use of the word *homousion*, which they imagined might easily bear a Sabellian interpretation. Against nine bishops, who openly defended the Anomæan errors, and particularly against Acacius of Cæsarea, the leader of the party, they pronounced sentence of deposition. But the ten deputies of the council were compelled by the emperor, with whom Acacius and Eudoxius possessed great influence, to subscribe to the formula of Rimini, and thus to resign their term *homoiusion*. In a council at Constantinople, in 360, the Acacians sacrificed their chief, Aëtius, but, in compensation to themselves, the slightest pretexts were sufficient for them to depose the leaders of the Semiarians. Eudoxius made himself master of the episcopal see of the imperial city, and Arian bishops were placed in the

---

* " Ingemuit totus orbis et Arianum se esse miratus est."—Adver. Lucif. c. 7.

Churches as far as his power extended. All the bishops of the east and the west were menaced with exile, unless they subscribed to the formulary of Rimini: only a few, in comparison, resisted, and amongst these was the pope Liberius, Vincentius bishop of Capua, and Gregory of Elvira. But in the meantime, many, particularly of those who had been banished, retracted their signatures, and a synod of Gallic bishops, in 360 or 361, rejected the formularies, and excommunicated all the Arian bishops in the west. By the arbitrary caprice of the civil power, an awful confusion was introduced into the Church: the orthodox bishops saw themselves placed in opposition to each other against their will, and thrown into society with their ancient enemies, the Arians. Despair at this melancholy sight drew from St. Hilary, and more particularly from Lucifer of Cagliari, expressions of severity, and almost of disrespect, against Constantius,—a dereliction of the duty of subjects to their sovereign, which only the extreme necessity of the Church could excuse.

SECTION III.

THE LAST PERIOD OF ARIANISM.—THE LUCIFERAN AND MELETIAN SCHISMS.—THE MACEDONIANS.*

WHEN the emperor Julian, after the death of Constantius, granted to the banished bishops permission to return to their Churches, those unnatural bonds, which had hitherto fettered the Church, fell away, and Arianism, no longer supported by the power of the state, sunk into the insignificance of an ordinary sect. Many numerous communities, and many bishops, at once renounced the formula of Rimini; and the synod of Alexandria,—over which St. Athanasius, who had again

---

* Faustini, Libellus Precum, in Sirmondi opp Paris, 1696, fol. tom. i —S. Hieronymi, Dialogus Orthodoxi et Luciferani.—S Basilii, Epistolæ; opp. ed. Garnier. Paris, 1721, † iii. Epiphanius, Hær. 74.

returned to his see, presided,—made their reconciliation with the Church as easy and as light as possible. Only the severe Lucifer of Cagliari required the deposition of all the bishops who had signed the formula; and when he found that he could not prevail, he placed himself at the head of the schismatical party, named from him the Luciferans, who declared that the Catholic Church had been defiled by receiving the fallen prelates; and that as they alone were untainted, they had separated themselves from its communion. One of them, the deacon Hilarius, went so far as to rebaptize the converted Arians. Another schism, the Meletian, which sprung from Arianism, agitated and troubled the Church of Antioch. After the deposition of Eustathius, the Catholic bishop, in 330, there was formed in this Church a Catholic community of Eustathians, which held itself separated from the Arian bishops. Meletius, bishop of Sebaste, was, in 360, placed by the Arians in the see of Antioch, but unexpectedly shewing himself inclined to the Catholic faith, he was expelled by the Arian Euzojus; and as Lucifer, the chief of the Eustathians, had consecrated the priest Paulinus, there were, at one and the same time, three parties and three bishops at Antioch.

St. Athanasius and St. Hilary endeavoured to conciliate the Semiarians by the declaration, that they considered them as brethren in the faith, who were divided from them only by a word, and that this impediment might easily be removed. But a more important point than the word *homousion* now became the subject of discussion between the Semiarians and Catholics. This was the divinity of the Holy Ghost. From amongst the Semiarians there arose a party, who were called Pneumatomachi, impugners of the Spirit, and also Macedonians, from Macedonius, a Semiarian, who was bishop of Constantinople from 341 to 361; and from whom originated, and by whom was spread, the doctrine that the Holy Ghost was a creature, and in all things dissimilar from the Father and the Son. Those Semiarians who would not adopt this doctrine, although their synod of Lampsacus, in 364, renewed the Antiochian formulary of 341, united themselves more closely with the supporters of the Nicene symbol, whilst the breach which separated the sects of the Eunomæans and Macedonians from the Catholic Church was more violently enlarged. The artful Acacians, in the meantime, knew well how to serve their own interests, by declaring for the Catholic doctrines under the emperor Jovian, and for the Anomæan under Valens.

For whilst Valentinian granted universal freedom of religion in the west, his brother Valens, a scholar of the Arian Eudoxius, raised a new persecution against the Catholics and Semiarians in the east. In 367, he commanded that the bishops who had been deposed under Constantius, should be again banished from their Churches. St. Athanasius was accordingly compelled to leave his see for the fifth time; but the fear of a tumult at Alexandria caused his speedy restoration. Eighty bishops went from Nicomedia to Constantinople to implore the protection of the emperor, in favour of the Catholics in the imperial city, against the barbarous cruelties of the Arians. Valens gave orders that the ship, in which they returned, should be set on fire, so that they all perished either in the flames or in the sea. At Alexandria, and in other parts of Egypt, many Catholics were tortured to death, when, after the decease of St. Athanasius, in 373, Peter, whom he had recommended for his successor, was expelled by the Arian Lucius. But the immediate effect of the persecution was, that those Semiarians who had not joined the sect of the Pneumatomachi, united themselves entirely with the Catholics. Their deputies, Eustathius of Sebaste, Silvanus of Tarsus, and Theophilus of Castabala, presented to pope Liberius, in the name of fifty-nine bishops, a profession of faith, in which the consubstantiality of the Son with the Father was unequivocally expressed. They were, therefore, received by the pope into the communion of the Church.

One of the most prejudicial consequences of this long-protracted religious controversy was an evil spirit of dogmatical strife which invaded all classes of society, and more particularly in the east. Men of every degree, from the emperor to the beggar, now accustomed themselves to make the most sublime mysteries of faith the subjects of their daily disputations. This we learn from St. Gregory of Nyssa, who tells us that, at Constantinople, money-changers, cooks, and dealers in clothes, might be seen in the streets, and in the marketplace, dogmatizing, amidst their ordinary occupations, upon the generation or non-generation of the Son, of his subjection to the Father, and upon other such exalted themes. Such a disposition could be only favourable to the progress of Arianism; but, happily, the Catholic Church possessed men, even after the death of St. Athanasius, who strenuously combatted against Arianism, and prostrated it before them. This was done by the three great Cappadocian doctors, St. Gregory Nanianzen, in his theological discourses; by St. Basil, bishop of Cæsarea; by his brother St. Gregory, bishop of Nyssa, in their writings against Eunomius; and at Alexandria, by Dydimus, the blind, in his book on the Trinity. In the west, the Nicene creed was universally adopted; if we except Milan, where Arianism was protected by the bishop Auxentius, who was succeeded, in 374, by St. Ambrose, and Illyrium, where there were several Arian bishops, six of whom were deposed by a synod which assembled in that country. In the east, on the contrary, where the Arians had gained over to their interests the emperor, the court, the prefects, and the vicars, they were enabled, by artifice and violence, to gain possession of the greater number of Churches: only in Cappadocia was the Catholic cause preserved triumphant, by the exertions and influence of the great St. Basil. As in the different Churches, after the expulsion of the bishops, the people were instructed and strengthened in the faith by the monks and anchorites, the anger of the emperor was now turned against them. In Syria, their cells, and the produce of their labours, were burnt: in Egypt, and particularly in the desert of Nitria, troops of them were murdered, others were banished, and doomed to labour in the mines. In the midst of these triumphs, Euzojus, the chief of the Arians, died in 376; and in 378, the cruel Valens perished in his unfortunate war with the Goths. A short time before his death he had granted some degree of peace to the Catholics, and had permitted the exiled bishops and priests to return to their Churches.

The emperor Gratian also gave full freedom to the Catholics: still, however, when Theodosius ascended the throne, in 379, the Arians were in possession of nearly all the churches, in Syria, Palestine, in many other provinces, and in the capital of the empire. But in 380 appeared the celebrated edict, which commanded all to embrace the faith professed by the pope Damasus, and by Peter of Alexandria, and to declare themselves Catholic Christians. At Constantinople, the Arians were obliged to vacate the churches, of which for forty years they had held possession: in 381, all meetings in the city were prohibited to them: all the churches in the east were taken from them; and thus fell Arianism, cast down by the same power by which it had so long been supported, and so widely propagated. All those, whom force or fear, or a desire to obtain the favour of the powerful, had attached to it, now naturally fell from it: an attempt of the real Arians (the Acacians and Eudoxians), to strengthen themselves by a coalition with the Eunomians, failed, through the condition required by the latter, that the condemnation pronounced in 360, of Aetius, and his writings, should be revoked: both parties differed every day more bitterly, and at length destroyed themselves by internal dissensions.

In 381, Theodosius convoked a great council of the east at Constantinople. One hundred and fifty bishops appeared there, and amongst them were thirty-six, who adhered to the sect of Macedonius, from the country on the Hellespont. These latter persevered in their rejection of the *homousia* of the Son and of the Holy Ghost with the Father. But the council ratified the creed of the Nicene synod, and added to it, as the necessity of the times required, that to the "Holy Ghost, who proceeds from the Father, the same adoration and glory are to be paid as to the Father and to the Son."*

By the acceptance of the pope, and the western bishops, this synod acquired the authority of a general council. In the west, the empress Justina endeavoured, during the minority of her son Valentinian, to restore the Arians again to power: but she was defeated by the immoveable constancy of St. Ambrose; and a second Auxentius whom Justina had nominated bishop of Milan, could not obtain, although violent persecution was raised to procure it, a church for his party in or near the city.

After a duration of eighty-five years, the schism at Antioch, which had produced a temporary separation between the eastern and western Churches, was at length happily closed. The pope, the western, and the Egyptian bishops, recognized Paulinus as bishop of Antioch, whilst the oriental Catholics adhered to Meletius. The two Catholic parties at Antioch had mutually agreed, in 378, that the survivor of the two rival prelates should be acknowledged by all as sole bishop. But when Meletius died, in 381, at the council of Constantinople, over which he presided, his friends elected the priest Flavian to succeed him; their choice was approved by the council, and when, in 388, Paulinus died, the Eustathians appointed Evagrius to fill his place. Evagrius died in 392, and Flavian persuaded his adherent not to choose a successor. In 398, he procured, through the mediation of St. John Chrysostom, and Theophilus of Alexandria, the recognition of the holy see. A party of the Eustathians, however, persevered in their separation until the year 415.

---

* "Qui ex Patre procedit, qui cum Patre et Filio simul adoratur et conglorificatur." From a similar necessity, the word FILIOQUE, after the words *Qui ex Patre*, was afterwards added by the council of Lyons, as we shall see hereafter.

SECTION IV.

PHOTINUS AND APOLLINARIS.—THE PRISCILLIANISTS.
—MINOR SECTS.—INDIVIDUAL HERETICS.*

DURING the controversies created by the Arian heresy, an old and long refuted error was renewed by Photinus, bishop of Sirmium. This man denied the threefold personality of God; and asserted that the Logos, the Word, was nothing more than a divine energy, which, emanating from the Deity, manifested itself and operated in the man Jesus; who, being exalted by this influence, and by the indwelling of this Divine power, was called the Christ, the son, (the adopted son) of God, and might be named, in an improper sense, God, although his kingdom ceased when he gave back his power to God, and when the divine Logos departed from him. On account of this doctrine, which approached nearest of any other to that of Paul of Samosata, Photinus was condemned by the Semiarians in a synod at Antioch, in 344, again by the western bishops assembled at Milan, in 347 or 349, and was finally deposed by a council of oriental bishops at Sirmium, in 351. From them he appealed to the emperor, and requested that he might

---

* Concerning Photinus, see the Antitheses of Antioch and Sirmium, in St. Athanasii De Synodis; Socrates, H. Eccl. ii. 19.—On Apollinaris, S. Gregorii Nysseni Antirrheticus in Zaccagni Monumentis, Romæ, 1698.—Leontii Byzant adversus eos qui proferunt quædam Apollinarii, in Basnage Canisii, Thesaur. i 597.

On the Priscillianists, Sulpicii Severi, Hist Sacra, ii. 46-51.—Orosii Commonitorium de Errore Priscillianistarum et Origenistarum, in opp. Augustini, tom. viii.—Leonis P Epist. xv. ad Turibium —On the Euchites, Epiph. Hær. 80, Theodoret. Hær. Fab. iv 11; Hist. Eccl. iv. 10 —On the Audians, Epiph. Hær. 70; Theodoret Hær. Fab. iv. 10, Hist. Eccl. iv. 11.—On Aerius, Epiph. Hær. 75, Philistratii, Hær. 75, Augustini, De Hæres, c 83.—On Helvidius, Hieronymus, adv. Helvidium, opp. tom. ii.—Gennadius de Viris Illustribus, c 32; Augustini, de Hær. c. 84.—On Jovinian, Hieron. adv Jovin. lib. ii. opp. tom. ii.; Siricius epp. 7, 8, in Constant. ep. Pontiff i. 663 —Ambrosius, Ep. ad Siricium.—Augustini de Hær. c. 82 —On Vigilantius, Hieronymus adv. Vigilantium, opp. tom. ii.; Epist. ad Vigilant. ep ad Riparium

be heard in a public disputation with Basil of Ancyra, in the presence of imperial judges. He was heard, but the consequence of the conference was, that he was sentenced to exile. In the reign of Julian, he returned to Sirmium, but was again expelled, in 364, by Valentinian. He formed around himself a sect, who were called Photinians, who soon, however, disappeared after the death of their chief. Not many years later, in 391, arose Bonosus, who like Photinus denied the divinity of Christ, and named him only the adopted son of God. Hence the Photinians and Bonosians are by the ancients often confounded.

On the relation of the human to the Divine nature in the person of Christ, Apollinaris, bishop of Laodicea, was the first who asserted an error. He had been a determined opponent of the Arians, and was led into his erroneous doctrines by a mistaken zeal for the unity and divinity of Christ. Of the nature of Christ, he taught that Christ possessed a human body, and the inferior faculties of the soul, ($\psi \upsilon \chi \eta$), by which this body was animated; but that *spirit* ($\nu o \upsilon \varsigma$, $\pi \nu \varepsilon \upsilon \mu \alpha$), was supplied by the Logos, the Divinity. He therefore denied to Christ the most essential part of human nature, the rational soul, and therefore admitted not the real and perfect incarnation of the Word,—an error which was destructive of the whole system of our salvation, for as it destroyed the incarnation of Christ, it destroyed also the mystery of our redemption. Apollinaris taught that the freedom of Christ from sin, could not have been compatible with his union with a human soul, which is essentially corrupt and sinful, and that an unity of person could not be made to consist of two things, of which each was distinct from the other, and perfect in itself,—the divinity and humanity. It was necessary, therefore, he added, that as soon as his doctrine was forsaken, and two contrary and independent natures were asserted, to admit two Sons and two Christs. The Apollinarists were accustomed to write upon their houses, as a fundamental truth of their doctrines, that the faithful should adore not a man who bore within himself a God, but a God who bore human flesh: they named their opponents Anthropolatrai, accusing them of idolatry in adoring a man. In 362, a synod at Alexandria declared what was the true Catholic faith, in opposition to the above errors. St. Athanasius combated them in writing, but without naming Apollinaris, with whom he was connected by friendship; but the chief refutation of Apollinarianism was by St. Gregory of Nyssa. The pope Damasus, in a synod held at Rome, in 378, (and at which St. Peter of Alexandria was present), condemned the doctrines of Apollinaris, and deposed him and his disciple, Timotheus, bishop of Berytus. This condemnation was confirmed by the synod of Antioch, in 379, and by the synod of Constantinople, in 381 At Antioch, Vitalis, the chief of the followers of Apollinaris, assumed the title of bishop of the sect. Another of his disciples, Polemo, taught that the flesh of Christ was immortal, and had descended from heaven, that it was united in one substance with the Divinity, and was thus divine. The adherents of Polemo were the forerunners of the Eutychians; but as we learn from Timotheus, Apollinaris himself had taught the same doctrine. Thus, according to St. Augustin, there arose three sects of the Apollinarists: the first, like the Eunomians, asserted that Christ did not possess a true human soul; the second, that he had not the higher faculties of the soul, whilst the third taught that his body formed a part of his divinity. These sects all became extinct in the course of the fifth century.

Towards the end of the fourth century, Manicheism, under the name of Priscillianism, spread itself through Spain. An Egyptian, named Marcus, introduced into that country, and Priscillian, a rich, eloquent and learned man,—but proud of his learning, and vain in the practice of severe external mortification,—embraced the error with ardour and zeal. Under his patronage, the new doctrines were rapidly extended, and infected even some amongst the bishops, as Instantius and Salvianus. Although condemned by a council at Saragossa, these bishops were not deterred, and presumed so far as to constitute Priscillian bishop of Avila. The emperor

Gratian expelled them from Spain, and they immediately went to Milan and to Rome, to gain to their interests the pontiff Damasus and the imperial court. They succeeded by their arts in the latter attempt. Their chief opponent, Ithacius bishop of Ossonoba, was obliged to leave Spain, but in a short time laid his complaint before the new emperor, Maximus, who, after the death of Gratian, began to rule from Treves over the western provinces of the empire. The usurper commanded the chiefs of the Priscillianists to appear before a council at Bourdeaux. Here Instantius was deposed: but Priscillian appealed to the emperor; and the council, which ought not to have been diverted by this artifice from pronouncing over him sentence of deposition and excommunication, granted to him his request. Priscillian, therefore, and his followers, on the one side, and Idacius, bishop of Merida and Ithacius, on the other, met at Treves. Ithacius, a short-sighted zealot, persuaded Maximus to violate the promise which he had made to St. Martin of Tours, that he would not shed the blood of Priscillian. The prefect Evodius conducted the examination according to the Roman forms, with the application of the torture, and the emperor signed the sentence of death. Priscillian, the widow Euchrocia, and five others, were accused of odious crimes, and beheaded in 385; Instantius and others were excommunicated.

The system of Priscillian had for its foundation the Manichean dualism. It taught that an evil principle, which had sprung from chaos and eternal darkness, was the creator of the lower world · that souls, which are of a divine nature, were sent by God from heaven, to combat with the powers of darkness and against their kingdom, but were overcome and enclosed within bodies. To free these souls, the Redeemer descended from heaven, clothed with a celestial body, which was, in appearance only, like to the bodies of ordinary men. By his sufferings,—which, according to Priscillian, were only apparent and symbolical,—he erased the mark which the evil spirits had impressed upon the souls when they confined them within material bodies. This sect prohibited the use of marriage, commanded abstinence from animal food, and rejected the belief of the resurrection. Their mysteries were not less abominable than those of the Manichees. To conceal their own doctrines, and to calumniate the Catholics, by lies and false swearing, they considered perfectly justifiable.

Maximus informed pope Siricius of all that had occurred at Treves; but the pontiff, and the most distinguished bishops of the west, St. Ambrose of Milan, and St. Martin of Tours, condemned the severity with which Ithacius and his friends had punished the heretics with death: they excommunicated the Ithacians, and in 389, Ithacius was deposed. In the meantime, the harsh conduct of Maximus served only to strengthen and to extend the heresy: the Priscillianists honoured their master as a martyr, and in a short period they won over to their sect nearly the whole of the population of Gallicia. At the council of Toledo, in 400, two Priscillian bishops, Symphosius and Dictinius, returned into the Church; but the sect continued long to exist, and as late as the year 563, the council of Braga found it necessary to form new regulations against them.

The sect of the Messalians or Euchites (which Hebrew and Greek appellations signify *Supplicators*), appears to have arisen amongst the anchorites of Mesopotamia. Notwithstanding the exertions against it of the bishop Flavian, in a council at Antioch, in 390, the sect continued to increase. It existed for a long period, and frequently reappeared from time to time. The members of this sect called themselves also Adelphians, from Adelphus, their chief. They delivered themselves up to that false asceticism, to that pretended quietism, which has since frequently appeared in the Church, and manifested itself in an endless variety of forms. Each individual, (so the Euchites taught), is under the dominion of a demon which he has inherited from his parents, and which can be overcome and expelled only by unceasing prayer: when this has been effected, the Holy Ghost takes possession of the soul, deifies it, and elevates it to a state of impeccability and impassibility. They rejected all external asceticism, especially the practice of fasting, and manual labour, as unworthy of a spiritual man, of whom prayer should form the only occupation. They considered the reception of the eucharist as unnecessary, as the sacraments were without signification for men who had been raised to a divine perfection in knowledge and in action. They wished, however, to remain in outward communion with the Church. The pagan Messalians or Euphemites, of whom St. Epiphanius speaks, were similar to the Hypsistari in Cappadocia, to whom the father of Gregory Nazianzen had belonged, only that the latter, together with their belief in one God, joined the Jewish observances, a distinction of meats, and of the Sabbath.

The Audians were an almost unknown sect in Mesopotamia. Its founder, Audius, had been excommunicated on account of his reckless zeal for severity towards heretics: he at length formed a schism, and drew many bishops and priests into his sect. As with all other parties that had separated themselves from the Church, so it was with the Audians: they celebrated Easter, as Quartodecimans, 'with the Jews: they had anthropomorphistic, or rather Manichean, representations of God: they dispensed with the canonical penance, and required of penitents no more than that they should confess their sins, and pass through two piles of the sacred books. This sect arose in the middle of the fourth, and disappeared at the end of the fifth, century. The Arian, Aerius, once a companion of Eustathius of Sebaste, taught, with his followers in Pamphylia, the equality of bishops and priests, inveighed against the paschal solemnity as a Jewish superstition, rejected the fasts commanded by the Church, and prayers and good works for the dead, as useless to those for whom they were offered.

How far the enemies of the Church sought to falsify its truth by practices opposed to it, and how well the Church knew how to defend its doctrines and its rites against contradictory pretensions and errors, is clearly exemplified on the one side in Eustathius, and in Helvidius, Jovinian, and Vigilantius, on the other. Eustathius, bishop of Sebaste, in the Roman Armenia, who died an Arian in 330, in the pride of a mistaken asceticism, made propositions and advanced assertions, which the synod of Gangra (we know not in what year), opposed in a series of canons. He and his sect declared the use of flesh unlawful, forbade marriage as impure, prohibited all society with a married priest, and fasted, contrary to the law of the Church, on Sunday. On the contrary, Hélvidius, a scholar of the Arian Auxentius, the monk Jovinian at Rome in 388, and the Gallic priest Vigilantius, in 402, dared to teach that the state of virginity possessed no preeminence over the state of marriage. The weak Jovinian instilled into his followers his errors on the fruitlessness of fasting and abstinence, on the inamissability of grace acquired in baptism, and of the equality of rewards in the future life. Vigilantius was also an enemy of fasting and of continency; he combated also the honour which the Church paid to the martyrs, to their tombs and relics; he declared the invocation of the saints to be vain, and called those, who honoured them, venerators of ashes, and servers of idols. Against both these teachers of error, St. Jerome wrote with great vehemence and force: the doctrine of Jovinian was condemned also by a council of Milan, in the year 390.

Controversies arose also, during this period, respecting the blessed Virgin, the mother of Jesus Christ, and the honour and veneration which are due to her. Jovinian taught that, by the birth of Jesus Christ, she ceased to be a virgin. Helvidius and Bonosus went further, and asserted that after giving birth to Christ, she bore other children. Against the first, St. Jerome wrote; against the latter, St. Ambrose. In Arabia, the Antidicomarianites, who were refuted by St. Epiphanius, also denied the virginity of the holy mother of Christ, whilst the Collyridianerians in the same country offered to her divine honours.

SECTION V.

CONTROVERSIES ON THE DOCTRINES OF ORIGEN.*

THE doctrines, which were advanced in his numerous writings by the great Alexandrian doctor, Origen, were fully calculated, sometimes clearly and decidedly, at others only by inference, and with a tone of doubt, to produce in the Church long controversies and violent confusion. Nurtured in the study of the Hellenic, particularly of the Platonic, philosophy, and necessitated by his position in the catechetic school of Alexandria, to represent to the philosophically educated pagans the Christian doctrine in as comprehensible a form as possible, he formed a system in which the simple truths of Christianity were expounded in philosophic terms, strange and harshly contradictory to ecclesiastical tradition. For although he retained a respect for the doctrines of the Church, and professed subjection to its authority, yet he imagined that in an age, when the Church had not yet spoken definitively upon many of the dogmas of faith, being carried away by the caprice of his allegorical interpretations, transforming the positive into the figurative and symbolic, and in which he made Scripture and tradition subservient to his own views,—he imagined that there was ample space for the propagation of his own ideas. He taught indeed, that the world had been created from nothing, that is, he rejected the pagan idea of a formation from pre-existing matter,

---

* The Epistles of Jerome, Epiphanius, and Theophilus, collected in Hieronymi Opp. ed. Vallarsi, tom. i.—Hieronymus ad Pammachium et Oceanum de Erroribus Origenis.—Rufini Apologiæ II. and Hieronymi Apolog. adv. Rufinum; Opp. ed. Vallarsi, tom. ii.—Palladius de Vita Chrysostomi, Paris, 1680, 4to.—Epistles of J. Chrysostom and Honorius, in Palladius and Sozomen; Extracts from the Synod at the Oak, in Photius, Biblioth. Cod. 39.

P. D. Huetii Origeniana, in the fourth volume of the works of Origen, by De la Rue.—L. Doucin, Histoire des Mouvemens arrivez dans l'Eglise au sujet d'Origène, Paris, 1700.

but he maintained at the same time that creation was eternal, for as we cannot imagine any change in the Deity, so we cannot imagine in Him any beginning of action. He taught that the present visible world had sprung from a series of others which had preceded it, and that it should be followed in succession by many yet to come. In the beginning, a world of spirits, in every respect equal, was formed by an act of the Divine will. Of these many had for a long time deprived themselves of their original justice and happiness, by turning their wills from God; and this perversion of the free will with which they had been endowed, was the fall into sin: this sin is different in different spirits, hence the cause of generic and individual differences amongst them. All souls are, therefore, fallen heavenly spirits, which are placed in bodies in a state of penance, and purification: to the higher spirits, the stars of heaven, which they animate, serve as bodies: those which have fallen lower, the human souls, dwell in earthly bodies. The Son or the Logos, who before time was, was hypostatically united with the pure and sinless soul of Christ, took to himself, in time, a human body, to redeem all the fallen spirits, not only those on earth; that is, he descended upon earth to make possible their return to God. Again, he taught, that as all punishments are intended to produce a salutary effect, and as the eternal duration of hell is repugnant to the essence of created things, namely to their instability, there would come at length (*in consummatione sæculi*), an universal apocatastasis or restoration, when even the demons would repent, and be pardoned; and when the reconciliation of all rational creatures with God should then take place, God would be truly all in all.

A system such as this, if advanced openly, and without disguise, must necessarily have caused excitement in the Church, which would reject it as a tissue of errors. But Origen himself complained that his writings had been corrupted by heretics: he was then careful not to change any thing in the ordinary forms of speech employed by the Church, and in his popular discourses and writings observed a prudent reserve: again, these doctrines were generally announced only obscurely; they appeared to have been explained away by contradictory assertions, and were never, with the exceptions of some books written in his youth, proposed consecutively. They, therefore, occurred not to many of his readers: others remarked in his writings something only objecttionable, which they easily pardoned to so great and meritorious a man; and although attacks were made upon him from time to time, yet the veneration and authority in which he lived in the memory of men were undiminished till towards the close of the fourth century. Methodius, bishop of Tyre, who was martyred in 309, attacked the doctrine of Origen on the resurrection, although Origen himself, in his later writings, in his refutation of Celsus, expressed himself clearly and correctly on this subject. Methodius might, with greater reason, have assailed Origen for his system of the eternal creation, and of the pre-existence of souls. On the other side, the priest Pamphilius of Cæsarea, a contemporary of Methodius, commenced an extensive apology for Origen, which, after his martyrdom, was completed by his friend, Eusebius. At the outbreaking of the Arian conflict, the Origenian controversy reposed, but was again awakened, and with greater violence, in the year 394. At this time the chief seats of Origenism were in Palestine and Egypt, where it was upheld and strengthened by the celebrated Didymus the blind, the most famed theologian of his age. At Jerusalem, John the bishop of that city, and Epiphanius bishop of Salamina in Cyprus, entered into a violent contest with each other, the former as the defender, the latter as the opposer, of the Origenists The same subject engaged also St. Jerome and Rufinus, a priest of Aquileia. They had both before been disciples of Didymus, and united in the strictest friendship. St. Jerome engaged in the controversy on the side of Epiphanius, Rufinus on that of John, from whose communion St. Jerome, and the monks of Bethlehem, withdrew themselves.

Epiphanius wrote an epistle, in which, according to the translation of it by St. Jerome, he seems to impute to John, to Rufinus and to others, the real and capital errors of Origen: John and his adherents, at the same time, accused Epiphanius of anthropomorphism, or the doctrine which teaches that God has a body like to that of man. Theophilus, bishop of Alexandria, at length effected a peace in Palestine, in 397; but as Rufinus, after his return to Aquileia, published a translation of the work of Origen, *On Principles*, in which he softened down or changed the objectionable passages, the contest was renewed between him and St. Jerome, in a series of empassioned letters. The Roman pontiff, Anastasius, when made acquainted with the dangerous character of the work of Origen, by the true translation of St. Jerome, condemned the doctrines contained in it, and in 401, called Rufinus to Rome to answer for his belief. He there endeavoured to justify himself by a profession of orthodox faith.

In the meantime, the anthropomorphist and Origenist monks were engaged in fierce controversial warfare in Egypt, and Theophilus, importuned by the former, condemned the books of Origen, in a synod, in the year 400; and in his paschal circular, in 401, expressed himself against the Origenists, with a vehemence that was not to be expected from one who had before defended them. The Origenist party of the Nitrian monks refused to discontinue the reading of the works of Origen, as required by the synod, under the pretext that each one was capable of judging of the good and evil which they contained. By this opposition they drew upon themselves a persecution, the circumstances of which were not, it is said, honourable to Theophilus; and fifty monks, with the four, so called, "Tall Brothers" at their head, fled to Constantinople, to seek protection from the patriarch St. John Chrysostom. The greater part of these monks were, in a dogmatical sense, no more Origenists than was this holy patriarch; but the credulous Epiphanius, who had been won over by Theophilus, thought that it was his duty to meet and combat Origenism in the capital of the empire. In 403, he went to Constantinople, and required of the bishops, who were there, to condemn Origen; and, as they refused, he left the city without waiting the arrival of Theophilus, and died on his return. Theophilus, who had been accused of great offences by the Nitrian monks, had been summoned to Constantinople, by the emperor Arcadius, to defend himself before an ecclesiastical tribunal, over which St. John presided. But through the influence of the all-powerful empress, Eudoxia, who had been embittered by the severe reproofs of the patriarch, Theophilus entered the city rather as a judge than as an accused man. In 403, a synod of bishops, of whom some were Egyptians, and others personal enemies of St. John, assembled at a place called *The Oak*, a suburb of Chalcedon. These bishops allowed themselves to publish against the holy patriarch a document replete with falsehoods, distortions of facts, and trifles; and as the patriarch refused to appear before them, when cited, he was deposed by them, and exiled by the emperor. But the unequivocal symptoms of discontent in the people, when they saw themselves deprived of their beloved bishop, terrified the empress; the patriarch was recalled after a few days, and conducted back in triumph to his church. But two months did not pass away before he again called down upon himself the anger of Eudoxia, by his reproval of the improper proceedings which accompanied the dedication of a statue erected in her honour. In one of his discourses he made an allusion to the enraged Herodias, who demanded the head of John in a dish; with which the empress became so infuriated that she vowed his destruction. Theophilus, who, at the request of the bishops assembled at *The Oak*, had been reconciled with the monks of Nitris, and had hastened back to Alexandria, to preside there over a great council, directed from a distance the machinations of those that were united in hatred against the holy patriarch. They employed against him the Antiochian canon, which declared that a bishop, who, having been deposed by a council, should again take possession of his church, without the authority of another council, had thereby become irregular. St. John was again banished, first to the Caucasus, on the borders of Armenia, and afterwards to Pityus, on the Black Sea. He died on his way thither, in 407.

CHAPTER THE FOURTH.

HERESIES AND CONTROVERSIES ON GRACE AND THE INCARNATION, FROM THE BEGINNING OF THE FIFTH CENTURY TO THE END OF THE PERIOD

Section I.—Pelagianism.*

THE attempt to rationalize the doctrines of the Church, had, in its first appearance, in the form of Arianism, suffered an entire defeat. But although it had failed in its attack upon the doctrine of the Trinity, it now directed itself against two other fundamental dogmas of the Christian faith: the incarnation and grace. From the school of a celebrated and influential teacher, Theodore, bishop of Mopsueste, in Cilicia, there went forth men, who reared into maturity the seeds which they had received there, of the closely connected errors of Nestorianism and Pelagianism; errors, of which the former produced a contest that long and deeply shook the Churches of the east, whilst in the west the latter was happily subdued with less effort, and before it had produced so great confusion in the Church.

According to the narration of Marius Mercator, Rufinus, a Syrian, (who is not to be confounded with the

---

* S. Augustini Opp. Edit. Bened. tom. x , S. Hieronymi, Epist. 138, ad Ctesiphontem, et Adversus Pelagianos Dialogi III.; Orosii Apologeticus contra Pelagianos de Arbitrii Libertate; Marii Mercatoris Commonitorium adv. Hæres. Pelagii, Opp edidit Garnerius, Paris, 1673, fol.

Henrici Norisii, Historia Pelagiana. Petavii, 1673 —Joh. Garnier, Dissert VII. quibus integra continetur Pelagianorum Historia, in his edition of Marius Mercator, Paris, 1673.—Scip. Maffei, Histoiia dogmatum de Div. Gratia, Lib. Arbitrio et Prædestinatione, Latine edid F. Reiffenbergius, Francof. 1756, fol.—Laur. Alticotii, Summa Augustiniana, Romæ, 1755, 4to. tom. iv. v. vi.—(Patouillet), Histoire du Pélagianisme, Avignon, 1763.

priest of Aquileia, of the same name), a disciple of Theodore, was the first who taught the doctrine that human nature is free from original, inherited guilt. He commenced his teaching at Rome, in the pontificate of Athanasius, who governed the Church from 398 to 402. This doctrine was reduced to a system by Pelagius, a British monk,—a learned man, celebrated then by his writings, who, in an ill-guided zeal against that slothful timidity, which excuses its neglect of the Divine law by its feigned inability to observe it, endeavoured to exalt the freedom and moral power of man. The following were the doctrines contained in this system, as Pelagius developed them, partly in the beginning and partly during the course of the controversy. Not to offer too violent an opposition to the universal belief of Christianity, Pelagius by degrees conceded many things respecting grace which did not originally enter into his cause. The following is a brief statement of his doctrines.

The first man was created mortal, and must consequently have died, whether he had sinned or not. As death is therefore not the effect of sin, sin has no influence generally on human nature; and being a thing unsubstantial, it cannot effect or change our nature. Children are born therefore in the same state in which Adam was before his fall, and men are as free now as he was in Paradise. The words of the apostle, "*that in Adam all have sinned,*" are to be understood to signify only that all imitate the first man in the sin which he committed, for that which is unavoidable is no sin, and concupiscence, even in its present state, is not evil. All men can consequently exist free from sin, and observe all the Divine commandments. That man can desire and perform what is good, is a power which he has received from God; and it is in the bestowing of this power,—that is, free will or the power not to sin,— that Divine grace chiefly consists: grace, therefore, is an assistance which God grants to us, that we *more easily* perform those things which he has commanded us to perform by virtue of our free will; this grace is no other than the law, the doctrine and the example of Christ, then the remission or non-imputation of sin, referring only to the past, not connected with an interior sanctification or strength for the avoiding of future offences. In addition to these external, Pelagius, during the contest, allowed there were other interior and supernatural graces, such as the in-dwelling of the Holy Ghost; which, however, produced no more than an enlightening of the understanding, not that sanctifying grace which immediately affects and guides the will, and which infuses charity into the soul of man. Of this doctrine the consequence was, that we are not to pray to God that he would grant us his grace to love and do what is good, but only the grace to know it. When, therefore, Pelagius spoke of the necessity of grace, he thereby understood no more than the first, the grant of free will; and this he defined to be a state of indifference, or equipoise of the will between good and evil: the assisting or helping grace, which he admitted was not *necessary* to man for overcoming temptation or for fulfilling the commandments, but with it man was enabled to perform good *more easily:* it is not a free gift of God, but merited by man by the good use of his free will; for God gives it to every one, who, by the sole, proper, due employment of his natural faculties, disposes himself to receive it. By the power of his free will alone, man can attain to the true faith, can merit the second (the assisting) grace, can resist every temptation, and comply with all the commandments. Baptism is necessary to adults for the forgiveness of sins; but to children, who are born without sin and without guilt, it is necessary only that they may obtain the adoption of children of God, and the inheritance of the kingdom of heaven; for children who die unbaptized, and pagans who have lived unstained by crime, enjoy eternal life; not, indeed, in the kingdom of heaven, which is open only to those who have been baptized, and who have been made partakers of the grace of Christ.

Celestius, the friend and scholar of Pelagius, who

attacked principally the doctrine of original sin, as Pelagius did that of grace, was first excommunicated, in 412, by a synod at Carthage, at which the bishop Aurelius presided, and before which Paulinus, a deacon of Milan, accused Celestius as a teacher of error. From this synod he appealed to the Roman pontiff; he did not, however, wait for the answer to his appeal, but went to Ephesus. Pelagius had in the meantime gone from Rome to Jerusalem, where he won for himself the favour and protection* of the bishop John. His writings, and in particular his commentaries on the epistles of St. Paul, were read with delight by the Roman ladies at Jerusalem, at the time when St. Jerome, who was then at Bethlehem, combated his assertion,—" that man may, when he pleases, become entirely free from sin,"—in a letter to Ctesiphon. Orosius, a Spanish priest, who had been sent by St. Augustin to St. Jerome, now arrived in Palestine, and in a synod of the clergy, held at Jerusalem, in 415, accused Pelagius, that he maintained the same errors that had been condemned in Celestius, by the council of Carthage. But as the bishop John openly favoured Pelagius, and as on account of the difference of their language, and the incapacity of the interpreter, it was difficult to arrive at a mutual understanding, Orosius appealed to pope Innocent for a decision. Not long after, two exiled Gaulish bishops, Eros and Lazarus, prompted probably by St. Jerome, addressed a letter of complaint against Pelagius to Eulogius, the metropolitan of Cæsarea. Eulogius thereupon assembled, also in 415, a council of fourteen bishops, at Diospolis. Pelagius here defended himself by those equivocal terms, and that dishonourable form of words of double meaning, for the use of which his contemporaries so severely and so often accused him. He confessed the necessity of grace, but he understood by this grace, the gift of free will; all that he had said on the sufficiency of free will, he wished to be said without any injury to grace: he declared that he had no other faith than that of the Church: he condemned in words the errors which had been imputed to him, and by this means obtained absolution. Whilst the Pelagians in Syria, made haughty by this triumph, used acts of violence against St. Jerome, in his cloister at Bethlehem, Pelagius wrote circular letters, boasting that the synod had declared free of all blame, his doctrines, which had in other places been so violently assailed.

At the first appearance of Pelagianism, a mighty champion of the Catholic faith arose in Africa, in the person of the great bishop of Hippo. For twenty years he continued to combat, untired, against this heresy, with all the powers of his rich mind, and of his profound and enlightened piety. In 412, at the request of the tribune Marcellinus, he wrote his books *On Merit and the Remission of Sin:* in 414, he refuted the work of Pelagius *On Nature,* by his work *On Nature and Grace;* and in 416, incited by the issue of the council of Diospolis, he wrote his book *On the Actions of Pelagius.* The doctrines which, in the name of the Church, (we speak not here of his own private views or of expressions which escaped from him in the heat of controversy), St. Augustin opposed in these works to the errors of Pelagius, were in substance the following:

Since the fall of our first parents by sin, man is not in that primitive state in which Adam was created, but, in consequence of that sin, has lost sanctifying grace, is subjected to death and corporal sufferings, and feels within himself the sting of concupiscence, or an impelling inclination to evil. Hence the free will of man is now different from that which was in Adam before his fall. Of free will, such as Pelagius understood it, that is as a state of equilibrium between good and evil, or a perfectly equal facility of performing good or evil, it must now be said, that it has been destroyed by original sin; that man, by the concupiscence which dwells within him, is more inclined to evil than to good, and that he, therefore, stands in need of grace, in order that his original state of indifference or equilibrium may be restored. But free will was not in reality destroyed or annihilated by the fall, it was deprived of its original justice, it was weakened and wounded. The power of choice was still left to man: when he commits that which is evil, he is not borne irresistably onwards to the commission; and when he performs that which is good, he is not overpowered by the impulse of grace; but in both cases he acts with liberty, and feels that he can choose either the good or the evil. He receives, however, the power of doing that which is good, from sanctifying grace, which was merited for him by the blood of Christ, and which is not a mere assistance or help, but a remedy, a medicine. This interior grace, which enlightens the mind, and influences the will, must precede the will, and raise it above its natural powers: it is an entirely free gift of God, which we have not merited, nor could ever merit, and without which it were impossible for man to perform any supernatural or meritorious action. Even with grace, man cannot totally free himself from the weakness and infirmity of his fallen nature: the best of men, and the most exalted by grace, will sometimes yield to temptations to less sins.

When Orosius, in 416, returned to Africa with letters from Eros and Lazarus, a synod at Carthage threatened to pronounce an anathema against Pelagius and his disciple Celestius, unless they should immediately condemn their errors: the council sent a request to pope Innocent, supplicating him to confirm their sentence. At the same time Innocent received letters from the Numidian synod of Mileve, and from five African bishops, amongst whom was St. Augustin, calling upon him to oblige these heresiarchs to retract their errors, to summon Pelagius to Rome, and to demand from him a full declaration of his faith. Innocent answered them, by the declaration, that if Pelagius and Celestius persevered any longer in their errors he would immediately excommunicate them. It was then that St. Augustin, in an address to his people, exclaimed: "Already have two councils sent their judgments in this cause to the apostolic see: the desired rescripts have come thence, and thus the affair is ended: would that the error were ended too!" Condemned by a synod of Antioch, and banished from Jerusalem by Praylus, the successor of

John, Pelagius sent declarations of his obedience and of his orthodoxy to Rome, where Zosimus, a Greek, had succeeded Innocent; and, about the same time, Celestius, who had been driven from Constantinople by the patriarch, Atticus, arrived in Rome to clear himself, as he said, from the errors which had been unjustly imputed to him. He presented to the pontiff a profession of faith, which was Catholic, even on the point of original sin: he declared that he was willing to condemn all that the holy see should pronounce censureable. Zosimus, who was not sufficiently instructed in the true nature of the controversy, and who entertained suspicions against Eros and Lazarus, gave credit to Celestius too easily, and suffered himself to be deceived. He received the profession of faith which Pelagius had addressed to him: he wrote, in a tone of censure, to the African bishops, as if they had acted with too great precipitation and severity towards Pelagius and Celestius, whom he called victims of calumny; but he deferred absolving them from excommunication until he should have heard from the African bishops. These bishops remained firm: they assembled to the number of two hundred and fourteen at Carthage, in the year 417; they determined to adhere to the former decrees against Pelagius, and particularly to those of pope Innocent; and exposed to Zosimus the insufficiency of the explanations of Celestius. In 418, a plenary synod of Africa was convened at Carthage; and, in eight canons, it condemned the principal of the Pelagian errors. Zosimus had, in the beginning of this year, discovered the deception which had been practised upon him, and in a second assembly of the Roman clergy, cited Celestius to give a more explicit declaration of his faith. Celestius did not appear, and the pope, therefore, in an epistle (*Tractatoria*), addressed to all the bishops of the Christian world, pronounced sentence of condemnation upon Pelagius and Celestius. This epistle was every where received and subscribed by all the bishops, with the exception of Julian of Eclanum, and fourteen Italian bishops, who refused, and were thereupon deposed by

Zosimus. An imperial edict, which was soon after published against all obstinate Pelagians, exiled them from their country.

This Julian afterwards proved himself the most learned and powerful advocate of Pelagianism; St. Augustin found in him an opponent worthy of his own talents, and the contest between the two was continued unto the death of the holy bishop of Hippo. Julian, however, was not a harsh Pelagian, but approached in his doctrines nearer to those which the Semipelagians afterwards maintained. He granted that there was a grace which moved the will, but taught that it was not necessary for man, even with his corrupt and weakened nature, was capable of willing, and beginning good, but that this grace supported him and enabled him to lead the good, already commenced, to perfection. This grace was given to man on account of his own merit, for it can be merited by a natural desire of good, by faith and by prayer. Hence he taught also, that infidels by their mere natural powers, without the aid of grace, may possess all the virtues even in their perfection. Whilst St. Augustin was engaged in refuting these errors, two other subjects were drawn upon the scene of controversy,—concupiscence and the state of matrimony. Concerning the former, Julian asserted, that it was not evil, but a natural and beneficial gift of God to man. St. Augustin, on the contrary, maintained and proved, that it was a defect, a depravation of nature, an effect of the sin of Adam, a chastisement from God, and which he might, after the example of St. Paul, call by the name sin. "If, then," asked Julian, "if concupiscence be an evil, a consequence of the sin of Adam, and if all children are born in sin, matrimony must be the cause, the principal of this evil; how, therefore, can it be tolerated?" St. Augustin answered this objection, in 418, in his work *On Matrimony and Concupiscence,* in which he proves that chaste matrimony is justified before God and man. He replied to Julian's answer in an extensive work, in six books, and he had commenced to refute another work of his adversary in an equal number of books; but before the completion of this his last undertaking, God took him from this world of strife to himself.

Julian and his party were not inactive in defending themselves and their doctrines. They accused their adversaries of Manicheism, as they admitted a radical corruption of our human nature, and the existence of substances which were not created by God, as they must consider matrimony a work of the devil; they accused them, moreover, of having introduced fatalism, under the name of grace. Against these accusations, St. Augustin wrote the work which, in 420, he addressed to pope Boniface. Julian and the seventeen Italian bishops appealed from the constitution of Zosimus to a general council: in a letter to the Roman clergy, Julian asserted that he and his adherents did not defend the tenets that were attributed to them, and required of those bishops who opposed him, that they should condemn the "Manichean errors" of which they, the Pelagians, accused them. But when they saw that these arts were of no avail, Julian, and those who were with him, went into Cilicia, to Theodore, bishop of Mopsueste, the real author of these errors; and it is probable, that Theodore composed about this time the work described by Photius, "against those who teach that man sins by nature, not by his will." In this work, he designated St. Jerome as the author of a new heresy, attacked St. Augustin, and represented the Catholic doctrine in the same manner as Julian had described it before him. After the death of the emperor Honorius, Pelagius and Celestius returned to Italy, and sought, but in vain, from pope Celestine, that their cause might be again examined. They then journeyed to Constantinople, but were soon compelled, by the patriarch, Atticus, to leave that city. They were more favourably received by Nestorius, the successor of Atticus, a disciple of Theodore of Mopsueste. But as letters from the pope, and a memorial from Marcus Mercator, who was then at Constantinople, exposed the errors of the Pelagians, Nestorius dared not to declare himself openly in their favour, and in 429 an imperial edict obliged them again to depart. At the general council of Ephesus, the acts respecting Pelagianism were read, and the papal decrees condemning it were confirmed. Thus, in a space of nineteen years, the Pelagians were condemned by four popes, and by more than twenty councils. The death of its author, and of his few adherents, extinguished this heresy,—which possessed this peculiarity, that it never formed a sect, but being defended only by a few learned men, remained almost unknown to the people.

SECTION II.

THE SEMIPELAGIANS.*

Pelagianism in its severe form, which was repugnant to every Christian feeling, was now subdued; but the error which exalted the will and the self-sufficiency of man, at the cost of Divine grace, was renewed in the milder, less unchristian, but still objectionable, form of Semipelagianism. St. Augustin, in his latter works against the Pelagians, had employed expressions which were harsh, and not in perfect conformity with the tradition of the Church, on the necessity of sinning, and on the irresistible operations of grace,—expressions, however, which were greatly softened by connecting them together, and by contrasting them with many others in his writings; but which, even then, could not be received as declaratory of the doctrine of the universal Church. Many persons, however, drew from them an apparent occasion to declare against the works in which they were contained, even where these works

---

* Joh. Cassiani, Collationes PP. Scet. Opp. ed. Al Gazæus, Atrebati, 1628, folio —Fausti Regiensis opp. in Biblioth. Max. PP. viii 523 et seqq.— S. Prosperi, Opp. Paris, 1684.— Joh. Maxentii Scripta in Biblioth. Max. PP. ix. 539 et seqq.; Prædestinatus S. prædestinatorum hæresis et libri, S. Augustino temere adscripti, confutatio, in Biblioth. Max. PP. tom. xxvii.

spoke the essential doctrines of the Church, and to form for themselves an entirely different system on grace and free will, which is known by the name of Semipelagianism.

In the year 426, the monks of the monastery of Adrumetum in Africa, thought that they discovered, in the works of St. Augustin, doctrines which would destroy the free will of man. This great doctor of the Church then wrote, for their instruction, his two works, *On Grace and Free Will*, and *On Correction and Grace*. Soon after this, two laymen from Gaul, Prosper and Hilary, informed him, that many priests and monks, at Marseilles, were dissatisfied with his doctrines, and taught that the operations of the will of man must go before grace, and that man himself must place the beginning of his own justification and salvation. These opponents St. Augustin answered, by his two books, *On the Predestination of the Saints*, and *On the Gift of Perseverance*. In these works he speaks to his adversaries with great mildness, as to brothers, who, although in error on an important subject, were yet far removed from Pelagianism. But not all those, whom Prosper calls adversaries of St. Augustin, were in reality Semipelagians: for St. Hilary, bishop of Arles, who rejected the doctrine of St. Augustin on predestination, had not embraced the Semipelagian errors. These errors were defended by Faustus, bishop of Riez, and by Cassian, who, having dwelt for a long time with the Egyptian anchorites, and with St. John Chrysostom in Constantinople, went to Marseilles, where he founded a large monastery, over which he presided as abbot. In his book of *Conferences*, he repeats the discourses which he held with his monks. In the thirteenth Conference, he teaches that a good will, which often comes from the powers of nature, is not always to be ascribed to grace. It is probable that the priest Gennadius of Marseilles, who, about the year 495, continued the work of St. Jerome, *On celebrated Ecclesiastical Men*, belonged also to this school. The doctrines of St. Augustin were powerfully defended by Prosper, who died a layman in

463, and later by Fulgentius bishop of Ruspe in Africa, who died in 533. The book *On the Vocation of the Gentiles*, in which the too harsh assertions of St. Augustin are modified, bears little evidence of being a work of St. Augustin, and is attributed by some writers to the pope St. Leo, and by others to St. Prosper.

In the year 431, Prosper and Hilary complained to pope Celestine, that there were priests at Marseilles, who openly taught erroneous doctrines, of which the bishops of Gaul appeared to take no notice. The pope immediately wrote to the bishops, reprehended their silence and inactivity, and praised the doctrines, on these disputed points, of St. Augustin, whom the Roman See, he says, had always considered one of the first teachers of the Church. He adds, however, " On those profound and difficult subjects, which the opposition of heretics have caused to be so extensively discussed, (such as the nature of original sin, and the cause of predestination, which St. Augustin has treated), we do not wish to speak with disapprobation, neither do we confirm them, for sufficient is contained on these questions in the papal decrees." The Scythian monks thought far otherwise. In 520, they wished to see the writings of Faustus, bishop of Riez, condemned, and wrote in anger against the pope Hormisdas, because in his epistle to the bishop Possessor, he had stated no more than that these works were of no authority in the Church. The African bishops, who had been banished to Sardinia, thereupon condemned them, and deputed Fulgentius to refute the errors contained in them, which he did in his work, *On the Incarnation and Grace of Our Lord Jesus Christ*.

The Semipelagians admitted that the natural powers of man had been weakened by the fall; but they maintained, at the same time, that man can, by the powers which have been left in him, arrive at the beginning of faith and justification; for by those emotions of faith, of a desire of salvation and of the Divine assistance, which of himself he can awaken within his soul, he can merit this first grace. They compared man to a sick person, who first knows his disease, then calls a physician, to whom he confides himself, and employs the remedies prescribed; and thus they taught that the beginning of salvation is to come from him who is to be saved, not from him who is to save. Hence it would follow, that God is prepared to bestow his grace, without distinction, upon all, and waits only for the spontaneous call of his creatures to distribute it to them: and this proposition, which is in itself perfectly true, " that God wills the salvation of all, and that Christ died for the whole human race," was erroneously interpreted by them to signify, that by the merits of Christ, a treasure of grace had been opened to all men, from which each one, by his own natural desire of salvation, can draw what, and as much as he pleases. The example of two children, of whom one dies baptized, and the other without baptism, was objected to them; and they answered, that God foresaw that in the one a good will, a desire of salvation would have been formed, and, therefore, he imparted to that one the grace of baptism; which he denied to the other, in whom this will would not have been formed. They denied, also, that a perseverance in good was a particular grace, as St. Augustin had taught, but maintained that it was a free act of the will; and, finally, when they asserted, as many fathers and theologians have asserted, that the decree of God respecting the salvation of the elect, was formed on his foresight of their merits, they understood thereby not merits acquired by grace, but by the use of man's own natural powers.

These errors were condemned, in 529, by the council of Orange (Aurusicanum) at which there were present, thirteen Gallic bishops, under the metropolitan, St. Cæsarius, of Arles. The Catholic doctrine, as opposed to Semipelagianism, was drawn up by the council, in twenty-five canons. It taught, that even the first emotion of faith in him who justifies the sinner, the invocation of divine grace, and the desire of man to be freed from his sins, were all effects of grace—an infusion of the Holy Ghost: that man, by his own powers, can do, think, and choose, nothing towards his salvation; and that, consequently, grace cannot be merited by any thing which precedes it, but that free grace goes before, that we may act meritoriously; and, that whatever good there is in man, comes from God, as man from himself has nothing but lies and sin: even those who have been regenerated, and those who are holy, must unceasingly implore the grace of God, that they may arrive at a happy end, and may persevere in good. Pope Boniface II confirmed these canons in 530; since which time, they have been considered as a rule of faith in the universal Church.

Diametrically opposed to the errors of the Pelagians, was the doctrine of the Predestinarians, of whom history has preserved the name of only one, Lucidus, a priest of Gaul. But Lucidus presented to the bishops, assembled in council at Arles in 475, a writing, in which he retracted the tenets which he had before defended, having been convinced of his errors by Faustus of Riez. The doctrine of the Predestinarians was, that God, by an absolute, necessitating decree, which preceded all foresight of merit or of guilt in man, has predestined a portion of mankind to eternal perdition, and to the sins which lead to it; that, consequently, he does not will the salvation of all men, but only of those whom he has destined to beatitude, and that Christ died only for the elect; lastly, that free will was destroyed by the first fall of man, and that the sacraments are of no avail to those who are doomed to eternal death.

SECTION III.

NESTORIANISM.—THE COUNCIL OF EPHESUS.*

As early as the year 418, Leporius, a Gallic monk, and afterwards a priest of Hippo in Africa, had advanced

---

* Fragments of Theodore of Mopsueste, in the Acts of the Fifth General Council, Harduin, Coll. Conc. iii. 1, et seqq.—Writings of

the doctrine, that in Christ there were two independent subjects; that the divine subject could be attributed only to the Logos, the Word—and the human, only to the man Jesus. He pursued this doctrine into its consequences, and asserted, therefore, that the man Jesus, separated from the Divinity, suffered on the cross, and Christ did not come to effect the redemption of the human race, but only to present to man the example of a holy life. These errors were condemned by the bishops of Gaul; Leporius was convinced of them by St. Augustin, and induced to retract them. But that which had been in the West only the ephemeral error of an individual, was, when embraced by a famed theologian in the East, and protected by the authority of a patriarch of the capital of the empire, the cause of a melancholy schism and heresy, which to this day exist. Theodore, bishop of Mopsueste, who had been before a priest of Antioch, in his contest with Apollinarism, which confounded the two natures of Christ, and almost destroyed his human nature, had formed the opposite error into a system, which separated the two natures so far from each other, as to leave only a moral external union, between the Logos and the man Jesus. Within the Antiochian patriarchate, this doctrine was widely diffused by the writings of Theodore, and by the attachment of many of his scholars to their master, when Nestorius, a priest of Antioch, celebrated for his elo-

---

Nestorius, his Homilies, collected by Garnier, in Opp. Marii Mercatoris, n 5; his Letters to Pope Celestine, to S. Cyril, to the Emperor Theodosius, in the Collection of Councils; Fragments of his writings in the works of St Cyril, and in the Acts of the Ephesine Council — S Cyrilli Alexandrini, Opp. ed. Aubert, Paris, 1638, 7 vols. fol.— Theodoreti, Reprehensio XII; Anathematismorum Cyrilli, Opp. ed. Schulze, tom. v.—Liberati, Breviarium Causæ Nestorianorum et Eutychian ed. Garnier, Paris, 1675. — Irenæi Tragœdia S. Comment. de rebus in Synodo Ephesina et in Oriente toto gestis, in a Latin translation, in Variorum Epistolæ ad Concil. Ephes. pertinentes, ed. Chr. Lupus, Lovan 1682, 4to —Acta Synodi in Harduin, Concil. Coll. i 1271, et seqq; Leontii Byzantini, contra Nestorium et Eutychen, in Canisii Thesaur. Monum. ed. Basnage, t. i.

Garnier, De Hæresi et Libris Nestorii, in his edition of Marius Mercator, tom. ii —L. Doucin, Histoire du Nestorianisme, Paris, 1698, 4to.

quence and the austerity of his life, introduced it, with himself, into Constantinople, whither he was called, in 428, to succeed the patriarch Sisinius. The system of Theodore and Nestorius—for between the two there was scarcely a discernible difference—was the following:—

Jesus Christ is properly only man, who was united with the Word, and filled with the power of God more than any of the prophets or saints had ever been. God, the Logos, and Jesus of Nazareth, are two subjects, or persons, entirely distinct, which, however, had been associated the one with the other; and this union is more close than that of man with the garment which he has on his body, or of the temple with the Deity that dwells therein. The man Jesus received the God within himself; the Logos dwelt in man; it clothed itself with human nature, that he might reveal his glory beneath this veil, and employ it as an instrument for our salvation. The son of Mary is not truly God; he is no more than man, who bore in his person the Divinity: he was filled, or possessed by God; he is called God, because in virtue of the relation in which he stood to God, he partakes of his honour and prerogatives: he is, however, improperly called God, as when in the Scripture Moses is named the God of Pharaoh, and Israel the Son of God. The Incarnation is therefore no more than the indwelling of God, the Word, in man: the Eternal Word was not made man; it only united itself with man; the Word was not born of the Virgin mother, nor did it suffer: it took up its abode only in him who was born of the Virgin, in him who suffered and died; for the Creator could not be created, life could not die, the Omnipotent could not experience weakness. The blessed Virgin is, therefore, not mother of God, (Θεοτοκος), but mother of man, mother of Christ. The name Christ does not signify a Man-God, but a man united with God: now, an union or association necessarily implies two persons, who may form a moral *one*, but who, in their physical or substantial functions and properties, which limit individuality, must be distinct. The man Jesus could not therefore communicate his properties to the Logos, with which it was united. Thus taught Nestorius, and hence, in the anathemas which he opposed to those of St. Cyril, he said, " Anathema to him who shall say that the Emmanuel is true God, and shall not say that God only dwelt in human nature! Anathema to him who shall say that after the assumption of human nature by the Logos, the Son of God was naturally one, or that the man who was born of the Virgin was the only begotten Son of the Father."

This doctrine recommended itself to the understanding by the greater facility with which the mind could form to itself an idea of a man filled with the power of God, compared to the difficulty of imagining a God-man. An appearance also of Scriptural truth might be given to it, by applying to it those parts of the sacred writings which speak of Jesus as the Son of Man, of his humiliations, of his sorrow and grief. To this we may add the intentional change of expression, " God died," " the Deity suffered:" for if the Logos, the Word, that was made flesh, that is, which united itself in its essence with human nature, suffered and died, it was indeed God that suffered and died, but not the Deity, for he suffered only in one of his two natures, whilst the other, the Deity, continued impassible and immortal. But the Nestorians transferred to the nature, that which belonged only to the person, and declared it blasphemy to assert that the Deity was capable of suffering or of death.

As God had before called the holy Athanasius to combat victoriously against Arianism, and St. Augustin to subdue the Pelagians, so his providence now disposed, that in the eastern Church there should be found a man, who strenuously defended the true Catholic doctrine on the Incarnation, and who successfully pursued this new heresy through all its artful windings and subtleties. This was St. Cyril, patriarch of Alexandria. He confuted Nestorianism, as well by exposing the consequences to which it conducted, as by opposing to it, and by establishing, the true doctrine of the Church. Draw as closely as you please, he said, the union between the son of Mary and the Logos, if this be not an internal, essential union, it never can serve as a cause that *he* should be adored as God, who in essence is not different from creatures. The adoration which is due to God alone cannot be given to another; and if Jesus Christ, according to Nestorius, may be adored, this would be contrary to the first commandment of the decalogue; for man cannot have been made equal to the Eternal, by having been employed as an instrument by the Logos. Again, if he that suffered be not the same who raises the dead to life; if the one does what the other cannot do; if one be by grace, that which the other is by nature (Son of God), then there must be not only one Son but two,—the one a real, the other an adopted Son: Christ would be not only one, but two persons, both of which bear the same name, but from very different causes. We cannot say that God, the Word, is our Redeemer, if it were not he who was delivered to death for our sins: the Word would have had no other part in our redemption than to have disposed, taught and encouraged the man Jesus; but the apostle, on the contrary, says, that " God spared not his *own* Son." His own Son can be no other than he who sprung from his essence, and was given for us. Thus did St. Cyril prove how repugnant was the Nestorian system to the whole economy of the Christian doctrine of the redemption. His exposition of this Christian doctrine was this:—

As the mother of a man is mother of his whole person, and not simply of his body, although his soul come from another origin,—as she gives birth not only to the body, but to the whole individual, which is composed of a real and essential union of body and soul,—so the holy Virgin Mary, although she by no means gave birth to the Divinity, by which the Word is equal in essence to his Father, yet she is truly and really the mother of the Word, for the flesh of the Word was formed in her womb, and she brought into the world the person of the Eternal Word, who was clothed with our nature. This union of the Word with man, is hypostatical, (that is an union with a subject) and physical,—that is a true and internal union of natures, not a mere relative (σχετικη) and external union, by which the human nature, existing as an independent subject for itself, is admitted to a participation of the majesty and honour of the Word, as Nestorius taught. Those passages of the Scripture, therefore, which speak of Christ, must not be divided, so that some may be applied only to the Man, and others only to the Word. For he was one and the same who said, "I am the resurrection and the life," and "My God, my God, why hast thou forsaken me?" and to this one undivided Emmanuel, there must be given one and undivided praise and adoration. His flesh is vivifying, for it is the flesh of the Word, of him who is "the life." And as man dies, although only his body, and not his soul, is destroyed by death, so the Word was crucified, and tasted death, though only in the flesh; for all the actions and sufferings of the flesh were truly and properly the actions and sufferings of God, the Word, for it was the true flesh of God.

Nestorius first directed his attacks, at Constantinople, against that title of the blessed Virgin, which had long been used by the fathers of the greatest authority,— Mother of God. This word (Θεοτοκος) was a stone of scandal to Nestorianism, and was the shortest symbol of the Catholic faith, as the word *consubstantial* (ὁμοουσιος) had formerly been in the times of the Arians. In his sermon on the festival of the nativity of our Lord, in 428, Nestorius said, "To call the Holy Virgin Mother of God, was to justify the folly of the heathens, who gave mothers to their gods." The Christians of the imperial city immediately perceived that Nestorius and his Antiochian priests designed to introduce a new doctrine amongst them. Proclus, the nominated bishop of Cyzicum, openly opposed the innovation; and when Dorotheus, of Marcianople, pronounced, with the silent approbation of the patriarch, who was present, anathema against all those who should call the Holy Virgin Mother of God, the people remained away from the church, and many priests and monks refused to join with him in communion. Nestorius hoped to break down this opposition by severity, depositions, and threats of exile; but his persecuted victims complained to the emperor, and prayed that a general council might be convened. In the meantime, a collection of the discourses of Nestorius, with the title of *A Treatise on the Incarnation*, was circulated in Egypt, and read with great eagerness by the monks. St. Cyril warned them of the new doctrines which were contained in this work, but, from motives of prudence, he neither named nor alluded to Nestorius. When the epistle of St. Cyril to the Egyptian monks was known at Constantinople, Nestorius no longer concealed his bitterness, and in the correspondence which ensued between him and St. Cyril, he treated his opponent with revolting haughtiness and contempt. At the same time, he wrote to Pope Celestine, complaining that his adversaries did not hesitate to apply to the blessed Virgin the odious title of Mother of God. Celestine lost no time in gaining full information of the nature of the controversy: the abbot Cassian discharged himself of the duty which was imposed upon by Rome, to examine the writings of Nestorius, the errors of which he exposed in an extensive work; and when the report, which St. Cyril had been desired to send, arrived in Rome, the pope convened a synod, in the year 430. In this synod the pontiff declared, "If Nestorius do not retract his errors within ten days after the receipt of this decree, let him be deposed and excluded from the communion of the Church." St. Cyril was appointed legate of the pope in this affair, and charged with the execution of the sentence. But before his messengers, who were the bearers also of a third dogmatical decree issued by a synod held by St. Cyril, could arrive at Constantinople, the emperor Theodosius, urged on even by Nestorius and his adherents, had proclaimed the convocation of a general council. The twelve anathemas of St. Cyril, which contained in a negative form the Catholic doctrine on the incarnation, were opposed by as many opposite anathemas, by

Nestorius; although his friend and countryman, and former fellow-student, John, patriarch of Antioch, earnestly counselled him to make the required retractation, and to approve of the title, Mother of God, which could not be rejected without great danger. Thus pressed by so many opponents, at home and abroad, Nestorius declared, in a sermon, that he was willing to tolerate and even to employ this expression, but only so far as to signify that the temple of God (the man Jesus), who was formed in the womb of the Virgin Mary, was united to God. In a conference with Theodotus of Ancyra, at Ephesus, he went so far as to say, that he could not recognise as God a child of two or three months old. But now John of Antioch changed his sentiments. His attachment to the doctrines of Theodore of Mopsueste, who was highly honoured at Antioch; respect for the many scholars and followers of Theodore in his patriarchate; the representations of Nestorius; and the fear of the increasing power of St. Cyril, which was confirmed by the bishop of Rome; all combined to effect a change in his sentiments, and to determine him to pass over to the party of Nestorius. He allured also two bishops of his patriarchate,—Andrew of Samosata and Theodoret of Cyrus,—to oppose the anathemas of St. Cyril.

Two hundred bishops, amongst whom there were one hundred metropolitans, from Palestine, Asia Minor, Macedonia, the Islands, Hellas and Egypt, assembled, in 431, at Ephesus. St. Cyril presided as plenipotentiary of the pope, who sent also two bishops and a priest as his legates. For a long time the council awaited the coming of John of Antioch, many of whose suffragan bishops had already arrived at Ephesus. The heat and unhealthiness of the season produced diseases amongst the bishops, many of whom died: others began to suffer from want, and all dreaded a long absence from their flocks. When their impatience had arrived at its highest point, two metropolitans arrived, who announced the near approach of the patriarch John. For three days they expected him in vain: they then determined to open the sittings of the council, when it appeared that John had purposely delayed, that he might not take part in the condemnation of his friend Nestorius; and the two metropolitans now declared, in his name, that they might commence the synod, without further expecting him. The imperial deputy, Candidian, opposed himself, in evident partiality for Nestorius, to the opening of the synod, which took place, at length, sixteen days after the term appointed by the emperor. Nestorius, who had surrounded his house with soldiers, refused to admit the bishops, who were commissioned to convey to him the citation of the council. The council, therefore, caused his answer to St. Cyril, and extracts from his works, to be read, and pronounced the judgment, "obliged," as it said, "by the canons and by the epistle of pope Celestine," that Nestorius should be deposed and excommunicated. Candidian then intercepted the letters of the synod to Theodosius, and to other persons in Constantinople, and joined with Nestorius in deceiving the emperor by false reports.

Six days after the deposition of Nestorius, John, accompanied by fourteen bishops, arrived at Ephesus; and he, who fourteen days before had written a letter filled with expressions of affection and of the highest esteem towards St. Cyril, now, immediately after his arrival, held in an apartment of his lodgings an assembly of the friends of Nestorius, and of his own followers. This convention, at which there were present forty-three bishops, passed a sentence of invalidation against the decree of the council; condemned, without reading them, the anathemas of St. Cyril as heretical; and declared him and Memnon bishop of Ephesus, deposed from their episcopal dignity. At the same time, John declared, also, that the bishops who had formed the council were excommunicated until they should condemn these anathemas, should subscribe the Nicene symbol without any additions, and should unite with the oriental bishops, who formed the true (his) council of Ephesus. This council did not, however, positively approve the doctrines of Nestorius. The real and true council, at which the papal legates had now arrived, after repeated citations to John and his party, pronounced against them sentence of suspension; the more severe punishment of deposition was reserved for the pontiff. At Constantinople, the misguided emperor commanded that Nestorius, Cyril, and Memnon, should continue deposed; and John, the imperial minister, who proceeded to Ephesus to execute this sentence, guarded the three prelates as prisoners, and exerted himself in vain to induce the bishops of the council to unite with the orientals. The council, St. Cyril, and Memnon, now contrived to send three letters to Constantinople by means of a poor mendicant. The emperor then permitted that the bishops of both parties should send to him delegates, whom he admitted into his presence at Chalcedon, and commanded that St. Cyril and Memnon should be restored to their liberty, that the bishops might be permitted to return to their churches, and that the delegates should consecrate a new patriarch for the capital of the empire. This was immediately done, that the priest Maximian might be ordained; and now the schism of the Antiochians openly declared itself. John, on his return from Ephesus, held a synod of the bishops of Cilicia, at Tarsus. These bishops, who were devoted disciples of Theodore and zealous Nestorians, resolved never to depart from their resolutions taken at Ephesus, and deposed Jevenal the metropolitan of Jerusalem, Theodotus of Ancyra, Acacius of Miletene, and the other two delegates, of the council, because they had presumed to consecrate a new bishop of Constantinople. In a numerous synod at Antioch the sentence of deposition against St. Cyril, and the condemnation of his anathemas, were renewed. Theodoret wrote against them his *Pentalogion*, an extensive work, which, with the exception of a few fragments, is now lost. This must have been an unfair and a designedly distorted controversy, when Theodoret could again and again object to St. Cyril, that he taught that the Logos had a beginning, that it was changed into flesh, and that he asserted with Apollinaris that this flesh had no other soul than the Logos. Repeatedly, and on express purpose, had St. Cyril declared the immutability of the Logos, and the perfect human nature, composed of a body, and a rational soul with which it was united. The expression "one nature of the Logos, made flesh," which he had on one occasion employed, was now most actively turned as a weapon against him by Theodoret, by Alexander of Hierapolis and others. It was in vain that he protested that he had used the word "nature" according to the ancient usage, to signify individual or person, and that he professed in Christ two substances, the divine and human: his enemies insisted that he admitted these two substances only in succession; and that his proposition, "God suffered in the flesh," had no other signification than that the Deity which was incapable of suffering, was subjected to it when it was changed into flesh.

The emperor, and the pope Sixtus III, who were most anxious to re-establish the peace of the Church, induced Acacius of Beræa, a venerable man, one hundred and ten years of age, and who was respected by all, to take upon himself the task of negociation. John of Antioch, awed at beholding Rome, Alexandria, Constantinople, and Jerusalem, ranged against him, and himself standing alone with the bishops of his patriarchate, and of some of the provinces of Asia Minor, displayed dispositions favourable to reconciliation. But he feared the obstinacy of his bishops, many of whom would withstand until St. Cyril had retracted his anathemas, and all that he had written before the council of Ephesus; but, by the exertions of Paul, bishop of Emesa, and by the prudent measures of St. Cyril, peace was at length restored in 433. A profession of faith, which the delegates of St. Cyril presented to John, was so altered by him, as nearly to resemble that which the oriental bishops, assembled at Chalcedon, had sent to the emperor. It was only by these changes, he wrote to St. Cyril, that he could persuade his bishops to enter into a reconciliation: to Theodoret, and to those who thought with him, he wrote that St. Cyril had yielded, and that the expressions which had given them offence, such as consubstantiation, hypostatical union, and one nature in

Christ, had been withdrawn. St. Cyril, for the sake of peace, permitted these changes which were not essential, and received the formulas, which expressed, though perhaps not with equal precision, the true doctrine of the Church. John and his bishops now addressed the pope, Cyril, and Maximian, to declare to them their wish to enter into communion with all orthodox bishops; that they approved of the ordination of Maximian, and of the deposition of Nestorius; and that they condemned the doctrines of the latter. But the obstinate Nestorians, at whose head was Alexander of Hierapolis, rejected every offer of peace, because, as they said, the innocent Nestorius had been sacrificed, because the Egyptian had not been required to condemn his anathemas, and because the metropolitans, Helladius of Tarsus, Eutherius of Tyana, Dorotheus of Marcianopolis, and Himerius of Nicomedia, who had been deposed by Maximian, had not yet been restored to their churches. Entire provinces now abandoned the patriarch John. Helladius and Eutherius sought to gain over even pope Sixtus to their party; and a synod at Anzarbe renewed the resolutions of the Antiochian schism at Ephesus. The embarrassed John turned himself to the imperial court, to obtain the assistance of the civil power to enforce conformity, and was necessitated to have recourse to the same means which (if we may believe the letter of the archdeacon of Antioch, in the collection of the Nestorian Irenæus, to be genuine) St. Cyril employed both during and after the council of Ephesus,—rich presents to the ministers and attendants of the court, to avert, or to render less injurious the power of the state in ecclesiastical affairs. The emperor published an edict, in which he threatened with exile those bishops who should persevere in the schism; whereupon Theodoret again united himself with John, but without giving his sanction to the deposition of Nestorius, or to the condemnation of his doctrines. The bishops of Ephratesia, Isauria, and the two Cilicias, followed the example of the influential bishop of Cyrus, but at first protested also against the condemnation of

Nestorius and of his doctrines, and against the anathemas of St. Cyril: but a second edict commanded all bishops to receive the council of Ephesus, to acknowledge as just the deposition of Nestorius, and to anathematise his doctrines. Nearly all now surrendered, although in some cases in equivocal terms. Helladius of Tarsus, and Himerius, yielded at length, and were permitted to retain their churches: but Alexander of Hierapolis, the Coryphæus of the Nestorians, Meletius of Mopsueste, Eutherius of Tyana, and Dorotheus of Marcianopolis, with some others, remained inflexible, and many of them died in exile. With the defiance and haughtiness of true schismatics, Alexander and his followers declared, that it concerned them not, how many or how few were attached to their cause: faith had suffered universal shipwreck: the monks might raise all the dead to life to strengthen their Egyptian impiety, but they would remain firm in the faith and in the knowledge which God had given to them. Nestorius, who, after the council of Ephesus, had retired to his ancient convent at Antioch, was banished by the emperor to an oasis in Egypt, where he died after twenty years of heresy, misery, and exile.

An imperial edict prohibited the Nestorians, who were still numerous in the capital, to hold assemblies, and commanded that they should be called Simonians.

Peace was now externally restored to the universal Church; but theological warfare had struck its roots too deeply to render it possible that opposition in doctrine should cease with ecclesiastical divisions. The supporters of the doctrine which Nestorius had most strenuously defended, thought now no more of his person, and spoke of him only in general terms: but the authority of Theodore, and of his writings, was still unshaken. Under the protection of this respected man, the doctrine of which he was the author was praised and propagated: extracts from his works, and from the writings of his scholar Diodorus of Tarsus, were translated into the languages of Syria, Persia, and Armenia; and a work in which, to the anathemas of St. Cyril, contrary passages from the works of Theodore were opposed, was widely circulated. The seat of these machinations was at Edessa, and in the celebrated theological school of that city, the seminary of the Persian clergy. Rabulas, the zealous Catholic bishop of Edessa, had, therefore, in 432, anathematized the person and writings of Theodore, and was for that reason attacked by the priest Ibas, in his disgraceful letter to Maris. Acacius of Melitene, and Rabulas, warned the bishops of Armenia of the dangerous tendency of the writings of Theodore: these bishops applied for instruction on this subject to Proclus, who, in 434, succeeded Maximan in the patriarchal see of Constantinople, and who had been one of the first assailants of the errors of Nestorius. Proclus replied in 437, in a dogmatical epistle (Tomus), which he sent to John of Antioch, with a request that he would cause it to be subscribed, as a sign of unity of faith, by his bishops, and particularly by Ibas, bishop of Edessa, who was accused of Nestorianism. The orientals subscribed the Tomus, but not the appendix to it, in which Proclus, without naming him, condemned many parts of the writings of Theodore. St. Cyril also, at this time, wrote a work, now lost, against Theodore, to which Theodoret replied. When St. Cyril beheld the inflexible obstinacy of the orientals in favour of their cherished master, Theodore, whose authority they would not see diminished, he desisted, and requested the patriarch Proclus to allow the affair to repose, lest, as he writes, the wounds of the Church should again be torn open, and an evil, greater and more incurable than the former, should be produced.

SECTION IV.

EUTYCHES.—THE LATROCINIUM.—THE COUNCIL OF CHALCEDON.—THE MONOPHYSITES. THE HENOTICON.*

It is a phenomenon of frequent appearance in the history of the Church, that scarcely does one error assume a determined form, before it calls into existence another directly opposed to it; and it is, therefore, the ever-recurring duty of the Church to defend the true Catholic doctrine, which lies in the mean between these two extremes ; and to protest equally against, and equally to condemn, both errors. Thus it was that Nestorianism called forth the heresy of Eutyches. Eutyches, an aged archimandrite of a cloister at Constantinople, imagining to himself that he could not go too far in his aversion to Nestorianism, taught that after the incarnation of our Lord, only one substance or nature was formed of the Divine and human natures of Christ, and denied that Christ, in his humanity, was in essence like to us. Eutyches did not indeed acknowledge the consequence that must naturally flow from the assertion of only one nature in Christ, that there had been a mingling, a commutation, or an absorption of the one by the other nature, but he insisted upon this that there had been two natures before the union ; so that, as St Leo remarked, he appears to have admitted, like Origen, a preexistence of the human soul of Christ. After the union, only one, the Divine nature, remained , consequently, according to Eutyches, it was the Deity that immediately suffered, and was crucified. To him it appeared no contradiction to say, " the Word was made flesh," and to assert that after the union of the natures,

---

* Breviculus Historiæ Eutychianistarum (to 480, by Gelasius I.?) in Mansi, Coll. Concil. vii 1060 et seqq.—Liberatus Breviarium, &c. Acta Concilii Chalcedonensis, in Harduin, tom. ii., Mansi, tom. vi.— Theodoreti, Evanistes seu Polymorphus. Opp. ed. Schulze, tom iv.

the nature of the flesh no longer existed: and as the flesh by its union with the Godhead had become deified, and had passed into another nature, the body of Christ, said Eutyches, was not the body of man, but only a human body, that is human in its outward form, not in substance. The mystery of the incarnation was, therefore, destroyed by the Eutychian, no less than by the Nestorian, error. If Christ had not been true man, he could not have been our Redeemer, our model, and our guide; and if the sufferings and death, by which we were redeemed, be transferred to the Divinity, which could not suffer but by the medium of the humanity, the virtue and the intent of these sufferings would be destroyed. It is certain that Eutyches did not contemplate all these consequences of his doctrine, for he was a devout, though short-sighted man, and void of all theological penetration; but the haughty obstinacy, with which, notwithstanding all admonition, he defended the doctrine which led to these results, made him a heretic. He subjected himself, he said, only to the Scriptures, the testimony of which was stronger and more decisive than that of the fathers, and yet he appealed to the holy fathers, Cyril and Athanasius, who had spoken of the one nature of the Word made flesh.

Domnus, bishop of Antioch, was the first who, in his letter to the emperor, censured the doctrine of Eutyches. He was followed by Eusebius, bishop of Dorylæum, who, when yet a layman, had been one of the first opposers of Nestorianism, and who now, in 448, appeared as an accuser of Eutyches, before a synod at Constantinople. At this synod, Eutyches refused to retract his error on the one nature of Christ, and was, therefore, excommunicated by his patriarch, Flavian. But Eutyches enjoyed the favour of the all-powerful eunuch Chrysaphius: he implored the protection of the pope; and so far prevailed with the emperor as to induce him to recommend his cause to the pontiff, and to procure the convocation of another council, over which Thalassius, bishop of Cæsarea, presided, which was to examine the acts of the former, which he said had been falsified.

The see of Alexandria had been occupied, since 444, by the ambitious Dioscorus, who saw in the Eutychian controversy an opportunity to humble the orientals, who, he pretended, were Nestorians, and to revenge himself on Flavian, against whom he entertained a personal hatred. He and Chrysaphius, to whom he lent himself as an instrument, and who then persecuted Flavian, persuaded the weak emperor to convoke a general council, not to extirpate the new errors, but, as it was set forth in the imperial edict,* to expel the abettors of Nestorianism from the Church. St. Leo thought that a general council was then unnecessary, and considered, that if convened, it were better that it should meet in Italy rather than in the disturbed east; but he at length consented. He appointed three legates to preside over the council, and addressed to Flavian the celebrated dogmatical epistle, in which, with a refutation of the extreme errors of Nestorius and Eutyches, he unfolded, with the greatest clearness and precision, the doctrine of the Church on the mystery of the incarnation.

The council was opened at Ephesus, on the 8th of August, in the year 449. About one hundred and thirty bishops, from Egypt, Asia, Pontus, and Thrace, were assembled, but the whole power was in the hands of Dioscorus, to whom the emperor had assigned the presidency of the council. To the abbot Barsumas, a friend of Eutyches, and of Dioscorus, a place and a voice amongst the bishops were given, as to the representative of all abbots and archimandrites,—a thing before unknown in the history of councils of the Church. The very first acts of the synod proved that not right and truth, but force and fraud, were to prevail: the papal legates were deprived of their prerogative of presiding, and the patriarchs Domnus and Flavian were compelled to sit below Juvenal of Jerusalem. Dioscorus commanded that the cause of Eutyches should be first examined. Eutyches appeared, and presented the Nicene creed as his profession of faith, and complained vehemently against Flavian and Eusebius of Dorylæum, accusing them of arbitrarily deposing bishops, and of other tyrannical acts. It was in vain that Julius, bishop of Puzzuoli, and the deacon Hilarius, the legates of the pope, required that the epistle of Leo should be read: this was overruled by Dioscorus: and Eutyches objected to the legates, whom, he said, he must view with suspicion, as the friends of his adversary, Flavian. When the acts of the council of Constantinople were read, the storm burst forth; and when Eusebius asked, "if Eutyches admitted two natures in Christ?" the bishops exclaimed, "Death by fire to Eusebius, tear him in pieces! as he hath divided, so let him be divided!" At the proposal of Dioscorus, anathema was pronounced against all who should assert two natures in Christ after the incarnation: he, who could not make his voice to be heard in the council, was to signify his approbation by raising his hand: those, who would not assent, were threatened with exile, as Nestorians. Soldiers with chains, enraged monks, under the command of Barsumas, the troops of Alexandria, the body-guard of Dioscorus, stood ready to obey the nod of the tyrant, and to inflict the worst of cruelties on all that should be delivered to them. Eutyches was absolved, and restored to his former dignity, as were also thirty monks, whom Flavian had, on account of their opposition, excluded from the use of the sacraments. Dioscorus then proposed that Flavian and Eusebius of Dorylæum should be deposed, under the vain pretext, that by introducing the doctrine of two natures in Christ, they had offended against the command of the first council of Ephesus, which forbade that any additions should be made to the creed of the council of Nice. Many of the bishops, falling prostrate at his feet, conjured him to abstain from this extreme severity; and when he saw that the number of his opponents increased, he called in the proconsul with a body of armed men, and caused the bishops to be confined in the church until the evening. Thus forced, they all at length subscribed, with the exception of the Roman legates, of whom one, the deacon Hilarius, escaped by flight from further violence. Theodoret, and Ibas of Edessa, and, after three days, Domnus of Antioch, who had withdrawn his extorted subscription to the deposition of Flavian and Eusebius, were also deposed. Flavian was led away to Hypepa in Lydia, where, after a few days, he died, from the effects of the cruelties which were inflicted on him in the *Latrocinium*, or *Council of Robbers*, the name by which this council of Ephesus has since been known. He had delivered to the legates an appeal from the council to the pope, on which account, in particular, he seems to have experienced greater cruelty from his enemies.

The triumph of Dioscorus might now appear complete, for an edict of the emperor Theodosius approved and confirmed the decrees of the council, and more especially the deposition of the bishops; but it would at the same time seem that an indelible stigma had been impressed upon the oriental Church, which was borne down by the double yoke of ecclesiastical tyranny and temporal power. Even the bishops of the Antiochian patriarchate, notwithstanding their inherited aversion to any expression that approached to the doctrine of the unity of natures in Christ, now implored forgiveness from Eutyches, named him their spiritual father, and endeavoured to conceal their ignominy under the pretence that the synod had decreed nothing new in faith. But that, which no one in the east dared to attempt, was effected by the holy pope Leo, who, by his immoveable firmness and wisdom, saved the Greek Church, and, we might almost say, against its own will. In his letter to the emperor, he declared that the iniquitous conventicle of Ephesus could not bear the name of a council, and that all its proceedings were invalid: he expressed a wish that a council should meet in Italy; and at his request, and with the same views, Valentinian III, and the empresses Placidia and Eudoxia, wrote to Theodosius, the father of the latter. The *Latrocinium* was condemned by a synod at Rome, and by the whole western Church; but Theodosius, ruled by the sycophant Chrysaphius, adhered to it to the hour of his death. A new prospect of affairs, however, opened, when Pulcheria the sister of Theodosius, and her husband Marcian, ascended the throne in 450. Anatolius, although he had been created patriarch of Constantinople through the influence of Dioscorus, held a synod in presence of a delegation from the pope, in which the letter from Leo to Flavian was subscribed, and Eutyches condemned. Many of the bishops, who had signed the decree of Ephesus, now returned, some immediately, others by means of Anatolius, to the pope: in their repentance they declared that only fear and violence had caused them to fall, and they now supplicated that they might be restored to the communion of the Church and of the see of Rome. The pope empowered Anatolius to receive them into communion, after he had imposed a penance on them, and after they had condemned Eutyches. He considered that the convocation of a general council was now unnecessary, as the subscription to his epistle to Flavian was sufficient to restore tranquillity, and as it would be impossible for the western bishops to take part in the assembly: but Marcian, before he had learned the mind of the pontiff, had called the council, first at Nice, and afterwards, on account of its proximity to Constantinople, at Chalcedon.

This fourth general council of the Church commenced its deliberations on the first day of October, in the year 451. Never, either before or since, did the eastern Church behold assembled together so great a number of bishops. Five hundred and twenty prelates, with four papal legates, at the head of whom was Paschasinus, bishop of Lilybæum, formed this august assembly. Dioscorus here found himself in the situation of a criminal. The reading of the acts of the Ephesine conventicle, and the testimony of several bishops who had been present, exposed the disgraceful injustice and violence of its proceedings. Dioscorus, who, it now appeared, had proceeded so far as to excommunicate the pope, was deposed first by the legates, and afterwards by the judgment of the council: but Juvenal of Jerusalem, Thalassius of Cæsarea, Basilius of Seleucia, Eusebius of Ancyra, and Eustathius of Berytus, who had headed the *Latrocinium*, were absolved: the whole council was favourable to them, as their guilt did not appear greater than that of the other bishops who had signed its decrees. The epistle of St. Leo to Flavian was then read; at its conclusion all exclaimed, "Peter hath spoken by Leo." It was received as a rule of faith, and subscribed by all except the Egyptian bishops, who could not sign before their new patriarch (who had not yet been chosen) had subscribed it. At first, the synod did not wish to draw up any new formulary of faith, as the subscription to the dogmatical epistle of the pope was considered sufficient to dispel the errors of Eutyches: but it was afterwards seen that another formulary was necessary, and the formation of it occupied the council in its sixth session. But a controversy arose on the expression, "*of* two natures:" instead of this, the papal legates wished to insert the form "*in* two natures." They at length prevailed, and the profession ran thus; "Christ is entire according to his Divine, and entire according to his human nature, true God and true man, existing in a rational soul and of a body, like in essence to the Father, according to the Divinity and to us according to his humanity; who is like to us, in all things, except in sin, born of the Father, according to his Divinity before all time, and in these last days, for us, and for our salvation was born, according to his human nature, of Mary, mother of God: one and the same Christ, Son, Lord and only begotten, *in* two natures, without mixture, without change, without division, without separation." The Greek text of this profession has, indeed, "*of* two natures," but this is evidently a modern alteration, for Evagrius, Euthymius, and Leo of Byzantium, all give the profession with the particle *in*; and in the conference between the Catholics and the Severians, in 533, it was acknowledged that the council had used this word. The formula further declared, that both natures remained unchanged in Christ, and were united in one person or hypostasis. Marcian in the meantime arrived at Chalcedon, and was present at the seventh session, in which the profession was signed by three hundred and fifty bishops. A law, which had before been made by the emperor, was approved, which prohibited, under pain of severe punishment, all public disputations on points of faith, the origin of all the evils in religion in the great cities of the east. In the following sessions, Theodoret, (who had appealed from the sentence of deposition passed upon him at Ephesus) and Ibas, were restored to their sees : they were required, as a condition, to condemn Nestorius, to which, after some resistance, Theodoret at length consented.

How great was the degeneracy of the oriental Church at this period, was shewn by the confusion which arose after the council of Chalcedon, first in one part, then in another, and which finally reigned in Palestine and Egypt. Theodosius, a monk and an ardent Eutychian, hastened, during the celebration of the council, from Chalcedon to Palestine, where, through all the monasteries, he announced, that Nestorianism had triumphed in the council, that Dioscorus was deposed, and Eutyches banished. By this inflammatory language he excited a commotion, from which the patriarch Juvenal, upon his return to Jerusalem, was compelled to seek safety by flight during the darkness of the night. The empress Eudocia, who was passing her widowhood in a convent at Jerusalem, favoured the Eutychians : Theodosius allowed himself to be chosen patriarch, and together with his inflamed monks, persecuted all who would not anathematize the council of Chalcedon. For twenty months, he defied the power of the emperor, but was at length obliged to leave Jerusalem, and towards the end of the year 453, Juvenal was enabled to regain possession of his Church. At Alexandria, the clergy had elected the worthy priest Proterius to fill the see of Dioscorus, who died in 455, in exile at Gangra, in Paphlagonia. But a powerful party amongst the clergy and populace still adhered to the cause of Dioscorus : a report was spread, that St. Cyril had been condemned at Chalcedon : a false translation of St. Leo's epistle to Flavian was circulated, and thus was raised a bloodstained tumult, in which the imperial soldiers were burnt to death in the ancient temple of Serapis. Tranquillity was restored, but, at the death of Marcian in 457, a new and more obstinate disturbance burst forth. The faction of Dioscorus raised up a monk, named Timotheus Ælurus, as patriarch, and Proterius, with six of his priests, was murdered in the baptistry of his church. Timotheus now raged against the memory of his victim; took into his society all the enemies of the council of Chalcedon; pronounced his anathema against that synod, and deposed all the Egyptian bishops and priests who dared to withstand him. Four bishops of his party appeared at Constantinople, before the new emperor Leo, with the request that another council might be called. But the pope strongly resisted. The decrees of the council of Chalcedon, he wrote to the emperor, could not be called in question: the contest, moreover, would thereby be made endless and irremediable. But as a powerful Eutychian party, in the capital, was not inactive, the emperor addressed a circular to all the metropolitans, requiring them to hold synods in their provinces, in which they might consult freely and deliberately on the authority of the definition of Chalcedon, and upon the person and cause of Ælurus. All answered that the decree of the council of Chalcedon was sacred and irrefragable, and that the criminal, Ælurus, was worthy not only to be deposed, but to be for ever excommunicated from the Church. Amphilochius, with his synod of Perga, in Pamphylia, was alone in condemning the council. The emperor, exhorted by the pope, and by Gennadius, the new patriarch of Constantinople, exerted his authority: the murderers of Proterius were punished; Ælurus was exiled, first to Gangra, and later to the Chersonesus; and in 460, the truly Catholic Timotheus Salophachiolus ascended the patriarchal throne of Alexandria. Unintimidated by these events, another monk, in 470, undertook to act the part of Ælurus, at Antioch. Peter, (surnamed the Tanner, from his former employment in a monastery at Constantinople), contrived, under the protection of the governor Zeno, and with the assistance of the Apollinarists, to be consecrated bishop: he introduced Eutychianism, and consecrated bishops like himself; but the emperor commanded him to be driven into exile: he fled and concealed himself, and Julian—the lawful patriarch, Martyrius, had resigned,—was elected patriarch.

Under the short rule of the usurper Basilicus, in 476, Eutychianism again raised its head. Ælurus returned to Alexandria, where Salophachiolus was compelled to retire before him. Peter the Tanner came forth from his hiding-place, and, in an encyclical letter, the tyrant commanded all bishops to condemn the epistle of Pope Leo to Flavian, and also the decree of the council of Chalcedon. So low had the oriental Church now fallen, that five hundred bishops obeyed this iniquitous command: only Acacius, patriarch of Constantinople, remained firm. But when Basilicus heard the loud murmurs and threats of the people of that city against the enemy of the Catholic faith, he recalled his letter, and, in a new edict, himself condemned Eutyches. The emperor Zeno also, after his restoration in 477, annulled all that had been done to the prejudice of the faith: the intruded bishops, Peter the Tanner, John of Antioch, and Paul of Ephesus, were made to give place to Catholic prelates. Ælurus destroyed himself by poison, and Salophachiolus returned again to his see: but the Dioscorians elected another monk, Peter Mongus (the Stammerer), who had taken part in all the tumults of his predecessor; and although he was soon driven from the episcopal residence, he remained concealed in Alexandria. But Zeno, under the influence of the ambitious Acacius, an inveterate enemy of the pope, approached every day nearer to the enemies of the council of Chalcedon: he was told, that by surrendering the authority of this council, peace would be restored to the Church; and, in 482, he published the *Henoticon* (or deed of union), in which, proclaiming himself master and legislator in matters of faith, he declared that no symbol of faith, other than that of Nice, with the additions of 381, should be received. He condemned, indeed, Nestorianism and Eutychianism; and without attributing any authority to the council of Chalcedon, he spoke of it in terms at least equivocal. Zeno and his counsellors imagined that the Monophysites (Eutychians) and Catholics, could, without prejudice to their dogmatical differences, be drawn by this edict into communion with each other: but they deceived themselves. The great majority of Catholics spurned the edict. Zeno, although he assured the pope, Felix, of his unalterable attachment to the council of Chalcedon, was, in fact, the patron and protector of the Monophysites; of those at least who received his *Henoticon*. He drove from their sees, Calendio, patriarch of Antioch, and John Talaia of Alexandria; and these great Churches were again doomed to fall into the unworthy hands of Peter the Tanner and Peter Mongus. Thus was the Church of the east split into three, or, more properly, into four parties:—the Catholics, who continued stedfast in their attachment to the see of Rome; the momentarily-dominant faction of the adherents to the *Henoticon*, to whom belonged all the patriarchs, even Sallustius of Jerusalem, who acted through timidity; and the ardent Monophysites, whom the suspension of the decree of Chalcedon, and the rejection of the epistle of pope Leo, could not satisfy. This faction, and especially that part of it which separated from Peter Mongus when he received the *Henoticon*, were named the Acephaloi (without a head or chief) and were soon divided into many sects. In 484, pope Felix, in a synod of seventy bishops, passed sentence of deposition upon Acacius, the cause and origin of all this confusion: some monks of the monastery of Acomete affixed the sentence to his mantle; an act of boldness which cost them their lives. Whilst thus nearly the whole east, in fear of the power of the emperor, ranged itself with Acacius, a separation between the eastern and western Churches ensued; and as the succeeding patriarchs of Constantinople, although some of them rejected the *Henoticon*, did not erase the name of Acacius from the diptycs, as the popes required, the schism continued for thirty-five years.

The emperor Anastasius (491-518) followed the example of his predecessor. Although he had presented to the patriarch of Constantinople a written declaration of adherence to the decree of Chalcedon, yet, during his reign, no one could ascend to the rank of patriarch who had not first signed the *Henoticon.* The two leaders of the Monophysites, Xenaias, or Philoxenus, bishop of Hierapolis, and the monk Severus, a master in the art of sowing dissension and strife, were all-powerful with Anastasius. The first raised up Syria in opposition to the patriarch Flavian of Antioch, whilst Severus, at the head of two hundred violent monks, spread confusion through Constantinople. The addition which Peter the Tanner had, in a Monophystic sense, made to the ancient hymn of the Church, the *Trisagion*—" Thou who wast crucified for us "—the emperor and Severus endeavoured to introduce into the liturgy of Constantinople; but a tumult was excited amongst the people by this innovation, which the emperor subdued, and for which he banished the patriarch, Macedonius. He then caused him to be judged by some bishops of his court, and transferred his authority to the unworthy but obsequious Timotheus, who did not cease to persecute most cruelly the friends of Macedonius. A synod at Sidon, acting according to the will of the emperor, was about to annul the council of Chalcedon, which, it was said, had sanctioned the heresy of Nestorius; but the patriarchs, Flavian of Antioch, and Elias of Jerusalem, dissolved the synod before such a resolution could be formed. Anastasius, however, deeply revenged himself; for he caused Flavian to be dispossessed of his patriarchate by Severus, and Elias by John bishop of Sebaste. The oppressed bishops of the east now wrote to the pope, Symmachus, imploring him to withhold from them no longer his communion and protection, on account of the schismatical Acacius. At Constantinople, the attempt of two officers of the state, Marinus and Plato, to introduce into the principal church of the city the Monophystic addition to the Trisagion, again aroused the indignation of the people. Vitalian, a general in the imperial army, turning the oppression of the Church and the banishment of the patriarchs into a pretext for his revolt, conducted his troops even to the gates of the capital, when Anastasius, contemplating his danger, prayed for the mediation of the pope, and purchased peace by a promise to recall the exiled patriarchs, and to suffer a general council to be convoked under the pope, to apply a remedy to the evils of the Church. He entered into negotiations with the pontiff, and sent to him an orthodox profession of faith; but availed himself of the cause of Acacius, in which Rome could not yield, but in which he had in his favour the voice of the people of Constantinople— to whom the memory of this patriarch was dear—to prevent a conclusion of peace. As soon as he thought himself safe from his enemies, he sent back the papal delegates, wrote to the pope to say that he would not endure to be commanded, and obliged the two hundred bishops who had met for the council, to return to their homes. In the east, Severus, without dread of punishment, made the blood of the Catholics to flow in torrents; and the new patriarch of Constantinople, John the Cappadocian, signed the condemnation of the council of Chalcedon.

But the death of Anastasius changed the scene. On the first Sunday after the enthronement of his successor, Justin (518-527), the people, in the church, obliged the patriarch, John, to pronounce anathema against Severus, and to profess his adherence to the council of Chalcedon. A synod of eighty bishops, hastily collected, confirmed this act; and an edict of the emperor obliged all the bishops of the empire to acknowledge the Chalcedonian decrees. The edict was almost universally obeyed with gladness. Severus and Julian of Halicarnassus, the chiefs of the Monophysites, fled to Alexandria; and peace with pope Hormisdas was so concluded, that all his conditions were accepted; and not only the names of Acacius, Zeno, and Anastasius, but those also of the respected patriarchs, Euphemius and Macedonius, who refused to condemn Acacius, were taken from the dyptics. On Maundy Thursday, of the year 518, the five papal legates, and the patriarch John mutually gave and received the kiss of peace: they then partook together of the body of our Lord, and thus the long desired union of the two Churches was effected. In honour of the council of Chalcedon, the institution of a particular festival, which is still observed in the Greek Church, was ordained. In Egypt, however, the dominion of the Monophysites continued unbroken.

The dispute on the addition to the Trisagion was now renewed, although in a different form. Four Scythian monks, who had come to Constantinople, exerted themselves to obtain the approbation of the Church to this proposition, "One of the Trinity died on the cross." This proposition, in itself true, excited suspicion, as it sprung from the Monophysites, Severus and Xenaias, and, in their mouths, had the signification that the Divinity itself, the substance of the Trinity, had suffered. If it had run thus, "One of the three persons of the Trinity suffered death on the cross,"—it would have contained nothing suspicious; but in this form, it displeased the monks, as the word *person* ($\pi\rho o\sigma\omega\pi o\nu$) might be taken, as it was by the Nestorians, in a purely moral sense; and thus by the proposition, "He who was crucified was one of the three Divine Persons," we should not profess that this person was substantially God.

In 519, the monks went to Rome to gain over the pope, Hormisdas, to their ideas, that this proposition was a necessary antidote against Nestorianism; and, as it has been mentioned above, they mingled themselves in the controversies of the Semipelagians. But their opinion, that the council of Chalcedon required this explanation and addition, was displeasing to the pontiff, and as they persisted in their refusal to admit, instead of their proposition, which might be so easily misunderstood, that which was more definitive, "One of the three Persons suffered in the flesh," Hormisdas dismissed them, as intentional or unconscious abettors of Eutychianism.

Justinian (527—565) was for a long time so zealous a defender of the synod of Chalcedon, that he with pleasure bore the name of the Synodite. To reconcile the Monophysites, or Severians, with the Church, he spared no exertions, and promised himself the most happy results from a conference, which, in 533, was held in his palace between five Catholic, and six Monophysite bishops. On the part of the Catholics, Hypatius, bishop of Ephesus, addressed the assembly: of the number of the Monophysites, four were bishops from Lower Syria, amongst whom was Sergius of Cyrus; the other two were from Cyprus. They felt no difficulty in condemning Eutyches as a heretic, on account of his doctrine that Christ was not consubstantial with his mother: but they at the same time defended the orthodoxy of Dioscorus, and of his two Ephesine synods, although they had acquitted Eutyches of heresy. When the dispute turned upon the council of Ephesus and its definitions of faith, the Catholic prelates declared that the testimonies of pope Julius, of St. Gregory Thaumaturgus, and of St. Dionysius the Areopagite, which the Severians had adduced in confirmation of their doctrine, that after the union of the two natures in Christ there existed only one, were spurious and false. Hypatius rejected in particular, as supposititious, the writings attributed to the Areopagite, which were now mentioned for the first time. The doctrines of St. Cyril were next brought into discussion: the Severians complained that the œcumenical councils had been inserted in the dyptics, that the council of Chalcedon had declared Theodoret and Ibas orthodox; and they objected to the Catholics, that they would not admit that God, or one of the Trinity, had suffered in the flesh; and that the sufferings and miracles were to be attributed to one and the same person. The conference produced this result, that one of the Monophysite bishops, Philoxenus of Dulichiana, and many priests and monks, were converted from their error.

Not long after, the dispute concerning this proposition "that the crucified was one of the Trinity," was revived. The Nestorians drew, from the reluctance of the Catholics to admit this proposition, consequences favourable to their own doctrines. As there are, they said, only three persons in God, and if you refuse to say, that the Crucified was one of these three persons, it is clear that the Crucified was not God, and that Mary was not mother of God. In the east, therefore, this proposition had found almost universal acceptance, as a sure shibboleth against Nestorianism : only the monks of the order of the Acomæte objected to it. Justinian, who was always ready to make laws in religion, published an edict in which the controverted proposition was approved, and sent two metropolitans to pope John II, to obtain his sanction. After a delay of a year, the pontiff, in 534, confirmed the edict, and received a profession of faith, presented to him by the two delegates, from the emperor. The learned African deacon, Ferrandus, when interrogated on this subject, replied with great earnestness, that it was correct to say that " one of the three Divine Persons had truly suffered," and that it was not customary to add " in the flesh," except in instructions to the people, as the addition was always implied.

SECTION V.

RENEWAL OF THE ORIGENIST CONTROVERSY.—THE CONTROVERSY ON THE THREE ARTICLES (TRIA CAPITULA).—THE FIFTH GENERAL COUNCIL.—SCHISM.*

THEODORA, the wife of Justinian, and a secret friend of the Monophysites, had, by her machinations, raised to the see of Constantinople, Anthimus, the Monophysite bishop of Trebizond: but pope Agapite, who, being

---

* On the Origenist Controversy, Cyrilli Scythopilitani, Vita S. Sabæ, in Cotelerii Monim. Eccles Græcæ, tom. iii.—On the Three Articles, The Acts of the Fifth General Council, in Hardouin, tom. iii. pp. 1-214; Facundi, Ep. Hermianens, libri xii. pro defensione Trium Capit. ad Justinianum.—Liber contra Marcianum Scholasticum, in Biblioth. PP. Max tom. x.—Rustici, Diaconi, Rom. Dialogus adversus

driven from Rome by the Gothic king Theodatus, came to Constantinople in 536, and convinced the emperor that Anthimus was infected with the errors of the Monophysites. He was, therefore, deposed, and succeeded by Mennas, whom the pope himself consecrated. The new patriarch, soon after the death of the pope, called a council of seventy bishops, in which, together with Anthimus, the other chiefs of the Monophysites, Severus, Peter of Apamea, and the monk Zoara, (who, under the protection of Theodora, had all come to the imperial city), were anathematized. An edict of the emperor ratified this sentence, and forbade all heretics, the followers of Nestorius, Eutyches, and Severus, either to hold assemblies, or to administer baptism. Theodora now endeavoured to effect her purpose of establishing Monophysitism by the instrumentality even of a Roman pontiff. The Roman deacon Vigilius, whom Boniface II had, contrary to the canons, destined as his successor, had continued at Constantinople after the death of Agapite, and now promised the empress, that if, under her protection, he should ascend the pontifical throne, he would annul the synod of Chalcedon, and restore Anthimus, Severus, and the other chiefs of the Monophysites, to the communion of the Church. Armed with gold, and a notification to the Greek general, Belisarius, Vigilius went into Italy. Belisarius made himself master of the person of the pope Sylverius; and, as the holy pontiff refused to decree any thing against the council of Chalcedon, he was banished to Patara in Lycia. Justinian, who knew nothing of the violent actions of Theodora, sent the pope back to Rome, but Vigilius again instigated Belisarius to drive him into exile to the island Palmaria, where, in 540, he was murdered by order of Antonina, or where, according to

---

Acephalos, ibid.; Fulgentii Ferrandi, Diaconi Carthag. Epistola ad Pelagium et Anatolium, R. Ec. Diaconos, in Bibl. Max. PP. tom. ix.

Norisii, Dissertatio de Synodo Quinta, Opp. tom. i.; Against this, Garnerii, Diss. de Synodo V. in Theodoreti Opp. ed. Schulze, tom. v.

In defence of Noris, Ballerinorum, Defensio, Dissert. Norisii, De Synodo V. adversus Dissert. Garnerii, in Norisii Opp. tom. iv.

another account, he died of starvation, being deprived of all food by the servants of Vigilius. Vigilius, who had thus opened for himself the path to the highest dignity in the Church, had written in 538, after Belisarius had extorted his election from the Roman clergy during the lifetime of Sylverius, a letter to the heads of the Monophysites, in which he professed himself of their doctrine, and condemned the dogmatical decrees which had sanctioned the epistle of St. Leo, but requested them to keep his letter, for the present, secret. But God was still watching over his Church. After the death of Sylverius, Vigilius, who was now lawful pope, proved himself an altered man. He refused the empress the decree which she required of him in favour of the Severians: he wrote to Justinian and to Mennas, declaring his firm adherence to the four general councils, to the doctrines of his predecessors, Leo and Agapite, and declared Anthimus and Severus excommunicated. When reproached by his former friends with his want of faith to his promises, he solemnly declared that he was willing to efface them with his blood.

The confusion which was occasioned in the oriental Church by the heresy of the Monophysites, was increased by the sudden reappearance of Origenism. Two men, Nonnus and Leontius, who were zealous adherents to this doctrine, had insinuated themselves amongst the monks of Palestine, who lived under the direction of the holy abbot St. Sabas. They seduced two of the younger monks, Domitian, and Theodore Askidas, of whom the one was afterwards bishop of Ancyra, the other bishop of Cæsarea in Cappadocia. As the number of the Origenists increased in Palestine, and more especially in the old and new Laura, the excitement amongst them became more vehement. Ephram, the patriarch of Antioch, therefore, convened a synod, in which Origenism was condemned. Pelagius, the papal legate, upon his return from Palestine, took with him to Constantinople messengers from Peter, patriarch of Jerusalem, and from the Catholic monks, whom the Origenists named Sabaites, or followers of Sabas, and obtained for them, with the co-operation of Mennas, an introduction to the emperor. Theodore Askidas, who lived as a courtier bishop, more at Constantinople than in his diocese, knew well that he could preserve the favour of the emperor only by the appearance of orthodoxy, in which he had concealed himself; and Justinian, to whom this opportunity of exhibiting himself again as a theologian and ecclesiastical legistor, was most welcome, presented to Mennas a treatise in the form of an epistle, in which many passages from the work of Origen, *On Principles*, were collected and condemned. Not only Mennas and Pelagius, but Theodore also, and Domitian, subscribed this edict. The patriarch, moreover, called together, in a synod, by order of the emperor, the bishops who were then at Constantinople (σύνοδος ένδημούσα), and to this synod probably belong the fifteen anathemas, that were afterwards attributed to the fifth general council. In this synod the following doctrines were condemned as Origenistic: the pre-existence of human souls; the original equality and immateriality of all rational creatures, which, in consequence of their fall from God, were enclosed in bodies, more subtle or more gross (in the stars, in human bodies, and as demons in bodies cold and dark), and which thus first became individually different; that amongst all the spirits, only Christ persevered in his love and honour of God, that as a pre-existing substance he was united to God the Word, and that as an universal Redeemer, he took different bodies, and was thus all to all; that after his resurrection his body was ethereal and of a spherical form, and that the bodies of men at their resurrection would assume the same quality and figure: the doctrines of a final annihilation of all matter, and of the establishment of a world of pure spirits, of the apocatastasis, or restoration of all things, even of the demons, to their original state; of the destruction of all individuality, and of the renewal of primeval equality of creatures, were also condemned.

When Peter, the patriarch of Jerusalem, in obedience to the imperial edict, banished the Origenist monks,

Theodore Askidas intimated to him that he would work his degradation, and Peter was weak enough to revoke his censure, and to receive two Origenistic monks into his household. From that time the faction of Nonnus triumphed in Palestine, and persecuted the disciples of St. Sabas, who were insulted and ill-treated in the public streets of Jerusalem: the greater part of the monks joined the faction, and so far were they powerful as to place one of their own body, Georgius, in the great Laura, as abbot. The episcopal sees were occupied by Origenists, and Macarius, the successor of Peter at Jerusalem, belonged to that party. But that party was now divided into two violently contending sections, the Protoctisti and the Isochristoi. The former, who asserted that the (pre-existing) soul of Christ was the first and most perfect creature of God, were called, by their adversaries, Tetraditi, as by their exaltation or deification of the human soul of Christ, which was united with the Word, they introduced a *fourth* person into the Trinity. The Isochristoi, on the contrary, arguing from their hypothesis of the original equality of all created intelligences, taught that this equality would be restored, and that all souls would thereby be made equal to Christ. To this sect belonged Theodore Askidas, to whom is attributed this question: " If the apostles and martyrs performed miracles, and received great honours, how can this restoration of all things to their primitive condition, affect them otherwise than by raising them to an equality with Christ?" The Protoctisti feared the superior power of the Isochristoi, and they therefore united themselves with the Catholics. Their leader, Isidore, after a conference with the abbot Conon, renounced the doctrine of the pre-existence of souls. Conon, thereupon, went to Constantinople, where he consulted with the emperor, and procured the deposition of Macarius, and the election of the Catholic Eustochius to the see of Jerusalem. The new patriarch obliged all the bishops under his jurisdiction to sign the edict of Justinian: all, even those of the Origenist faction, obeyed, with the exception of Alexander of Abyla, who was deposed. The chief seat of this heresy, the new Laura, was freed from it by the expulsion of the Origenist monks: it was given to Catholics, and thus was peace at length restored to the churches and cloisters of Palestine. But Theodore Askidas directed his machinations so well, that, in 563, he enabled Macarius to expel Eustochius from Jerusalem, and to replace himself in that see;—not, however, before he had removed from himself all suspicion of Origenism. The supposition that the general council of 553 renewed the condemnation of Origen and of his writings, arose, in all probability, from the error of confounding a synod held by Mennas with the fifth œcumenical council.

Theodore Askidas, pretending that by the condemnation of the *Three Articles* (Tria Capitula), it would be easy to unite the Monophysites with the Catholics, and to obtain from them a recognition of the council of Chalcedon, involved the emperor in a far-spreading and most intricate controversy. By this means, that artful man thought to revenge himself on the adversaries of Origenism, to withdraw the attention of the emperor from that error, to serve the desires of Theodora, and to plunge the Church into a state of confusion favourable to his own party. By the three articles were meant the writings of Theodore of Mopsuesta, of Theodoret against St. Cyril, and the epistle of Ibas, bishop of Edessa, to the Persian Maris. It must be confessed that there was something here left to be done by the Church. Theodore was the real author of Nestorianism: Nestorius was no more than his disciple. Not to drive the Antiochian school, which then ruled almost the whole of the east, to extremes, the writings of Theodore, the favourite and most influential master of this school, had hitherto been left uncondemned: this school now no longer existed; but there existed not only in the Roman, but also in the Persian, empire, a numerous and powerful party of Nestorians, who, forgetting Nestorius, revered Theodore as their founder, and gave an almost symbolic authority to his writings. The writings of Theodoret against St. Cyril, and the epistle of Ibas to

Maris, in both of which St. Cyril is accused of the Apollinarian, Manichean, and other errors, his anathemas rejected, and the authority of the council of Ephesus denied, in which Theodore is praised, and Nestorius declared free of error, must have been to the Catholics, and much more to the Monophysites, an unceasing source of irritation. Amongst the latter, there was a party that was named the *Waverers*, who did not entirely reject the council of Chalcedon, nor would they receive it until some difficulties, which prevented them, had been removed: it is more than probable that the condemnation of the three articles would have gained these over to the Church. Even the Severians, in the conference at Constantinople, had declared that the absolving of Theodore, Theodoret, and Ibas, was their chief objection to the council of Chalcedon. On the other side, the Catholics of the west adhered with unshaken fidelity to the council, and to all that it had decreed: they would not suffer a syllable to be called in question, and any attempt of the kind on the part of the orientals, (for whom the bishops of the west entertained no high consideration, on account of their unsteady character), excited suspicion, and the fear that they designed to undermine the entire authority of the council. The bishops of the west, who, for the greater part, were ignorant of the Greek language, knew not the contents of the writings of Theodore, Theodoret, and Ibas: they knew only that the authors had been declared orthodox by the council of Chalcedon, and they, therefore, imagined that their writings had been approved, and particularly the epistle of Ibas, which was read before the council. But in this they deceived themselves; for at Chalcedon, Ibas, by a declaration opposed to his epistle, and by signing the letter of St. Leo to Flavian, had condemned his epistle, which was defended as orthodox not by the synod but only by Maximus of Antioch.

With the assistance of Theodore, Justinian, in 544, drew up a theological edict, condemning the three articles; which, according to his despotical custom, he sent to be signed by the patriarch, with an intimation that deposition and exile awaited his refusal. Mennas subscribed it, but with the condition of its being approved by the pope. Zoilus of Alexandria pleaded as his excuse for having signed it, the violence that was employed against him: in the west, and more particularly in Africa, it met with the most decided opposition. Justinian therefore called the pope Vigilius to Constantinople, and at his arrival, in 547, received him with every demonstration of respect. Vigilius saw that in this affair the bishops of the east were in understanding with Justinian, and that an obstinate resistance on his part might occasion another separation of the east from the west, and from the papal see. He therefore consented to the condemnation of the three articles; but first in a letter to the emperor, which was yet kept secret, for he feared the Latin bishops, amongst whom Facundus was then writing his defence of the articles, or rather of the council of Chalcedon, which he imagined to have been assailed. At length, after Vigilius had held a council, in 548, of the bishops then at Constantinople, he publicly condemned the three articles, with the condition that the strife should now cease, and with an express prohibition of any invasion of the authority of the council of Chalcedon. And now there occurred an event like to which another happily had never been. Hitherto the bishops of the west had ever stood united with the pope,—oftentimes in opposition to the bishops of the east,—but now the pontiff ranged himself with the orientals, whilst the prelates of Illyria, Dalmatia, and of Africa, separated themselves from him. Even two Roman deacons, and the nephew of the pope, wrote into all the provinces against the *Institutum*, the document in which Vigilius had condemned the articles, proclaiming that he had given to the Acephali arms which they would turn against the Church. In this emergency, the emperor and the pope determined to convoke a general council; and in the meantime, Vigilius recalled his decree, and forbade all controversy on the subject of the three articles. He wished that the council should assemble in the west, but he was compelled to yield to the emperor, who had appointed Constantinople as the place of meeting. It was resolved also, that an equal number of western and of oriental bishops should be summoned. But as only a small number of bishops from the west attended, Justinian, at the instigation of Theodore, published in 551 a new edict, which was also a profession of faith, and a theological treatise against the three articles. By this act, Justinian violated the compact into which he had entered with the pope. Vigilius opposed himself to this edict, and excommunicated the bishops who had signed it. The emperor thereupon resolved to cast him into prison; guards were sent to apprehend him, and were about to drag him from a church into which he had fled for safety, when they were intimidated by the resistance of the people. From the church the pope returned to his residence, after the emperor had sworn that he should suffer no violence. But it was not long before he found himself exposed to ill-treatment, and to violent threats: he therefore fled in the night, across the Bosphorus, to Chalcedon, where he retired into the church of St. Euphemia. Here he made known a decree which he had formed five months before, by which Theodore, the disturber of the Church, was deposed, and Mennas and his bishops were suspended: he addressed also, to the universal Church, an encyclical letter, in which he detailed the late events and justified his own conduct. But he now beheld a splendid proof, that the dignity and authority of the papal see, even in him, persecuted as he was and oppressed, drew from his enemies submission and subjection. Mennas, Theodore Askidas, Theodore of Antioch in Pisidia, Peter of Tarsus, and many other bishops, addressed to him an epistle, in which they declared that they received the four general councils in which the popes had presided by their legates or vicars, and likewise all decrees of the popes regarding faith, and by which they had confirmed the councils; that they condemned all that had been written against the three articles, and now implored his pardon for all that had passed. Vigilius received their submission, withdrew his censure, and returned to Constantinople.

After his return, he refused to open the council until a sufficient number of Latin bishops had arrived: but these bishops came not, dreading lest Justinian might employ against them violent measures, such as they had seen employed against Decius of Milan, Reparatus of Carthage, and other bishops. The council was however at length opened, by the command of the emperor, but contrary to the will of the pope, on the fifth of May, in the year 553. About one hundred and fifty prelates, (amongst whom were Eutychius, the successor of Mennas, Apollinaris of Alexandria, Dominicus of Antioch, and five African bishops) were present. The first sittings or conferences were passed over in fruitless attempts to induce the pope to join them. Although the three patriarchs, at the head of eighteen bishops, chiefly metropolitans, visited Vigilius to entreat him, he remained unmoved in his resolution neither to attend nor to approve the council, which was composed almost exclusively of Greek bishops. In the fourth, fifth, and sixth sittings, the three articles were examined with all possible diligence and care, and this question in particular was discussed, whether it were permitted to anathematize persons who had died in the communion of the Church? Precedents in the history of the Church sanctioned an answer in the affirmative, and it was ascertained that the name of Theodore of Mopsueste had been struck from the dyptics of his own church. During these proceedings of the council, there appeared a decree, named the *Constitutum*, addressed by the pope to the emperor. In this he condemned sixty propositions extracted from the writings of Theodore, the same passages which the bishops, in their fourth session, had deemed sufficient to call for his condemnation: but Vigilius at the same time declared, for reasons many of which were weak, that he would pronounce nothing against the person of Theodore, and that he would not consent that others should do so: he also forbade the controverted writings of Theodoret and Ibas to be condemned, and recalled his *Judicatum*, which he had addressed to Mennas. The emperor concealed this document, and ordered the former writings of Vigilius, which favoured the condemnation of the three articles, to be laid before the council. In the eighth session, the final sentence of the council was pronounced, without any mention of the papal decree. Vigilius still resisted, and was therefore driven into exile by Justinian, who commanded that his name should be erased from the dyptics, with the declaration, however, that union with the see of Rome should be preserved. Vigilius yielded at length to the heavy pressure of affliction. In a letter to the patriarch Eutychius, he condemned, but without mentioning the council, the writings and the person of Theodore, who had obstinately propagated and defended evident and dangerous errors. He condemned also all that Theodoret had written against the council of Ephesus, in favour of Nestorius and of Theodore, and against St. Cyril, as likewise the epistle of Ibas to Maris; finally he revoked all that had been written by himself or others in favour of the three articles. To justify his changeful conduct in these affairs, he produced the example of St. Augustin, who, when he saw the necessity, did not hesitate to retract what he had formerly written or said. And in truth, the consideration of the unexampled difficulties in which Vigilius was placed, must soften our judgment upon him. At one time, the danger that the Monophysites might employ the condemnation of the three articles to degrade the council of Ephesus, appeared to him greater; at another he dreaded a separation of the eastern from the western Church; and now the threatened desertion of the western prelates terrified him; whilst perhaps a just judgment, which as the consequence of his iniquitous seizure of the pontificate, weighed heavily upon him, deprived him of light and of strength from above, till he was tossed to and fro, like a helmless bark in this tempestuous commotion. But his changings had no reference to dogmas of faith; in these he was ever the same; for even in his *Constitutum*, he condemned the propositions drawn from the writings of Theodore, and all that Theodoret had written against St. Cyril. He varied only on this question of ecclesiastical economy, whether it were prudent to condemn writings which the council of Chalcedon had spared, and to anathematize a man who had died in the communion of the Church.

Pelagius, the successor of Vigilius, who died in Sicily on his return to Rome, had to combat with violent opposition to the fifth general council. Primarius, the new bishop of Carthage, held two synods, in which he prevailed upon the prelates of the proconsular Africa, and of Numidia to receive the decree of the council. Several of the bishops who pertinaciously refused, were banished. But in the north of Italy, and in Istria, a formal schism was the effect of the opposition of several bishops, at the head of whom were Paulinus of Aquileia and Vitalis of Milan. At a synod holden at Aquileia, in 558, the fifth council was condemned on account of its pretended contradiction to the council of Chalcedon. The schism continued under the succeeding pontiffs, until the time of St. Gregory the Great. It was in vain that the popes employed the assistance of the exarchs of Ravenna to lead back the schismatics into the Church: they were protected by the emperor Mauritius. In 602, four bishops, amongst whom were the bishops of Sabiona and Trieste, returned into the communion of the Church, but the bishops or patriarchs of Aquileia persisted in their schism. In 606, there was a Catholic patriarch at Grado, to which city Paulinus, flying in 568 before the Lombards, had transferred the see of Aquileia. But there still continued schismatical patriarchs of Aquileia, until the year 699, when Peter, in a synod of his suffragan bishops, having been conjured by pope Sergius, renounced the schism and acknowledged the authority of the fifth council.

SECTION VI.

INTERNAL HISTORY OF THE MONOPHYSITES.—CONTROVERSIES AND SECTS AMONGST THEM. THE NESTORIANS.*

One of the principal ends which the fifth general council had proposed to itself, was the reconciliation of the milder Monophysites with the council of Chalcedon. But this it did not obtain. The Monophysites, on the contrary, acquired a greater consistency, and placed themselves in more direct opposition to the Catholic Church. In Egypt, the Dioscorians had maintained the ascendancy since the time of Timotheus Ælurus, and, after the expulsion of Talaia, the Catholics had had no patriarch, until Justinian, in 538, sent to them the abbot Paul, who had been recommended by Pelagius, the papal legate. From that period the succession of Catholic patriarchs was continued until the Monothelite Cyrus. But the Monophysites also appointed their patriarchs, who lived sometimes in banishment, and sometimes concealed, and who at intervals came forth and acted in public. The Monophysites in Egypt were now divided into two sects, the Gajanites and the Theodosians, and

---

* Anastasii Sinaitæ, Οδηγος, in Gretserii Opp. tom. xiv. p. 2.—Extracts from the writings of Ephræm, bishop of Antioch (about 540), against the Monophysites, in Photii Biblioth cod. 228, 229.—Writings and Fragments of Eulogius of Alexandria (about 607), in Maximi Opp. ed. Combefis, tom. ii.; and in Photii Biblioth. cod. 225-250.—Gelasii Rom. Tractatus de duabus Naturis adv. Eutychianos et Nestorianos, in Biblioth. Max. PP tom. viii.—Vigilii Tapsensis (about 480), adv. Nestorium et Eutychen, lib. v. ibid.—Joannis Damasceni, Scripta adv. Monophystas, Opp. ed. Le Quien, tom. i —Leontius (about 610) De Sectis, Bib. Max PP. tom. ix.—Timotheus Presb. Constant. (about 630) De receptione Hæreticorum, in Cotelerii, Monum. Eccl. Græcæ, tom. iii.—Theodori Abucaræ (about 860), Opp. in Gretserii, Opp. tom. xv.

Assemani, Dissert. de Monophysitis, in the second volume of the Biblioth. Orientalis.—Renaudot, Historia Patriarcharum Alexandrinorum Jacobitarum, Paris, 1713, 4to.—Assemani, Diss. de Syris Nestorianis, Bib. Orient. tom iv p. ii.

hence it happened that at Alexandria there were often three cotemporary patriarchs. As after the time of Justinian, the Monophysites, although the greater part of the Egyptian people belonged to them, suffered many persecutions, their hatred against the Catholics, or Melchites (Imperialists—so they named the adherents to the council of Chalcedon, which was celebrated under the protection, and had been enforced by the edicts, of the emperor Marcian), daily struck deeper and stronger roots. The narration of sanguinary persecutions,—that means ever effectual of nourishing and strengthening their hatred against the Catholics, and abhorrence of their religion,—was employed by this sect: and in later times the Cophts hesitated not to declare, that Apollinarius, who had been sent by the imperial court to Alexandria, as patriarch, in 551, ordered the soldiers, who had come with him, to slay the defenceless people; and that in all Egypt, he ordered the deaths of no less than two hundred thousand persons. When, therefore, the Arabs burst into Egypt, the Monophysites, preferring the yoke of the Moslems to that of the Melchites, facilitated the devastation of the country, and in return were made the ruling party at Alexandria, as the conquerors thought thereby to confirm their hatred against the Byzantine court. All the churches were delivered over to them; and the Melchites, to whom belonged the Greeks and the officers of state, whilst nearly all the Monophysites were native Egyptians, could not for eighty years elect a Catholic patriarch, but received their bishops from the metropolitan of Tyre.

The Armenians also, as followers of the Monophystic doctrines, separated themselves from the Catholic Church. Nersapo, bishop of Taron, and the Syrian Abdjesu, contrived that a synod, held at Thevin in 535, should pronounce anathema against the council of Chalcedon, and against all who professed the belief of two natures in Christ. Pilgrimage to Palestine was prohibited in Armenia; as in the cloisters of Palestine there were many Armenian monks who still adhered to the Catholic faith. In 628, the emperor Heraclius called a synod at

Carin, or Theodosiopolis, in which the Armenian patriarch, and many other bishops, renounced their errors, and again joined the communion of the Church: but the clergy, and people of Persian Armenia, resisted the union. Equally fruitless were the endeavours of the emperor Constans, who, in 648, assembled a synod at Dovin, in which the patriarch Nerses, and the Armenian philosopher David, aided by a Grecian army, which was besieging the city, enforced the reception of the council of Chalcedon: but in 651 the new patriarch John, after he had escaped from the hands of the Greeks, convened a council at Manazkert, in which he anathematized the council of Chalcedon, and all those who received it. From that time, Armenia, as a nation, continued Monophystic, and separated, in government and religion, from the Grecian empire.

In Syria and Mesopotamia, the Monophysite party was indebted for its preservation to Jacob Baradai, a disciple of Severus, and from whom the entire sect received the name of Jacobites. Some bishops, who were confined in a castle, lest their sect might be deprived of bishops, consecrated this monk universal metropolitan. He wandered, in the garb of a mendicant, through all the oriental provinces, induced the Monophysites to cease their internal strifes, arranged their communities, and ordained, as modern writers relate, (perhaps with some exaggeration), eighty thousand priests and deacons. He gave also to the sect a new supreme head, which was necessary for its existence, for, after the death of Severus, in 539, he consecrated the Monophysite Sergius patriarch of Antioch: from him there has come down to this day an unbroken series of Jacobite patriarchs of the east, whose seat is at Ansida, or in the cloister of Barsumas, near Melitene. In a party, such as the Monophystic, which persevered in its enmity to the Catholics, and in its separation from their Church, trifling causes were sufficient to create new divisions and new sects. An occasion of this kind was produced by the question, whether the body of Christ were subjected to ordinary corporal affections and changes, such as hunger, thirst, and fatigue? Julian, bishop of Halicarnassus, denied this, and asserted that Christ did indeed suffer such sinless weaknesses, not indeed from any natural necessity, but only from his free will, and for the redemption of man. The supporters of this doctrine were called by their adversaries *Aphthartodochetes* or *Phantasiasts*, and formed at Alexandria the party of the Gajanites. Justinian, who was not fatigued, even in his old age, with the exercise of his theological despotism,'issued an edict, in 563, in favour of this doctrine, and sent it to the patriarchs, with a command to them to sign, if they wished not to suffer exile. This punishment was inflicted upon Eutychius, the patriarch of Constantinople, and other bishops; and would have visited also the respected patriarch of Antioch, Anastasius the Sinaite, had he not been saved by the death of Justinian in 565. Justin II, the successor of Justinian, recalled the edict.

Opposed to the Gajanites, or Julianists, were the Agnoetes, a Monophystic sect, whose author was Themistius, an Alexandrian deacon, about the year 540. The Agnoetes taught, that even the soul of Christ was subjected to many earthly defects, and that as man he was ignorant of many things, such as the tomb of Lazarus, and the day of judgment; and that they might, therefore, without blame, not pay respect to the not yet exalted man Jesus. Whilst the Monophysites of the party of Severus and Xenaias, notwithstanding their firm adherence to the one nature of Christ, conceded that he was true God and true man, and that the Divinity and the humanity had preserved their essential properties in him without mixture, the more consequent Stephen Niobes rejected this distinction of natures, which, he said, was absorbed by their union. The Monophystic patriarch of Alexandria, Damon, excommunicated him, and he then formed for himself a new sect, called from him Niobites. The doctrine of the Trinity, also, was another source of schism amongst the Monophysites. The philosophers, John Ascunages and John Philoponus, endeavoured to refute the conclusion that was drawn from the dogma, by the Catholics, that the ideas of nature and of person or hypostasis were totally distinct, for no one would designate the Father, the Son, and the Holy Ghost, as three natures. These new teachers denied the numerical unity of God, and would admit only of an unity of kind, so that the three persons of the Trinity were three individuals of the kind (or genus) Godhead, as three men or three angels are individuals of their kinds. This doctrine, which was correctly named *Tritheism*, for it supposed three Gods, drew after it many followers, and produced the sects of the Condobaudites and Cononites. Even the two chiefs of the Monophysites, Peter of Callinico, at Antioch, and Damian at Alexandria, disagreed on this new system. The latter, in his refutation of the Tritheists, fell into Sabellianism; for by the word hypostasis, he understood no more than personal signs of the Father, Son and Holy Ghost, or three names of one person: he thereby destroyed the personality of the three Divine Persons, and attributed to the Divine essence a subsistence distinct from the hypostases. From him arose a new sect named the Damianites. Philoponus and his disciples rejected also the dogma of the resurrection, (for with the form the matter also must fall); inasmuch as the resurrection will be a restoration of the bodies of the dead: they taught that as God will create a new world, he will also form new bodies in which men will arise. This error was opposed by the Cononites; so called from Conon, a bishop of Tarsis.

From the middle of the fifth century, the home of Nestorianism had been in Persia. Barsumas, bishop of Nisibis, and Maanes, bishop of Ardaschir, aided by many of the scholars from the seminary of Edessa, had by untiring exertions rendered this heresy triumphant in the greater part of the Persian empire. The Persian monarchs saw that it was advantageous to their policy, that their Christian subjects should be placed in a state of sectarian hatred against the Christians of the eastern provinces of the empire of Rome. Barsumas and his companions, confident therefore of protection, proceeded with acts of violence and cruelty to compel the opposing Catholics to embrace Nestorianism. The chief of the Nestorians was the Catholicus or universal bishop, at Seleucia, under whom were twenty-three suffragans, who received ordination from him. Still, however, several Catholic communities preserved their existence, and, being distributed in fifteen provinces, were under the jurisdiction of two Catholici, appointed by the patriarch of Antioch. In the Roman empire the Nestorians lost the principal seat of their doctrine, when their school at Edessa was destroyed, in 489, by command of the emperor Zeno: but this loss had no influence on the condition of the Nestorians in Persia, who continued to be, also, under the dominion of the Arabs, the most powerful party of the Christians. Their chiefs wished to lay aside the name of Nestorians, and to be considered disciples not of Nestorius, but of Theodore of Mopsueste.

SECTION VII.

THE MONOTHELITES.*

As the controversy on the three articles was a continuation, and an effect, of Nestorianism, which had now been attacked in its very origin, and defeated in its last resting place, so Monothelitism was in like manner one of the fruits of Eutychianism. This new doctrine found many powerful supporters, ecclesiastical and civil. The

---

* S. Maximi Opera, ed. Fr. Combefis, Paris, 1675, 2 vols. folio.—The Epistles of Cyrus, Sergius, Sophronius, Honorius, John IV, in Mansi Coll. Concil. tom. x. and xi.—Anastasii Bibliothecarii Collectanea, in Sirmondi Opp. tom. iii.—The Acts of the Lateran Councils, in Mansi. tom. x., and the Acts of the Sixth General Council, in Mansi, tom. xi.

Combefis, Hist. Hæresis Monothelitarum, in his Nov. Auctarium Biblioth. PP. tom. ii.—Tamagnini (Fouquière) Celebris Historia Monothelitarum et Honorii Controversia, Scrutiniis viii. comprehensa, Paris, 1678.—Jac. Chmel. Dissertatio de ortu et progressu Monothelitarum, in his Vindiciæ Concilii Œcumenici Sexti; Pragæ, 1777.

former, the bishops, those at least who acted with knowledge and design in this affair, sought to introduce the Monophysite dogmas, if not in the letter certainly in the spirit, by some unseen bye-path into the Church: the emperors allowed themselves to be led, on the one side by that mania, which seemed inherent to the Byzantine throne, of forcing their ideas as laws upon the Church; and on the other by political considerations, which dictated to them that Monothelitism might be a means of reconciling the Monophysites with the Church, and that the empire might thus gain in internal peace, and in external strength and power.

Theodore, bishop of Pharan in Arabia, and Sergius, patriarch of Constantinople, in an interchange of letters about the year 616, first expressed the idea, that from the unity of the person of Christ, the unity also of his operation and will must flow as a consequence. The human nature of Christ, which was united with the Logos, had, they acknowledged, its soul, and possessed all the faculties of the human mind, but they also maintained, it did not exert any peculiar operation, for all that was performed by the two natures must be ascribed to the Logos; so that in Christ there was only one operation, and only one power of will, springing as from its cause, from the Logos, which employed the human nature only as its instrument. Sergius endeavoured to gain over to his doctrines Paul, bishop of Theodosiopolis. The emperor Heraclius viewed these new doctrines as a means well adapted to effect a reconciliation between the Catholic and Monophystic systems, and therefore, in 622, addressed a letter to Arcadius, metropolitan of Cyprus, in which he forbade him to discourse further on the subject of two operations in Christ. Cyrus, who when bishop of Pharsis, had been instructed by the emperor and by Sergius on the unity of operation in Christ, undertook, in 630, when patriarch of Alexandria, to reconcile the Theodosians of that city with the Church. As the foundation of his attempt, he drew out, in form, the doctrine of the Church on the Trinity, and on the Incarnation, in nine articles. In the seventh article he stated, "it is the same Christ and Son, who performs Divine and human actions, by one only divine-human operation," (Θεανδρικη ενεργεια,—a phrase borrowed from the writings of the Areopagite), so that the distinction of Divine and human operations, exists only in our abstracting imagination. Sophronius, a monk, who was then at Alexandria, implored Cyrus not to make these articles public; but in vain. The union was solemnly celebrated, and the Theodosians, ecclesiastics and laics, received the communion in the principal church of Alexandria. "We have not," they exclaimed in triumph, "we have not gone over to the council of Chalcedon, the council has come to us; for he who teaches only one operation in Christ, confesses only one nature."

When Sergius beheld the opposition which his new form of doctrine had to encounter, particularly from Sophronius, who had in the meantime been elevated to the dignity of patriarch of Jerusalem, he endeavoured, in a most artfully composed letter, to gain to his side the pontiff Honorius. In this epistle, he described with great exaggeration the return of all the Egyptian Monophysites to the Church, and remarked that it would be distressing to compel these millions to fall back again into their heresy for the sake of an expression,—one operation in Christ; an expression moreover, which had been employed by many of the Fathers: he then suggested to the pope, that it would be most expedient that mention should not be made either of one or two wills and operations in Christ; not of one, for although the form of speech was correct, it was new, and might therefore be offensive to many: not of two, for thence two conflicting wills would follow, for it would be impossible that there should be in one subject two wills not opposed, and in conflict with each other. Honorius suffered himself to be misguided. His answer was almost an echo to the letter of Sergius, and betrayed an extraordinary dogmatical obscurity, and misconception of the subject in dispute. He viewed the opposition of Sophronius as a contest for words, which should be left to grammarians, and decreed that no ecclesiastical decision should be pronounced on the question:

but when he made the distinction of the two natures, which remained unmixed, and of the two operations peculiar each to its nature, he declared the true doctrines of the Church: he made mention indeed of an unity of will in Christ, but by that he understood no more than the conformity of the human with the Divine will, and rejected the idea that in Christ, as in sinful man, there was a law of the members combating with the spirit. Without, therefore, declaring for Monothelitism, he seemed to favour it, and to approach to it, by his unsupported interpretation of those texts so decisive for the cause of the two wills: " Father, let this chalice pass from me; *yet not my will, but thine be done ;*" which words, he said, were uttered by our Redeemer, only to teach us to conform our will to the will of God. From this inconsiderate letter of Honorius, matter was drawn in later times both for his condemnation and exculpation. Pope John IV, in his apology of Honorius, addressed to the emperor Constantine, and the holy Maximus Martyr, pleaded his cause on this ground, that by asserting an unity of will in Christ, he wished only to oppose the idea of a twofold will in Christ, of the flesh and of the spirit. Leo II, in his brief to the bishops of Spain, and to the emperor Constantine, places the error of Honorius in his inactivity, by which he gave support to the heresy, and caused confusion in the Church: but the sixth council condemned him, because he followed the advice of Sergius, and thus strengthened his errors. Such was this affair, although we are fully authorized to suppose, that Honorius thought much more correctly than he had expressed himself.

Sophronius sent to the pope, and to the bishops of the principal Churches, his synodical letter, written against the new errors: but Honorius, both in his answer to him, and in his letters to Cyrus and Sergius, persisted in his command that both parties should observe silence, and that there should be no controversy on the subjects of one or two operations. In 639, an edict, called the Ecthesis, or explanation, of Heraclius, drawn up, however, by Sergius, was made public. In the Ecthesis every thing was expressed according to the will of Sergius: it was decreed that no more should be said on two operations, nor (to spare the weakness of some), of one operation in the Lord made man; but it was asserted, that in Christ there was only one will, as to profess otherwise would be to declare that in Christ there were two conflicting wills. Sergius, and his successor Pyrrhus, assembled synods, in which they caused their adherents to sign this edict: Cyrus received it with joy at Alexandria; but in Rome, where John IV had succeeded to Honorius and Severinus, it met not with equal favour. Sophronius, not daunted by the unfavourable opinion of Honorius, had sent Stephen, bishop of Dora, to Rome, to lay before the pope full information of the real nature and consequences of the controversy. The pontiff John rejected the Ecthesis, first in a synod in 640, and afterwards in his letter to Pyrrhus. Heraclius, thereupon, wrote to the pope, a short time before his death (641), and declared that it was only after the repeated supplications of Sergius, the author of the Ecthesis, that he had signed his name to that decree. The decree, however, was still publicly maintained in Constantinople, notwithstanding the exertions of the pope Theodore; for Paul, the new patriarch, was a firm supporter of Monothelitism: in Africa, on the contrary, both Monothelitism and the Ecthesis were condemned by the bishops in 646. At that time—after the death of Sophronius—the abbot Maximus, the most learned and acute theologian of his age, stood at the head of the Catholics, who were engaged in combating the error of the Monothelites. In a conference with Pyrrhus, who had fled into Africa from the hatred of the people, he reduced him to the necessity of confessing that the doctrines which he had maintained were false. Pyrrhus went from Africa to Rome, where he presented to pope Theodore an abjuration of his errors, but it was not long before he fell into them again at Ravenna.

In this conference we may view in the clearest light the arts employed by the Monothelites to support their doctrines, and the arguments adduced by the Catholics to cast them down. The Monothelites pretended that by denying that there existed a human will (the root of sin), in Christ, they established most firmly his impeccability: for, they said, every created will is capable of sin, and two wills in the same subject must necessarily come into conflict, and the rebellion of the human against the Divine will is sin. We must, therefore, they added, repudiate the idea of two wills in Christ, or we must suppose two subjects possessing the power of willing, consequently two Christs. They taught that the human soul of Christ, like an instrument, was put into operation by foreign impulse; and that the Divinity, supplying the place of the natural powers of the soul, produced in the soul of Christ the same effects that were produced by a rational soul in the body of man. The Catholics granted that the human soul of Christ was indeed under the impulse and guidance of the Divinity, but without being deprived of its natural liberty: they observed that the will forms a part of the nature not of the person, and that we distinguish natures only by operations, and that God had together with human nature taken also to himself the human will. They added that Christ had shewn obedience to his Father, and that he had subjected himself to the law; and that without this assumption of the human will by him, the human will could not have been freed in man. They in particular demonstrated that Christ had himself distinguished between his human will "that the chalice of his sufferings might pass away from him," and the will of his Father, consequently his own divine will; and that in the passage of St. Matthew (xxiii, 37), he speaks only of his Divine will.

In 648, the patriarch Paul persuaded the emperor Constans to publish another edict, named the Typus, which he had himself composed to replace the Ecthesis. Without pronouncing, as the Ecthesis had done, on the dogma, the new edict prohibited, under pain of the severest punishments, all further controversy on the operation and will of Christ. But the see of Rome, and the Catholic bishops in general, withstood this ordinance, which, in itself despotical and unjust, placed truth on an equality with error, and imposed silence on a question, which was most intimately connected with fundamental dogmas of the Christian religion,—the Incarnation and the Redemption. Theodore pronounced sentence of excommunication and deposition against Paul and Pyrrhus; and his successor, Martin, convened in Rome a synod of one hundred and five bishops. At this synod, there appeared, as accusers of the Monothelites, Greek abbots and monks, who had sought in Rome an asylum from their persecutors at Constantinople. Theodore of Pharan, Sergius, Cyrus, Pyrrhus, and Paul, were anathematized. The Ecthesis and the Typus were condemned; but, to spare the emperor, the latter was named only as the work of Paul. The enraged Constans immediately sent orders to the exarch Olympius to enforce throughout all Italy subscription to the Typus; but his attempts were vain. With the exception of Paul, bishop of Thessalonica, who was afterwards deposed by the pope, all the bishops of the west and of Africa adhered faithfully to the decree of the Lateran council. But the new exarch Calliopas, more artful than his predecessor, caused the infirm pontiff to be taken from the church, in which he had sought refuge, and to be conveyed, in 653, to Constantinople. Upon his arrival, he was exposed on the shore, during a whole day, to the derision of the populace: he was then left to languish for three months in a dungeon, and was at length placed before a tribunal, where suborned witnesses accused him of conspiracy with the Arabians against the emperor. The emperor had the heart to behold him treated with cruelty and scorn, as the worst of malefactors, in the court of the imperial palace: in 655, he was banished to the Chersonesus, where he died after four months of confinement and privation. A more severe doom awaited the holy Maximus and his two disciples, who were both named Anastasius. They were first sent into Thrace: but as they still persisted in their refusal to receive the Typus, or to enter into communion with the new patriarch Peter, they were, in 662, recalled to Constantinople. Here a synod pronounced anathema against them,—against Martin, Sophronius, and all their other adherents, that is, against all Catholics. They were then scourged, deprived of their tongues, and of their right hands, and conducted through the city as objects of derision and contumely. They were at length banished to Lazia, where Maximus died soon after their arrival. Whilst the tyrant was thus engaged in deeds of cruelty against innocent and defenceless priests, he suffered the provinces of his empire to fall one after another into the power of the infidel Saracens.

After the death of Constans, in 668, the affairs of the east experienced a happy change. The Typus indeed still retained the force of law, although the emperor Constantine Pagonatus, who was not infected with Monothelitism, most earnestly desired the reconciliation of the oriental Church with the see of Rome. At Constantinople, the Catholic patriarchs Thomas, John, and Constantine, had succeeded the Monothelite Peter. But Theodore, who filled that see in 676, was a Monothelite. He and Macarius, patriarch of Antioch, wished to strike from the dyptics the names of the popes who had followed Honorius, as heretical Duothelites. In 678, the emperor wrote to the pope Donus, requesting him to send legates to Constantinople, there to terminate the disputes which agitated the Church. Donus had died before the arrival of the imperial letters; but they were received by his successor Agatho, who, in 680, called a council of one hundred and twenty-five bishops, for the selection of his legates, and in preparation for a general council to be holden in the east. And now at length the oriental Church freed itself from this heresy. On the 7th day of November, in the year 680, the sixth general council was opened in the presence of the emperor, of the papal legates, of the deputies from the west, and of the patriarchs, George of Constantinople, and Macarius of Antioch. In the first three sittings, the acts of the four preceding councils, and in the fourth, the two dogmatical epistles, which Agatho had written in his own name, and in the name of the Roman synod, were read. Macarius then presented to the council a collection of extracts from the writings of the fathers in favour of Monothelitism, but he afterwards confessed that they had been distorted and falsified. In the seventh sitting, the testimonies which pope Agatho had produced to confirm the doctrines of the Church were examined; and when they were found to be genuine, George, with the bishops of his patriarchate, declared that they received the doctrine delivered in the epistle of the pope Agatho. But Macarius was obstinate in his defence of the one will of Christ, and was, therefore, deposed. Sergius, Pyrrhus, Paul, Peter, Theodore of Pharan, Cyrus, and, finally, Honorius, were anathematized. A monk, named Polychronius, then presumed to make the offer to raise a dead man to life, in proof of the truth of Monothelitism; and the council, to undeceive the people, permitted the attempt. Failure in his endeavours on a corpse, that was brought before the council, did not shake the monk in his attachment to his error: he was, therefore, excommunicated and degraded from the priesthood. In the last sitting, on the 16th of September, 681, the epistle of Agatho, " by whose mouth, Peter had spoken," was confirmed: one hundred and sixty bishops, with the papal legates, and the emperor, signed the decree of faith, " that in Christ, there were two natural wills, and two operations, without division, without change, without confusion; that the human will did not conflict with the Divine will, but that it followed it, and was in all things subjected to it."

The attempt of the emperor Philippicus (Bardanes), sometime after the council, to restore Monothelitism, proves to us that this heresy still retained some adherents in the east. This emperor assembled a synod, in 712, which, as we might expect from the oft proved servility of the oriental bishops, condemned the sixth general council, and approved of Monothelitism, which they endeavoured to establish as the ruling dogma of the east. The names of Sergius and Honorius were again inserted in the dyptics; and even learned and respected prelates, such as Germanus of Cyzicum, and Andrew of Crete, had the weakness to yield to the torrent: only a few preferred exile to apostacy. In the west, however, the endeavours of Philippicus were vain. Constantine, the pope, condemned the epistle which the emperor addressed to him; and when Philippicus commanded that the representation of the sixth general council, which had been painted in the portico of the church of St. Peter, should be effaced, the people resolutely resisted, and declared that they would no longer acknowledge him as emperor. But the dominion of Monothelitism was terminated, in 713, by the dethronement of Philippicus, and the exaltation of Anastasius II.

This doctrine, indeed, continued for several centuries to possess some followers amongst the inhabitants of Libanus and of Antilibanus,—the Maronites, who were descended from the ancient Phœnicians. They had their own patriarchs, probably since the time of Macarius, who was deposed by the sixth council. One of these patriarchs, John Maron, was in the seventh and eighth century, civil as well as ecclesiastical chief of his people, who successfully defended their independence and liberty against the power of the Saracens, and from him was derived the name which designated at once a nation and a religious party. About the year 1182, the Maronites renounced Monothelitism, and united themselves with the western Church and the see of Rome.

CHAPTER THE FIFTH.

CONSTITUTION AND GOVERNMENT OF THE CHURCH DURING THE SECOND PERIOD.

SECTION I.—RELATION OF THE CIVIL POWER TO THE CHURCH.*

DURING the first three centuries, the Church had enjoyed, under a pagan government, in the midst of external oppression and bloody persecution, the most perfect freedom and independence in its internal relations, in its doctrine and discipline. But it continued not so under the Christian emperors, who, accustomed to rule, on all sides, with despotic sway, sought to intrude into the province of the Church, and oftentimes with caprice and tyranny. Soon then did it become manifest that the Catholic Church had purchased the prerogative, which it obtained in the time of Constantine, of being the religion acknowledged, defended, and protected by the state, at the sacrifice of a part of its ancient independence. Constantine himself used the power in ecclesiastical affairs, which the gratitude of the Christians had awarded to him, in general with moderation. Not so his son Constantius, whose tyranny at length became insupportable: but his conduct, and the conduct of Valens, against the Catholic Church and its bishops, cannot be taken as examples of the relations which then existed between the Church and the power of the state, for it might be almost said of them, that, as the blind instruments of Arianism, they ranged themselves amongst the pagan persecutors of Christianity.

---

* The Ecclesiastical Laws of the Emperors, in the Codex Theodosianus, ed. Ritter, Lips. 1737, 6 vols. folio, and in the Codex Justinianæus.

The strongest and the most direct exercise of the power of the Christian emperors, in the Church, was with respect to the general councils. They it was, who called the bishops to these assemblies, who designated the place and the time of their opening, and they took part in them either in person or by their commissaries. They it was, who provided public conveyances for the journey of the bishops, who maintained those that needed their assistance during the celebration of the council, and who preserved order in its proceedings. Bishops, however, were always at liberty to assemble when they pleased, in less councils; and if sometimes the permission of the emperor were requested, this was contrary to the general practice. When this permission was once asked of Valentinian I, he answered, that it became not him, as a layman, to determine in ecclesiastical affairs, and that the bishops might meet in whatever place they might think proper. In the councils, the emperors left the bishops in full liberty to consult together, and to decree on articles of faith, and on the interests of the Church. Theodosius II forbade the Count Candidian, whom he sent to the council of Ephesus, to interfere in the deliberations and other ecclesiastical matters, which, he said, belonged exclusively to the bishops. The emperor Marcian declared to the fathers who had assembled at Chalcedon, that he came amongst them, like Constantine, not to exercise power or authority, but only to defend the faith by his imperial influence. This synod, at its termination, wrote to Leo, that he, the pope, had presided by his legates, as the head over the members, and that the emperor had been present for the preservation of decorum. Constantius indeed wished to compel the councils to frame their decrees according to his views, but all, whose faith was sincere, resisted this despotic violence. Athanasius, Honorius of Cordova, Hilary, and Leontius of Tripoli, boldly declared to him that, in spiritual things, he possessed no right, no authority; that in matters of faith, it was his duty not to dictate to the bishops, but to learn from them. Thus spoke also the holy bishop

Ambrose to Valentinian II, who wished to appoint a judge in the conference to be held between him and the Arian Auxentius, "in things of faith, bishops judge over emperors, not emperors over bishops." Theodosius I, whilst engaged in the east in the suppression of Arianism, acted as the protector, not as the judge or propounder, of faith; and when Constantine, according to the account of Eusebius, took so active a part in the council of Nice, as to dispute with some of the bishops who were inclined to Arianism, he appealed for his authority to the unanimous consent of the great majority of the bishops there assembled; and as he regulated his faith by this authority, which he himself named the voice of God, so he endeavoured to lead the Arians to the same profession. When the emperors passed laws on matters of faith, or confirmed the dogmatical decrees of councils, this was only to make the belief of the Church the law of the state, and deprive those who should oppose it of all civil protection. It was different with the Henoticon of Zeno, with the Ecthesis of Heraclius, and the Typus of Constans: these were rejected by the Church, partly for no other reason than that they were derived from sources which had no authority to issue such decrees; and as the pope Felix II declared to the emperor Zeno, it was not for him to prescribe laws to the Church, but to submit himself to her decisions. But in process of time, the ancient and just principles, with regard to the limits of the imperial power, were lost in the east, by the continually increasing dependence of the bishops on the court; and the holy Maximus Martyr was one of the last who undauntedly protested against the unceasing invasions of the emperors.

The elections of bishops were left entirely free; but the nomination to the principal churches was confirmed by the emperors, and in the see of Constantinople, particularly in troubled times, they exercised a direct influence. Thus Theodosius I selected from amongst the names that had been proposed by the bishops in the synod of 381, that of Nectarius: and thus Theodosius II called St. John Chrysostom from Antioch, after he had been chosen, indeed, by the clergy and people. The election of the Roman pontiff was also free. Odoacer, king of Italy, was the first who decreed that no one should be named bishop of Rome without his approbation. After him, this prohibition was recalled by the Gothic kings, although Theodoric promoted the elevation of Felix III, and Theodatus that of Silverius.

From the reign of Justinian the practice arose that each newly-elected pope should obtain the approbation of the emperor, and the pontiffs, after St. Gregory the Great, paid at their election a kind of tax to the emperors, until the time of Constantine Barbatus, who remitted it. Arbitrary depositions of bishops were frequent during despotic reigns, such as that of Constantius: but a bishop lost his dignity only by the judicial sentence of the Church, or of a synodical decree; and the emperors exerted their power only in executing the judgment that had been pronounced by ecclesiastical judges. Thus, Theodosius the Great banished the bishops and clergy of heretics, after the synod of 383 had passed against them sentence of deposition.

That ecclesiastical affairs could be decided only by ecclesiastical laws was generally acknowledged by the emperors. Hence Marcian declared that all imperial laws that were in contradiction to the canons were null and void. Valentinian I and Honorius decreed that on spiritual matters and persons, only the bishops should determine: Justinian also published a similar law. Some emperors did indeed think themselves authorized to give laws on subjects relating to ecclesiastical discipline; but, for the most part, these laws were intended either to restore ancient canons of the Church, or to establish their authority. Justinian, who more frequently than any other emperor published such laws, proclaimed that he was no more than the protector and avenger of ancient ecclesiastical discipline; and, at the council of Chalcedon, the imperial officers declared with the bishops, "that against the canons no civil law ($\pi\rho\alpha\gamma\mu\alpha\tau\iota\kappa\text{o}\nu$) could prevail." The laws of Justinian regarded chiefly the form of ecclesiastical trials, the employment of the goods of the Church, and elections; also some abuses which had shewn themselves amongst the clergy and in the monasteries.

Appeals from a decision of the ecclesiastical to the civil power, were forbidden both by the Church and the emperors. Thus the synod of Antioch, in 341, decreed, that any ecclesiastic or bishop, who, being deposed by his ecclesiastical judges, should have recourse to the emperor, should never be restored to his lost dignity; and Justinian sanctioned, that appeal against excommunication passed by a bishop, should be made not to the power of the state, but to the metropolitan. The bishops did indeed sometimes call to their aid the arm of the civil power, not to obtain from the emperor force and validity for their decrees, but only when those who despised the censures of the Church rendered necessary the use of physical compulsion. This may be seen in the case of Cresconius, an African bishop, who had forsaken his own Church, and had forcibly obtained possession of another, and against whom the third synod of Carthage found itself obliged to invoke the assistance of the state.

The administration of the sacraments, and consequently the refusal of them, or the deprivation of the communion of the Church, were regulated, with full liberty, by the bishops, against the most powerful and the most exalted. Synesius, bishop of Ptolemais, excommunicated the prefect of that province. St. John Chrysostom publicly and frequently declared, that those who were unworthy, whether they were generals of armies, or prefects of provinces, even if they wore the diadem, should be driven from the table of the Lord: and when St. Ambrose, following this principle, closed the entrance of the Church against the emperor Theodosius after the massacre at Thessalonica, the humbled emperor submitted himself, received the penance which was imposed upon him, and extolled the constancy and fidelity of the holy archbishop. In this spirit, also, Gelasius wrote to the emperor Anastasius, that in the administration or refusal of the sacraments, it was his duty rather to obey than to proscribe.

The Civil Condition of the clergy was improved by Constantine, who granted to them the privilege, which freed them from the burdensome offices of the state. But as many enrolled themselves amongst the clergy solely to participate in this exemption, he decreed that only those whose poverty already freed them from these municipal duties, (and of those only as many as were sufficient to fill the places of deceased ecclesiastics), should be ordained. Valentinian I, also, in 364, forbade those who were rich to enter amongst the clergy. The later laws of Valentinian II, and of Theodosius the Great, permitted the wealthy and rich to embrace the ecclesiastical state, but, to enjoy the immunity attached to it, they were required to renounce their riches or to appoint an administrator.

The Judicial Authority of the Church was recognized by the state, and enlarged by it with new privileges. Constantine and the succeeding emperors confirmed, by a series of laws, the right of bishops and priests to be cited and tried, in spiritual affairs or for spiritual crimes, only by ecclesiastical judges, the bishops or synods. Ecclesiastics, in contests of any kind with other ecclesiastics, were not permitted to appeal to civil tribunals; and the synod of Chalcedon, in 451, threatened with deposition any ecclesiastic, who in such cases should deceive his spiritual judges. But in civil suits between a layman and a cleric, the latter was obliged to follow his opponent to the civil tribunal, where if a compromise were not effected, the cause was decided by the bishop; and according to a law of Justinian, a a complaint against a priest or a monk was to be referred to the bishop, and if either of the parties refused to acquiesce in his sentence, the cause was to be laid before a civil tribunal: if the decision of the judge should be different from that of the bishop, an appeal to the highest court was permitted. Any sentence pronounced by a civil judge in a criminal case against an ecclesiastic, could not be executed until the consent of the bishop had been obtained. Constantine had granted to bishops the privilege, that the judicial evidence of one of their body should be decisive, and that no other witness should be heard after a bishop. Justinian added to this, by conceding to them, that instead of appearing in person before the tribunal, they might give their testimony in their own houses and unsworn. Theodosius prohibited by a law, that priests should be subjected to the torture, which was often practised in the Roman courts, to obtain evidence. The jurisdiction of arbitration, which bishops had exercised in disputes amongst the faithful, since the times of the apostles, was confirmed by Constantine, for he granted to all parties the liberty of laying, with mutual consent, their causes before the bishop, whose sentence, from which there was no appeal, was to be enforced by the civil authority. Hence it happened, that not only Catholics, but persons also of other religious parties, would sometimes submit their causes to the bishop, who, as he was often overwhelmed with other affairs, employed ecclesiastics or even laics (as Sylvanus, bishop of Troas, did), as assistants in their court, the *audientia episcopalis*. In favour of those who had been condemned to death or to severe punishments, it was permitted to the bishop to interpose official intercession, and so generally was this considered connected with their rank and duty, that about the year 460, a community in Gaul opposed the consecration of a monk as their bishop, because, as it was said, not being accustomed to intercourse with the powerful, he might indeed be able to intercede with their heavenly judge for their souls, but not with their temporal judges for their bodies. The bishops took, in a particular manner, under their protection, those condemned or persecuted persons, who fled into the church for refuge : this right of asylum appears to have passed from the pagan temples to the churches of the Christians. The synod of Carthage, in 399, supplicated the emperor Honorius, that he would confirm this privilege, and forbid that those who sought an asylum in the church, should be taken violently from it. The same was sanctioned by a law of Arcadius and Honorius, in 414; whilst anterior laws of the same emperors excepted from the benefit of asylum all debtors of the public treasury, all who were worthy of death, and more especially such as were guilty of high-treason, and slaves who fled into the church with arms in their hands. Justinian, in 536, added to this exception, murderers and adulterers, remarking that the asylum of the church was not for the encouragement of evil deeds, but for the protection of those who were persecuted.

Great and beneficial was the influence exercised by the bishops in the various relations of social life. The pagan severity and cruelty, which had mingled themselves with so many laws of the empire, were by them greatly softened, and Christian principles substituted in their place. They watched that slaves might not be treated with barbarity by their masters; that exposed children might not be reduced to slavery: they visited and comforted the accused and condemned in their prisons. The emancipation of slaves, according to a law of Constantine, could take place in the church and before the bishops, for slighter and more simple causes than had before been admitted, and ecclesiastics could liberate their own slaves without any formality. The laws gave to the bishops a political authority and power for the suppression of immoral books, of gaming, of magic and of witch-craft. There are existing proofs that the bishops possessed a power even over the governors of provinces and other public officers.

But all these privileges and favours, which the state granted to bishops and priests, were granted only to those of the Catholic Church. Heretics were deprived of all pretensions to them by Constantine, who moreover prohibited all societies, separated from the Catholic Church, from meeting in public or private assemblies. The same was done by Valentinian I, with regard to the Manichees and Donatists, although, when he ascended the throne, he had promised to all parties a freedom of religious exercise. Gratian excluded the Eunomians, Photinians and Manichees, from the toleration which he had at first granted in a rescript from Sirmium; he soon afterwards published an edict against all sects without distinction. Theodosius I. forbade, in most decided terms, all heretics to hold religious meetings, and to possess churches not only in cities, but also in the country, and proclaimed that no other worship than that of the Catholic Church should be permitted. He and his sons, Arcadius and Honorius, proceeded even to greater lengths: they excluded heretics from all offices of the state, banished them, especially from the capital, and deprived them of the power of making wills and of inheriting property. The laws of Honorius, which not only thus incapacitated the Donatists, but which also inflicted on them fines and confiscations, were approved of by St. Augustin. From this period, this system of restraining heretics as much as possible, and this method of extinguishing heresy by depriving its professors of places of worship, and of all civil emoluments, continued to prevail in the Roman empire. The laws of later emperors, and in particular of Justinian, were directed to this end. If the power of the state proceeded with more severe vigour against the Manichees, and threatened them with the punishment of death, this was on account of the unnatural crimes of which they had been judicially convicted.

SECTION II.

SUCCESSION OF THE ROMAN PONTIFFS.*

To avoid omissions, we here now present the order of succession of the popes during the first three hundred

---

* Liber Pontificalis (by different authors, at different times, and lastly by the Roman Anastasius Bibliothecarius), ed. F. Bianchini, Romæ, 1718-35, 4 vols. folio; Vignoli, Romæ, 1724-53, 3 vols. 4to.

F. Pagi, Breviarium Hist. Chron.-Criticum, illustriora Pontific. Rom. Gesta complectens; Antverp. 1717, 6 vols. 4to. (The last volume by Ant Pagi goes down to Gregory XIII)—Gius. Piatti, Storia Critico-Chronologica de Rom. Pontifici; Napoli, 1765-70, 12 vols. 4to (As far as Clement XIII.)—J. Cl. Sommier, Histoire dogmatique du S. Siège; Nancy, 1726, 7 vols. 8vo.

years. To these we annex the series extending to the end of the Second Period.

Peter, to the year of Christ 67; Linus, Anencletus, Clement; (to 77?) Evaristus, Alexander, Xystus, Telesphorus, Hyginus, to 142; Pius, to 157; Anicetus, to 168; Soter, to 177; Eleutherius, to 193; Victor, to 202; Zephyrinus, to 219; Callistus, to 223; Urban, to 230; Pontianus, to 235; Anterus, to 236; Fabian, to 250; Cornelius, from 251 to 252; Lucius, to 253; Stephan, to 257; Xystus II, to 258; Dionysius, from 259 to 269; Felix, to 274; Eutychianus, to 283; Caius, to 296; Marcellinus, to 304; Marcellus, after a vacancy of four years, from 308 to 310; Eusebius, from the 20th of May to the 26th of September, 310; Melchiades, from 311 to 314; Silvester, from 314 to 335. Almost immediately after his accession, this pontiff sent his legates to the synod of Arles. The synod, at its termination, sent its decrees to him, that he might make them known to the faithful. That in the year 324, he baptized at Rome the emperor Constantine, is a fable, which most probably took its origin from the fact, that a brother of the emperor, of the same name, was baptized in that city. Mark was chosen on the 18th of January 336, and died on the 7th of October of the same year. Julius I, from 337 to 352, the steadfast defender of St. Athanasius: he wrote in 342 the celebrated epistle to the Eusebians in favour of the deposed Catholic bishops; absolved Marcellus of Ancyra; and pardoned the Arians, Ursacius and Valens, who hypocritically pretended conversion to the Catholic faith. The less steadfast Liberius, from 352 to 366, purchased, in 358, his return from exile by an ill-placed condescension to the demands of the Arians. He, however, soon redeemed the honour which he had forfeited by this step, by his condemnation of the council of Rimini, for which act he was again driven from his Church. During his banishment, the Roman clergy were compelled to elect the deacon Felix in his place, or probably only as administrator of the Roman Church. When Liberius returned to Rome, Felix fled from the city, and died in the country, in 365. Damasus, from

366 to 384, by birth a Spaniard, had, at the very commencement of his pontificate, to assert his rights against a rival named Ursicinus, who obtained consecration from some bishops a few days after the election of Damasus. The faction of Ursicinus was the cause of much bloodshed; and although he was twice driven from the city, and at last banished, by the emperor, to Cologne, he for sometime maintained a schismatical party; against the calumnies of which pope Damasus defended himself in a synod at Rome in 378. The riches and splendour possessed by the Roman see, as early as his pontificate, were offensive to the pagans. Siricius, from 385 to 389, was, although Ursicinus again endeavoured to intrude himself, unanimously chosen by the clergy and people. His decretals are the most ancient possessed by the Church: they have passed into all collections of canon law, and consist of answers to questions proposed to him by a bishop, Himerius of Tarragona, on various subjects of ecclesiastical discipline.—Anastasius, from 398 to 402; a pontiff, highly extolled by his successor, and by St. Jerome, of whom the latter says, that he was taken early from this earth, because Rome was not longer worthy of him, and that he might not survive the desolation of the city by Alaric. He was succeeded by Innocent I, from 402 to 417. To him St. John Chrysostom appealed after his deposition: the pope annulled the acts of Theophilus and his party, although Theophilus had sent delegates to Rome to gain the pontiff. St. John wrote to him letters of thanks from the place of his exile. After his death, in 407, Innocent refused all communion with Theophilus and the oriental bishops, until they should replace the name of the holy patriarch in the dyptics. Alexander of Antioch was the first to yield, and, by messengers to the pope, prayed to be admitted into the peace of the Church. Atticus, of Constantinople, was more obstinate, and, although he frequently sent delegates to Rome, he was not received by the pope into communion, before he had complied with all the conditions by him required. During the possession of Rome by Alaric, Innocent went to Ra-

venna, to supplicate the emperor, in the name of the Romans, to conclude a peace with the Goths. The pontificate of his successor, the Greek Zosimus, was only of twenty one months. The election of Boniface, from 418 to 422, was disturbed by the violence of the archdeacon Eulalius, who had attached a small party to his interests. The contest was referred to a synod in the imperial palace at Ravenna: but as Eulalius, contrary to the commands of the emperor, returned to Rome before the conclusion of the synod, he was banished, and Boniface was immediately installed. He was followed by Celestine I, from 422 to 432, the combatant of Nestorianism and of Semipelagianism. To Sixtus III, from 432 to 440, the metropolitans, Helladius of Tarsus, and Eutherius of Tyana, appealed, when they were threatened with deposition at the peace between St. Cyril and John of Antioch. Leo the Great, from 440 to 461, is the first pope of whom we possess a collection of writings: they consist of ninety-six discourses on festivals, and one hundred and forty-one epistles. By his high and well-merited authority, he saved Rome, in 452, from the devastation of the Huns; and induced Attila, named "the scourge of God," to desist from his invasion of Italy. Again, when, in 457, the Vandal king Geiserich entered Rome, the Romans were indebted to the eloquent persuasions of their holy bishop for the preservation, at least, of their lives. His successor, the Sardinian Hilarius, from 461 to 468, had been one of his legates at the council of Ephesus in 449. He obliged the emperor Anthemius, under whose protection the Macedonian heretic Philotheus sought to form new sects in Rome, publicly to swear that he would not sanction his proceedings. The zeal of Simplicius, from 468 to 483, was called into action chiefly by the confusion occasioned in the east by the Monophysites. The same may be said of Felix II (or III) from 483 to 492, in whose election the prefect Basilius concurred, as plenipotentiary of king Odoacer. Gelasius I, from 492 to 496, and Anastasius II, laboured, but in vain, in endeavouring to heal the schism, formed by Acacius, at

Constantinople. This schism occasioned a division in Rome at the election of a new pontiff. The senator Festus had promised the emperor that he would enforce the reception of the Henoticon at Rome ; and by means of corruption, established against the deacon Symmachus, who had in his favour the majority of voices, a powerful party, which chose Laurence as antipope. Again was a double election the cause of bloody strife in the streets of Rome, until the Arian king, Theodoric, at Ravenna, declared for Symmachus, who gave to his rival the bishopric of Luceria. But after a few years the contest was renewed. Some adherents of Laurence accused Symmachus to the king of great crimes ; and even Peter, bishop of Altinum, whom Theodoric sent as his commissary to Rome, joined with the schismatics. Two synods were hereupon held in Rome, in 502 and 503. The first (Synodus Palmaris), to the decision of which the pope had willingly subjected himself, declared him innocent of the crimes with which he was charged : in the second, Ennodius presented his defence of the proceedings of the former synod. Laurence was then condemned as an obstinate promoter of confusion, deposed, and banished. More tranquil was the pontificate of the succeeding pope, Hormisdas, from 514 to 523, and made illustrious by the restoration of peace, in 519, in the eastern Church.—John I died at Ravenna, in 519, in prison, into which he was cast by the suspicious Theodoric, after his return from Constantinople.—Felix III (or IV) from 526 to 530, was chosen by the Romans, at the command of the king. At short intervals, followed Boniface II, from 530 to 532 ; and John II, from 533 to 535.—Agapite I. went, at the desire of the Gothic king, Theodatus, to obtain peace from the emperor, to Constantinople, where he died in 536.—Sylverius died, in 540, during his second exile, on the island of Palmaria. A suspicion of a friendship between him and the Goths, the revenge of the empress, and the ambition of his successor, conspired to effect the ruin of this holy martyr. Vigilius, who was ordained in 537, and who became lawful pope in 540, was compelled to remain in the east, from 546 to 554, sometimes a prisoner in Constantinople, and sometimes in exile. He died at Syracuse, on his return to Rome, in 555. Pelagius I, from 555 to 560, found difficulty in obtaining an acknowledgement of his election, as, by his condemnation of the three articles, he was considered in the west as a traitor to the council of Chalcedon, and because there existed a suspicion that he was accessory to the death of Vigilius.—John III, from 560 to 573, beheld the commencement of the Lombard dominion in Italy.—Benedict I, from 574 to 578, and Pelagius II, from 578 to 590, ruled the Church during the melancholy times of the Lombard devastations. One of the most splendid appearances in the series of the Roman pontiffs was that of Gregory the Great, from 590 to 604. He was first prætor of Rome, then a monk, and was afterwards ordained by Pelagius II one of the seven deacons of Rome. From 579 to 584, he was apocrisarius at Constantinople, and was finally elected, by the unanimous choice of the clergy and people, although he himself offered strong opposition, to fill the chair of St. Peter. His epistles, of which eight hundred and forty have been preserved, prove with what untiring zeal he laboured both in the west and in the east, as vindicator of the faith against the Arians, Donatists, and schismatics, and as the defender of ecclesiastical discipline: they prove too, how, in the most difficult times and circumstances, he provided with paternal care for the temporal as well as the spiritual welfare of his people. He laboured, and with success, in the conversion of the Arian Lombards, and, as we have seen at length, of the pagan Anglo-Saxons: with firmness and dignity did he defend the poor inhabitants of the provinces against the oppressions of the Byzantine court. Although afflicted with many corporal diseases, and overwhelmed by a multiplicity of affairs, he found strength and time to compose a number of theological works. In his time the Roman Church held, (besides its possessions in the east, from which it drew a revenue of more than one hundred thousand florins), twenty-three extensive patrimonies in Middle and Lower Italy, in

Ravenna, Liguria and Istria, in Dalmatia and Illyricum, in the islands of Sicily, Sardinia, and Corsica, and even in the south of Gaul. Each of these patrimonies had its governor, who was named the defensor or rector, and was generally one of the chief of the Roman clergy. But, even in those early times, upon the pope devolved all the cares and anxieties arising from the dangers threatened by the Lombards, from the weakness of the Greeks, the government of Rome, and the necessities of the city. He was compelled to bear the expenses of the Lombard war, to provide corn for the people, and to become the medium of all intercourse with the imperial court. He was already, in fact, the temporal head of Rome. Even in Greek Italy, the popes now exercised a civil jurisdiction, for Honorius I sent two governors to Naples, and delivered to them instructions on the exercise of their power.

In rapid succession, followed Sabinian, from 604 to 605, Boniface III, 606, and Boniface IV, 607 to 614. The two former were, when elected, like St. Gregory the Great, deacons, and had been apocrisarii at Constantinople. At this period the election of Roman pontiff fell more frequently on deacons than on priests; as in Rome, the deacons, by their occupations in the most important civil affairs, were supposed to have acquired great influence. Boniface IV, with the consent of the emperor Phocas, converted the Pantheon of Agrippa into a Christian church, which he dedicated to God in honour of all the saints. Adeodatus from 615 to 618; Boniface V, from 619 to 625; Honorius I, from 625 to 638, whose memory has been in some degree darkened by his conduct in the Monothelite controversy, and by the anathema of the sixth general council. But Severinus, 640, who was consecrated after long delays occasioned by the imperial court, and died after a few months, repaired the evil occasioned by his predecessor, by condemning both Monothelitism and the Ecthesis. The same was done by the following popes, John IV, from 640 to 642, (who endeavoured also to exculpate Honorius, in an apology written in his defence), and

Theodore, from 642 to 649, a Greek from Jerusalem. Martin I, from 649 to 655, died a martyr. Eugene I, was chosen in 654, by the Romans, during the imprisonment, and with the approbation, of St. Martin, as they feared that the emperor would endeavour to force upon them a bishop of Monothelite principles. History relates little more of the remaining pontiffs of this period, than the part which they took in the controversy and suppression of Monothelitism. They were: Vitalianus from 657 to 672; Adeodatus II, from 672 to 676; Donus or Domnus, from 676 to 678, and Agatho, a Sicilian, from 679 to 682.

SECTION III.

THE SUPREMACY.*

THE name of pope (papa), was first applied exclusively to the bishop of Rome, by Ennodius and Cassiodorus, in the sixth century. By other writers it was given as late as the tenth age to all bishops in general. But there were not wanting names and titles, which, in the fourth and fifth centuries fully expressed the supreme ecclesiastical power and dignity of the pope. He was called father of fathers, the shepherd and guardian of the flock of Christ, the chief of all bishops, the guardian of the vineyard of Christ. The Church of Rome was named, by pre-eminence, the apostolic see, the chief of all Churches, the rock, the foundation of faith, the Church, which, as Prosper sings, possessed more by religion than the city had before possessed by arms, so that Rome had become more powerful by the see of the first bishop, than it had been in past ages by the throne of worldly dominion.†

---

* Epistolæ Rom. Pontificum, a S. Clemente ad S. Xystum III. ed. Petr. Coustant. Paris, 1721, folio.

† "Quidquid non possidet armis
Religione t net.

1. THE POPE, AS SUPREME TEACHER AND GUARDIAN OF THE FAITH.—That the decrees of synods regarding faith obtained their full power and authority only by being received and confirmed by the pope, was publicly acknowledged in the fourth century. Thus the synod held at Rome, 372, under the pope St. Damasus, declared that the council of Rimini, notwithstanding the great number of bishops who were there assembled, was invalid and null, because neither the bishop of Rome, whose decision should be awaited before all others, nor Vincent of Capua, and others, had decreed with them. The same pope was the first who condemned the heresy of Apollinaris, although it arose in the east; and by his decision, as Sozomen relates, the controversy of the orientals on the divinity of the Holy Ghost was ended. The fifth general council, held in 381, which was a council of only oriental bishops, acquired the authority of an œcumenical synod by the subsequent acceptance and confirmation of the pope: and St. Augustin declared, after the two African synods had been confirmed by the pontiff, that the cause of the Pelagians was terminated:—" Roma locuta est, causa finita est." Hence could Boniface, the successor of Zosimus, write to the oriental bishops, that a judgment of the apostolic see was inviolable, and that he who should presume to act against it, cut himself off from the Church. The proud pre-eminence of this see, that it never had been stained by error, was extolled by Theodoret. Peter, bishop of Ravenna, exhorted Eutyches to submit himself, before all others, to the pope and to the judgment which he should pronounce: and Avitus, bishop of Vienne, about 503, names the pope the pilot of the vessel of the Church, when assailed by the storms of heresy. The holy Maximus, in his controversy with the Monothelite Pyrrhus, declared to him that if he would free himself from heresy, he must make his peace with the see of Rome, for then all would believe him to be orthodox. About the same time, Sergius bishop of Cyprus declared that the see of Rome was, by virtue of the promises of Christ, the immoveable foundation of faith.

Thus also spoke Stephen, bishop of Dora, the delegate of Sophronius, patriarch of Jerusalem.

2. As the visible Representative of Ecclesiastical Unity, the bishop of Rome was the centre with which every other bishop was necessarily either mediately or immediately united. He, who was not in communion with him, who was not recognized by him, was not truly in the Catholic Church. Hence the blessed Ambrose, in the letter which he addressed to the emperor, in the name of the council of Aquileia, declares that the right of ecclesiastical communion flowed upon all from the Church of Rome: and his brother Satyrus, when on his death-bed, would receive the assistance of no other bishop than of one " who was in communion with the Catholic bishops, that is, with the Church of Rome." In the schism at Antioch, St. Jerome would acknowledge as bishop only him whom the pope directed him to acknowledge; for he who was not united to the see of Peter, was a stranger to him as to the Church. The same were the sentiments of those three chiefs of parties or bishops, in the same schism, at Antioch, Meletius, Paulinus and Vitalis, each of whom earnestly desired communion with the bishop of Rome. In his book against Rufinus, St. Jerome asks him, " Is your faith the faith of the Church of Rome? If so," he adds, "we both are Catholics." When, during the pontificate of Hormisdas, the schism which had been begun by the patriarch Acacius, was at length terminated after a duration of thirty-five years, about 2500 oriental bishops signed a formulary which had been sent to them by the pope; on which occasion they confessed, that he who was not in all things united with the apostolic see, was cut off from the Catholic Church.

3. The Pope in connexion with Councils. The six general councils of this period were convened immediately by the emperor: the approbation of the popes was sometimes, but not always asked. That St. Silvester called the council of Nice in conjunction with Constantine, is not mentioned by any contemporary authority: it is asserted, however, by the sixth general

council. The papal legates at the council of Chalcedon declared that it was a high misdemeanor of the second assembly at Ephesus, in 449, and a crime in Dioscorus, that he should presume to hold a general council without the authority of the apostolic see, a thing that had never been permitted. When Marcian and Pulcheria convoked the council of 451, they first sought and obtained the consent of pope Leo, although he had agreed with the emperor as to the place of assembly. Hence the bishops of Mæsia, in their epistle to the emperor Leo, declared, that it was at the command of the pope Leo that the bishops had assembled at Chalcedon. The fifth general council, which Justinian convoked against the will of Vigilius, was, in the beginning, not an œcumenical synod, and it acquired that character only by receiving the confirmation of the pontiff. Pelagius II therefore asserted, that the convocation of general councils was a prerogative attached to the see of Rome. That particular synods also were assembled by command of the pope, is evident from the narration of St. Augustin, that he and many other bishops had met at Cæsarea, in Mauritania, in obedience to directions sent to them by the pontiff Zosimus.

The right of presiding was conceded without contradiction, by all the general councils, to the pope, in the persons of his legates. That at Nice, Hosius bishop of Cordova, and the priests Vitus and Vincentius, presided as the legates of the pope, is clear from the order in which Socrates names those who were present, and from the testimony of Eusebius, cited by Gelasius. At Ephesus, St. Cyril presided as plenipotentiary of pope Celestine. At the *Latrocinium*, Dioscorus, in virtue of an imperial rescript, assumed to himself the right of presiding; which was, as were all the transactions of that assembly, a violation of ecclesiastical order. Hence, Prosper and Victor remark in their chronicles, that here Dioscorus had usurped the prerogative of the supremacy. Paschasinus and Lucentius, the legates of St. Leo, were the presidents of the council of Chalcedon; and the council, in its epistle to the pope, declare, that by his representatives he had presided over them, as the head over the members. Vigilius, although he resisted the convocation, was invited first by the patriarch Eutychius to assume the presidency of the fifth general council, and later by three patriarchs and seventeen metropolitans. Before this, Macedonius, patriarch of Constantinople, had declared to the emperor Anastasius, that in matters of faith he could do nothing without the authority of a general council, which should have at its head the bishop of Rome.

It was customary that a decree of the apostolic see should precede the dogmatical decisions of general councils, and this decree was the authority and guide of the council. The council of Ephesus, therefore, in forming its judgment against Nestorius, said, that it did so, "following the canons and the epistle of the pope." The same council, also, ratified without any further examination the papal condemnation of Pelagianism. At Chalcedon, the council, in drawing up its decision on the points in controversy, did not appeal to the synod which had been held at Constantinople, under Flavian, but only to the decree of the pontiff. In the judgment upon Eutyches, Cecropius, bishop of Sebaste, declared in the name of all his brethren, that the bishop of Rome had sent to them a formulary, that they all followed him and subscribed his epistle. The sixth general council in like manner declared that it adhered to the dogmatical epistle of pope Agatho, and by it condemned the heresy.

Thus, by the voice of the bishops assembled in a general council, and by the decree of the see of Rome, was formed the highest and inviolable authority of the decision in matters of faith of the representatives of the universal Church. Nor was it deemed superfluous, that the pope should confirm the decrees of councils although he had taken part in their formation. Thus the emperor Marcian requested the pope Leo to confirm the council of Chalcedon, that all doubt of his approbation of its transactions might be removed. The deacon Ferrandus asserted that it was by this confirmation that the council first acquired its authority; and in general, he declared, that œcumenical councils which had received the confirmation of the pope were in authority highest next to the Sacred Scriptures. The westerns, who were at a distance from these councils, and who could with difficulty be made acquainted with their decrees, anxiously adhered to the authority of the see of Rome; as for example, the council of Orleans, in 549, condemned the heresies of Eutyches and Nestorius, and in their condemnation appealed only to the judgment of Rome.

If particular councils formed decrees on subjects of faith, it was by the approbation of the supreme pontiffs that they acquired authority, as may be seen in the councils of Carthage and Mileve against Pelagius and his disciple Celestius. The bishops of these councils solicited the pope to strengthen their statutes by his high authority, to which, as they said, the heresiarchs would be more willing to submit themselves. Thus we are to understand what is said by Prosper, that the first condemnation of Pelagianism proceeded from Rome: he well knew that the first steps towards this condemnation were taken by these councils, for he himself declares it, but he knew also that their judgment was made decisive by being accepted by Rome. In the same manner, Flavian of Constantinople requested pope Leo to confirm the decision of the synod which had been held in that city on Eutyches, so that the convocation of a general council might not be necessary.

4. The Pope, as Legislator, as Guardian, and Administrator of the Canons. Of the papal decrees, prior to the time of pope Siricius, we have only occasional notices, for Dionysius Exiguus, when forming his collection of canons, could find, even in Rome, none more ancient than those of this pontiff. Siricius makes mention of an universal decree of pope Liberius, addressed to all the provinces, by which he prohibited that those who had been baptized by Arians should be again baptized. These decrees were generally directed to a particular bishop or metropolitan, or to the bishops of

various provinces, but they might be universally extended, and every where possessed authority. Thus the answers of Siricius to Himerius, bishop of Tarragona, contained provisions, which, the pope declared, were to be universally observed. For the oriental Church did the pope issue his decrees no less than for the western. Thus Innocent I gave directions to Alexander, patriarch of Antioch, on the ordination of bishops, on the division of metropolitan districts, and on the conduct to be observed towards those clerics who passed over from Arianism. But with perhaps greater care did the bishops of Rome provide that existing laws should be observed throughout the whole Church. In this they themselves set the first example, and appealing to the scrupulosity with which the Roman see honoured the canons, they exacted with severity a due observance of them from all other superiors in the Church. The pope Hilary immediately withdrew a rescript which he had issued, when he found that it was in contradiction to the rights of the metropolitan Church of Ebredunum. But wherever the welfare of the Church seemed to require it, the popes made no opposition to the grant of dispensations. Such exceptions or remissions in things of minor import, were granted by bishops, or by provincial synods, but in affairs of greater consequence, recourse to the apostolic see was necessary. Melchiades thus granted to the Donatist bishops permission to retain their sees, when they renounced the schism, so that when it happened that there would thus be found two bishops in one city, he who was first ordained would remain, and the younger was placed in another church. In similar circumstances, the African bishops applied to pope Anastasius, that he would dispense with the canons of the synod of Capua, in favour of the Donatist ecclesiastics. How often, though in vain, pope Siricius was requested by laymen and their friends, to dispense with the canons in their favour, that they might be consecrated bishops, he himself has informed us. And in fact the popes of this period appear to have acted always with the greatest firmness in maintaining the laws of the Church, and in rejecting cases of unnecessary dispensation.

5. AUTHORITY OF THE POPE OVER THE PATRIARCHS OF THE EAST. In the west, each metropolitan was in immediate connexion with the pope, who exercised over them and through them the highest jurisdiction. But in the east, where the patriarchal government had been fully organized, the patriarchs were in immediate subjection to the Roman pontiff; his intercourse was with them, and by their means his supremacy was rendered universally effective. Hence it was the duty of the newly-elected patriarchs to obtain confirmation in their dignity from the popes; and the *formatæ*, or letters of communion, which the popes addressed to the bishops of the principal churches, were at the same time letters of confirmation. Thus we see that Theodosius I sent a deputation of officers of his court, and of bishops, to the pope, to obtain from him his approbation of the election of Nectarius, as patriarch of Constantinople. For the same purpose, St. John Chrysostom sent to Rome, Acacius bishop of Beræa. The same was done by Anatolius, patriarch of Constantinople, to whom pope Leo, after a delay of two years, sent letters of communion and of institution, whence he afterwards declared, that by his consent, Anatolius had been made bishop of the capital. In like manner, Maximus was confirmed in the patriarchate of Antioch by Leo; and, at the council of Chalcedon, Anatolius asserted that all that had been done by the synod of 447 was invalid, except the raising of Maximus to the patriarchal dignity, for that had been approved by the pontiff. A synod at Alexandria prayed pope Simplicius to grant institution to John Talaia as patriarch of that city: the pope at first listened to their petition, but, at the representation of the emperor Zeno, recalled his grant. In the same relation to the popes stood also the exarchs, as long as they did not recognize an immediate superior in the patriarch of Constantinople: when, therefore, pope Leo resisted as invalid the election of Bassianus, as bishop of Ephesus, the council of Chalcedon adhered

to this judgment, although Proclus, patriarch of Constantinople, had acknowledged Bassianus. With truth then might pope Gelasius say, in his instruction to his legates, that either directly or indirectly, "the authority of all bishops was confirmed and ratified by the see of Rome."

As the immediate superior of the patriarchs the pope was also their judge. Without judgment from the Roman see, or without its consent, no patriarch could be deposed. When the oriental bishops who had assembled at Antioch, passed sentence of deposition against St. Athanasius, pope Julius wrote to them, saying, that even if Athanasius had been guilty, they should have informed him and have awaited his decision. Innocent I, for the same reason, annulled the judgment against St. John Chrysostom. Pope Celestine suspended sentence of deposition over Nestorius, after he had granted him time to retract his errors: he entrusted to St. Cyril the execution of the sentence, and the Ephesine council declared that it was necessitated to obey the papal decree against Nestorius. At the same council, Juvenal, patriarch of Jerusalem, appealed to the apostolical traditions and decrees, that the bishops of Antioch should be judged by the Roman see; and the synod itself reserved, for that reason, the cause of John, bishop of Antioch, and of the bishops who were united with him, to the judgment of the sovereign pontiff. At Chalcedon, the Roman legates proclaimed, that pope Leo, through them and that sacred synod, deposed the patriarch Dioscorus. During that awful confusion, which agitated the eastern Church after this council, Timotheus of Alexandria, Peter of Antioch, Paul of Ephesus, and Acacius of Constantinople, were deposed by the popes; and when Euphemius objected that his predecessor Acacius could be judged by no other power than a general council, the pope Gelasius replied, that in the last instance, judgment upon bishops was always the right of the Roman see, as Acacius himself had often acknowledged by executing similar papal sentences against others; and that, moreover, in the case of

Acacius, he had acted as vindicator and executor of the decree of the council of Chalcedon. Anthimus, who when placed in the see of Constantinople, had promised to perform whatever the pope might require of him, was deposed, in 536, as an abettor of the Monophysites, without the assembling of a council, by Agapite, who ordained Mennas to fill his place.

On the other hand, it was acknowledged to be the prerogative of the first see in the Christian world, that the bishop of Rome could be judged by no one. And, in fact, the synod of Rome, under pope Damasus, in its epistle to the emperor Gratian, declared that it was sanctioned by the custom of antiquity, that the bishop of Rome, when his cause was not submitted to a general council, should answer for himself before the council of the emperor; but this was to be understood only in accusations of civil and political offences. When, in 501, king Theodoric called a synod to examine the complaints that had been made against pope Symmachus, the bishops remarked to the king, that the pope himself must convene the synod, for it was a thing unheard of that the head of the Church should be placed in judgment before his own subjects. They at length pronounced that he was innocent before men, and left all to the tribunal of God. Ennodius, deacon, and afterwards bishop, of Pavia, in his apology for this Roman synod, asserted, that a council on more important affairs (*causæ majores*), could be assembled only by the pope, or at least must be confirmed by him. Avitus, bishop of Vienne, wrote at the same time, in the name of the bishops of Gaul, to the senate of Rome,—" that the pope, as superior, could be judged by no one, and that if that were attempted, the whole episcopacy would be shaken."

6. In virtue of their supremacy, the bishops of Rome possessed also the right of receiving APPEALS, and, in the last instance, to decide. Priests generally could not appeal to Rome, as they were to be judged, if they appealed from their bishop, by a provincial synod: bishops were entitled to appeal, although in general the

popes received only seldom the appeals of bishops of minor sees. But when this authority was called forth to oppose a powerful, heretical faction, or to defend, in the persons of persecuted, orthodox prelates, the faith also of the Church, then would the popes exert it in all its power and extent. Thus, the pope Julius received the appeals of the patriarchs, metropolitans, and bishops, Athanasius, Marcellus of Ancyra, Asclepas of Gaza, Lucius of Adrianople, and of others, who had been deposed by the Arians, and restored them to their churches. The fifteenth canon of the council of Antioch, in 341, has been so interpreted, as if it prohibited bishops to appeal from the sentence of a provincial synod: but it contains no more than the resolution, that the report of the bishops of another province, which the above-named canon had ordered to be received, should not be required, when the synod was unanimous in its judgment on the person accused. But a few years later, the great council of Sardica reduced the right of appeal to a more determined form. In its third and fifth canons, it introduced this new form, that the pope might command, if the bishop, who had been judged in his provincial synod, should desire it, that another examination should be made by the bishops of the neighbouring province; or if the accused should, in the second instance, appeal directly to the see of Rome, that the pope should send one or more persons, empowered by himself, to judge with these bishops. But if the bishop should desire an entirely new examination, he could, in the third instance, appeal to the pope, and, in that event, it was ordained by the fourth canon that his church could not be given to another until the pope had decided. This ordinance, however, became the less prevalent in the east, as only few of the oriental bishops took part in its formation: but this did not prevent many bishops of the east (and not the patriarchs only, such as St. John Chrysostom, Flavian, and John Talaia), from appealing to the apostolic see, when in their controversies with heretics they had been driven from their churches. This was done in 357, by Eustathius, bishop of Sebaste, when he had been deposed by the council of Melitine in Armenia: the council of Tyana reinstated him in his bishopric in consequence of a letter from the pope, which annulled the previous judgment. The same respect was shewn by the council of Chalcedon to the sentence of pope Leo, to whom Theodoret of Cyrus had appealed.

Between the years 418 and 426, a difference arose between the African bishops and the see of Rome, on the subject of appeals. A synod held at Carthage, in 393, had forbidden priests and the inferior clergy to appeal to Rome. Pope Zosimus, however, received an appeal from a priest named Apiarius, and sent legates to judge the cause, claiming his right to do so from the canons of Sardica, which he erroneously attributed to the council of Nice. The Africans, who were not acquainted with the Sardican canons, caused copies of the decrees of the council of Nice to be sent from the east, and again forbade appeals to be made beyond the sea. In the mean time, however, Celestine took under his protection Apiarius, who was indeed not worthy of it, and enjoined his legate, the bishop Faustinus, to procure his restoration. But the crimes of the man were made evident by the synod which Aurelius convened at Carthage to decide on this affair, and the bishops then wrote in an embittered tone to the pope, requesting that he would not for the future receive the appeals of priests, nor too easily those of bishops, before they came to him in due course, and that he would not restore to communion a bishop who had been excommunicated in Africa, until he had passed through the ordinary judicial proceedings. To this point, they were in the right; but they went too far, when, irritated by the party conduct of Faustinus, they disputed the authority of the pope to send legates into Africa. How Celestine answered their objections is unknown, but this we know, that African bishops continued to appeal to the pope as they had ever before done. St. Augustin makes mention of the bishops Priscus, Victor, Laurence and Anthony of Fussala, who appealed from Africa to Rome.

Some years later, the bishop Lupicinus, who had been judged in Africa, appealed to pope Leo, and was restored by him to the communion of the Church. In the Codex, as it is called, of the African Church, we find the canon of the second synod of Mileve, which, whilst it forbids priests to appeal beyond the sea, assigns to them the African synods and primates, as a third instance, adding these words, " as it has often been decreed with regard to bishops ;" but we are not to understand by this, that these were decrees forbidding bishops to appeal to Rome, for no such decrees indeed existed, but only that the plenary council, together with the primates, which, according to the canons, was the second judicial appeal for bishops, formed the third and last for other ecclesiastics.

7. Within the wide circle of the authority of the popes, were included also their decrees on subjects of importance, and their answers to questions of matters of doubtful or contested faith and of discipline. These subjects were generally proposed by provincial synods; as the council of Sardica declared that it was good and proper, " that bishops of particular provinces should direct themselves to their chief, that is, to the chair of Peter." That whole synods thus proposed questions to the popes, we learn, amongst other sources, from St. Jerome, who informs us, that he assisted the pope Damasus in answering synodal consultations, which came to him from all parts of the east and west. The same holy father obtained from the pope a decision on the propriety of speaking of one or three hypostases in God. The emperor Justinian wrote, that it was his desire, that all things which related to the Church should be submitted to the bishop of Rome, as to the head of all churches.—But in these affairs, and particularly in those of higher importance, the popes were accustomed to consult with their Presbyterium, and if necessary with a council of the suburbican bishops assembled in Rome.

Frequently were the popes, to perform more easily all the duties of their high station, obliged to send

LEGATES, with full power and authority, to remote parts of the Church. Thus pope Leo sent the bishop Luculentius and the priest Basilius to Constantinople, that together with the patriarch Anatolius, they might guard the faith which was endangered by the Latrocinium, and might reconcile with the Church those who had been led into error. He sent also another bishop into Africa, to take cognizance of certain abuses which had insinuated themselves into the ordination of bishops. At an earlier period, Lucifer of Cagliari and Eusebius of Vercelli had been sent as legates by Liberius to the emperor Constantius; and it is probable that Lucifer would not have dared, except in his capacity of papal legate, to have ordained Paulinus as patriarch of Antioch. Soon after this time, St. Basil, in his letter to St. Athanasius, expressed his desire, that the pope would send men of firm character, as his legates, to arrange the disturbed affairs of the Church. Again, some years later, the patriarch Acacius was commissioned by the Roman see, to act with decision in the two other patriarchates which were then agitated by the Monophysites; but he executed his duty with negligence. About the year 643, pope Theodore delegated to Stephan, bishop of Dora, power to depose the Monophysite bishops in Palestine; and in 649, Martin I conferred upon John bishop of Philadelphia a still greater power: he was authorized, as plenipotentiary extraordinary of the apostolic see, to appoint priests and deacons in the different cities of the patriarchates of Antioch and Jerusalem. The apocrisarii (*Responsales*), who from the time of Leo the Great, represented the popes at the imperial court, and were a medium of communication between them and the emperor, were another kind of papal legates. The other patriarchs had also their apocrisarii at Constantinople; those of the pope had no particular ecclesiastical jurisdiction, although we see that the deacon Pelagius, whom pope Agapite left at Constantinople, took the chief part in the deposition of Paul of Alexandria, and in the raising of Zoilus to the patriarchal dignity. The emperor Constantine Barbatus requested the pope to send to Constantinople an ambassador, who, in all dogmatical and ecclesiastical affairs, might represent the see of Rome, and who might be rather a legate vested with extraordinary powers than only an apocrisarius.

SECTION IV.

THE PATRIARCHAL AND METROPOLITAN CONSTITUTION IN THE WEST.

Those chief or parent Churches, which, from the first ages of Christianity, had risen above all others, and, as superior metropolitan Churches, had exercised influence and authority over a number of daughter Churches spread over a vast circuit around them,—Rome, Alexandria and Antioch,—were confirmed in this right, at the commencement of this period, by the sixth canon of the council of Nice. The council, compelled by the attempts of Meletius against the authority of the bishop of Alexandria, decreed that this prelate should exercise jurisdiction, according to ancient custom, over Egypt, Lybia and the Pentapolis; that as the bishop of Rome possessed such power, the authority and privileges of the Antiochian and other Churches should be, in like manner, preserved. The territory of a bishop, which comprised several provinces, was called a diocese, and the bishop was named archbishop or exarch of a diocese. The title of patriarch, which was borrowed from the Jews, was adopted after the time of the council of Chalcedon, for that council first employed the name, when speaking of the pope. The authority of these bishops was very unequal.

1. The bishop of Rome, together with the jurisdiction of supremacy over the universal Church, possessed patriarchal powers over a portion of the same. These powers were adduced as an example in the above-mentioned canon, in establishing the jurisdiction of the

bishop of Alexandria; and if in the exemplar from which the papal legates at Chalcedon read this canon, the superior power of the pope is expressed in the superscription (ἡ εκκλεσια Ρωμ. παντοτε εσχε τα πρωτεια), we are not thereby to understand, as it has often been erroneously supposed, that mention is here made of the supreme jurisdiction of the pope, but only of his patriarchal powers, for the authority of the bishops of Alexandria and Antioch is expressed by the same word, (πρωτεια). Rome was the apostolic parent Church, and therefore the only patriarchal Church of the entire west. Its patriarchal diocese included Italy, Gaul, Spain, the islands of Sardinia and Sicily, with the provinces of eastern and western Illyricum. The power of the popes over the churches of these countries was analagous to that which the oriental patriarchs possessed over the churches subjected to them. Hence the bishops of the council of Arles, in 314, addressing pope Silvester, said, that he possessed the "greater dioceses," for his patriarchate included six or seven large dioceses: hence also, St. Basil designates the pope as Coryphæus of the west, as St. Augustin names pope Innocent, head of the western Church. From the same cause, St. Jerome places together, the west, with its chief, Damasus, and Egypt with its head, Peter of Alexandria; and, on another occasion, speaks of the Churches of the east, of Egypt and of the apostolic see, to distinguish the patriarchates of Antioch, Alexandria and Rome. In the decrees of the bishop of Rome, however, the distinction between their supreme and patriarchal jurisdiction is not always fully observed: the latter is often supported and exalted by the former; the one influences the other, and not unfrequently both flow on together; that is, the bishops of Rome perform many things both as popes and patriarchs. The popes themselves do not always draw the precise line of distinction: they possessed indeed both powers as successors of St. Peter, and often appeal, even in acts which were connected immediately with their patriarchal authority, to their supreme pontifical power.

When, therefore, Rufinus explains the sixth canon of

the council of Nice, as referring to the power of the pope over the suburbican provinces, he must have understood by that term the ecclesiastical constitution, as it at that time existed. At that period, the close of the fourth century, the popes had contracted their ancient immediate patriarchal rites, by the appointment of apostolic vicars, and by the institution of metropolitan churches. They continued to exercise their full and primitive patriarchal jurisdiction only over the suburbican provinces, that is, over the ten provinces of middle and lower Italy and Sicily, (Sardinia already possessed its own metropolitan, in the bishop of Cagliari), so that they ordained the bishops of all these provinces, and these bishops could not, as Gelasius writes, without the permission of the popes, dedicate churches or oratories. The relation, therefore, of the bishop of Rome with these provinces was the only one, which, at the time of Rufinus, could be compared to that of the bishops of Alexandria with Egypt, the bishops of which were ordained by him and were in perfect dependance on him.

In the other parts of Italy, Milan was the first which obtained the rank of a metropolitan Church, probably a short time before St. Ambrose: soon after, and as it appears in the time of the bishop Chromatius, the same honour was accorded to the Church of Aquileia. To the metropolitans of these Churches, the popes granted the power of mutually ordaining each other, as their distance from Rome, and the difficulties of the journey, would render it burdensome to them to travel to that city to receive ordination. This practice continued until the schism which arose on the subject of the three articles, when the bishops of Milan were ordained by the bishops of their own province, but always with the consent of the popes. Between these two metropolitans, the seven provinces of northern Italy were divided, until the year 430, when by a decree of the pope, and with the approbation of the emperor Valentinian III, the Church of Ravenna was raised to the dignity of metropolitan. This happened under the bishop John, who, like his successor St. Peter Chrysologus, was ordained by the pope, either as metropolitan, or because it had hitherto been customary, that the bishops of Ravenna should be ordained at Rome. Another John, bishop of Ravenna, in his epistle to Gregory the Great, confessed that his Church had received all its privileges from the bishops of Rome. About the year 660, when Ravenna was the seat of the imperial exarchs, the bishop Maurus endeavoured to free his Church (not from the supremacy, but) from the patriarchal authority of the pope. It was complained of as a grievance, that the bishops of Ravenna, when they went to Rome for consecration, were too long detained there, that they were compelled to pay a tribute for the use of the pallium, and that they were called to Rome every year. It was not difficult for Maurus to obtain from the emperor Constans, who was hostile to Rome, a decree which declared the independence of the Church of Ravenna: the pope Vitalian issued a document which confirmed this declaration. But under the bishop Theodore, and the popes Agatho and Leo II, this autocephalia of Ravenna was revoked: the *Typus* of Vitalian was withdrawn, and the emperor Constantine cancelled the decree of his predecessor. It was arranged, that the bishops of Ravenna should continue at Rome only eight days after their consecration, and that they should not go in person, but should send their legates, annually to Rome. The people of Venice also, were accustomed to obtain their bishops from Rome, as we learn from a letter of pope Honorius.

The metropolitan form of ecclesiastical government was introduced likewise into Gaul, about the end of the fourth century. In the Latin text of the canons of Sardica, that which in the Greek is granted to the metropolitan, is extended to the nearest bishop: hence we find that in Gaul, at the synod of Valence in 374, Phæbadius, bishop of Agen, presided, although his Church had never acquired the rank of metropolitan; and the acts of the synod of Turin, in 401, shew that the metropolitan dignity was then a new institution, and only in the state of introduction. The same is proved by the contest between the bishops of Arles and Vienne, both of whom claimed this authority over the province of Vienne, and by the varying state of the right to consecrate bishops, which was then claimed and exercised by many. This contest was terminated by pope Zosimus, in 417, in favour of the bishop of Arles. This bishop, as successor of St. Trophimus, who had been sent to that country by Rome, was to possess metropolitan jurisdiction over three provinces, that of Vienne and the two of Narbonne. At the same time Zosimus deprived Hilary, bishop of Narbonne, of the right of metropolitan over the first province of Narbonne, which he had obtained by fraud from the apostolic see : he annulled also the decree of the synod of Turin, which gave to Proculus, bishop of Marseilles, the second province of Narbonne, and at length deposed Proculus, who resisted his ordinance. But the succeeding pontiffs, Boniface and Celestine, acting on the principle that no metropolitan should possess more than one province, and that the ecclesiastical should not exceed in extent the civil provinces, took from the Church of Arles the two provinces of Narbonne. It now happened that Hilary, bishop of Arles, in a synod over which he presided, deposed a bishop who belonged to another province,—Celidonius of Besançon. Celidonius appealed to the pope, at the same time that the bishop Projectus was also appealing against Hilary, complaining that during his life Hilary had appointed him a successor. The accused metropolitan also appeared at Rome, but when he saw the unfavourable turn of his affairs, he hastened to leave the city. The indignant pontiff, in 445, deprived him of his metropolitan jurisdiction over the province of Vienne, and tranferred it to the bishop of that province. At the same time, Valentinian III published an edict, in which he commanded the bishops of Gaul, and of every other province (of the west), to submit themselves in all things to the authority of the see of Rome, and to appear before the pope whenever their presence should be required. Hilary sought by his supplications to appease the pope, and after his death, in 449, the bishops of the province entreated the pope, for the sake of St. Trophimus, who had been sent thither by the see of Rome, to grant to Ravennius, the new bishop, the privileges which that see had conferred upon the Church of Arles. The pope Leo then divided the province between the bishops of Arles and Vienne. The bishops of Arles, as vicars or delegates of the Roman see, had received from it a kind of primacy over the entire Church of Gaul: in virtue of this jurisdiction, they could convoke synods of all or any of the provinces: they gave to ecclesiastics who were travelling to Rome, letters (formatas) of communion and recommendation: it was their duty to watch over the Churches of the provinces, and to report, when circumstances should require it, any occurrences to the pope. Leo took from Hilary of Arles the right of convening synods, and transferred it to Leontius, bishop of Frejus, but it was soon again restored to the bishops of Arles. Pope Hilary, however, sent notice to Leontius of Arles that he should not interfere in the case of Hermas, who had invaded the see of Narbonne, as that event occurred in a province which was within his own "monarchy." When the popes appointed a vicar of this nature in Gaul, when they determined and divided provinces, conferred or withdrew metropolitan jurisdiction, they then exercised their patriarchal, as distinct from their supreme, authority. After the baptism of Clovis, St. Remigius, bishop of Rheims, obtained the jurisdiction of apostolic vicar over the Churches in nine of the kingdoms of the Franks. The vicarial authority was, however, still granted to the bishops of Arles in the sixth century.

In the fourth century also the metropolitan authority was first known in Spain. The bishop of the first see, who is mentioned in the decree of the council of Elvira, was no other than the senior in ordination. But towards the end of the fourth age, there was established in Spain five metropolitan Churches, Tarragona, Seville, Emerita, Toledo, (or Carthagena, before its destruction?) and Bracara: in the year 569, a sixth was added to these, the Church of Lugo, when the synod of Lugo divided the province of Gallicia into two metropolitan districts.

That the bishops of Rome consented at least to this establishment and division of the metropolitan authority, is evident from the complaints of the Spanish prelates, who accused the bishop Silvanus of having violated the papal ordinances in the consecration of a bishop. We must recognize the patriarchal authority of the pope in the decrees respecting bishops, as we read them in the epistle of pope Innocent to the prelates of the council of Toledo, and in the prayer of the Spanish bishops, that the pope would confirm Irenæus in the see of Barcelona, which the pontiff refused. In the year 465, Ascanius, bishop of Tarragona, and his suffragans, laid before the pope Hilarius a complaint against Silvanus of Calahorra, that he had consecrated bishops without the permission of his metropolitan. Hilarius confirmed the bishops who had been thus irregularly ordained.

The bishops of Rome appointed their vicars also in Spain in the same manner as in Gaul. In the year 482, Simplicius constituted Zeno, bishop of Seville, his vicar in the provinces of Bætica and Lusitania. Before this, in the year 447, pope Leo had conferred upon Turibius, bishop of Astorga, extraordinary powers to call a synod against the Priscillianists. But the power of the Roman vicar in Spain was not always confined to one Church, nor did it at all times extend over an equal territory. Hormisdas granted this jurisdiction to John, bishop of Illice. It was the ordinary duty of these vicars to watch over the observance of the canons and of the decrees of the popes, to provide for the maintenance of the rights of metropolitans, and to report to the pope causes of greater importance. To these powers was also added that of calling bishops of other provinces to attend a council. When the synod of Braga decreed, in 563, that the liturgy of the mass should be celebrated in the form which the metropolitan Profuturus had received from the apostolic see, we here see exercised the patriarchal authority of Rome. During the course of the seventh century, the popes appear to have discontinued the practice of appointing vicars in Spain. After the conversion of Reccaredo from Arianism, the Spanish

Church was in a flourishing and well ordered condition: its zealous and learned bishops held frequent national synods, in which the subjects of discussion were decided according to the canons of councils, and the decrees of the popes, (*synodalia et decretalia constituta*). St. Gregory the Great once interposed, when two bishops, Januarius of Malaga, and Stephen, had been deposed by the secular power. He appointed the priest, John Defensor, whom he sent into Spain, to restore these bishops, if they should be found innocent.

If the popes willingly conceded that in Gaul and Spain, bishops should be ordained by the metropolitans, and these by provincial synods, they acted otherwise towards eastern Illyricum. This at first was a part of the western patriarchate, and formed two dioceses, the Macedonian and Dacian. The former comprised six provinces, Achaia, Macedonia, Crete, Thessaly, Old and New Epirus; the latter five, the two Dacias, Mæsia, Dardania and Prævalitana. Pope Damasus, in the fourth century, appointed the bishop of Thessalonica his vicar in these provinces, and succeeding popes did the same. On account of the peculiar circumstances of the Illyrican provinces, and as it was to be expected that the neighbouring bishop of Constantinople would endeavour with the aid of the emperor, to subject these provinces to himself, more ample powers were entrusted to the vicar of the Roman patriarch. "No bishop," said Siricius, in his instruction to the vicar, "no bishop shall be ordained without his approbation: he shall be ordained by him or by another bishop, empowered by him so to act." But Sixtus III and Leo the Great granted to the metropolitans power to consecrate their suffragans, and reserved to the vicars the ordination only of the metropolitans. An epistle of pope Leo conveyed to the metropolitans of the province the notification, that they should obey his vicar in the exercise of all the faculties that had been given to him, that he could convene synods from all the provinces, but that greater causes and appeals should be referred to the apostolic see. It was thus, that Perigenes, who had been ordained bishop of Patræ, was translated to the see of Corinth only by the permission of pope Boniface, to whom the Corinthians had sent a supplicatory address; and when some of the bishops questioned the right of Perigenes to the Church of Corinth, they were severely reprimanded by the pope. These were probably the bishops, who, when the eastern Illyricum had been incorporated with the eastern empire, obtained, in 421, in conjunction with the patriarch Atticus, a rescript from Theodosius II, decreeing that doubtful cases occurring in these provinces should not be decided without the knowledge and consent of the bishop of Constantinople. But the emperor Honorius requested his nephew to cease from this attack upon the privileges of the Church of Rome, which their fathers had confirmed. His request was granted, and Illyricum continued to form part of the Roman patriarchate down to the time of Leo the Isaurian. The vicarial powers of the bishop of Thessalonica were withdrawn, when Andrew and Dorotheus took part in the schism of Acacius. The popes would no longer grant them; and in 516, forty Illyrian and Greek bishops separated themselves from Dorotheus to maintain communion with their patriarch, the bishop of Rome. A new attempt of Epiphanius, patriarch of Constantinople, occasioned by the contested ordination of Stephan of Lerissa, failed in its object of obtaining influence in these provinces. At this period, in 531, in a synod held at Rome, under Felix II, Theodosius, bishop of Echinus in Thessaly, clearly distinguished between the supremacy and the patriarchal power of the pope, stating that to the apostolic see belonged jurisdiction over the entire Church; and that to it, from all parts of the Church, appeals must be made, but that it had reserved to itself, in a particular manner, the provinces of Illyricum. The vicariate of Thessalonica, when it had been again restored, was contracted in the extent of its jurisdiction, for Justinian obtained from pope Vigilius that Illyricum should be divided; that the provinces in which the Latin language was spoken, together with the second Macedonian province, be be subjected to the jurisdiction of the bishop of his native city Justinianea Prima, as vicar of the Roman see, whilst the other provinces, in which the Greek tongue was used, remained under the bishop of Thessalonica. In Dalmatia, which belonged to the western Illyricum, the metropolitan, the bishop of Salona, was ordained by the bishops of the province, but always with the knowledge and consent of the pope, as we learn from the epistles of Gregory the Great.

The patriarchal authority of the popes in the provinces of Illyricum could not have sprung from the dependance of daughter Churches on their parent and mother Church: for there were in these provinces Churches which could trace back their origin to an antiquity equal, if not superior, to that of Rome. This authority then must have been derived from an apostolical ordinance, or from a special reservation of the immediate successors of St. Peter. The African Church had been planted by apostolical labourers from Rome, and yet the indications of patriarchal authority, exercised over it by the Roman see, are fewer and more obscure than in any other part of the west. That, in 313, the two bishops, Eunomius and Olympius, were sent from Rome to Carthage, and that they terminated the schism there by the ordination of a new bishop; that the synod of Cella, in 418, drew many of its canons from the epistle of pope Siricius; that pope Agapite, in 535, restored to the bishop of Carthage the rights of metropolitan, which had been lost during the Vandal invasion,—these and many other events declare evidently the supreme jurisdiction of the Roman pontiffs; and when we remember that in the African Church there arose circumstances and regulations, differing from those of any other Church in the west, we are led to believe that the autocephalia of this Church must be dated from a very early age. To these peculiar circumstances must be attributed the greatly disproportionate number of bishops which we find in Africa, where, in 411, there were five hundred and ten Catholic sees—a greater number than in all the other parts of the west. To these same circumstances belong also the constitution of metropolitans: in the six provinces, into which northern Africa had been divided, since the time of Constantine, (the proconsular Africa, Numidia, Byzacena, Tripoli, and the two Mauritanias) the bishops, who were seniors in ordination, enjoyed the rights of metropolitans, with the name of primates; so that when, in 401, two Numidian bishops contested with each other for these rights, the cause was decided by determining who was the elder bishop. This regulation existed in the sixth century, and was certainly accompanied, as St. Gregory the Great remarked, with this disadvantage, that the metropolitan was oftentimes the bishop of a small town or village. Without the consent of these primates, no bishop could be ordained in their respective provinces; they convoked synods, and received appeals from ecclesiastics. The primacy of the proconsular province, together with a superiority over all the others, was possessed by the bishop of Carthage. He could call a plenary synod of all the provinces, and could receive appeals from the decisions of the other primates: he addressed circulars to all the bishops, confirmed the primates, visited the provinces, and sent to the Churches, that applied to him, bishops and priests, who had received ordination from him.

In the management and decisions of ecclesiastical affairs, the bishops of Rome were assisted by their synods. These synods were convened regularly once in every year, and more frequently if circumstances should so require. The particular synods, with which they generally consulted, were composed of the priests of Rome and the neighbouring bishops, who formed the consistory of the pope. At the *metropolitan* councils of the pontiffs, the bishops from all parts of Italy were accustomed to assist as late as the end of the fourth century; after that time, when the metropolitan Churches of the north of Italy arose, only the bishops of middle and lower Italy attended. A council of this kind was holden by Julius I in 342, and by Siricius in 386, at which eighty bishops were present. They formed a more extensive consistory, and there and it was after their deliberations that the popes sent forth those synodal letters, during the contests occasioned in the east by Nestorius, Acacius, Peter Mongus, and others. But the definitive decision, on the subjects proposed for consultation in these councils, was reserved to the pope. This was declared by the synod at Rome, under Felix III, in 484: " That as often as the bishops of Italy assemble on ecclesiastical affairs, it is his (the pope's) duty, as head of all, to determine all :" and in their subscription, the bishops of this synod confess, "that they follow the authority of the apostolic see." Hence, at the head of the acts of a council, which was held by Gregory the Great, we read, " I, Gregory, decree." Of the *patriarchal* synods of the bishops of Rome, together with the bishops of Italy, the bishops also of Gaul, Spain, Illyricum, and Britain, formed parts. These bishops were summoned to meet in national councils, either by the apostolic vicars, or by letters addressed to them immediately by the pope, as when the general synod of Spain was called by Leo I. These national synods constituted component parts of the Roman patriarchal council. Thus, in the dogmatical epistle which the pope sent to his legates at the sixth general council, it is said: " Agatho, bishop, servant of the servants of God, with all the synods, subjected to the council of the apostolic see." He had a short time before ordered that synods should be convened in Gaul and the above-named nations, delegates from which assisted at the patriarchal council, at which he had himself presided, at Rome. If it were intended to convoke a synod, on any subject appertaining to faith, within the boundaries of the Roman patriarchate, it was necessary first to obtain the approbation of the pontiff. " Without the consent of the bishop of Rome, we can do nothing in matters of faith," said St. Peter Chrysologus, in his letter to Eutyches. The bishop of Rome confirmed the great councils of the east, as supreme head of the Church; and as the assent of the entire west was comprised in that of its patriarch,

As patriarchs, the popes were accustomed to send the pallium to particular bishops. This ecclesiastical ornament was not a robe, but only a narrow band, and ordinarily was worn only during the celebration of the Holy Sacrifice. It was not at first the emblem of extraordinary jurisdiction, but it was sent mostly only to metropolitans; sometimes, however, as in the case of the bishop of Autun, who received it from Gregory the Great, it was granted also to other bishops. The first instance on record of a grant of the pallium by the pope, is that of Symmachus to Cesarius of Arles, and to Theodore, metropolitan of Laureacum: but it is evident from this fact that the custom was more ancient, for Symmachus speaks of the practice of his predecessors. We are told also, in the *Liber Pontificalis*, that the pope Mark appointed, in 336, that the bishop of Ostia, when consecrating the pope, should wear the pallium. The popes generally granted the pallium to those bishops whose predecessors had received it, but only after a formal petition. If Vigilius and Gregory the Great first obtained the approbation of the emperor, before they gave the pallium to certain bishops of Gaul, for whom their king had requested it, this was only to prevent Byzantine suspicion, which might have considered this transaction as an undue familiarity of the popes with a foreign power. St. Gregory appears to have been the first who sent the pallium to metropolitans in confirmation of their authority.

SECTION V.

PATRIARCHAL AND METROPOLITICAL AUTHORITY IN THE EAST.—THE PATRIARCHS OF CONSTANTINOPLE.

1. At the commencement of this period, the bishop of Alexandria, whose Church derived its pre-eminence from its founder, St. Mark, and through him from St. Peter, was next in rank to the bishop of Rome, and was therefore the first bishop of the east. The Churches of

Egypt, Thebais and Lybia, were so entirely subjected to him, that he ordained all the bishops, and, according to his pleasure, the priests of the different communities. In his diocese, therefore, there was no metropolitan; and the bishops of the chief cities had no more power than the patriarch was pleased to confer on them; as Synerius, bishop of Ptolemais, the capital of Cyrenaica, testifies of himself. So great was this dependence, that, as we have seen, the Egyptian bishops at the council of Chalcedon, most suppliantly requested the assembled fathers not to oblige them to subscribe to the letter of the pope, as all Egypt would rise up against them if they should dare to take such a step without the consent of their patriarch.

2. The patriarchal diocese of the bishop of Antioch, comprised Cilicia and Isauria, Syria, Phœnicia, Arabia, Euphratesia, Osroene and Mesopotamia. The island of Cyprus also, appears to have formed at one time part of his diocese: so, at least, it was asserted by the bishop Alexander, in his epistle to pope Innocent, to whom he complained, that the Cypriots, during the confusion occasioned by the Arian heresy, first asserted their independence. But the bishops of Cyprus, who were present at the council of Ephesus, in 431, maintained that they had always been independent of the see of Antioch. The council decided in their favour, and granted to the bishop of Constantia metropolitan authority, "as the bishop of Antioch had not ancient prescription on his side." Palestine was never subject to the see of Antioch, although St. Jerome once wished to prove, from the sixth canon of the council of Nice, that it was so subjected. The high rank of the Church of Antioch, and the great power of its see, were derived from St. Peter, who had been its bishop; but this power was not so great as that of the patriarch of Alexandria. In the patriarchate of the east, the metropolitan authority was fully developed. The patriarch ordained only the metropolitans of his provinces; the metropolitans ordained their suffragan bishops. Pope Innocent indeed, wrote to the patriarch Alexander, that he could not so permit

suffragan bishops to be ordained without his consent, so that the more distant should be ordained by the metropolitans, empowered so to act by writing from him, and that those who were nearer, should receive consecration from himself. But this regulation was never carried into effect. The patriarch John was the first who ordained bishops in the provinces, the Nestorian metropolitans of which obstinately refused to join in the peace with St. Cyril. Theodoret complained bitterly of this violation, as he called it, of metropolitan rights.

3. The bishops of Cæsarea, Ephesus and Heraclea, were, or became during the course of the fourth century, superiors of large dioceses, with powers like to those of the bishop of Antioch, which were confirmed to them by the canons of the council of 381. The bishop of Cæsarea possessed jurisdiction over the diocese of Pontus, which included the provinces of Galatia, Bithynia, Cappadocia, Pontus Polemoniacus, Helenopontus, and the Lesser Armenia: he was accustomed also, towards the middle of the fifth century, to ordain the Catholicus of the Greater Armenia. The Asaitic diocese, to which belonged the provinces, Asia, Hellespont, Pamphylia, Lydia, Phrygia, Caria, Pisidia, Lycaonia, with the adjacent islands, had been, from the times of the apostles, under its parent Church of Ephesus. To the bishop of Heraclea was, in a short time, subjected the Thracian diocese, that is, the provinces, Europa (Byzantium), Thrace, Hæmimontium, Rhodope, the Lower Mæsia, and Scythia.

The bishop of Ælia, which city had risen from the ashes of the ruined Jerusalem, was, with the other bishops of Palestine, under the metropolitan of Cæsarea: but as an apostolical Church, the Church of Ælia enjoyed a pre-eminence of honour, which was confirmed to it by the council of Nice, with the reservation however of the metropolitan rights of the bishop of Cæsarea. But there soon arose between the bishops of Ælia, which was now again named Jerusalem, and the bishops of Cæsarea, a contention for superiority. Cyril yielded to Acacius, who was supported by the Arians; and in

415, the bishop of Cæsarea presided over the synod of Diospolis, although John of Jerusalem was present. On the other hand, not only did Juvenal of Jerusalem assume to himself the rights of the bishop of Cæsarea over the bishops of Palestine, but entered also into the diocese of the bishop of Antioch, whose authority had greatly fallen during the Arian controversies, and ordained bishops in Phœnicia and Arabia, having been probably empowered so to act by an imperial rescript. This contention was terminated at the council of Chalcedon, by an agreement, which was sanctioned by the papal legates, between Juvenal and Maximus of Antioch. Phœnicia and Arabia continued in the patriarchate of Antioch; to the bishop of Jerusalem were conceded the three provinces, Palestine, Samaria, and Galilee, which he was to govern with patriarchal authority. From that time, Jerusalem ranked as the fifth amongst the patriarchal churches.

The bishops of Byzantium, afterwards named Constantinople, even after their city had become the capital of the east, were for a long time under the bishops of Heraclea : but during the Arian contests, the bond which united the two Churches was greatly loosened, and St. John Chrysostom was consecrated by Timotheus, patriarch of Alexandria. But before this time, the council of 381 had, in its third canon, given to Constantinople, the New Rome, the first rank after the Church of Rome, and to its bishops, precedence before the bishops of Antioch and Alexandria; an ordinance with which the pope was displeased, which the bishop of Antioch received with indifference, and the bishop of Alexandria with opposition. Hence Dioscorus accused the Antiochians of having betrayed the common rights of both Churches. Although the above canon conveyed to the bishop of Constantinople no particular jurisdiction, and assigned to him no particular diocese, many things now concurred to place him in possession of both : amongst these, the most powerful was the constant synod (σύνοδος), which was formed by the bishops, who resided at Constantinople, and to which, causes occurring in the neighbouring districts were referred for judgment. St. John Chrysostom exercised jurisdiction not only in the dioceses of Pontus and of Thrace, but, having been invited by the Asiatic bishops, went also to Ephesus, where he held several synods, deposed six bishops, who had been convicted of simony, and, together with their successors, ordained a bishop of Ephesus. Theophilus, in his accusations against the saint, forgot not to produce this "illegal innovation;" but the succeeding bishops of Constantinople proceeded in the path which had been opened before them. The attempt of Atticus to subject to himself the eastern Illyricum indeed failed; but in compensation for his disappointment, he obtained a rescript from the emperor, which forbade any bishop to be ordained in Asia Minor, or in Thrace, without his consent. From this sprung the practice, by which the metropolitans of these two dioceses generally received ordination at Constantinople: the bishops of the Asiatic diocese, in particular, during the confusion of the Church of Ephesus, which was disgraced by the worthlessness of its bishops, willingly subjected themselves to the see of Constantinople. Anatolius ventured to exercise an almost boundless jurisdiction even in the patriarchate of Antioch: he divided Phœnicia into two metropolitan districts, he threatened the bishop of Tyre with excommunication and deposition, and consecrated a bishop of Antioch at Constantinople. It was in conformity, therefore, with this order of things, that the council of Chalcedon, in its sixth and seventeenth canons, decreed that those who had a complaint against their metropolitan, should lay the same before the primate of the diocese, (the bishops of Ephesus and of Cæsarea in Pontus) or before the bishop of Constantinople. But the pretensions of the Byzantines were not yet at an end: their Church must be a patriarchal Church, and the first in the east: if possible it must be, in the east, what Rome was in the west. To obtain this pre-eminence a favourable opportunity seemed to present itself, a short time before the end of the council. By the deposition of Dioscorus, the see of Alexandria had been made vacant, and Maximus of Antioch was indebted for his elevation to the influence of Anatolius: Thalassius of Cæsarea had been ordained by him: Ephesus was without a bishop, and the bishop of Heraclea was absent. The clergy of Constantinople, encouraged by the absence of so many prelates from the council—only two hundred were then at Chalcedon, and amongst them there were no Egyptians—procured the formation of a new canon in favour of their own Church. As the papal legates had departed, not a voice was raised in opposition, and a new canon, the twenty-eighth, referring to the similar canon of the council of 381, decreed that the New Rome, which was ennobled by the residence of the emperor and the senate, and which enjoyed privileges equal to those of the ancient Rome, should be equally exalted, also, in its ecclesiastical relations, and that the metropolitans of the dioceses of Pontus, Asia, and Thrace, and the bishops of countries within those dioceses, possessed by the barbarians, should be ordained by the bishop of Constantinople.

As formerly the sixth canon of the council of Nice, when confirming the patriarchal rights of the bishop of Alexandria, appealed to the similar rights of the bishop of Rome, so now was the same patriarchal authority of the Church of ancient Rome brought into comparison, when there was question of conferring like authority on the Church of New Rome: but to do this with an appearance of truth, these rights were called privileges, "which the fathers had conceded to the bishop of ancient Rome, the residence of the emperor and of the senate." The supremacy of the bishop of Rome over the universal Church was not here spoken of: this was declared in the next sitting to the protesting legates by the imperial commissaries. "The supremacy over all," ($\pi\rho o\ \pi a \nu\tau\omega\nu\ \tau a\ \pi\rho\omega\tau\epsilon\iota a$) said they, "remains inviolate to the bishop of Rome:" to the bishop of Constantinople, this canon gave only an equal rank, (as patriarch), and patriarchal rights over the three dioceses. In its address to the pope, also, the synod declared that by its canon, it had only raised ancient practice, (by which the

Byzantine bishops ordained the metropolitans of the three dioceses) to the dignity of a law, and had confirmed the opinion of the council of 381, that the bishop of Constantinople should stand in rank next to the bishop of Rome. The Byzantines might indeed have imagined that the patriarchs of the east were dependant on theirs, and that he could exercise the same authority in the patriarchates of Alexandria and Antioch, as did the pope in the west: but they had never thought that their patriarch was independant of the bishop of Rome, or that he could compare himself in all things with him. The council, the emperor Marcian, and Anatolius himself, confessed in their epistle to the pope Leo, that the decree respecting the elevation of the Church of Constantinople required his confirmation, and Anatolius expressly declared, even after Leo had made known his disapprobation of the canon, that its whole force and validity depended on the consent of the pontiff. The following patriarchs, who omitted nothing to maintain their authority in the east, in terms the most unequivocal professed the higher authority of the pope, and their subjection to him. Anthimus pledged himself, at his ordination, to follow in all things whatever should be prescribed to him by the bishop of Rome, and wrote to the other patriarchs stating that he in all things obeyed the apostolic see. Mennas, at the council of 536, declared, "as you know, we follow and obey the apostolic see in all things;" and the emperor Justinian asserted in his laws, that he did not permit, in ecclesiastical affairs, any thing to be determined, which had not first been submitted to the pope, who was the chief of all bishops.

The protest, which the Roman legates, on the following day, entered against the twenty-eighth canon, was confirmed by the pope, who persevered in rejecting the canon, as by it the sixth canon of the Nicene council was annulled, and the ancient order of the patriarchs reversed: he exhorted the patriarchs of Antioch and of Alexandria, also to resist it: and so far gained his object, that the emperor Marcian surrendered the canon and extolled the constancy of the pontiff in maintaining the rights of the Church. The whole western Church repudiated the canon, and the Greeks themselves, until the time of Photius, did not place it in their collections: hence Theodore Lector and John Scholasticus, who lived in the sixth century, enumerate only twenty-seven canons of the council of Chalcedon. But Acacius exerted himself to gain the authority which the canon gave to his see: he was opposed by the Monophystic party, and by the emperor Basiliscus: this opposition, however, was rather favourable than prejudicial to Acacius, for it would seem to be only one of the consequences of the rejection by the Monophysites of the whole council of Chalcedon; and in 476, he obtained from the emperor Zeno a rescript, which granted to his see patriarchal rights in their fullest extent. The bishops of the Asiatic diocese immediately and submissively implored his pardon for having so long refused his yoke: but as soon as he had obtained his end, he himself, as author of the Henoticon, rejected the council of Chalcedon; and, secure of the protection of the emperor, acted the part of a tyrant in Antioch and Alexandria, deposing and instituting patriarchs at his pleasure. After his time, also, several patriarchs of Antioch and of Alexandria were ordained at Constantinople, although, as the Carthaginian deacon, Liberatus, remarked, in 560, the apostolic see refused to receive the twenty-eighth canon, which was defended, however, by the emperors. It was confirmed also by the council of Trullo, in 692, in its thirty-sixth canon.

The bishops of Constantinople expressed their pretensions to ecclesiastical jurisdiction over the whole of the eastern Roman empire, by the name of "œcumenical patriarch," which they now assumed. By the word οἰκουμενη, the Greeks understood the dominions of the emperor. This title had been applied by the council of Chalcedon to pope Leo: Justinian employed it, in one of his rescripts, when speaking of the patriarch Epiphanius, and it was given by the councils of 518 and 536, to the patriarchs John and Mennas. Hence the patriarch, John the Faster, rashly presumed to convene a general council of the east, at Constantinople, in which it was his intention to depose Gregory, patriarch of Antioch, and in his letter of convocation, styled himself œcumenical patriarch. The pope, Pelagius II, reprobated this two-fold assumption—of the title, (which he translated by the words, *Patriarcha universalis*), and of the convocation of a general council, which was the exclusive right of the pope. More strongly than Pelagius, did Gregory the Great declare himself against this title, which appeared to him to bear, or might be made to bear, the signification, that the bishop of Constantinople was the universal, that is the only true, bishop in the Greek empire, and that all others were no more than his representatives, professing only a power delegated by him. He, therefore, himself declined the appellation, when it was given to him by Eulogius, patriarch of Alexandria. Although neither John, nor his successor Cyriacus, would resign the title, yet they both, together with the emperor, continually acknowledged that their see was subject to the Church of Rome. During this dispute, the priest John of Chalcedon, appealed from the sentence of the patriarch to the pope; and the patriarch himself, to facilitate the judgment which was to be given in Rome, sent thither the acts of the process. It appears that Boniface III, although the representations of Gregory to the emperor Mauritius had proved fruitless, obtained from Phocas a rescript which prohibited the patriarchs of Constantinople from assuming the contested title: for in this signification must be understood the assertion in the biographies of the pope, and in the writings of Paulus Diaconus, "that Phocas confirmed to the Church of Rome, the supremacy which was assumed by the Church of Constantinople." But after the death of Phocas this rescript was no longer respected: at the sixth general council, the patriarch George asserted his right to the title of universal patriarch, which was given to the pope by his legates in their subscriptions.

From the time of Constantine there had been, in the

east, an endeavour to adapt the division of the Church, into metropolitan districts and patriarchal dioceses, to the political division of the empire. But, when the boundaries of provinces and the divisions of them were frequently changed, an unceasing source of ecclesiastical disputes, and of ambitious contentions, was created. When Valens divided Cappadocia into two provinces, Anthimus, bishop of Tyana, asserted his metropolitan rights over the new province, whilst St. Basil defended the jurisdiction of his Church over the whole of Cappadocia. Alexander of Antioch proposed to pope Innocent the question, whether the ecclesiastical division of the provinces were still to follow the changes which were then made by the civil government: the pope replied in the negative, as that would subject the Church to the varying circumstances of political events. The council of Chalcedon, also, forbade bishops to take to themselves metropolitan rights, because they had obtained from the emperor a rescript by which a province was divided into two parts. Thus Theodosius II divided Phœnicia, that he might raise the bishop of Berytus to the rank of metropolitan; an innovation, which was condemned by the council, with the assent of Marcian. The bishop of Tyre, therefore, recovered his jurisdiction over the whole of Phœnicia. But the principle, that the ecclesiastical should be accommodated to the civil boundaries of provinces, still remained, with some exceptions, in the east: it was on this, that the patriarchs of Constantinople grounded their pretensions; although the Greeks, in a later age, had recourse to the fable that the Byzantine Church was founded by the apostle St. Andrew.

Both in the east and in the west, it was, and still is, the first and chief prerogative of metropolitans to confirm the election of their suffragan bishops; to ordain, or to empower others to ordain, them. According to the sixth canon of the council of Nice, no one was to be considered as bishop who had been ordained without the consent of his metropolitan; but it was the duty of the metropolitan to act in unison with the majority of his bishops. The provincial synod was, according to a frequently renewed law, holden twice in each year by the metropolitan: he presided in it, and, with its assistance, decided on ecclesiastical affairs, heard complaints against the bishops, and judged on controversies which might have arisen amongst themselves. The synod could not, without his consent, either assemble or form decrees; neither could he determine on important matters without the consent of his synod; he could not alone ordain a bishop, nor interfere with his suffragans in the internal administration of their districts. But when one of the Churches of his province had lost its bishop, the care of the vacant see devolved upon the metropolitan, who generally entrusted it to a neighbouring bishop, until a successor to the deceased prelate should be elected.

SECTION VI.

BISHOPS AND THEIR DIOCESES.—CHOREPISCOPI AND PARISH PRIESTS.—THE OTHER CLERGY.

That in one city there could be only one bishop was decreed by the council of Nice, in reference to the Novatian bishops, who had been converted to the Catholic Church: but it was decreed also that the bishop, when the infirmity of age, or of disease, or the multiplicity of his occupations, might require it, should associate with himself a coadjutor signed with the episcopal character. Thus, Maximus of Jerusalem took to himself Macarius; John of Apamea, Stephen, and Valerius of Hippo, St. Augustin, as coadjutor bishops. By the sixth canon of the council of Sardica, it was ordained, that in villages and small towns, in which a priest was sufficient to perform the spiritual duties, a bishop should not be appointed, that the episcopal character might not be degraded: but in the east, and in Africa, there were many bishoprics which comprised only small hamlets, and the adjacent country; for there it was permitted to each bishop, with the permission of the metropolitan and the provincial synod, to divide his diocese, as we know it was done by St. Augustin: metropolitans also could erect new bishoprics, as St. Basil did, by appointing bishops to insignificant places, to repair the loss which he had suffered from the pretensions of Anthimus.

Often was the law renewed, that no ecclesiastic or layman should be admitted to communion in a foreign diocese, unless he had brought with him testimonies or letters of communion from his own bishop. Public instruction, during the divine worship, continued to be the duty of the bishop: in the east, priests performed this office, but by the order, and in the presence, of the bishop: in the west, St. Augustine was the first priest who preached in public. St. John Chrysostom places the visitation of his diocese among the first duties of a bishop: during the visitation, the bishops were wont to administer the sacrament of confirmation to those who had been baptized by the priests or deacons.

Thirty years was the age required for the consecration of a bishop. There are instances, indeed, of men of great merit and promise, such as Athanasius and Remigius of Rheims, who were consecrated when under that age. The departure from the rule more frequently occurred when the new bishop was chosen from the diocese which he had to govern. The community itself sometimes elected a stranger, as when the inhabitants of Vercelli called St. Eusebius, whom they had never seen, to govern their Church. Another law, which was likewise sometimes overlooked, required that only he should be elected who had passed through the lower degrees of the hierarchy, and whose conduct therein had been approved: according to the tenth canon of Sardica, the bishop elect must have been lector and deacon or priest; but a decretal of pope Siricius required that he should have been lector, acolyth, subdeacon, deacon, and priest, ten years. But it was not generally considered necessary that a bishop elect should have been in all the inferior grades: for not unfrequently were deacons, and even subdeacons, and lectors, chosen to be consecrated. Nectarius was yet a neophyte, Ambrose a catechumen, when the election fell on them. In such cases, however, the person received, in a short period, the intermediate orders. Thus we are told, in the life of St. Ambrose, that he first exercised all the ecclesiastical functions, and in eight days was ordained bishop: thus also St. Epiphanius ordained Paulinian, the brother of St. Jerome, in one morning, deacon and priest.

According to the most ancient practice of the Church, bishops were elected by the communities which they had to govern: the clergy confirmed the choice of the people, determined in doubtful elections, and when there was danger that the election might fall on an unworthy subject, directed it into another course: the provincial synod then approved of the proceedings, and the metropolitan, with the co-operation of two or three bishops, consecrated the prelate elect. In some places it was customary for the bishops to designate three persons, one of whom was chosen by the clergy and people, or sometimes the people selected three, one of whom was ordained by the metropolitan. In contested or divided elections, the metropolitan decided. The bond which united the bishop to his Church, was considered almost as indissoluble as the bond of marriage: hence the councils of Nice and of Antioch prohibited the translations of bishops from one see to another; and at Sardica, the removal of a bishop from a less to a greater church was more particularly forbidden. The same synod also decreed, that a bishop should not absent himself more than three weeks from his see.

The order of *Chorepiscopi*, which appeared in the east about the end of the first period, was introduced, though not universally, by degrees into the west. In Africa, where the number of bishoprics was great, and their extent proportionally small, this order was unknown. In Gaul, the synod of Riez, in 439, permitted Armentarius, the deposed bishop of Embrun, to enjoy the title of Chorepiscopus, and this is the first mention that is made in the western Church of this institution.

The council of Seville, in 620, declared that the chorepiscopi were in all things like to priests. The council of Laodicea decreed, that in the country and in villages, not bishops but *visitors* (περιοδευται) should be appointed This has generally been interpreted as an attack upon the order of the chorepiscopi, but the visitors, who are here mentioned, could have been no other than chorepiscopi, whose duty it was to perform the visitations of the country; and the synod could have intended no more than the council of Sardica, which forbade the appointment of bishops in villages and small towns. Before the council of Laodicea, the chorepiscopi were sometimes bishops; after the council they were only priests. But amongst many restrictions, they enjoyed, also, some privileges : they could ordain the inferior ecclesiastics, and give letters of peace to the clergy of their districts : they assisted at councils and subscribed the decrees after the bishops : from the second canon of the council of Chalcedon, we learn that they were ordained by a peculiar rite, and only by bishops. How numerous they were in the east in the fourth century, we learn from the fact, that St. Basil had fifty of them in his diocese. The great distinction between a true bishop and a chorepiscopus was, that although the latter might have received the episcopal ordination, it was not in his own, but in another's diocese.

Parish churches, which were served by priests, as at present, were known only in the country : in cities the faithful were not divided into congregations, but all formed one community, which assembled in the cathedral church to assist at the holy sacrifice, which was offered by the bishop. The other churches in the city (*oratoria, martyria, memoriæ*) were employed, not for the celebration of mass, but for psalmody and prayer. If a priest should form a congregation distinct from that of the bishop, he was viewed as a schismatic. When those who met in the cathedral church were very numerous, the holy sacrifice was repeated. Only in Rome, in Alexandria, and perhaps in some other large cities, were the people divided into parishes. But even in Rome, the priests of the city churches (*tituli*) of which each had two priests, could not, as late as the beginning of the fifth century, consecrate in these churches, but distributed to the people the eucharist, that had been sent to them by the bishop. Parishes then existed only in the country, and the name parish (παροικια), was used to distinguish them from the churches in the city. The priests of these parish churches baptized, and offered the sacrifice of the mass, whereas the priests in cities conferred baptism and celebrated mass, only by the permission of the bishop, or by delegation during his absence. The revenues of the parish churches were at first delivered entire to the bishop, or were administered by his procurator. In Africa, the property of these churches was removed from the administration of the bishops, early in the fifth age; in other places, the oblations made to the episcopal treasury by the parishes, were confined to the third or fourth part, and the *cathedraticum*, or offering to the visiting bishop by the parish, was established at two solidi.

The *archpriest* (named by the Greeks the *protopresbyter*, and later *protopapas*), a word first employed by St. Jerome, was the priest, in each church, who was eldest in ordination; but in the east a younger priest sometimes held this rank. He was, when the bishop was absent or was prevented from the performance of his duties, his general vicar, and frequently his successor. But greater privileges and greater influence were possessed by the archdeacons, a title that was first given to Cæcilian of Carthage. The archdeacon was the right hand of the bishop, and appears to have been elected, in earlier ages, by the deacons; he was afterwards always appointed by the bishop. To him was entrusted the administration of the episcopal revenues, and under the direction of the bishop, the expenditure of the same, and the distribution of the alms of the church: he possessed a kind of jurisdiction over the lower clergy, who were sometimes instructed by him. At the ordinations, he presented to the bishop those who were to receive orders, and he gave his testimony of their character. In short so great was his power, that the ordination of an archdeacon to the priesthood was sometimes considered a degradation, and we know that pope Leo severely reproved Anatolius of Constantinople, who had ordained the archdeacon Ætius, that he might take from him his influence and authority. The *defensors* (εκδικοι) were, in the Greek Church, some ecclesiastics and others laymen, whose duty it was to defend the possessions of the Church, and to protect ecclesiastics before civil tribunals: they guarded ecclesiastical privileges and exercised authority over the inferior orders of clerics.

Of these inferior orders, the Greek Church had, in the fourth century, the hypodiaconi, lectors, cantors, exorcists, ostiarii; the Latin Church, (according to the enumeration of the fourth synod of Carthage), the subdeacons, acolythes, exorcists, lectors and ostiarii. Youths of eight or nine years of age were often taken into the order of lectors, although Justinian decreed that no one under the age of eighteen years should be thus chosen. The cantors or psalmists conducted the music of the church, but they do not appear to have formed a distinct ecclesiastical order, at least in Africa, for there they were created by priests without the knowledge of the bishop. St. Epiphanius mentions also, the Hermeneutists, whose duty it was to interpret those portions of the Scripture, which were read in the churches, and to explain the sermons to the people, who were ignorant of the Greek or Latin languages. In the time of Constantine the copiati *(fossarii)* were introduced: they provided for the burial of the dead, particularly for the gratuitous sepulture of the poor. At the same time, the Parabolani, for the care of the sick, were instituted in large cities, and especially at Alexandria; they were numbered amongst the clergy and were subject to the bishop. Deaconesses were chosen from amongst widows advanced in years, who had been only once married, and from virgins. In Gaul, the institution of these ecclesiastical servants was forbidden by several councils, after the fifth century; yet we read that Medardus, in the sixth century, ordained the queen Radegunda a deaconess. In the east, particularly at Constantinople, the order continued to exist to a later period: the synod of Trullo, in 692, ordered that women, whose husbands had been consecrated bishops, should be made deaconess, if they were found worthy of that honour.

Schools of theology, and communities for the education of the clergy, had not yet been formed in the west. In the east, the catechetical school of Alexandria had existed since the second century: it was originally intended for the instruction of catechumens, which was often, indeed, a preparation for an ecclesiastical education. In this school, from the year 180, there were superiors or catechists, Pantœnus, Clement, Heraclas, Dionysius, Pierius, Theognostus, and in a later age Didymus. A similar school was founded at Cæsarea in Palestine, towards the close of the third century, by the priest and martyr Pamphilus, and about the same time, a theological school was founded at Antioch, into which the martyr Lucian, and, after him, Diodorus of Tarsus, introduced the study of Biblical criticism and exegesis. The school of Edessa, for the education of the Persian clergy, was founded by St. Ephræm, the Syrian: after its destruction, in 489, it was succeeded by the school of Nisibis. In the west, Cassiodorus, in concert with pope Agapite, projected the formation of a theological school at Rome; but he was prevented from his purpose by the invasion of Italy. In Italy, the parish priests were careful to form the young lectors to their ecclesiastical vocation, a practice which the synod of Vaison, in 529, wished to introduce into Gaul.

In the ordination of the superior clergy, and particularly of the priests, the voice of the people had great weight. The people were accustomed to express their testimony by the exclamation, "Thou art worthy!" Strangers from another diocese were not easily ordained, neither were those who had been once subjected to public penance, who had belonged to any heretical sect, or who had been guilty of any public crime after baptism. Absolute and unconditional ordinations, as we see them in modern ages, were not permitted: every ecclesiastic was by his ordination bound to some Church, and to a determined service. Exceptions, few indeed, may be found. Paulinus was ordained priest at Barcelona, with the condition that he should be free, and not attached to that Church; the monks, Barses and Eulogius, were consecrated bishops at Edessa under the same condition. The council of Chalcedon afterwards issued an universal prohibition against these ordinations. Bishops could not ordain in the dioceses of others, nor foreign clerics in their own. In the fourth century, it happened not unfrequently that persons were ordained with violence and against their own will, after the reiterated solicitations of the people. Nepotian, Martin of Tours, the hermit Macedonius, Augustin, Paulinus of Nola, Paulinian, and others, were ordained in this manner. This, however, took place only when their refusal sprung from humility or timidity. The canons of later councils forbade these violent ordinations. A repetition of ordination was no more permitted than a repetition of baptism: the ordinations of schismatics and heretics, as long as they preserved a succession of bishops, were esteemed valid.

In the first centuries the *revenues of the Church* consisted of the voluntary oblations of the faithful. Of these oblations some were placed weekly upon the altar, during the holy sacrifice, or were taken to the residence of the bishop: others were placed monthly in the treasury *(corbona)* of the church. The former were chiefly the productions of nature, the first fruits: the latter were generally made in money: both were divided amongst the clergy once in each month. These offerings were in some churches so abundant and so rich, that the superfluities were employed to succour more indigent communities: this was an early practice in the Church of Rome. A catalogue of the donors and of their gifts was read publicly in the church by the deacon: those who were sparing in their gifts were admonished of their duty by the bishop. Some churches appear to have possessed immoveable property in the second century: these goods were confiscated in the persecution of Diocletian, but were afterwards again restored. From the time of Constantine, the Church could possess free property, both moveable and immoveable, by purchase, by gift, or by legacy. Valentinian I passed a law, restricting legacies, to prevent surreptitious wills, by forging which many ecclesiastics had disgraced themselves and the Church. By a provision of Constantine, which was abrogated by Julian, and restored, in part, by Jovinian, the clergy received a yearly portion from the public treasury. The administration and expenditure of the ecclesiastical revenues were regulated by the bishop with the assistance of the deacons, and to such a height did the increasing wealth of the Church soon amount, that the most zealous in the service of the bishops found their employment a heavy burden. Hence we observe in the fifth century, the institution, in the oriental Church, of ecclesiastical procurators, to whom the administration of the revenues were entrusted, with the obligation of submitting their accounts to the bishops. In the west, was introduced, about the same time, the division of the Church revenues into four unequal parts, for the bishop, the clergy, the poor, and the building or repairs of the Church, and the public divine service. By this division the portions allotted to the clergy and the poor were in the power of the bishop. In the alienation of Church property, the bishops were first restricted in Africa, where the fourth and fifth councils of Carthage declared that for the validity of such an act, the consent of the clergy and primate of the province was necessary.

SECTION VII.

FORMATION OF ECCLESIASTICAL RELATIONS IN THE
NEW CHURCHES OF GERMANY.—THE CHURCH IN
THE KINGDOMS OF THE FRANKS AND WEST-GOTHS.*

In the revolution and destruction of all civil relations, in the fall of all political institutions, which succeeded to the emigration of the Germanic tribes, the Church alone stood unshaken in her strength and influence. She passed, despoiled, it may be, of many of her external possessions, but in her essence uninjured and the same, from the civilized Romans to the barbarous nations of the north : or rather, she was the happy mediatrix between the oppressed and the victor : she protected the one, whilst she taught, instructed, and formed the other.

Nowhere was this mediating and protecting influence more required than in the kingdom of the Gallic Franks. The endless family wars amongst the Merovingians, the revolutionary contests which laid waste the Austrasian, Neustrian, and Burgundian states, the hostilities between the nobles and the cities, the continual changing of possessions and of benefices, (grants made to the nobles, but which might be recalled), the assumption of a weak but despotic power, from the kings by the majores domo, and again from the majores domo by the kings and the nobles, all this, united with a general rage for plunder, and a no less general immorality, produced an universal destruction of all civil and social relations, amidst which the Church of Gaul, strong in the unvarying character of her doctrines, in the learning which she alone possessed, in the internal stability of her constitution, in the ecclesiastical unanimity of her bishops, formed the only power which could preserve, heal, and regenerate

---

* Gregorii Turonensis, (who died in 594), Historia Francorum, collected by Bouquet, in his Recueil des Histoires des Gaules, Paris, 1738, tom 2, 3, 1, fol., Collectio Canonum Ecclesiæ Hispaniæ, Matrit. 1808, folio.

the state. During the latter years of the Roman dominion, the bishops, as heads of the municipal magistracies, had arrived at the first rank in the government of the cities: they not unfrequently filled civil offices, and were the natural protectors of the Gallic-Roman population, to which they themselves belonged until the end of the sixth century. Before the year 560, we find no bishops of Frank descent; after that time they were numerous. Hence it was that the synods, which were regularly holden until the year 680, and were then discontinued until the time of St. Boniface, consulted on civil as well as on ecclesiastical affairs, and formed many laws most beneficial to the state: they provided for the care of the poor and imprisoned: they examined the condition of the prisons: they excommunicated the powerful who oppressed the weak, and those who reduced freemen to slavery: they emancipated slaves, (Desiderius alone, in 610, freed two thousand), and employed their influence over the administration of justice, to succour and to protect the defenceless. If they sometimes inherited vast possessions for their churches, those, who were bound to these lands, passed under the mild authority of the Church, under a government that was most solicitous even for the temporal happiness of its subjects.

But to all this power and influence of the Gallic Church, there was united a dependance on the civil power, sometimes most prejudicial in its consequences. The kings did not, indeed, like so many of the emperors, mingle themselves, or interfere with affairs of discipline and faith, but they were the more arbitrary in their interference with persons. They invaded the freedom of the election of bishops; for instead of merely confirming, as they had formerly done, the choice of the clergy and people, they began to nominate bishops themselves, and often did a royal mandate *(præceptio)*, transform in a short time a laic into a bishop. The synod of Paris, in 615, placed the nomination of a bishop, by the king, on an equality with the election by the clergy and people. Hence the bishoprics fell towards the close of the sixth century, generally into the hands of Franks. There were, indeed, amongst them many most holy and worthy men, but there were many also who passed from the court or from the army into the sanctuary,—worldly men, who relaxed the bonds of discipline, destroyed the authority of the Church, misemployed its riches, and thereby presented to powerful laics a welcome pretext to seize and alienate them. The synods, particularly the greater synods, in which the bishops of an entire kingdom assembled, were frequently either called by the king or held with his permission; and as the decrees of these councils often comprehended civil affairs, the confirmation of the monarch was sought, or they were promulgated in his name. But that any royal commissaries were present at the synods cannot be shewn. Whenever a freeman attached to the military service wished to enter the ecclesiastical state, it was first necessary that he should obtain the royal consent.

The persons of ecclesiastics and the property of churches were under the immediate protection of the king. The high dignity of the ecclesiastical state was expressed by the Ripuarian law, which determined the fine, which defended a priest from violence, to be equal to that of the antrustio of the king, and of a subdeacon as equal to that of a noble Frank. Several synods forbade civil judges to cite, to imprison, or to punish an ecclesiastic, without the knowledge of his bishop, under pain of excommunication: all, even the inferior ecclesiastics, and the servants of the Church, were judged by mixed tribunals, composed of laics and ecclesiastics, and, when convicted, were punished according to the canons. In purely civil cases higher ecclesiastics were exempted from secular jurisdiction by a law of Clothaire II, in 615. Bishops, even in cases of high-treason, were judged by their peers, that is by the synods, and even kings appealed against bishops to these assemblies; as when Childeric accused the bishop Prætextatus before the synod of Rouen. Another law of Clothaire II empowered the bishops, in the absence of the king, to examine and to amend the unjust sentences of secular judges. The privilege of asylum in churches was confirmed, and extended even to the residences of bishops. A person pursued, having sought refuge therein, was to be surrendered only when a declaration, confirmed by oath, that his life should be spared, had been received. Freedmen, also, were under the especial guardianship *(mundiburdium)* of the Church: widows and orphans could be tried only at tribunals, at which either the bishop or his archdeacon was present. To excommunication a civil effect was annexed, for by a law of Childebert, in 595, whoever had been excommunicated by his bishop, was to absent himself from court: his goods were confiscated, and conferred upon his relatives: more courageous bishops employed the weapon of excommunication even against kings. Thus Nicetius of Triers excommunicated Clothaire II, by whom he was therefore banished; and Germanus of Paris, in like manner, excommunicated Charibert, the son of Clothaire.

By presents from kings, from bishops, from nobles, and from every class of society, the Gallic Church in an early period acquired so great wealth, that, in the sixth century, king Childeric proclaimed, "Our revenue is impoverished: our riches have passed into the Church, and now only the bishops rule." The Church, in fact, granted out of its possessions benefices, for a yearly rent, in the same manner as did the kings; and as the bishops, and even abbots, possessed larger benefices, whole cities sometimes and entire districts, on the same conditions as those held by temporal antrustiones, they had their armed followers, their vassals, and friends, *(amici)*, whom they formed into troops, and who drew the sword often in private quarrels. The payment of tithes was required: they are first mentioned by the bishops of the province of Tours in 567, who exhort the people to pay the tenth of all their goods, even of their slaves: the council of Macon, in 585, commanded the payment of tithes under pain of excommunication. But they were not universally introduced before the following period. In general the property of the Church was not exempted from tax: some churches and monasteries enjoyed immunities by privilege: at one time Clothaire II exempted all the churches of his kingdom; whilst at another he exacted from them a third part of all their revenues.

All these circumstances concurred together to exalt the bishops to the highest influence in the state. The people honoured them, not only on religious grounds, but as their natural guardians also and their protectors; for under the oppression of an ill ordered, and often despotical government, the people were indebted, for nearly all the benefits which they enjoyed, to the power of their bishops. The bishops took their seats in the council of the king, which was composed of the nobles of the court and provinces. The great council, convened by Clothaire II, in 615, to deliberate on the most important affairs of the nation, was attended by the bishops and feudal lords,—the holders of royal benefices: this is the first mixed council *(concilium mixtum)* of this nature upon record. On account of their superior learning, the bishops also were employed as chancellors, as ambassadors, and in many other high offices of the state; they sat in the royal tribunals, and, in some cases, by royal appointment, held the chief magistracies in cities, as the bishop of Tours, who was named count of Tours, and the bishop of Maurienne, who by a grant of king Guntram obtained the lordship of the city of Suze. Thus was prepared the way to that high station, attained in later ages by the bishops. The relations of the Gallic Church, under the dominion of the Franks, with the see of Rome, remained as in former times. The popes continued, even at the request of the kings, to confer the authority of vicar-apostolic on the bishops of Arles. That the right of appeals was still acknowledged is shewn from the history of the bishops, Sagittarius of Gap and Salonius of Embrun, who having been deposed by a synod, went to Rome, with the permission of king Guntram, and were restored by pope John III. They were again deposed after some years, but in consequence of new crimes. Synods were held, not only by the papal vicars, but were convened also immediately by the popes. Queen Brunhilde, in 602, requested Gregory the Great to send a representative empowered to hold a council: the great synod of Nantes, in 658, was assembled by order of the pope. When Leo, bishop of Sens, opposed the erection of a bishopric at Melun, which was intended by the king, he appealed to the decision of the pope, or of a synod to be called by him. Frequently were the popes requested by the kings to confirm foundations which they had instituted. But after the middle of the seventh century, when the country was thrown into confusion, and the Church disturbed, the communication with Rome appears to have been less frequent; the authority of the metropolitans, which had been supported by the councils which they were accustomed to convene, was weakened when these councils ceased.

In Spain also, on account of the connexion of the Church with the West-Goth states, the Catholic sovereigns soon began to interfere with the hitherto free election of bishops. The fourth council of Toledo, in 633, decreed indeed that bishops should be elected, according to ancient usage, by the clergy and people, and that the election should be ratified by the metropolitan: but, soon after this period, it appears to have been the practice, that the king should select one from a list of names sent to him, and the twelfth synod of Toledo, in 681, empowered the bishop of that city, as he was near the person of the king, to confirm the choice which the king should make with his advice, and that he should consecrate the person elected: the new bishop was required to present himself to his metropolitan within three months after his consecration. After the year 589, the national synods were convened by the command or with the permission of the sovereign: the canons were, by his confirmation, made laws of the state, and the transgression of them was therefore punished, not only by ecclesiastical, but also by civil pains. The Spanish synods permitted an appeal to the king in ecclesiastical affairs. The thirteenth synod of Toledo declared it to be lawful to appeal from one metropolitan to another, and from him to the king. But nowhere were the political influence and power of bishops greater than in Spain. The Spanish bishops, in the synod of 633, determined the order of succession to the throne, which had not yet been regulated by law: they decreed that the successor of a deceased monarch should be chosen in a council of bishops and nobles. The next synod, in 636, pronounced excommunication upon him, who, without an unanimity of voices in his election, should seek to seize the crown. From this period the synods were formal assemblies of the state, in which civil laws were made, and the most important affairs of the kingdom considered. Secular nobles and palatines (officers of state), who accompanied the king to the synods, and whose consent to their acts is mentioned by the sixth council of Toledo, in 633, took a conspicuous part in the deliberations of the eighth council, in 653, in political matters, and subscribed the decrees. The seventeenth council, in 694, ordained that on the first three days of the synods, only ecclesiastical affairs should be discussed without the presence of laics, and that then the deliberations on the affairs of the state should commence. These assemblies, in which the numerous body of the bishops, whose office obliged them always to be present, possessed a decided superiority over the few nobles, who were called according to the caprice of the king, were in reality a limitation of the regal power: the king was accustomed to present to the council, in writing, the subjects of deliberation; but he was bound to respect and to observe its decisions. Excommunication was threatened, if he should presume to violate them: such at least was the threat of the thirteenth synod of Toledo, which accompanied its decree against the employment of torture.

The relations of the Spanish Church with the see of Rome, appear to have been so far altered after the conversion of the West-Goths, that then the nomination of apostolic vicars ceased. But the right of appeal continued in all its force. When in 603, Januarius of Malaga and Stephen of Oreto, who had been deposed by a synod, appealed to Gregory the Great, this pontiff sent into Spain, John Defensor, as papal judge; he restored Januarius to his church, deposed the usurper, and sentenced all the bishops who had taken part in this unjust proceeding to solitude and penance. The West-Goth bishops, in the decrees of their synods, appealed to the authority of the papal laws, and to the decisions with which the popes had replied to interrogatories of the Spanish prelates.

In the kingdom of the Lombards, after the conversion of the Arian people, and after the succession of Catholic to Arian kings, there arose no direct connexion of the Church with the State. The bishops took no part in civil affairs, not even in the eighth century, when there were amongst them many of Lombard descent. Even the Arian bishops — for in the Lombard cities there were for a long time Arian and Catholic bishops — possessed no political authority, and it does not appear that the kings regularly exercised any influence in the election of the prelates. When king Agilulf, who was then still an Arian, after the death of Constantius, bishop of Milan, sought to direct the Milanese in the choice of his successor, Gregory the Great wrote to them declaring that he never would recognize a bishop who had been elected by Lombard influence. An example of a synod convened by a Lombard king is presented to us by that which the Catholic Cunibert assembled at Pavia in 690: at this council the bishops who still adhered to the schism of Aquileia, returned to Catholic unity: with the co-operation of the king, both parties sent an embassy to pope Sergius, and the late schismatics acknowledged him to be the supreme head of the Church.

SECTION VIII.

CELIBACY.

As our Saviour Christ, who was born of a virgin mother, extolled the state of virginity, when it was chosen for the sake of the kingdom of heaven; as the apostles forsook all things, even their wives, to follow their Divine master, and to serve him more perfectly; so, from the very beginning of the Christian Church, it has been an universal principle, that they were the most proper for the priesthood, who, to offer the holy sacrifice with a becoming purity, and to present themselves to their faithful flocks as models of the most difficult virtues; and who, to attend to the obligations of their sacred calling freely and undisturbed, lived in perpetual continency. As a second marriage, after the death of a wife, generally bespoke a defect of continency, St. Paul (1 Tim. iii. 2, 12), forbade that a person, who had been thus twice married, should be ordained, even as a deacon. That a successive, not a simultaneous bigamy, is here spoken of, is shown, both by the nature of the case itself,—for he who lived in simultaneous bigamy, or adultery, would not have merited the name of Christian; and, again, by a similar ordinance of the apostle (v. 9), that those widows should be elected deaconesses, who had been the wives of only one husband. From the times of the apostles, it had been an universal observance, and it soon became an express law, that no priest could marry after his ordination; should he do so, he was immediately degraded, as it was decreed in 314, by the council of Neocæsaria, in its first canon: nor can an example of the contrary be produced. The want, indeed, of a sufficiency of unmarried, virtuous men, obliged the Church to receive amongst her ministers many persons who were in the married state: they then generally separated themselves from their wives; this was, however, not required by law, but was left to the conscience of each individual. By the synod of Ancyra, it was permitted to deacons to marry after their ordination, only upon condition that the bishop was willing to ordain them, after they had declared their intention of so doing. According to Socrates and Sozomen, it was proposed, at the council of Nice, that all ecclesiastics who had been married before their ordination, should live separate from their wives; but, at the proposition of the Egyptian bishop Paphnutius, the council determined that this subject should be left, as it had before been, to the free choice of each person. Hence, the synod of Gangra defended the cause of married priests, against the Eustathians, who, as they rejected matrimony, forbad married priests to offer the holy sacrifice.

St. Jerome asserts, that in the Egyptian and Syrian Churches, celibacy was universally practised by the clergy. The same is asserted by St. Epiphanius of the Church in general; but his words, "this is the custom wherever the laws of the Church are duly observed," prove to us that a contrary practice had extended itself in the east. That in Egypt, the bishops, at least, lived in perfect continency, is proved by the case of Synesius, who refused to become bishop of Ptolemais, because he would have been required to live separate from his wife. The assertion, therefore, of Socrates, that bishops, even after their consecration, were the fathers of children, must be confined to the patriarchate of Constantinople, to which this historian belonged; in this patriarchate, in the diocese of Pontus, St. Gregory Nazianzen was born, after his father had for some time been bishop. A relaxation of discipline, and degeneracy of morals, now assumed the ascendency in the east; and the council of Trullo, which was held by the bishops of the Constantinopolitan patriarchate, in 692, adhered only to an appearance of the ancient discipline, for it, in fact, destroyed ecclesiastical celibacy. It, indeed, declared the marriage of a priest, contracted after his ordination, to be invalid; but it declared, also, that only bishops were required to live in perfect celibacy, and that their wives were to reside in cloisters, at a distance from them;

that priests and deacons were not obliged to promise continency at their ordination, and that there was no impediment to cohabitation with their wives: it was required, only, that they should live continently during the time of their ministry at the altar. This has since continued to be the discipline of the Greek Church.

Far different was the practice of the west. The Spanish synod of Alvira, about the year 306, decreed, that all ecclesiastics who should refuse to separate from their wives, whom they had espoused before their ordination, should be deposed. This severe discipline continued to be the law of the entire western Church: it was absolutely required, by the popes Siricius and Innocent I: and if, according to Socrates, perfect continency was observed by all ecclesiastics of the higher orders in Thessaly, Macedonia, and Achaia, this was because these provinces formed part of the Roman patriarchate, in which St. Jerome states, that celibacy was practised in its fullest extent, as in the Churches of Syria and Egypt. The African Church followed the same discipline. Two synods of Carthage, the second in 390, and the fifth in 401, renewed the laws, commanding the entire celibacy of the clergy, appealing to the apostolical ordinances, and to the usages of the ancient Church. So obligatory was the law on this point, that St. Augustin could appeal to the example of priests, who had been ordained against their will, but who willingly bore the heavy weight of continency. That this law was frequently violated, we know, from the complaints of St. Ambrose, and from the interrogatories of many Gallic and Spanish bishops, addressed to the popes; and, in truth, the virtue of ecclesiastics must have been firm, and the grace of God in them must have been powerful, which enabled them to comply with a law, of which the pope St. Leo I said: "that without separating themselves from wives whom they had married before ordination, it was difficult for them to live with them as sisters, and to transform their former carnal, into a spiritual marriage." But the Church would not relax the severity of its law: it sought to avoid it, by admitting, as seldom as possible, married persons to holy orders.

The purity requisite for the oblation of the holy sacrifice, and the administration of the sacraments, was the chief foundation of the law of celibacy. The oriental Church acknowledged this, but thought, particularly after the Trullan synod, that this duty should be left to the conscience of each individual, and the more, as its priests were not every day called to the altar. In the Latin Church, on the contrary, the law of celibacy was extended, in the fourth century, to subdeacons, as they were then employed in the service of the altar. This law was first made in Africa: in Spain and Sicily, subdeacons, as late as the sixth century, were permitted to live with wives, married before ordination. But the synod of Toledo, in 527, prohibited this in Spain, and in Sicily it was prohibited by Pope Pelagius II.

SECTION IX.

ASCETICS AND ANCHORETS.—THE ORIGIN OF MONASTERIES.—SPREAD OF THE MONASTIC INSTITUTE IN THE EAST AND WEST.—THE BENEDICTINE ORDER. —CLOISTERS OF NUNS.*

The necessity of leading a life in the greatest possible abstraction from earthly things, in a communion with God, uninterrupted and undisturbed by this external

---

* J. Cassiani Opera, ed. Al. Gazæus; Atrebati, 1628, folio.—Palladii, Historia Lausiaca, in Cotelerii Monum. Eccl. Græcæ, tom. iii.— Theodoreti, Historia Religiosa, Opp. ed Schulze, tom. iii.—J. Moschi, Pratum Spirituale, in Cotelerii Monum. tom. ii.—Gregorii Magni, Vita S. Benedicti, seu Dialogorum Liber II, in Actis Sanctorum Ord. S. Benedicti, edid. D'Archery et Mabillon; Paris, 1668, 9 vols. folio, tom. i.—Luc. Holstenii, Codex Regularum Monasticarum, ed. Mar. Brockie.

Alteserræ, Asceticon, seu, Origines Rei Monasticæ; Paris, 1674, 4to. —Martene, De Antiquis Monachorum Ritibus; Lugd. 1690.—Mabillon, Annales Ord. S. Benedicti; Paris 1706, 5 vols. folio.

world, and of working out salvation far from its troubled and troubling scenes, is purely Christian. In its every form, the monastic life belongs essentially to the Christian religion, and has always been found in it. From the times of the apostles, there had been virgins, laymen, and ecclesiastics named Ascetics, who sought to remove themselves from the corruption and contagion of the world, who, dedicating themselves to exercises of most fervent piety, lived in continency, renounced all worldly possessions, and subjected themselves to rigorous and almost continual fasts. The ancient fathers designated this kind of life, which appeared to approach nearest to the ideal of evangelical perfection, by the name of the higher Christian philosophy. This word, when used in the sense in which it was employed by antiquity, does not signify a mere speculative system, but a life regulated by the first principles of truth. It is related of many martyrs, that they bore the pangs of the Roman torture the more courageously, the more they had inured themselves to sufferings by their ascetic lives. As these primitive ascetics, although they sometimes resided in cities, and even within the circle of their own families, had learned to free themselves from the bonds of ordinary life, so there were many others about the middle of the third century, who were driven at first by the persecution, or were afterwards led by inclination, into the desart, and thus first formed in Egypt the anchoretic mode of life. Thus Paul, about the year 251, fled into the Desart of Thebais; and about 270, there were many hermits, who dwelt not in the wilderness, but in the neighbourhood of villages. At that time, the Egyptian Anthony, admonished by the words of our Lord (Matth. xix. 21), sold his rich possessions, and distributed the price to the poor; he then placed himself under these ascetic hermits, and in 285, after he had passed fifteen years of severe mortification and of severer temptations, he crossed the Nile, to the desart on the shores of the Red Sea, where, sometimes visited by his friends, he spent twenty years in acts of penance and prayer. The fame of his wisdom, and of the miracles which he wrought, drew many persons around him, who became his disciples and imitators, and lived, under his direction, in separate dwellings. When, in 311, he went to Alexandria, to console the persecuted Christians, and again, in 325, to oppose the progress of Arianism, he was honoured and admired even by the pagans, many of whom he converted to the faith. The community of virgins over which his sister presided, is the first of the kind recorded by history. Amon, a contemporary and friend of Anthony, founded, in the region of Nitria, in Upper Egypt, communities of holy men, who lived in separate cells, but who, on Sundays, met to celebrate the divine mysteries; before the end of the century, their numbers amounted to five thousand. The holy Hilarion, a disciple of Anthony, chose for his abode the desart between Gaza and Egypt. The fame of his sanctity, attracted many into his wilderness, to follow his guidance in a spiritual life, so that when he visited their cells, he found himself surrounded by two thousand brethren. The desart of Scete also, in Egypt, soon after St. Macarius had selected it for his solitude, became peopled with hermits.

All these holy men lived as hermits: monasteries were first founded by St. Pachomius. By means of the hermit Palæmon, who had been trained in the severe discipline and the exercises of the fervent piety of the Egyptian anchorets, he formed, in 325, a community at Tabenna in Upper Thebais, and soon after, eight other cloisters, to which he gave the rule, which has been preserved in the Latin translation of St. Jerome. The monks were divided into different classes, according to their occupations and employments: a procurator attended to the temporal affairs of the order: a noviciate, or state of probation, was soon introduced. Manual labour occupied a great portion of their time, and its produce supported the brethren, of whom only a few, at least at the time of their entrance into the order, were priests.

From Egypt the claustral institute passed into Palestine; and during the fourth century flourishing monasteries arose on mount Sinai and in the desart of Raithu, not far from mount Horeb. About the year 580, St. John Climacus, abbot of a cloister on mount Sinai, dedicated his work, *The Ladder*, to the abbot of Raithu. In Syria, Charito founded first at Pharan, and then at Suca, a *laura*, that is, an union of many distinct cells, the inhabitants of which assembled on Saturdays and Sundays in the Church of the laura to offer the holy sacrifice. Mesopotamia and Persia received the cœnobitic order of life from Syria: into Armenia and Paphligonia it was introduced by Eustathius, bishop of Sebaste: St. Basil was its chief promoter in Cappadocia and Pontus. This great saint drew up a rule for his disciples,—for those who lived in community as well as for those who dwelt in solitude.

Those anchorets, who continued with the cœnobites, but who, after having been formed in the cloisters, frequently retired to attain to a higher degree of perfection in solitude, lived in caves, in cells, and even in tombs, were named *Memoritai*. When many dwelt together in a desart in separate cells, at a short distance from each other, the residence was denominated a laura. Some of these holy men, after St. Simon Stylites had set them the example about the year 440, lived in prayer under the open heaven, on the summits of columns. Soon after St. Simon, the holy Daniel lived in this manner in the neighbourhood of Constantinople. Others, without any fixed abode, lived upon the mountains, supporting themselves upon wild herbs: others enclosed themselves in narrow cells, in which they remained during the whole of their lifes. But the most holy men, and the greatest fathers of the Church, gave the preference to the life of monks in community. There was also an intermediate kind of monks, named Sarabaites, who lived together in parties of two and three, without any superior: by their contentions and vanity, and by their excesses, which were often mingled with their fasts, they obtained for themselves a discreditable reputation.

In the west, St. Athanasius, during the time in which he sought refuge in Rome, to excited an inclination towards the monastic life, by his descriptions of the life of St. Anthony, and by the monks, who had accompanied his flight. St. Jerome makes mention of the nunneries, and great numbers of monks, who were at Rome in his time. At Vercelli, the holy bishop Eusebius introduced the severe discipline of the oriental monks amongst his clergy, both by his word and his example. Before the gate of Milan there was a cloister of monks, under the protection of St. Ambrose. Many of the smaller Italian islands had already been peopled with anchorets. In Gaul, St. Martin of Tours founded the first monastery. When his corpse was borne to burial, it was accompanied by two thousand monks. About the same time, (the end of the fourth century), the first cloisters arose in Africa, at Carthage, Tegaste and Hippo; and the Donatists, who objected to the introduction of the monastic life to St. Augustin, asked of him, where in the Scriptures there was mention of a monk? This great doctor had, when a priest, founded a cloister at Hippo, in which, with other clerics, he lived in humility and in a community of goods: when bishop, his episcopal residence was converted into a cloister for ecclesiastics.

Monks both in the east and in the west were originally only laymen, and a long time seems to have passed before the monastic was united with the ecclesiastical state; for, according to the canons, a priest could be ordained only for a particular church. But in the greater monasteries, which were at a distance from an episcopal or parish church, the want of priests was soon felt; and as by a law of Theodosius the Great, in 392, it was granted to monks to settle in cities, there soon arose in the greater cities of the east large monasteries, of which the superiors, (archimandrites), were generally priests. In general, however, monks were enumerated amongst laymen, as at the council of Chalcedon. But the cloisters might be considered as seminaries for clergy. A law of the emperor Arcadius had exhorted the bishops to select, in case of necessity, their clergy from amongst the monks; and they did so the more willingly as the popes (Siricius and later pontiffs) had counselled them in like manner. In a short time, the bishops, through the whole of the east, were chosen by preference from the cloisters; and the sixth *novella* of Justinian says, in a few words, that bishops should be selected from the clergy or from the monks.

Persons connected with the tribunals were excluded by imperial laws from the ecclesiastic and monastic state, unless they surrendered their property to others, who would perform their duties. Neither slaves, without the permission of their masters, nor spouses without mutual consent, nor children, without the approbation of their parents, dared to enter into a cloister. A law of Justinian seems to have granted to either spouse the right of separation without the consent of the other party; but this was never sanctioned, at least in the west, by any law of the Church. That children who had been consecrated to a cloister by their parents might return to the world, when arrived at the age of discretion, was forbidden by the fourth council of Toledo, contrary certainly to the spirit of the Church at all other times.

A particular form or colour of dress was not usual amongst the monks: in the east, the disciples of St. Pachomius appear to have distinguished themselves by their habit. The monks in the west wore the ordinary dress of the country, but of coarser materials. Vows were not yet introduced. The rule of a monk was, that he should be poor, without possessions, and should support himself by the labour of his hands. Those who entered monasteries generally distributed their wealth amongst the poor: the Egyptian monks in particular adhered so strictly to poverty that their cloisters possessed no goods or revenues. Whatever was given to them they bestowed immediately on the indigent. Bodily labour was enforced amongst them, and the dangers of idleness to monks were most forcibly pourtrayed in the works of the spiritual writers of the age. St. Augustin wrote a work expressly to prove the duty of labour amongst monks. The poor were entitled to all the produce of their labour, which was not necessary for their immediate support. Perpetual chastity was only tacitly promised: but, although perfection might not be acquired by some in their cloisters, it was not permitted, or rather it was considered criminal, to return again to a worldly life. The council of Chalcedon pronounced excommunication against any monk or nun who should marry. Immediate and willing obedience to superiors was deemed the first duty of the monastic state: the monk, as St. Basil says, was to deprive himself of his own will, and to follow, with unconditional confidence, the guidance of his superiors. These superiors were named abbots, hegumeni, and archimandrites: they possessed supreme authority within their monasteries; they regulated the order of the Divine worship and of the public prayers; they watched over discipline and decreed punishments. They were also the spiritual directors of their monks. The punishments which they inflicted were temporary deprivation of the sacraments, corporal chastisements; and, if these failed, expulsion from the monastery. But both abbots and monks were subject to the bishops. By the fourth canon of the council of Chalcedon, it was sanctioned that cloisters should not be erected without the permission of the bishop of the diocese, whose duty it was to protect and watch over them when erected. Complaints against the monks were to be laid before the bishop. In the west, also, monasteries were under the same episcopal jurisdiction.

A flourishing colony of monks was established on the island of Lerins, on the coast of Provence, where Honoratus, afterwards bishop of Arles, founded the first monastery in 410. From the same cloister, of the inmates of which some lived in community, and some as anchorets, there came forth the pride of the Gallic Church, Hilary of Arles, Lupus, bishop of Troyes, Valerian, bishop of Cimelia, Vincent, the author of the well-known *Commonitorium*, and other great men. About the same time, Cassianus, who had lived in a monastery at Bethlehem, and had thence passed into Egypt to reside with the holy hermits there, founded two cloisters at Marseilles. He was in the west the classic author of the monastic institute: he collected in two works the result of his observation. In one of these works, the *Institutions,* he describes the manner of life, and the regulations of the oriental monks: the other, the *Conferences,* contains his conversations with the anchorets of Scete on a contemplative life, and on continual prayer. The orientals possessed similar works in the writings of St. Nilus, who, after many years of an eremitical life in the desart of Scete, died about the year 430; and in *The Sacred Ladder,* of St. John Climacus, who was abbot on mount Sinai about the year 580. This work describes the different degrees and virtues of a spiritual life.

We have seen that the cloisters were, as schools of preparation for the clerical state, of the greatest service to the Church This was kept in view by St. Patrick, who had himself been formed in the monastery at Tours, in all those which he founded in Ireland, and it continued to be one of the principal objects of those which arose after his death. Ailbe, Fiech of Sletty, Mel of Ardagh, Moitheus of Louth and others, founded similar cloisters or seminaries, towards the close of the fifth century. In western Britain, the great abbey of Bangor contained, in the sixth century, in each of its seven divisions, three hundred monks, who lived by the labour of their own hands. In Ireland, also, there was a numerously peopled monastery of the same name, from which went forth St. Columban, the founder of the abbies of Luxeu, Fontaines and Bobbio. His rule, which was observed in most of the monasteries of Gaul, before the introduction of St. Benedict's, and which was the only one in the north of Italy as late as the ninth century, was approved by the Gallic bishops at the synod of Macon, in 624, notwithstanding the objections that were raised against it by a monk named Agrestius. From this we may learn what was the order of life in the numerous cloisters of Ireland. Unconditional obedience, silence, abstinence from all flesh meats, and the procuring their own support by labour, were the chief duties of the religious. A considerable time was dedicated in the Irish monasteries to study, to the transcription of books, and to the duty of teaching. In Gaul, Cæsarius of Arles had formed a rule, about the year 520, according to which, all the monks lived together in one large apartment, and divided their time between prayer, study and labour. The merit of having made the duty of transcribing books an ordinary occupation of monks, is due to the learned chancellor Cassiodorus, who founded two monasteries at Squillace, his native city, one for cœnobites, the other for hermits, and who himself died a monk, about the year 565.

But all the monastic institutes of the west were obscured, and gradually destroyed, by the order of St. Benedict. This patriarch of the western monks was born in the territory of Mursia in Umbria, about the year 480. In his youth, he retired into a solitary cave at Subiaco, where for three years he lived in entire concealment. As soon as he became known, many were attracted by his sanctity, and in 520 he founded twelve monasteries, each with twelve religious, all of whom were under his direction. Roman senators entrusted their sons to him: two of these youths, Placidus and Maurus, became his most worthy disciples, the former of whom carried the rule of his master into Sicily, the latter into Gaul. In 529, St. Benedict founded the celebrated abbey of Monte Cassino, which was plundered by the Lombards, forty years after its erection; he established some time after the monastery of Terracina. He was visited in his solitude by Totila, the king of the Goths, and died in 543.

Until this period an uniform rule had been observed in few monasteries. They possessed the rules of St. Basil, of Macarius and Pachomius, the Institutions of Cassian, the lives of the Egyptian and Syrian anchorets, the traditions of their founders, and first superiors: from all these an order of life was drawn, in which the precepts and customs depended on the good will of the abbot, and on the greater or less zeal of the monks. The monasteries, therefore, did not present an uniform, nor an entirely different method of life but by this partial dissimilarity, they were soon divided into distinct orders. The rule of St. Benedict, therefore, wrought a great change, for he obliged his disciples by a solemn vow to observe it, and as it was preferred to all others in the west, it was introduced into all new establishments, and was soon adopted in the more ancient. St. Benedict endeavoured to make a monk, by an abstraction from the things of the world, by a separation from external temptations and cares, by poverty, labour and obedience, by daily contemplation and continual prayer, a sincere adorer of his God in spirit and truth. Only the humble and persevering suppliant could be received in the cloister, and admitted after a noviciate of a year to the solemn and irrevocable obligation of his vows: even priests passed through this probation, but they were in rank next to the abbot. At midnight the nocturnal office was sung; and during the day, the religious met seven times in the church to chant the other parts of the office and to pray. Seven hours of the day were dedicated to the labour assigned to each one by the superior, two hours to study, and the rest of the day to relaxation and repose. From their simple but sufficient diet, flesh meat was excluded. The monks wore the ordinary dress of the poor and peasants. No one possessed property: all things, even their dress, belonged to the monastery, and that the religious might more readily hasten to the church at the first signal, they slept in their habits. The punishments in use were, separation from the community, corporal chastisements, and lastly, expulsion: the expelled brother could, however, be received again three times, if he shewed repentance for his fault. The abbot was chosen by all: he named the prior and the dean (*decanus*, superior of ten): in affairs of difficulty he sometimes consulted the whole community, but was not bound to follow their advice.

The rule of St. Benedict was at first received entire by only a few monasteries. An ancient tradition tells us that it was first given to the monastery of Glanfeuil, on the Loire, by St. Maurus. In other places, it was adopted according to choice, and in part with other rules. The pope St. Gregory the Great, although, in his life of St. Benedict, he highly extols his rule, seems not to have introduced it entire into his cloister of St. Andrew, in Rome. This house was intended to be a seminary for priests and missionaries; and hence St. Gregory devoted to study the time allotted by St. Benedict to labour. The cloister which his disciple St. Augustin founded in Canterbury, followed, we are told by pope Honorius, the rule of St. Gregory. The same might be said of the filiations of this parent house in England, whilst the monks in North Britain adhered to the rule which the Irish St. Columban had established on the island of Hy. In Spain, we find vestiges of only a partial adoption of the Benedictine rule, before the eighth century, so that the great diffusion and prevalence of this rule must have commenced in the next period.

The jurisdiction of bishops over monasteries was still undiminished: the privileges which bishops granted to particular monasteries, and which popes and kings sometimes confirmed, regarded the free election of the abbot or the protection of the property belonging to them. The first exemption from the spiritual jurisdiction of the bishop recorded in history, is that granted in 670, by the pope Adeodatus, to the monastery of St. Martin of Tours: but as the pope himself says, in the grant, it was contrary to the practice and tradition of the see of Rome, and was made only at the instance of the bishop of Tours and other bishops. The synod of Carthage, in 525, had contracted the jurisdiction of bishops over cloisters in Africa, and had transferred the immediate jurisdiction to the primate of Carthage: in the patriarchate of Constantinople, also, we find several cloisters, in the seventh century, exempted from the jurisdiction of the bishop of the diocese, and subjected to the patriarch, or to an exarch, delegated by him for the government of monasteries. This connexion of the patriarch was made known by the erection, at the cloister, of the patriarchal cross.

Virgins consecrated to God existed in great numbers

in the earliest ages. They lived with their relatives, but their obligation to perpetual chastity was inviolable, and a violation of it was designated, by St. Cyprian, as no less a crime than adultery against their spouse Jesus Christ. A virgin, who wished to dedicate herself to God, professed her intention in the church, before the bishop, and received from him the virginal habit, to which the veil, and a head dress *(mitrella)* of gold, particularly belonged. If she should afterwards marry, she was excommunicated, according to a canon of the council of Chalcedon; and the man who should marry her was declared, by a law of Jovinian, punishable with death. The consecration of such a virgin was reserved to the bishop: in Africa, it might be performed by a priest, to whom the bishop had granted permission. If more ancient canons, (such as those of the third synod of Carthage), require that the age of the virgin to be consecrated, should be from seventeen to twenty-five years, it is certain that the age of forty years was required by later councils of Gaul and Spain.

Cloisters for nuns arose at the same time with cœnobia for monks. The sisters of the saints Anthony and Pachomius, were superioresses of female communities. St. Pachomius compiled a rule for women, whose occupations were to be similar to those of religious men; and when he speaks of cloisters which followed in common his rule, we are to understand cloisters of men and of women, which were near to each other and separated only by a river. In the time of Theodoret there were many cloisters, each containing two hundred and fifty nuns, who employed themselves in manual occupations, particularly in weaving wool. In the west, these communities are mentioned about the end of the fourth century. St. Augustin, whose sister presided over one of them, composed a rule for nuns, by which they were placed under the direction of a superioress, (called in Syria *Amma*, mother) and of a priest, but principally of the bishop. In Gaul, the rule of St. Cæsarius of Arles was generally observed. In the east, the hair of the virgin entering the cloister was cut off, a practice not observed in the west. Besides the nuns living in community, there was still many virgins consecrated to God, who resided in their own families: this we learn from a canon of the fifth synod of Orleans, which mentions also, that enclosure was observed in some, but not in all communities, and that the noviciate continued for a year. Marriage was forbidden to nuns, and declared invalid, by many synods in Gaul. St. Gregory the Great, in whose time there was three thousand nuns in Rome, decreed that to each cloister there should be attached an experienced priest, that the nuns might attend to the duties of their vocation, undisturbed by temporal affairs. At first, these cloisters possessed only domestic oratories, and the nuns went on Sundays to the public church: after the sixth century, however, they had their own churches, that every occasion of passing the threshold of their house might be taken away. In the east, and in Spain, the cloisters of monks and nuns were united, and were called double monasteries, that the religious of each might mutually assist each other by their labours. Justinian forbade monasteries of this kind to be divided.

SECTION X.

COLLECTIONS OF CANONS.—BOOKS OF ECCLESIASTICAL LAW IN THE GREEK AND LATIN CHURCHES.*

The Church, in its first ages, was governed, not by written laws, but by the traditions of the apostles, and of their immediate and most holy successors. The most ancient work, in which the laws, customs, and ordinances of the Church are contained, are the first six

---

* Voelli et Justelli, Bibliotheca Juris Canonici Veteris; Paris, 1661, 2 vols. folio.—Beveregii, Synodicon, seu Pandectæ canonum ab Ecclesia Græca receptorum; Oxonii, 1672, 2 vols. folio.—Jos. Sim. Assemanni, Bibliotheca Juris Orientalis Canonici; Rom. 1762-60. 3 vols. 4to.

Sylloge, De vetustis Canonum Collectionibus collegit Andr. Gallandius; Venet. 1778. folio.

books of the so-named *Apostolical Constitutions*, of which the author, probably a Syrian bishop, or priest, who lived towards the close of the third century, has presented, in the form of apostolical epistles, the duties of ecclesiastics and of laymen, the sacred mysteries, the festivals, and the Christian doctrine, in opposition to the prevailing heresies of the time. They are, in all appearance, the same as the "apostolical teaching" ($διδαχη$), which, St. Athanasius says, was read to the catechumens and neophytes. Some time later, but before the council of Nice, a seventh book was compiled, of almost similar contents, with the addition of liturgical formularies; it was, at first, a separate work, and by a different author. Finally, in the fourth century, the eighth book, an episcopal ritual, or pontifical, was added to the preceding.

The first synods, the canons of which were received into later collections, are those of Ancyra and Neocæsarea (314). But the greatest authority was always attached, both in the east and in the west, to the canons of the council of Nice, and next, to those of the council of Antioch, of the year 332 or 341. These were followed by the decision of the synod, held, at what time is uncertain, at Gangra, in Paphlagonia. At the time of the council of Chalcedon, the authority of another collection, composed of the same materials, had been widely extended; and at the council, canons, which were appealed to, were read from it. In the same manner, the canons of anterior councils (consequently the canons of the councils of 381 and of 431, the former of which were cited at Constantinople), were confirmed in their authority as laws. Hence, the Codex, of which many bishops at the council had copies, was acknowledged as an authentic book of ecclesiastical law. About the time of the council of Chalcedon, the first collection, containing fifty, of apostolical canons, appears to have been compiled. The author, who also probably was a Syrian, borrowed much from the apostolical constitutions, and from the decrees passed at Antioch, and who has collected much that belonged to the apostolic times.

second, third, and fourth centuries, to gain greater authority for his work, attributed it to the apostles. By a later addition, by another hand, the number of canons was made to amount to eighty-five. In the collections made after the year 451, after the canons of Chalcedon, came the decrees of the council of Laodicea, which were only an abridgment of others more ancient than those of Constantinople, Ephesus, and Sardica. All these, together with eighty-six canons of St. Basil, and the eighty-five apostolical canons, were comprised in a collection by Joannes Scholasticus, first a priest of Antioch, and in 565, patriarch of Constantinople. The imperial laws, on ecclesiastical affairs, were collected in 534, in the Codex of Justinian. Of the later *novellæ* of Justinian, a compendium was given by the above named Joannes, in a collection of eighty-seven chapters. In the seventh century, appeared another extensive collection of the novellæ of Justinian and Heraclius. The Trullan synod, which was held in 692, as a supplement to the two last general councils, which had not decreed anything on ecclesiastical discipline, enumerated the canons which had the authority of laws in the Greek Church. They are, together with the apostolical canons, and those of the above councils, the laws of the African Church, as they were confirmed and promulgated by the synod of Carthage, in 419, and the canonical epistles of Dionysius and Peter of Alexandria, of Gregory Thaumaturgus, Athanasius, Basil, Gregory of Nyssa, Gregory Nazianzen, Amphilochius, Timotheus, Theophilus, Cyril and Gennadius, patriarch of Constantinople. To these, it added its own one hundred and two canons, the future fountain-head of Greek ecclesiastical law.

The Roman Church had for a long period no authentic collection of canons. Pope Innocent I (402-417) declared that the Apostolic See recognized no authority in any decrees of councils, other than those of the council of Nice. By these, we must understand also the canons of Sardica, which were considered as a continuation of the Nicene canons, and were often called by the same name. The popes promulgated their decrees at synods, or addressed them to metropolitans, by which means they became known: the Roman archive, in which they were preserved, rendered an authenticated codex unnecessary. Latin translations of the canons of oriental synods, had existed as the works of individuals, since the fifth century: as soon as they were adopted as books of law, the decretals of the popes were inserted in them. Before the time of Dionysius, there were three collections, which contained the canons and decretals. The *Collectio Prisca*, which appeared in Italy about the middle of the fifth century, comprehended only the canons of the oriental synods, with those of Sardica. The most celebrated work of this kind, in the west, was the collection of Dionysius Exiguus, a Scythian monk, who, at the desire of Stephan, bishop of Salona, about the year 525, brought into one collection, first fifty apostolical canons, then the decrees of oriental councils, as far as the Chalcedonian, in a new translation, and the Sardican and African canons. In a second part, edited later, he added the decretals of some of the popes, from Siricius to Anastasius II, who died in 498.

The Spanish Church had an ancient collection, which contained none of the apostolical canons, but in which were found the decrees of several Gallic councils. About the year 610, a new and more comprehensive collection was formed, perhaps by St. Isidore of Seville; it contained the oriental and African canons; the decrees of seventeen Gallic and fifteen Spanish synods; the papal decretals, from the time of Damasus; and was gradually enriched by the ordinances of later synods and popes. The Gallic Church possessed no authentic codex of canons, before the eighth century. The oriental and African canons were first reduced into systematic but compendious form, about the year 540, by the African deacon Fulgentius Ferrandus, in his *Breviatio Canonum*. In a still shorter form, we find the oriental canons in the collection of Martin, Bishop of Braga, about the year 570. Lastly, Cresconius, an African bishop, in 690, reduced the contents of the collection of Dio-

THE SACRAMENTS, WORSHIP AND DISCIPLINE OF THE AN-
CIENT CHURCH, DURING THE FIRST SEVEN CENTURIES,
OR THE FIRST AND SECOND PERIODS.

SECTION XI.—THE CATECHUMENATE, BAPTISM, AND CONFIRMATION.*

In the primitive ages of the Church, the apostles baptized their converts without any preparation, more than a profession of faith in Jesus Christ; but when the Church had acquired extension and form, the catechumenate was introduced as a state of trial and preparation. The reception into this state, was performed by the imposition of hands with prayer, and by signing the person to be received with the sign of the cross. The time of this probation was not always the same, and depended chiefly on the qualities and circumstances of the catechumen: for those, who, before their entrance into it, had been guilty of great crimes, or who committed them whilst in this state, the time was prolonged. In the fourth century, the catechumens, of their own will, deferred their baptism; and thus, many remained for years,—many even for their whole lives, out of the Church; some, perhaps, to live more freely,—others, in the hope, that if they received the sacrament in their last infirmity, they should depart this life pure from sin, and certain of their salvation. Hence, the frequent exhortations of the fathers to the catechumens, not to defer too long their serious preparation for baptism.

---

* C. Chardon, Histoire des Sacremens; Paris, 1745, 6 vols.—Jos. Vicecomitis, Observationes Eccl. de antiquis baptismi ritibus; Paris, 1618.—Jo. Morini, De Cathechumenorum expiatione et ad baptismi susceptionem præparatione, in ejusd. opp. posthumis; Paris, 1703, 4to.—G. Walli, Historia baptismi infantum, Latinè vert. Schlosser; Bremæ, 1748, 2 vols. 4to.—J. Sainte Bœuve, De Sacr. Confirmationis et Extremæ Unctionis; Paris, 1686, 4to.—Morini, De Sacr. Confirmationis, in opp. posthumis.—J. A. Orsi, De Charismate Confirmatorio; Mediol. 17 , 4to.

According to the synod of Elvira, and to one of the novellæ of Justinian, the ordinary period of the catechumenate, was two years; but, according to the Apostolical Constitutions, it was three years: by degrees, it was abridged; and the synod of Agde, in 506, prescribed eight months for a Jew. In danger of death, it was terminated at once by baptism.

The catechumenate was divided into three classes. In the first, were the *hearers;* a name which was afterwards applied in general to all. These were instructed in the first principles of faith, and assisted at the mass of catechumens; that is, they heard the lecture of the sacred Scriptures, and the exhortation of the bishop; after which, they were dismissed. The *kneeling*, those of the second class, remained during the following prayers, and received the episcopal benediction. The third class were the *elected* (*competentes*, $\phi\omega\tau\iota\zeta o\mu\epsilon\nu\alpha\iota$), who, having completed their probation, were destined to be baptized at the next ensuing solemnity. The profession of faith, and the Lord's prayer, were first made known to these, and were committed by them to memory. At first, the precise words of this prayer were not delivered to them, but were paraphrased. In the explanation of St. Augustin, however, we find the words themselves. Ordinarily, the mysteries of faith were first explained to the *competentes*. Forty days before Easter, their names were entered. By fasting, by prayer, by continency, and by a confession of their past sins, they prepared themselves to receive baptism. Now, also began the scrutinies or assemblies, for the purifying and probation of the *competentes;* these were at first seven, afterwards five, and for children three. In these scrutinies, it was customary to perform the exorcism on the catechumen, by prayer, by the invocation of the name of Christ, by signing with the cross, and by insufflations. At Rome, the chief scrutiny took place at the mass, on the Wednesdays of the four ember weeks: the catechumens were signed with the cross by their sponsors, and by the clergy; blessed salt was put into their mouths—a ceremony frequently repeated in

Africa: they were exorcised, their ears were opened, that is, touched, and the introduction to the four gospels was read to them. After this, the paper containing the symbol, was returned, and then followed the solemn profession of faith, and the recital of the Lord's prayer. When, in a later age, baptism was administered generally to children, these ceremonies, which originally were performed at different times, followed each other, in one action, at the baptism.

The catechists *(doctores audientium)* were commonly taken from the clergy; deacons and lectors were often employed, and sometimes laics. Directions for their use, are contained in the work of St. Augustin, *De Catechizandis Rudibus.* The *Catecheses* of St. Cyril of Jerusalem, show us the order and contents of their instructions. The *competentes* were instructed by the bishop himself, or by an experienced priest, in one or two discourses. Immediately after the baptism in Easter week, a knowledge of the practical mysteries, of the sacraments, and particularly of the eucharist, was imparted in a series of instructions to the neophytes. Of this kind, are the five mystagogic catecheses of St. Cyril, and the instructions of Gaudentius, bishop of Brescia, and of St. Augustin.

To the ceremonies immediately preceding baptism, belonged the washing of the head, which was performed on Palm Sunday, and of the feet, on Maundy Thursday. On the Saturday, a custom, as ancient as the times of the apostles, the renunciation (ἀποταξις) of Satan, his works, and angels, was practised. This renunciation was pronounced twice or thrice by the catechumen, standing, and turned towards the west; then, turning again to the east, he vowed his adherence to Christ. He was next anointed with exorcising oil: in the east, he was anointed over the whole body; but in the Latin Church, only on the head, on the breast, and between the shoulders. Lastly, he was interrogated on his faith of the principal articles of belief; of the Trinity, of the Catholic Church, of the remission of sins, and of the resurrection

In the first ages, baptism was administered in any place,—in houses, in prisons, or on rivers. After the cessation of the persecutions, it was conferred only in the baptisteries, which were circular buildings, divided from the Church, and generally on the south side. In large cities, they were so spacious, that councils were sometimes held in them; they had altars, at which mass was celebrated, and from which the communion was given to the neophytes. In the earlier centuries, each diocese possessed only one baptistery, which was connected with the cathedral. Only Rome possessed more than one—as until the end of the seventh century, only the bishops ordinarily baptized, or priests and deacons, by power received from them. In cases of extreme necessity, indeed, laics could baptize; but, according to the 38th canon of the council of Elvira, this power was confined to those who had not been twice married, and who had not violated their baptismal vows by deadly sin. In the west, the validity of baptism, conferred by laics, was universally acknowledged, but in the east, the power to baptize appears not to have been conceded to them. St. Basil expressly states, that baptism administered by a laic, should be repeated; and in the Apostolical Constitutions, baptism given by a woman is rejected in the strongest terms.

Baptism was administered by an entire immersion in water; this immersion was three times repeated, as expressive of the faith in the Trinity, a custom which was ascribed to an apostolical ordinance, or to a command of Christ. But St. Gregory the Great declared that a single immersion was valid, and even recommended it, in opposition to the Arians, who, by their three-fold immersion, wished to signify their belief in the essential distinction of the Father, and of the Son, and of the Holy Ghost. Hence, the synod of Toledo, in 633, decreed, that the counsel of the pope should be considered as a law. In the east, on the contrary, Eunomius, who referred his baptism only to the death of Christ, was the first who introduced the single immersion; so that there the Church, as we see in the 50th of the Apostolical canons, forbad this kind of baptism under pain of deposition. Baptism, by immersion, continued to be the prevailing practice of the Church, as late as the fourteenth century. Infirm persons, to whom immersion would have been dangerous, were baptized by having the water poured on the head, or on the body *(baptismus clinicorum)*; but many synods declared, that those who had been thus baptized, as they had been induced to receive the sacrament only by the fear of danger, were rendered incapable of being received amongst the clergy. The baptismal water was consecrated by a blessing, of which St. Cyprian makes mention, and which St. Basil ascribes to an ordinance of the apostles; this blessing at first consisted of prayers, of the sign of the cross, and an invocation of the Trinity; in later ages, there were added the insufflations which accompany exorcisms, the mingling of the sacred chrism, and the immersion of the paschal candle. To this water, the fathers ascribed a peculiar power of purification and benediction: the faithful took it to their houses, and employed in in various benedictions.

That baptism was administered in the earliest ages, in the name of the three Divine persons, we learn from the testimony of St. Justin. The anointing with chrism, after the immersion (the introduction of which was attributed by the Pontifical Book to St. Silvester), first mentioned by Innocent I, was not generally employed, and was unknown in the Greek Church. The neophyte then received a wax taper, which he lighted, and for eight days was clothed in long white garments. As a sign of brotherly love, and of reception into the Church, the faithful (in the west), kissed him, and gave him blessed milk and honey, or wine and honey, to taste: in some churches, the washing of feet followed these ceremonies. Godfathers, who presented the catechumen to be baptized, and who received him coming from the water *(susceptores)*, and who gave pledges of his future faith *(sponsores)*, are mentioned in the second century. The adoption, at baptism, of a new Christian name, which was generally that of an apostle, or a martyr, was not universal; but many examples of it may be found. Solemn baptism was generally administered at Easter, and afterwards at Pentecost, and on the eve of the festival. Pope Siricius prohibited the administration of solemn baptism on the festival of an apostle or martyr. The custom of baptizing on the Epiphany, was condemned by the synod of Auxerre, in 578; but in the east, and in Africa, baptism was usually administered on that day.

Baptism of infants, is declared by Origen to have been a custom extending as far as the times of the apostles. St. Irenæus presupposes this practice, when he speaks of the regeneration, not only of adults, but also of infants. Tertullian, indeed, advised that baptism should be conferred in a mature age; but the synod of Carthage, in 252, decreed that children should be baptized as soon as possible, without waiting even for the eighth day. But this was not generally practised: St. Gregory of Nazianzen wished baptism to be administered to children in the third year of their age: and in the Churches of Thessaly, and also in Spain, and in Gaul, it was the custom, when no danger threatened, to defer the baptism of children to the festival of Easter.

The difference of opinion, as to the validity of baptism administered by heretics, continued for a long time after the controversy which arose in the middle of the third century. The question was decided by the council of Arles, in 314, and according to its decree, that baptism was to be considered valid, when it was conferred in the name of the Trinity. At Nice, the baptism of the Paulinians, (that is, not only of the followers of Paul of Samosata, but in general, of all the opposers of the Catholic doctrine of the Trinity), was rejected. The baptism of the Novatians, on the contrary, was pronounced valid. This decision was too general, to produce uniformity on this subject in the Oriental Church; for, after this synod, several fathers, Athanasius, Cyril, Optatus, considered the baptism of such heretics, although they invoked the sacred Trinity, as of no avail. The council of 381, however, named many heretical sects, the members of which were not to be rebaptized, when converted to the Catholic Church.

Baptism, or spiritual regeneration, was followed by the imparting of the Holy Ghost by the sacrament of Confirmation (*chrisma, signaculum, perfectio, confirmatio,* σφραγις, μυρον, βεβαιωσις της ομολογιας), by which the baptized person was raised to the dignity of a perfect Christian. This sacrament was administered by the imposition of hands, and by anointing with the sacred chrism. In the eastern Church the anointing (with these words, " the seal of the gifts of the Holy Ghost") was considered the chief part of the sacrament, for by it the seal of the Holy Ghost was impressed upon the soul. But the imposition of hands, with which was united prayer to obtain the gifts of the Holy Ghost, formed also a part of the sacrament, as we learn from the expressions of Fermilian, St. John Chrysostom, and Theodoret. The chrism was applied in the form of a cross, on different parts of the body, as on the ears, the eyes, the mouth and the feet: but the principal unction, and in the west the only one, was on the forehead. The chrism, from the earliest ages, was consecrated by the bishop at the altar; and St. Cyril, in his *Catecheses*, declares that by this consecration it was made a gift of God, and capable of operating the sanctification of the soul. In the oriental Church, the consecration of the chrism, which was in later times reserved to the patriarchs, was considered one of the most sacred and most solemn of ecclesiastical functions. In the west the right of consecration was preserved by all the bishops; and from the fifth century was prescribed to be performed on holy Thursday; on which day, also, was consecrated the oil for the sick, and the oil of exorcisms or of the catechumens. In Gaul, when a person, baptized on account of danger, could not receive confirmation from the bishop, the priest, who baptized him, anointed him on the crown of the head, whence, according to a canon of the council of Orange, every priest who had the faculty to baptize, always kept a portion of the chrism in his possession.

Adults as well as children, when the bishop, or a

priest in his presence, baptized, received immediately the sacrament of confirmation: in other cases the neophyte awaited the arrival of the bishop, but was in the meantime admitted to the eucharist. For this reason the synod of Elvira decreed that those who had been baptized by a priest or a deacon should be presented to the bishop to receive the *perfection* from him; and as early as the time of St. Jerome, bishops were accustomed to visit the distant parts of their diocese to confirm the neophytes. As confirmation impressed a character ($\sigma\phi\rho\alpha\gamma\iota\varsigma$) on the soul, it had always been taught, that it never could be repeated when it once had been received in the Catholic Church. With regard to the validity of confirmation administered by heretics, opinions and practice were various. St. Cyprian and those who followed him, naturally considered it, as they did the baptism of heretics, as invalid; but in the Roman Church, the opposite opinion was defended, and when heretics were received into the Church, an imposition of hands, not sacramental, with prayer, was practised, by which the Holy Ghost was invoked to pour down his graces upon the soul of him in whom heresy had hitherto impeded the effects of the sacrament: hence we sometimes find in the briefs of the pontiffs, the gifts of the Holy Ghost attributed as an effect of this imposition of hands. The African Church, after the fourth century, imitated the practice of the Church of Rome in this respect; and the more so, as the first synod of Arles, in 314, decreed in favour of this practice. But in the oriental, Spanish, and Gallic Churches, heretics who were not rebaptized were received by a formal confirmation, administered by anointing, and the imposition of hands. In the east, three classes of heretics were distinguished in the fifth century; one of these, the Marcionites and Manichees, received baptism upon their conversion; the second class, the Novatians, the Arians and the Macedonians, received only confirmation: those of the third class, the Nestorians and Monophysites, were received into the Church after only a profession of Catholic faith.

As the apostles completed by confirmation that which others had commenced by baptism, so it continued to be the law of the Church, that bishops should be the ordinary ministers of confirmation. In the east, however, priests were admitted to this right; first and principally in Egypt, from which country, the usage extended to other parts of the Greek Church. In the west, (in Gaul, namely, and in Spain), priests were permitted to confirm in cases of necessity, and in the absence of the bishop. St. Gregory the Great granted the same privilege to the priests of Sardinia.

SECTION XII.

THE LITURGIES OF THE ANCIENT CHURCH.*

A CERTAIN order of worship, a series of prayers and ceremonies, which accompanied the oblation of the holy sacrifice, was, as we learn from the writings of St. Paul, instituted by the apostles. By this means a conformity, in the different churches, in the principal parts of their liturgies, in the order of their liturgical acts, and in their prayers, was almost necessarily established. Still there existed a freedom in the introduction of new forms: a zealous priest, yielding to the impulse of his piety, might introduce new prayers when offering the

---

* The Liturgy of the Apostolical Constitutions, in Cotelerii Patres Apostolici, tom. i.; Amstel. 1724.—Renaudot, Liturgiarum Orient. Collectio; Paris, 1716, 2 vols. 4to.—Muratori, Liturgia Romana Vetus; Venet. 1748, 2 vols. folio.—Pamelii, Liturgicon Ecclesiæ Latinæ; Colon. 1751, 2 vols. 4to.—Mabillon, De Liturgia Gallicana; Paris, 1729, 4to.—Leslei, Missale mixtum, dictum Mozarabes; Romæ, 1755, 2 vols. 4to.—Jos. Al. Assemani, Codex Liturgicus Ecclesiæ Universæ; Romæ, 1749-66, 13 vols. 4to.

Grancolas, Les anciennes Liturgies, et l'ancien Sacrementaire de l'Eglise; Paris, 1704, 3 vols.—P. Le Brun, Explication de la Messe, contenant les dissertations historiques et dogmatiques sur les Liturgies de toutes les Eglises; Liege, 1778, 8 vols.—A. Kraser, De Apostolicis necnon antiquis Ecclesiæ occidentalis Liturgiis; Aug. Vindel. 1786.— F. Lienha... le auti puis Li egis et d Di ciplina Arcani.

sacrifice, or he might abbreviate or lengthen those which had before been in use; but the bishops principally, preserving indeed the essential parts of the liturgy, might change or institute others. In a very early age, however, the suffragan Churches were accustomed to conform to the liturgy of their metropolitan, and this practice was enforced as a law by the synods of Vannes in 461, of Agde in 506, and of Epaone in 517. The fourth synod of Toledo, in 633, commanded that, in the whole of Spain, one and the same liturgy should be observed.

In the first ages of the apostles, and for some time after them, it does not appear that any prescribed liturgy had been established. From the writings of the fathers of the second century we learn that permanent liturgical forms and customs were then in use : they were, for a long time, delivered orally from one priest to another, and the laws of Justinian even commanded bishops and priests to learn and to teach these forms. In what age liturgies were first committed to writing, it is now impossible to determine; it was perhaps in the third century : this is certain, that it was not so late (the fifth century) as some modern writers have erroneously stated. St. Jerome ascribes to St. Hilary of Poitiers a book of mysteries, that is a codex of the sacraments and liturgies. St. Paulinus of Nola compiled a sacramentarium; according to St. Gregory Nazianzen, St. Basil wrote an order of prayers, or a liturgy ; and the perpetual tradition of the Greek Church ascribes its liturgies to him and St. John Chrysostom. It is probable, that, as Proclus states (437) these fathers reduced the more ancient liturgies into a shorter form.

The order of the liturgies, in the four first centuries, may be gathered from the scattered notices in the writings of those times, independently of the liturgies themselves. It was in substance the following :—The bishop offered the sacrifice, assisted by the priests and deacons. The liturgy commenced with the salutation, " The Lord be with you :" then followed the reading of the sacred Scripture : in the east, from the prophets and apostles, as we are told by St. Justin; in the west, generally from the apostolic epistles; a psalm was sung and the Gospel read. The bishop then addressed to the people his discourse or homily. When the catechumens and penitents had been dismissed, and the faithful alone were present, the prayers destined for them were repeated. The altar was now covered with linen: the bishop and the priests at the altar washed their hands, and the faithful (in the east and in Gaul) gave to each other the kiss of peace. All present then made their offerings. The bread to be consecrated, and the chalice, containing wine and water mixed, were presented to the bishop. Before and after the *preface* many prayers were said—for the bishop and the clergy, for the emperor and the empire, for the preservation of peace, for the public necessities, and for all those who had died in the communion of the Church. Commemoration was made of the martyrs, particularly of those who had been members of that community. The preface began with the words " Sursum corda," and ended with the " Sanctus." At the consecration, during which the sign of the cross was employed, the words spoken by our Lord, when instituting the eucharist, were repeated: to these where added a prayer of thanksgiving, and an invocation to the Almighty God, that he would change the bread and wine into the body and blood of Christ. After the prayer of the canon, the faithful answered, "Amen." The hosts were divided for the communion, and the Lord's prayer was recited, after which the bishop blessed the people with upraised hands. In the Italian and African Churches, the salutation and kiss of peace were now given. After the exclamation, " Holy things for those that are holy," the veil which had before concealed the sacred mysteries, was removed: the bishop first partook of the sacrifice, and then distributed to the faithful the body of the Lord, whilst the deacons administered the chalice. All adored when receiving the Divine body: the bishop said, " The body of the Lord," and the communicant answered, " Amen." A prayer of thanksgiving concluded the liturgy; the bishop saluted the people, as at the beginning, with these words, "Peace be with you;" to which they replied, "And with thy spirit."

The liturgies which were used by the principal Churches, were called by the name of the founder of the Church, or of one of its most celebrated bishops. Thus the liturgy, which was observed in the Church of Jerusalem, was named the liturgy of St. James; that of Alexandria, the liturgy of St. Mark; that of Milan, the liturgy of St. Ambrose; and that of Constantinople, the liturgy of St. John Chrysostom: although it is probable that both St. Ambrose and St. John were, in a later age, designated as the authors of these liturgies, on account of changes introduced by them into the liturgies which had existed before their time.

I. THE ORIENTAL LITURGIES. The most ancient liturgy that has come down to us, is contained in the eighth book of the apostolical constitutions, and is distinguished by the ancients as the liturgy of St. Clement: it appears to have been committed to writing about the commencement of the fourth century, and may be judged, from nearly the whole of its contents, to belong to the third: only the mention of the *hypodiaconi* would seem to indicate the fourth century. Distinguished by the length of the prayers, which in the later liturgies are short, it coincides almost entirely with the liturgy of St. Cyril of Jerusalem, as he taught it in his mystagogic catecheses. The mention that is made in it of Evodius, bishop of Antioch, who is always named with St. James and St. Clement, would lead us to conclude that this liturgy was used at Antioch or in some church of the patriarchate.

The liturgy of the Church of Jerusalem or of St. James, by which name it was cited by the Trullan synod in 692, has received several additions of later times, which however are all antecedent to the reign of Justinian (the $\dot{o}\mu oo\upsilon\sigma\iota o\varsigma$ and $\Theta\varepsilon o\tau\iota\kappa o\varsigma$ and the symbol which was received in the liturgies in 519.) The liturgy of St. Cyril is distinguished only in these points, that it prescribes the washing of hands, which is omitted in the former, and passes over the kiss of peace at the oblation. The liturgy of St. James was observed by many Churches, particularly the Syrian, until the liturgy of Constantinople began to prevail amongst the orthodox Syrians; and even then the liturgy of St. James was used on his festival, the 23rd of October. The Church of Constantinople had, in an early age, two liturgies: the one, that of St. Basil, which exists also in a Syriac and Coptic imitation, is in its present form much altered; for the prayer, which was extracted from it by Petrus Diaconus in 520, is found in it at present, greatly mutilated: the other, that of St. John Chrysostom, is, with the exception of some changes, the original liturgy of the Church of Constantinople, which Leontius ascribes to the apostles: it did not receive the name of the holy archbishop before the eighth century. The liturgy of St. Mark, or of the Church of Alexandria, called also the liturgy of St. Cyril, which was first written in Greek and afterwards translated into Coptic and Arabic, is, according to all authority, the true, ancient liturgy which was in use in Egypt before the Monophystic schism, as the Catholics there continued to observe it, after the time of Dioscorus. Besides this, the Egyptian Jacobites used two others, of which one bore the name of St. Basil, the other that of St. Gregory Nazianzen. The Ethiopians derive their twelve liturgies from the Egyptian Jacobites; two of these, one named the liturgy of Dioscorus, and the other of Jesus Christ, were written in an early age, probably before the end of the fifth century. The Nestorians have three Syriac liturgies:— the ancient liturgy of the Syrian Church, or, as it is called, of the apostles; the liturgy of Theodore, or of the Church of Mopsueste, which is spoken of by Leontius as infected with the errors of Theodore; and the liturgy of Nestorius, which was introduced into the Church of Constantinople with the changes favourable to the doctrines of Theodore and Nestorius. The Armenians also have a liturgy peculiar to themselves, rich in most beautiful prayers and of a high antiquity.

II. LITURGIES OF THE WEST.—The popes Innocent I

and Vigilius, derive the substance of the Roman liturgy from apostolical tradition. But if the conjecture of St. Gregory the Great, that in the consecration, the apostles added nothing to the words of institution but the Lord's Prayer, be correct, we must place the origin of the prayers which follow the consecration in the canon, in the second or third century. The same pope speaks also of a prayer, which accompanied the words of consecration, which was composed by a *scholasticus*, or learned ecclesiastic. But however these things may be, this is certain, that the Roman canon of the mass existed in the beginning of the fifth century in almost the same form in which we now read it. Leo the Great added the words, *sanctum sacrificium, immaculatam hostiam*, which Gelasius transcribed in his *Sacramentarium*. In 538, Vigilius sent it into Spain. Gregory the Great transferred the Lord's Prayer, which had hitherto been repeated after the breaking of the host, to the place which it now occupies, and added to the prayer *Hanc igitur*, the formula *diesque nostros in pace disponas*. From the year 600 it has preserved its present form entire.

1. The most ancient sacramentary of the Church of Rome (the *Sacramentarium Leonianum* of Muratori), of which the latest editions are of the fifth century, in which there is commemorated no festival of a confessor, and in which not the Vulgate but the old Itala version of the Scriptures is used, has been by some attributed to pope Leo I, but it is more probable that it was compiled by some private hand, a short time before pope Gelasius. 2. The sacramentary of Gelasius is a collection of liturgical formulas, many of which are of the earliest age of the Church, others are of the time of pope Leo: to these Gelasius added some prayers and prefaces. In its present form it has received many additions of later times. 3. The sacramentary of Gregory the Great is the Gelasian, changed by St. Gregory by the addition of some prayers, and by the omission of others, and arranged in a different order: copies of this sacramentary have been made very unlike the original

by many and modern interpolations. The *Ordines* of the Roman Church serve to complete the forms of prayer in these sacramentaries: these ordines describe the rites and the order of the liturgical ceremonies: the most ancient of them, published by Mabillon, are of the seventh century. The form of the African liturgy appears to have corresponded in general with that of Rome: it had some prayers peculiar to itself, and the lessons from the Old Testament.

The liturgy of the Church of Milan, or the Ambrosian, is, in its chief parts, more ancient than the time of St. Ambrose: it departs in many points from the Roman, and approaches near to the oriental liturgies. How far St. Ambrose changed it is not known: only this is certain, that he introduced the alternate singing of hymns and psalms according to the usage of the east. The Ambrosian liturgy has three lessons, one from the prophets, and the Greek form of consecration; the Lord's Prayer is recited after the breaking of the host, and the *Agnus Dei* is said only in masses for the dead. Another liturgy is contained in the six books of the Sacraments, which have been erroneously ascribed to St. Ambrose: they are of an age more modern. The Church, in which this book was compiled, followed, for the most part, the Roman liturgy: it had, however, some peculiarities, such as the washing of the feet of the neophytes.

The liturgy of the Church of Gaul was, as the first founders and bishops of this Church came from the east, of oriental origin. It had one lesson from the Old Testament,—a canon, which changed with the mass, and which was much shorter than the Gregorian: at the commencement of the masses of the saints their acts were recited. We have, as monuments of this liturgy, four missals or sacramentaries; the Gothic-Gallic, which was in use in the Gallic province of Narbonne, which was subject to the Goths; it is of the seventh, or commencement of the eighth century; the Frank, in which there are many things corresponding with the Roman liturgy, and is of the eighth century: another Gallic, which belongs to the beginning of the eighth century;

and, lastly, that which has been discovered at Bobbio, and which is of the seventh century. This is probably the ancient Irish liturgy, the *Cursus Scotorum*, which St. Patrick received from the Gallic bishops Germanus and Lupus, and which he took with him into Ireland: for a century it was the only one in use in that country; and even in a later age, when others had been introduced, it was preserved by the order of monks founded by Comgall, and by the followers of St. Columban; it appears to have been taken by the latter to Bobbio.

In Spain, the synod of Braga, in 561, decreed the introduction into the Church of Galicia, of the canon of the mass, which had been sent by pope Vigilius; but it was superseded, according to the decree of the abovementioned synod of Toledo, in 633, by the Gothic-Spanish liturgy, which from the time of the dominion of the Arabs in Spain was named the Mozarabic, as the Christians, who lived amongst the Arabs, were called Mostarabes. In this liturgy there is no admixture of the Roman or Ambrosian rites, whilst there is not another of the Gallic liturgies without them. It is throughout rich in the abundance of its prayers: it mentions daily communion, the elevation of the host, at the time of its being broken, that it might be seen by the people; and another division of one half into nine parts in commemoration of the nine mysteries of our Lord — his incarnation, birth, circumcision, epiphany, his passion, death, resurrection, glory, and dominion. Like the ancient Gallic liturgies, it has a lesson from the Old Testament together with the epistle, and a lesson of the acts of the saints on their festival days: in the Gallic liturgies, the place of the *preface* is supplied by the longer *contestatio* or *immolatio*, in the Spanish by the *inlatio*, and by a different one in every mass: instead of the canon of the Roman mass, they have the prayer of praise and thanksgiving, the *post sanctus*, after this the sacramental words, and then the short formula *post mysteria* or *post secreta*, which is different in different masses, and, in the Spanish liturgies, is called the *post pridie*. Lastly, between the Lord's Prayer and the Communion there is a solemn benediction, which also varies in its form. The great similarity of these liturgies explains to us why Charles the Bald, when he wished to learn the ancient Gallic rite, caused mass, according to the rite of the Church of Toledo, to be celebrated in his presence.

SECTION XIII.

ORDER OF THE DIVINE WORSHIP: THE MASS OF THE CATECHUMENS AND THE MASS OF THE FAITHFUL.*

In the ancient Church the solemnization of the Divine worship, (the mass, *missa*, so called instead of *missio*, dismissal, because before the offertory the catechumens and penitents were dismissed from the church), was divided into two principal parts, the mass of the catechumens and the mass of the faithful. The first part consisted of the singing of psalms, the lecture of the Scripture, the sermon, and the prayers for the catechumens, the energumeni, and the possessed. Together with the catechumens, heathens, Jews, and heretics, were allowed to be present during the singing of the psalms, the lecture, and the prayers. In the first three centuries, the reading of the gospel and the sermon did not form part of the mass of the catechumens, who were not permitted to hear them before the fourth century; pagans and heretics also were then suffered to be present, although the synod of Laodicea commanded that the latter should be entirely excluded from the Church. The mass of the catechumens began with the singing of psalms: in the Latin Church, and in the liturgy of the

---

* Jo. Card. Bona, Rerum Liturgicarum, lib. ii.; Commentario auxit, Rob. Sala; Aug. Taurin. 1753, 3 vols. folio.—Bocquillot, Traité Historique de la Liturgie Sacrée, ou de la Messe; Paris, 1701.—Dom. Georgii, De Liturgia Romani Pontificis in solemni celebratione Missæ; Romæ, 1731, 3 vols. 4to.—Fre. De Berlendis, De oblationibus ad altare; Venet. 1743, 4to.—Orsi, De Liturgica S. Spiritûs Invocatione; Mediol. 1731, 4to.

Constitutions, it commenced with the lecture from the sacred Scriptures, between the parts of which verses of the psalms were sung, which were thence called responsaries. Pope Celestine I first introduced into the west, probably after the example of St. Ambrose, the custom of reciting a psalm at the beginning of the mass. In the first ages the psalms were sung by the whole assembly standing; after the fourth century the practice introduced by St. Ambrose from the east was adopted in the west, by which the psalms were sung in alternate chant by the congregation, divided into two choirs. The melodies in which they were sung were simple, almost recitative; but at the end of the fourth century, a more artificial song was introduced into some churches, as in that of Milan. The psalm, or antiphon, which was sung, whilst the priest ascended to the altar, by the people, and afterwards by the choir, was named the introit or *ingressa*. In later times, instead of the entire psalm, only some verses were sung, as we learn from the antiphonarium of Gregory the Great, and from the Gallic and Mozarabic liturgies.

The general confession made by the priest, for which there was at first no prescribed order, formed part of the preparation before his approach to the altar. The Kyrie Eleison, which in the Gallic and Mozarabic liturgies was preceded by the Trisagion, is found in all the ancient liturgies of the east, and was introduced into the Italian, at least, in the fifth century, and into the Gallic as early as the year 529: in the Greek Church it was chanted by the people; in the Roman, alternately, by the people and the choir. Then followed (but in Rome only on Sundays), the greater Doxology, the Gloria, which is found entire, with only a few variations from its present form, in the apostolical constitutions: in its more modern form it occurs in the Mozarabic liturgy and in the sacramentary of Bobbio. In the Gallic liturgies, instead of the Gloria, we have the prophecy of Zacchary, the canticle "Benedictus Dominus Deus Israel." After the salutation, "Peace be with you," or "The Lord be with you," there was sung a short prayer, addressed always to the Father, and concluding with an invocation of the Son, which was named the *Collect*, as in it the devotion of the whole assembly was offered up collectively by the priest. At the conclusion the people answered, " Amen."

The lessons from the Scripture were then read: besides the lessons from the apostolical epistles, many Churches read portions from the Old Testament: the Roman Church had only the former. Particular seasons had their proper lessons; thus, in the fourth century, the Acts of the Apostles were read between Easter and Pentecost; the Book of Genesis during Lent, and at Milan and Alexandria, the Book of Job in Passion Week. These lessons were contained in books called *lectionaries*, of which an ancient one, belonging to the Gothic Church, has been preserved. Sometimes, the bishops regulated the lessons at pleasure; and during the first four centuries, the writings and letters of celebrated men were read in the churches: but the synod of Laodicea, and of Carthage, in 397, prohibited to be read all writings, except the sacred Scripture. Between the lesson and the gospel, a psalm (*Gradualis*) was sung. The gospel was more anciently read by the lector; later, that is, from the sixth century, only by the deacon: while it was read, the people stood. After the gospel, the bishop addressed his discourse (ὁμιλια, *tractatus*) to the assembly, generally from his throne. In the east, priests, and even laics sometimes, who were requested by the bishop, delivered the sermon: in Africa, no one but the bishop preached before the time of St. Augustin. In Rome, according to the account of Sozomen, neither the bishop, nor any other person preached, a custom which could not be without exceptions, and which was certainly abolished by Leo I. It was often the practice, in the east, to deliver several discourses to one assembly. Many bishops preached on the days of the week, particularly on the festivals of martyrs, and during the fast of Lent; and sometimes twice,—first, in the mass of the catechumens, and, secondly, in the mass of the faithful, when they explained the mysteries and the sacraments. In churches in the country, there were few sermons, although the synod of Vaison, in 529, commanded that they should be frequently delivered in them. The best preachers were often loudly applauded by acclamations, or the clapping of hands: their sermons, particularly those which were delivered extemporaneously, were often copied in the church, either by private persons, or by public notaries, as were those of Origen, St. John Chrysostom, Atticus, St. Gregory Nazianzen, and St. Augustin.

In the oriental Church, after the dismissal of the infidels and catechumens, who were in the class of the hearers, particular prayers for the catechumens, penitents, and energumeni, were recited The deacon first exhorted the catechumens to pray, and the faithful to pray for them: after they were dismissed, he exclaimed, " Pray, ye energumeni, who are troubled by unclean spirits;" and when these had received a sign from the bishop to retire, the same was practised towards the penitents. Whether these particular prayers were recited after the gospel, in the west, is not certain: St. Augustin and St. Ambrose so express themselves, as if the mass of the faithful followed immediately after the homily of the bishop.

The doors of the church were now closed, and the mass of the faithful, who alone remained within, commenced: it consisted of three parts, the Offertory, the Consecration, and the Communion. According to the oldest liturgies, the silent prayer of the assembly (which silence was commanded by the deacon), was followed by an audible, alternate prayer ($\sigma\upsilon\nu\alpha\pi\tau\eta$, or $\pi\rho\sigma\sigma\phi\omega\nu\eta\sigma\iota\varsigma$), recited by the bishop or deacon, and the people, who were kneeling, for the bishop, the clergy, and the various classes of the faithful; and after this, the collect of the bishop ($\epsilon\pi\iota\kappa\lambda\eta\sigma\iota\varsigma$ or $\pi\alpha\rho\alpha\theta\eta\sigma\iota\varsigma$), wherein he recommended the prayers of the faithful to God. The Nicene creed, with the addition of the council of 381, was first received into the liturgy of Constantinople in 519; it was also received, also, into the Sunday liturgy of the Spanish Church, by the synod of Toledo, in 589; this example was followed by the Gallic, and, finally, by the Roman Church.

The offertory, or oblation, was preceded by the salutation of the priest to the people; and, in the east, by the kiss of peace. The faithful then presented their gifts of bread and wine. In the earlier ages, the first fruits formed a part of their offerings, and were blessed by the bishop: one of the apostolical canons permitted, with incense and oil, young ears of corn, and bunches of fresh grapes, to be placed on the altar. This mention of incense, proves to us its early use in the sacrifice; and as St. Ambrose speaks of the incensing of the altar, and St. Ephraem, the Syrian, of the burning of incense during the mass, this usage must have been introduced into some Churches as early as the fourth century.

From the oblations of the bread and wine, the deacon and subdeacon took what would be sufficient for the communion of the faithful; all that remained was divided amongst the clergy and the poorer members of the community. From those who were excluded from communion no offerings were received. Money, also, and other things for the wants of the clergy and poor, were offered, but were not placed upon the altar: the donor gave his name in writing (*nomen offerebat*) to the deacon, who read it aloud (the same was practised also, if the donor were dead), with the amount of the benefaction, in presence of the assembly. In the Roman and African Churches, if not in others, the names of the offerers and their gifts were commemorated in the prayer of the priest. The prayers found in the ancient Roman liturgies, and entitled *super oblata* or *secretæ*, contain the supplication that God would graciously vouchsafe to receive the gifts lying on his altar, and that the faithful, united together, might be as a sacrifice most acceptable to Him: then, as the Church offers first bread and wine, which were to be changed into the body and blood of Christ; next, this body and this blood themselves, and, lastly, itself as a sacrifice to God,—so the prayers before the consecration, and particularly the Secret and the Preface, clearly express this first oblation of the bread and wine, as the commencement of the holy sacrifice. But as the bread and wine become a perfect oblation by their conversion into the flesh and blood of the Lord, the sacrifice and the sacrificer were designated in these prayers as the sin-offering for our redemption, as the spotless victim coming from the womb of his virgin mother, our Lord and Saviour himself. In the preface it was said, that Christ presented himself as a suffering victim on the altar; and, as in the liturgy of Constantinople, it was said: "we offer to thee Thine from Thine" (τα σα ἐκ τῶν σῶν), that is, the flesh and blood of thy Son, formed from bread and wine created by thee: it was said, also, in the Roman canon, *de tuis donis ac datis*. From the sixth century, it was the custom to offer gifts to the altar only on Sunday. During the oblation, the choir, according to a practice first introduced in Africa, sung a psalm, and later, only a verse, which was called the antiphon or offertorium. As the number of the communicants became less, and as, in the seventh century, the then unleavened eucharistic bread was prepared by the clergy, the offerings ceased, or gifts of money were made instead of the ancient oblations of the fruits of nature. After the offertory, the deacon presented water to the priest for the washing of his hands, and all the men, who were present, at the same time washed their hands.

The preface (πρoλoγoς εὐχαριστια, and in the ancient liturgies of the west, *contestatio, inlatio, immolatio*), preceded, according to the example which Christ had given, as a prayer of thanksgiving, the act of consecration. The introduction spoken by the priest, with the answers of the people, is found in the liturgy of the apostolical constitutions, in perfect correspondence with the liturgies of our own times. In the east, the preface was the same in every mass, and contained a prayer of thanksgiving for all the gifts of God; but in the west, it changed with the festivals, so that in the old Roman Sacramentarium, there are 267 different forms of the preface: the Sacramentarium of St. Gregory contains only the few changes which are now in use. The preface was closed by those words of the seraphic hymn, which were sung by all the people, " Holy, holy, holy."

Now began the essential, the most sacred part of the mass,—the canon, as it has been called since the time of St. Gregory,—and which, before his time, was named *actio, secretum,* and by the Greeks, ἀναφορα. For the high antiquity of the Roman canon, testimony is borne by the fact, that in the book on the Sacraments, which was written soon after the time of St. Ambrose, the four principal prayers, *Quam oblationem—Qui pridie quam pateretur—Unde et memores—Supra quæ propitio,* are found, with only a few verbal variations. Pope Gelasius inserted it, as he found it in his time, in his sacramentary; and in this form, with the exceptions of the few changes of St. Gregory, we possess it at the present day.

In early ages, prayers for all the faithful were offered in the canon, namely, for the bishop, and in the east, for the patriarch, for the emperor, or king, for the benefactors of the Church, and for those who had presented oblations: the pope, also, was named in the liturgy, in an early age, both in the east and in the west, and his name was placed in the dyptics: in Gaul, this was commanded by the council of Vaison, in 529. The dyptics contained the names of all those for whom supplication was made: the deacon, and in later times in the west, the priest, read them aloud. In the east, a second prayer—the first was at the beginning of the mass of the faithful—was offered at the invocation, after the consecration, for the bishop, for the clergy, and for the different classes of the faithful: at first, only the priest offered this prayer; but, in later times, the faithful were admonished by the deacon to present a similar supplication to God.

After the living faithful, the saints in heaven, and in particular, the blessed Virgin and the martyrs, who were known and honoured in the community, were commemorated; for the mass was offered in communion with the saints, who were bound with the Church by love and by prayer. The most ancient fathers and liturgies speak of the oblation of the sacrifice for the martyrs and saints, meaning, thereby, that commemoration was made of them, to thank the Almighty for the graces that he had conferred upon them, and to implore him to hear and receive their prayers for their brethren who were still upon the earth.

In the Gallic and Spanish liturgies, after the Sanctus, followed a prayer *(Post Sanctus)*, which contained a doxology of the Son : then succeeded the consecration *(actio sacra)*, beginning with the words, *Qui pridie quam pateretur*. The Ambrosian canon has the three prayers before the consecration, that we find in the Roman, with only a few changes of expression. In the liturgy of the apostolical canons, the preface is followed immediately by the narration of the institution of the eucharist, and by the consecration, in the words of Christ: " This is my body, this is my blood." In all the Greek liturgies, to the words of the Lord is adjoined a prayer (ἐπίκλησις), in which God is invoked to send down his Holy Spirit, that he may change the bread and wine into the body and blood of Christ. A similar prayer, in the same place, is sometimes found in the Mozarabic liturgy : in the Roman canon, an invocation, in essence the same,—that by the grace and omnipotence of God, the bread and wine may become the body and blood of Christ, immediately precedes the recitation of the words of institution. Many of the oriental fathers express themselves as if they attributed to this prayer the power of consecration ; but others, and particularly St. John Chrysostom, unite with the Latins in ascribing this power to the words of consecration. But the prayers of the Church, which supplicate from God the realization of the sacrament, as they express the intention of the Church, and define the signification of the words of institution, belong, as an integral part, to the consecration ; and it was natural that the eastern fathers should ascribe to this invocation the power of changing the sacramental elements, as in their liturgy it formed the last part of the act of consecration. For that which God effects in a moment, is represented, in the language, prayers and actions of the Church, as proceeding successively and in parts; whence it happened, that now one part, and now another, is designated as the instrument and cause of the mystery.

The words of consecration, like the other prayers of the Greek Church, were spoken aloud, and the people answered, by saying: "Amen," or "We believe," ($\pi\iota\sigma\tau\epsilon\upsilon o\mu\epsilon\nu$). The Amen was introduced into the liturgy by a law of Justinian, who commanded that the prayers should be recited aloud, that the people might understand all that was said. The most ancient liturgy, that of the Apostolical Constitutions, places the Amen of the people at the end of the canon, and the practice of the oriental Churches, mentioned by St. John Chrysostom, of concealing, by a curtain, the more sacred part of the sacrifice from the gaze of the people, would seem to indicate, that the prayers of the canon were then read in silence. In the west, at least from the sixth century, the canon was recited in a low voice: but we have not sure data wherewith to determine this point.

By the consecration was perfected the sacrifice, which had been begun by the oblation of the bread and wine: in the moment, when by the substantial change, Jesus Christ, in the mystic separation of his body and blood, appeared on the altar as the living sacrifice for sin, he was presented to his Heavenly Father, in memorial of his death for man; and the faithful viewed the sacrifice of the mass as the continuation of the sacrifice which was offered on the cross, with which it was, in essence, one, and the fruits of which it imparted to their souls.

According to an apostolical tradition, prayers for the repose of the dead were said after the consecration: the names of those, who had departed in the communion of the Church, were inserted in the dyptics, and were read aloud: the bishops were first named, after them the other clergy, the emperors and the other faithful. As a preparation for the communion, the Lord's Prayer, with the very ancient introduction, mentioned in the same words in which we now read it, by St. Cyprian, was recited: only in the liturgy of the apostolical constitutions is this prayer not found. In the oriental and Gallic Churches, it was recited aloud or sung by all present. The *embolismus*, that is, the prayer *Libera nos*, which follows, as a conclusion to the Lord's Prayer, is found in the ancient Gelasian sacramentary. Immediately after this prayer, the bishop, in the Gallic and Spanish Churches, gave the people his benediction: in the oldest oriental liturgies, this blessing (παραθεσις) is expressed in the form of a prayer, that God would sanctify the bodies and souls of his people and prepare them for the sacred communion.

Here the priest, or the deacon, turning to the people, said: "Holy things for them that are holy." The people answered with a doxology and the Gloria, which in the eastern Churches was not said before this period of the mass. The breaking of the host was practised in all Churches; in the eastern and Milanese, after the consecration, and before the Lord's Prayer; in the Roman, after this prayer. The hymn *Agnus Dei*, which was sung by the priest and the people during the breaking of the host, was received into the Roman liturgy by Sergius I, in the year 687. The mingling of a part of the host with the consecrated wine in the chalice, is mentioned by the council of Orange in 441, and is prescribed in the liturgy of St. James. The salutation and kiss of peace were given, in the second centuary, as we learn from St. Justin, before the oblation; but in the oriental and Mozarabic liturgies they occur between the oblation and the preface: in the Roman and in most of the western Churches, they were given at the end of the canon. The priest kissed the deacon, the deacon one of the people, and the faithful then embraced each other.

In the Greek Church, the eucharist was solemnly exhibited to the people before the communion: the veil, which had concealed the sanctuary during the consecration, was removed, and the priest elevated the bread, which had been changed into the body of the Lord, that it might be seen and adored by all. This elevation, which occurs in all the Greek liturgies, except the most ancient, is mentioned, in 473, by Cyril of Scythopolis in the life of St. Euthymius. In the western Church, there was at this period no particular elevation; but according to St. Ambrose and St. Augustin, the eucharist was adored by all who received it.

The communion was first received by the priest, and then, in order, by the other clergy, by the ascetics, the deaconesses, the virgins, the widows, and the rest of the faithful. In the first ages, the deacons administered the eucharist under both forms; it afterwards became customary for the priest to administer the holy sacraments under the form of bread, and the deacons under the form of wine from the chalice. A deacon, however, could never administer the eucharist to a priest; and synods in the fourth century decreed that deacons should not take part in the administration in the presence of a priest, except in case of necessity. In the eastern, Spanish, and Italian Churches, only the priests and deacons could receive the communion within the sanctuary: it was given to the other members of the clergy at the entrance or in the choir, and to the faithful in the church beyond the choir. In the Church of Gaul, on the contrary, and probably in Egypt, this distinction was not observed. Each one received the eucharist standing (and on particular festivals kneeling), and expressed his adoration by an inclination of the head; the sacred host was given into the hands of the communicant, and the greatest diligence was observed, lest the smallest particle should fall to the ground. To the words of the priest "the body and blood of Christ," he answered, "Amen." In the time of Gregory the Great, the longer formula, "The body and blood of Christ preserve thy soul," had come into use. During the communion, psalms were sung. The prayer after the communion, *Quod ore sumpsimus*, is found in a sacramentary which was prior to the time of Gelasius. All the liturgies contain a prayer of thanksgiving after the communion; and the oriental, a benediction of the people given by the bishop; the deacon then dismissed the assembly with the words: "Go in peace;" in the west, with the words: "Ite missa (missio) est."

SECTION XIV.

ADMINISTRATION OF THE HOLY EUCHARIST: ITS ELEMENTS.—VARIOUS KINDS OF MASSES.—COMMUNION UNDER ONE KIND.—THE AGAPE.

The fervent Christians of the first ages communicated daily, or certainly as often as they assisted at the holy sacrifice. This was customary in the time of St. Cyprian, who therefore applies the petition for our daily bread contained in the Lord's Prayer, to the daily bread of the eucharist; and hence, some ancient laws of the Church (two of the apostolical canons and a canon of the council of Antioch, in 341), forbid the faithful to depart from the celebration of the sacrifice before they have partaken of the communion. In Cappadocia, it was the practice to celebrate mass and to communicate four times in the week; at Constantinople, three times, on Friday, Saturday, and Sunday; at Alexandria, twice: in the Roman, Spanish, and African Churches, the holy sacrifice was offered daily; we may, perhaps, except Thursday. St. John Chrysostom complained that in his time this practice of the ancient Church was neglected, and that there were many who received the communion scarcely once in the year. In the sixth century, those who should pass three successive Sundays without partaking of the holy sacrament, were declared excommunicated. The synod of Agda, in 506, ordained that all should approach the altar, at least three times in the year, at Easter, Pentecost, and Christmas. The great majority of Christians, however, continued to do this every Sunday. The sacred species that remained when the faithful had communicated, were in many Churches, such as those of Constantinople and Gaul, given to innocent children: in others, as at Jerusalem, they were burned.

The *Missa præsanctificatorum* (λειτουργια των προηγιασμενων) in which no consecration took place, and in which the communion was given from the species which had been before consecrated (presanctified) was introduced, in an early age, into the Greek Church. The synod of Laodicea had decreed that, in the time of fasting, mass should be celebrated only on Sundays and festivals; and in 692, the Trullan synod, in its fifty-second canon, commanded, that on other days, the faithful should receive the communion from the hosts which had been consecrated in the mass of Sunday, and that in the evening, before they broke their fast, they should celebrate the office of the presanctified. The Alexandrian Chronicle of the year 615, contains the description of this mass; and in the prayer which is there cited, is contained the form of adoration of the bread which had been changed into the body of Christ, by angels and by men. In the western Church, mass of this kind was celebrated only on Good Friday. Worthy of remark is the usage of the Gallic Church, which is, in some degree connected with the mass of the presanctified, and is mentioned by St. Germanus, about the year 550. It was there the practice to place on the altar at the beginning of mass, in a vessel of the form of a tower, a portion of the eucharist, that had been consecrated in the mass of the preceding day, and thus to perform the whole of the divine service in the presence of the body of our Lord.

The public mass, at which the people were present, was celebrated by the bishop, with the assistance of his priests and deacons, and sometimes of other bishops; in such a manner, that the people, by their offerings, their answers, and communion, cooperated in the oblation. Private masses of a single priest or bishop, and at which no laics communicated, were in use from the earliest times. Mass was frequently said in small chapels in the country, dedicated to the martyrs, and private houses, and frequently also in the prisons of confessors, who were condemned to suffer the death of martyrs. St. Paulinus, bishop of Nola, said mass when dying, on an altar which had been hastily erected near his bed. The elder Gregory Nazianzen often celebrated the holy mysteries in his private house. When the patriarch

John of Alexandria, about the year 609, saw one day the men leaving the church after the gospel, he called to them and said: " That it was for them he had come into the church, as he could have offered the sacrifice in his own dwelling." The synod of Toledo, in 687, declares in its canons, that only the communion of the priest is essential to the integrity of the sacrifice.

From the very first ages, masses were offered in honour of the martyrs on the anniversary days of their sufferings; but the sacrifice itself, as St. Augustine remarked in his epistle to Faustus the Manichee, was not offered to the martyrs but to God. In the two most ancient Roman sacramentaries, the Gelasian and that which existed before his time, there are many masses for the saints; and St. Gregory the Great says: " That in his time, masses were offered nearly every day in commemoration of the martyrs." These masses were distinguished by the particular lessons assigned to them, taken from the acts of the martyrdom, and by the prayers, in which thanks were given to the Almighty for the victory which he had enabled his servants to achieve, and in which also the intercession of these holy champions was implored. In the fifth century, masses in honour of other saints came into use. That mass was said for the *faithful departed*, and that it was repeated on the anniversary of their deaths, we are told by Tertullian; and St. Isidore of Seville remarks, "that this was a practice coming down from apostolical tradition." According to the liturgy of the Apostolical Constitutions, the memory of the dead was celebrated on the third, ninth, thirtieth, and anniversary day after their decease. That at the end of the seventh century, the liturgy for the dead was different from the ordinary mass, is seen clearly from the fifth canon of the seventeenth synod of Toledo, in 699. *Votive masses* for particular requests, or to thank God for favours conferred, were frequently solemnized. In the sacramentary of Gelasius, we find masses "for the health of the faithful—to obtain rain—to avert a failure of the fruits of the earth," and others of the same kind.

Nearly all the Churches of the east employed leavened bread in the eucharist; and hence St. Epiphanius reprehended the practice of the Ebionites, who used unleavened bread, as being a deviation from general custom. Some of the Churches, however, and in particular the Ethiopian, employed unleavened bread on Holy Thursday. The schismatical Monothelites introduced the use of unleavened bread, about the year 640, thereby to express their belief in the unity of the nature and of the will of Christ. In the western Church, the use of unleavened bread was also almost universal until the time of Photius: but some Churches of the west appear to have celebrated mass in unleavened bread at a much earlier period. Throughout the whole of the east and of the west, water was mingled with the wine destined for the altar; only some Monophystic sects, the Julianites, and the Gajanites, began in the sixth century to omit the water, that by the use of wine alone they might declare their tenet of one nature in Christ. The Armenians imitated them also in this particular point, in the year 640. The custom soon died away amongst the Monophystics, but was retained by the Armenians.

It was permitted to the faithful of the first ages to take the blessed eucharist with them to their homes, that they might partake of this sacred food on days when the sacrifice of the mass was not offered.* The Church could then confide the body of the Lord to the reverence of the people, and it is in reference to this practice, which had then been introduced in Rome, that St. Jerome observed, " Is it not the same Christ that you receive in your house or in the Church?" Hermits, who dwelt in the deserts, were careful to preserve the holy eucharist, that, when priests could not visit them, they might administer it to themselves; and, according to St. Basil, the Christians of his time, in Egypt, generally took the sacred species to their houses, that from time to time they might partake of them. As late as the sixth century, when a persecution was feared in Thessalonica, the eucharist was distributed to the faithful, for a long time, from baskets which had been filled with it. In the oriental Church this practice was long continued. The custom of receiving the eucharist fasting seems to have arisen amongst the people, without any express law, and to have sprung from respect to the sacred banquet of the Lord. Tertullian mentions this practice, and so general had it become in the fourth century, that the enemies of St. John Chrysostom adduced this, amongst other accusations, that he had admitted persons who were not fasting to communion. The synod of Carthage, in 397, ordained that each one should receive the communion fasting, with the exception of the Thursday in holy week, when, in honour of the institution of the sacrament, mass was celebrated in the evening.

The eucharist was preserved in the churches, generally in vessels of the form of a dove or of a small tower. The second synod of Tours, in 567, ordered, that the body of the Lord should be preserved on the altar, under the cross. But for this purpose there was frequently a small apartment at the side of the Church ($\pi\alpha\sigma\tau o\phi o\rho\iota o\nu$, *thalamus, sacrarium.*) According to the Roman and Gallic liturgies, a portion of the host consecrated in each mass was kept until the next, to be mingled with the sacred blood in the chalice, to signify the uninterrupted continuance, and the connexion of the eucharistic sacrifice, as well as to express the identity of the victim offered.

Anciently the holy sacrament was conveyed from the church, to those who could not assist at the sacrifice, by the deacons or other ministers. It is related of the acolyth Tharsacius, in 250, that when apprehended by the pagans, he chose rather to die than to deliver to them the eucharist, which he was carrying for this purpose. The bishops were accustomed to send the holy eucharist to each other, as a sign of communion, even to a great distance, as we learn from St. Irenæus, who informs us, that the bishops of Rome, before Victor, sent it, in this manner, to the bishops of Asia. The council of Laodicea forbade this custom, and the different Churches then began to send blessed instead of consecrated bread, as a sign of communion. This blessed bread, having been dipped in blessed wine, was given to laics, when they no longer continued to receive the communion as often as they attended the holy sacrifice; this bread and wine were made in some manner to represent the eucharist, and the remains of the bread and wine, that had not been consecrated at the altar, were blessed, and thus distributed. In the fourth and fifth centuries, it was customary, particularly in the Roman Church, to send the eucharist *(fermentum)*, which had been consecrated by the bishop on Sunday, to the smaller neighbouring churches: to more remote churches it was not sent; for as Innocent I says, " it is not proper to send the sacrament to a great distance." The eucharist was, however, taken on long journeys, on which danger was apprehended. The abuse of placing it in the mouths of dead persons, who had not been able to receive it before death, was abolished by several councils: but it was permitted to leave it on the breast of the deceased person, in the grave, and particularly at the funerals of bishops.

The blessed eucharist was ordinarily administered to the faithful in the ancient Church under both forms of bread and wine: but there never was a doubt that the substance of the sacrament was contained entire under either form, or that he, who received under either form, received a perfect sacrament, and all the graces that were connected with it; that he was incorporated with Christ, and was nourished with his body. It never was doubted, indeed, that the consecration of both species was essential to the integrity of the sacrifice; but it was at the same time believed, that a participation of either species, in the sacred banquet, was perfect and as full in its effects as the participation of both. The apostle had said,"Whosoever shall eat this bread, *or* drink the chalice of the Lord unworthily, shall be guilty of the body and blood of the Lord:"

worthy reception of one, he profanes both; as he, who receives only one species worthily, is made partaker of the graces that are contained under the two species. Communion under one form was, therefore, frequent in the ancient Church, perhaps more frequent than communion under both forms. For domestic communion, in which the faithful partook only of the consecrated bread, which they had taken with them to their houses, was, particularly in times of persecution, of more ordinary occurrence than communion in the church. Anchorets, in the wilderness, when they administered the holy sacrament to themselves, partook only of the consecrated bread, and, as St. Basil says, their communion was not less holy, nor less perfect, than that received in the church. To the sick, also, it was customary to administer only the form of bread, for it would have been difficult to have preserved the consecrated wine, particularly in hot climates, and to have avoided the danger of spilling. The most ancient examples of the communion of this kind prove to us that only the consecrated bread, generally steeped in water, was given to the sick: the communion of the penitent Serapion, mentioned by Dionysius, and that which St. Ambrose received, when dying, from the bishop Honoratus, were of this nature. The mingling together of the two species was a custom which was afterwards introduced: but the synod of Braga, in 675, which is the first to mention it, severely reprehends it. Children, to whom the eucharist was given immediately after baptism, and on other occasions, received only the species of wine: this we learn, amongst other sources, from the narration of St. Cyprian, that a little girl, to whom meat which had been offered to the idols had been given, could not swallow the sacred wine when poured upon its tongue by the deacon. Jobius, a Greek writer of the sixth century, speaking of the order in which children received the sacraments, says, " We are baptized, anointed (confirmed), and then thought worthy of the precious blood." But it was left to the faithful to receive, at their own pleasure, only one form, even in public communion. Hence the Manichees, who held wine in abhorrence, and who did not believe in the reality of the blood shed by Christ, and who, therefore, avoided the chalice, were enabled for a long time to elude the vigilance of the Church: for, the better to conceal themselves, they approached to the altar with the faithful, and with them received the body of the Lord, but did not partake of the consecrated wine. As many of the faithful received only the form of bread, the Manichees hoped to conceal themselves amongst them. Their continued and anxious avoiding of the chalice at length betrayed them. Pope Leo commanded that they should be driven from the Church, and pope Gelasius that all persons should receive under both forms; "for this separation of one and the same mystery, founded on a corrupt error, cannot," he says, "be attempted without sacrilege:"— not that the pontiff would wish to declare that the reception of only the bread or of the wine was a sacrilegious separation, but that the Manichean denial of the reality of the blood of Christ, and their rejection of onehalf of the sacrifice, was a sacrilege, "founded on corrupt error." In the Greek Church, as we have already seen, mass was solemnized, in the time of fasting, only on Saturday and Sunday: on the other five days of the week, the liturgy of the presanctified was performed, and the communion was given from the bread consecrated in the previous masses. In the Latin Church, the priest, the other clergy, and the people, communicated in the same manner on Good Friday.

After the example of Christ, who instituted the sacrament of his body and blood after the feast, which was commanded by the law, the apostles introduced the Agapè or love-feasts. These were feasts, at which the faithful assembled, and to which the rich contributed, and were followed by the celebration of the eucharist. The abuses which accompanied this practice, when the rich alone eat of what they had brought with them, and exhibited contempt rather than compassion for their poorer brethren, called for reproof as early as the time of St. Paul as we learn from his first epistle to the

Corinthians (xi. 22). It is probable, therefore, that the change, by which the celebration of the eucharist preceded the agapè, was also established by the apostles. These feasts continued for a long time; and Tertullian presents to us pleasing pictures of the temperance, modesty, and piety, with which the Christians there conducted themselves. The bishops and priests presided at them; and, as the holy sacrifice, nearly always, either preceded or followed, the word agapè was used to signify either the feast, or the sacrifice. The synod of Gangra defended the agapè against the Eustathians; but the council of Laodicea forbade them to be held in the church, and commanded that the clergy should not take to their houses any thing that they had received at them. At that period, however, the agapè were not at all connected with the eucharistic, but were celebrated in honour of the martyrs, in chapels dedicated to them, or at burials and marriages. As intemperance was then almost their necessary consequence, St. Ambrose abolished them at Milan: they fell away, in a few years, in the greater part of Italy; and St. Augustin counselled Aurelius, bishop of Carthage, to prevent them in Africa. At the third council of Carthage it was resolved to dissuade the people from them as much as possible. But St. Gregory the Great, to turn the minds of the newly converted English from the profane feasts of their false deities, permitted them to hold the agapè in their churches: in Gaul also, and at Rome, they continued for some time. In the east, no more was done than to renew the prohibition which excluded them from the Churches.

SECTION XV.

PENANCE.—THE CONFESSION OF SINS.— ABSOLUTION.*

For those, who after their baptism fall into sin, the only means instituted by Christ for recovering lost grace is the sacrament of Penance. This he instituted when he conferred upon his apostles the authority to judge upon the sins of the faithful. In the remotest ages of the Church, this sacrament was known in the east, and in the west, by the name of *Exomologesis*, by which was understood sometimes the confession of sin, and more frequently the whole exercise of penance. By the fathers, it is called "the second and laborious baptism, the last plank after shipwreck," and they distinguish it as a second penance, differing from the first, which was practised by the catechumens before baptism. It included a sorrow, and a confession, of the sins committed, together with the performance of the satisfaction enjoined.

1. The necessity of confessing in particular every mortal sin, even the most secret, was universally asserted, and declared to be connected with that power of binding and of loosing, which was united, by its Institutor, with the priesthood, and was declared to be the beginning of salvation for all who had fallen into sin. Those who shunned this duty, were compared by the fathers (in particular by Tertullian) to those sick people who, through a false shame, concealed from their physician the seat of their disease, and thus brought death

---

* J. Morini, Commentarius Historicus de Disciplina in Administratione Pœnitentiæ; Paris, 1651, folio.—Jac. Sirmondi, Historia Pœnitentiæ Publicæ; Paris, 1651.—D. Petavii, De Pœnitentia Publica et Præparatione ad Communionem; lib. viii. in ejusdem Dogm. Theol.; Antwerp, 1700, tom. iv.—Jac. Boileau, Historia Confessionis Auricularis; Paris, 1684.—Denis De Sainte Marthe, Traité de la Confession; Paris, 1685.—Orsi, Dissertatio Historica, De Capitalium Criminum Absolutione; Medial 1730.

upon themselves. St. Cyprian relates, that those who only in thought designed to save themselves from the persecutors by offering, or by pretending to offer, sacrifice, confessed their offence to the priests. The fathers also warned the faithful against any attempt to deceive the priest or to confess their sins only by halves: those, also, were severely reprehended, who confessed their sins, indeed, but who neglected to subject themselves to a proportionate penance.

The confession was in part public—before the presbytery and the community, or before the presbytery alone; and in part private, to the bishop or to a priest. Faults which, by their own nature or by accident, had become public, and had caused public scandal, ordinarily required a public self-accusation: but even secret sins were, in the first ages, oftentimes confessed either before the entire community or before the presbytery. This confession was dictated either by the impulse of the penitent or by the counsel of the priest to whom he had previously confessed in secret, and was then a part of the satisfaction, by which, after the guilt and the eternal punishment had been remitted, the remission also of the temporal punishment, and of the pains which would be inflicted on the remains of sin in the soul, was obtained. Hence the advice given by Origen: "the Christian must first examine and determine to what priest he will confess his sins, and if he (the priest) shall judge that a public confession before the whole community be advisable, he shall follow this advice and confess again, with more mature deliberation." But those to whom this open confession might bring evil consequences, were not subjected to it; and, according to the testimony of St. Basil, it was an ancient ordinance of the Church, that females who had violated their matrimonial vows, should not confess their crime in public, although a condign penance should be imposed upon them.

II. The discipline of penance was not uniform in different Churches. According to the variation of times, of countries and of circumstances, penance was administered with greater severity or with comparative mildness. The greatest severity was exercised in the second, and in the first part of the third, century: but after the persecutions under Decius, it was necessary to shew a greater degree of lenity to many of those who had fallen. In general, the penance was long and laborious: it was considered to be a longer and more painful cure than the regeneration of baptism: it was thought also, that not only the sinner, but others also, should be terrified and filled with a deep horror for sin, by the example of so difficult and so protracted a state of repentance. The Church wished likewise to effect a sincere and firm conversion, to give the sinner the opportunity of offering the greatest possible satisfaction to God and to cleanse his soul from the last remains of sin.

The permission to enter into the state of penance was granted, as a favour, only to those who had implored it by repeated and humble supplications, and who had besought their brethren to intercede for them. Public penance was imposed upon all, who had been guilty of the most grievous crimes, such as apostacy from the faith, idolatry, murder, and fornication: it was afterwards extended to other hated offences, such as usury, drunkenness, false testimony, and others connected with them. When these sins were secret, the penitent, by the advice of the priest to whom he had confessed them, submitted to the public penance. This, however, was not enforced, at least in the time of St. Augustin, under pain of excommunication. If public penance were not deemed necessary, other works of penance were imposed, and absolution was given, in secret, as the confession itself had been in secret. For less grievous sins, the practice of the contrary virtues was required, as also acts of prayer, fasting, and alms. The exercises of penance began by the imposition of the hands of the bishop and his presbytery on the sinner, and by prayer. This solemn act took place, in later times, particularly in the first week of Lent. The penitent was bound not only to deny himself all pleasures, but to live separate from his wife, whose consent he was, therefore, to obtain before he could enter upon his penitential course; his place, during the sacred mysteries, was in the most distant part of the church, or outside the door. Strewed with ashes, with his hair shorn, and clothed in poor garments, he cast himself upon the earth, and continued, through a long period, the exercises of abstinence and mortification, of humility and penance, required by the canons or by the circumstances of his case. In more ancient times, smaller sins deprived the offender of the use of the sacraments (ἀφορισμός, *segregatio*): but this was not viewed as a real penance.

But those who had been guilty of more enormous offences, were not permitted to be present at the holy sacrifice, and were doomed to practise the most rigorous fasts. Those who had committed crimes which were in their nature abominable, were entirely excluded from the assemblies: their names were struck from the lists of the faithful, nor were they permitted to approach the church (καθαίρεσις): it was not until after a long probation and repeated supplications, that they were admitted amongst the penitents. They then took part in the ordinary prayers, but were not suffered to assist at the holy sacrifice. Clerics, for small faults, were for a time suspended from the exercise of their offices; for greater offences, they were degraded and allowed to receive only the lay communion: more heinous offences deprived them even of this, and excluded them at once from the body of the faithful. Penance, properly so called, was imposed, during the first centuries, only by the bishop: ordinarily, it was imposed only once; and he, therefore, who by a fall into the same or equal crimes, again rendered himself guilty, was deprived of the communion of the Church unto the time of his death. In the year 589, the synod of Toledo renewed the laws relating to public penance, and to the rejection of the relapsed. But in the east, this severe discipline was long before relaxed, although it formed one of the accusations against St. John Chrysostom, that he admitted persons a second time to penance.

After the persecution of Decius and the Novatian

schism, a priest was appointed in the churches of the east, whose duty it was to perform that which had hitherto been the employment of the bishop and the presbyterian. He first heard, in secret, the confessions of the faithful, and then prescribed to each one the acts of penance which were proportionate to his offences: he determined what should be kept silent, and what should be made known, to increase the severity of the penance: he watched over the conduct of the penitents, and appointed the time when they should be permitted to receive the communion. Soon after that period, the order of penance was accurately defined generally through the east. The penitents were divided into four classes, those of the *mourners*, the *hearers*, the *prostrate*, and the *consistentes* (προσκλαυσις, ἀκροσις, ὑποπτωσις, and συστασις). St. Basil is the first who speaks of these four degrees collectively: before his time, they are mentioned only separately. The penitents of the first class (which existed as a distinct class only in the east) remained out of the church, in the vestibule: they could not be present at the lecture or the discourse, but prayed of those who entered into the church, to intercede for them with God and with the bishop. The *hearers* occupied the space immediately within the door, but were told to leave with the infidels and the simple catechumens, as soon as the mass of the catechumens commenced, that is, at the time of prayers, and of the imposition of hands for the *competentes* and penitents of the third class. In the west, the *auditio* is mentioned as a penitential station only once, in an epistle to Felix III. But the true expiatory and atoning penance, was performed in the third station, to which the other two were only preparations: the penitents continued in it for a longer period than in the others, and admission into it was considered the real entrance into the state of penance. Those, who were in this class, had their place in the church amongst the catechumens and the energumeni, in the centre of the basilica as far as the pulpit (*ambo*), and left the church together with the of the faithful. They were named the *Kneeling*, from the posture in which they received the imposition of the hands of the bishop, and in which they heard the prayers that were offered for them before their dismissal from the church. Those of the fourth class were suffered to take part in all the prayers and to be present at the sacrifice; but it was not permitted to them to make offerings nor to receive the communion, neither were prayers said for them, during the mass, as for the other faithful. • In this class, were often placed those who had been guilty of such smaller crimes as did not merit greater punishment, and those also, who, by their self-accusation and their willingness to undergo any penance, appeared worthy of some degree of lenity. For those who would not willingly confess their transgressions, but were convicted of them, were condemned to a more severe and a longer course of penance. If a bishop became acquainted with the crime of a Christian only by confession, he could not excommunicate him, or condemn him, against his will, to the public penance. But when a man had committed a public offence, his penance was announced to him, even before his confession. Many on their beds of sickness, obliged themselves, of their own free will, to enter upon a course of public penance, and upon their recovery were bound to the observance of their vow.

The office of the priest penitentiary was abolished at Constantinople, in the year 390, and soon after, in the other Churches of the east. A respectable female, in her public confession, amongst other things declared, that during the performance of the penance imposed upon her, she had suffered violence from a deacon. As this naturally excited great notice and caused great scandal, the patriarch Nectarius, to prevent all repetition of such an occurrence, with the counsel of the priest Eudamon, abolished the office of the penitentiary, and caused the use of public confession to be discontinued. He left it to the decision of the conscience of each one to determine how he should approach to the sacraments, that is, to make his confession and to perform his penance, which the penitentiary had before regulated in secret, and sooner or later to receive the communion. By this means, Nectarius introduced a practice into the administration of penance which is similar to the usage of the present day: each person might select his confessor, and the fulfilment of the penance either recommended or enjoined by him, was entrusted to the conscience of the penitent. The first, second, and fourth classes of penitents, therefore, fell away: in the third, only the dismissal at the commencement of the mass of the faithful was retained in some churches, although the penitents generally withdrew without any admonition. Thus the secret, judicial confession, which preceded the imposition of the penance, remained: by it, the priest determined how he should act in the exercise of his power of binding and of loosing, as he had done before the change of discipline: this change removed only the public confession which had hitherto been considered an act of penance connected with satisfaction for sin, and it was now left to the religious feelings of the faithful whether they would pass through the whole course of penance, or approach, without this long preparation, to the holy communion. In reference to this change, introduced by his predecessor, St. John Chrysostom says more than once in his homilies, "That he does not require that the sinner should accuse himself in public as in a theatre, but that it is sufficient if he acknowledge himself guilty to God alone." This same holy father of the Church, however, speaks again and again of the necessity of confession to the priest, and thus proves to us that the above acknowledgment before God, which he recommends, had taken the place of the former public confession which the penitent was required to make before the faithful. In the west also, pope Leo declared that confession made in private to the priest was sufficient; and, in his letter to the bishops of Sicily, he prohibited them from requiring a public confession of all sins, particularly of those which might draw upon the sinner the punishment of the state. To hear confessions was the peculiar office of the bishop and of the priests empowered by him to hear them : monks afterwards took part in this duty, but with certain restrictions, as when in 639, they were forbidden by the synod of Rheims to exercise this power during Lent. Some bishops exerted a great portion of their zeal in the tribunal of penance. Thus we know that St. Ambrose and St. Hilary of Arles dedicated the Sunday to this sacred duty. Towards the end of this period, princes and nobles had their own private confessor: the Abbot Ausbert was, about the year 680, the spiritual director of Dietrich, king of the Franks.

The canonical punishments and works of penance, were not considered as things depending on the caprice of men, or as having no relation to the sins committed: they were viewed in the light of tradition, and of the spirit of the prevailing penitential discipline. In the east, they were regulated by the canonical epistles of the most celebrated teachers of the Church, of St. Gregory Thaumaturgus, Peter of Alexandria, Athanasius, Basil, and Gregory of Nyssa; which epistles contain decisions on the nature of penances to be imposed for particular sins. The canons of the synod of Elvira (306), of Ancyra (314), and of Arles (314), together with one half of the apostolical canons, formed also a code of penitential laws. In extraordinary cases, application was made, in the west, to the pope. In a later age, books of penances were compiled for the guidance of priests, in the administration of the sacraments : these collections contained the forms of the confession and absolution of all kinds of sins, together with the different punishments to be inflicted. A work of this nature was composed by John the Faster, patriarch of Constantinople, at the commencement of the seventh century, and another in the west, about the year 670, by Theodore, archbishop of Canterbury. We may learn the penitential discipline of the fourth century, from the writings of the Spanish bishop Pacian (373), and from the book of St. Ambrose on Penance.

When the Montanists and Novatians denied to the

Church the power of absolving from the more grievous sins, such as apostacy, murder, and adultery, and therefore divided sins into the two classes, of remissible, and irremissible, the Church delayed not to defend the plenitude of its authority to grant pardon and absolution to all sinners, who truly repented of their crimes. But in some countries, during the second and third centuries, persons who had been guilty of these crimes, were subjected, even by Catholic bishops, to a course of severe penance, for the whole period of their lives, without offering them a hope of being received into the communion of the Church before the time of their death. St. Cyprian relates, that some bishops in Africa, before his time, condemned adulterers (and naturally, therefore, apostates and murderers), to be excluded for their whole lives from the communion of the Church; and it was, probably, this discipline that caused Tertullian to inveigh so bitterly against the decree of pope Zephyrinus, who commanded that even adulterers and fornicators should receive absolution, when they had merited it by their sincere repentance, and their course of penance. We find, also, that the canons of the synod of Elvira, in 306, imposed upon particular kinds of apostacy, adultery, and fornication, the severe penalty of perpetual exclusion from the holy communion *(nec in fine recipiat communionem).* It is probable that this severity was intended to repress a gross depravation of morals, which had found its way into Spain; but that it was carried to such an extreme, as to refuse absolution, at the time of death, to those who were truly repentant, is not credible. The decision of the council of Arles, which was held soon after, was more just, namely, that those, who after the commission of a grievous fault, absented themselves from the church, and sought neither penance nor absolution, should be deprived of the communion, even on their death-beds. In the east, a greater leniency appears to have been practised; for the council of Nice decreed, that the eucharist should be denied to no dying person, and the same was ordained by the popes Innocent, Celestine and Leo, during the fifth century. The milder discipline, therefore, of giving the holy eucharist to all dying persons who requested it, with signs of repentance, began to prevail, also, throughout the west. In the time of Nectarius, the penitential discipline was still so rigid in the east, that St. Gregory of Nyssa, in his epistle to Letoius, prescribes, that the penance for apostacy should continue during the whole life of the delinquent; for adultery, through eighteen, and for some less crimes, through nine years. Those penitents, who had been admitted to the peace of the Church, when in danger of death, were obliged in the west, in case of recovery, to complete the term of their penance : in the east, they were placed for a time in the class of the *consistentes*. If any one, who had commenced a course of penance, should interrupt it by returning to his ordinary mode of life, he was at once excommunicated. But the sixth synod of Toledo determined that such an offender should be compelled, even against his will, to continue his penance, in a monastery ; and that, in case of need, the aid of the civil power should be obtained,—the first example of the kind on record. Exile and imprisonment had been employed, before this time, as ecclesiastical punishments, in Spain. In the Roman and other western Churches, confinement was frequently employed, as a means of penance, as late as the seventh century, but always with the consent of the penitent. But the severity of the ancient penitential discipline, began now greatly to relax, even in the west. St. Augustin complained that, in his time, the bishops often could not subject a laic, whatever might have been his crimes, to public penance, or depose an ecclesiastic. From the seventh century, public penance was inflicted throughout the entire west, only on the most public offences, and such as were accompanied with great scandal : it was also granted, contrary to ancient custom, more than once. According to decrees of Popes Siricius and Leo, superior ecclesiastics were no more to be subjected to public penance : suspension and deposition were the ordinary punishment of their offences. By deposition, when not accompanied with excommunication, they were placed in the rank of lay-communicants (*communio laica*)—they still were members of the body of the Church, but they could no longer receive the communion as clerics, but only as laics, beyond the limits of the sanctuary. A lighter kind of censure was the placing of ecclesiastics in the class of those who were in foreign communion (*communio peregrina*), as it was then denominated. They were, by this, placed on an equality with those foreign ecclesiastics, who could not present letters of recommendation from their own bishops: they continued to hold their rank, and to partake of the revenues of the church, but they could exercise none of their functions. In like manner, ecclesiastics, who had been deposed on account of any crimes, although they might again acquire their former rank and precedence, were never again permitted to fulfil the duties of their ministry.

III. Absolution and reconciliation with the Church were granted, according to ancient discipline, only after the entire completion of the canonical penance. The reconciliation of public penitents was reserved to the bishop, and was performed during the celebration of the holy sacrifice, to which was attributed a peculiar grace for the remission of sins, before the offertory, and after the homily: it consisted of prayers in the deprecatory form, accompanied with the imposition of hands. In the Roman Church, Holy Thursday was the day appointed for this function; in the Spanish and oriental Churches, Good Friday, or Holy Saturday. The persons absolved immediately received the communion,— the body of the Lord, as the seal of their perfect reconciliation with God and his Church. This absolution (the *plena communio*, or *absolutissima reconciliatio*), was generally preceded by a less perfect reconciliation, by which the penitent obtained the peace of the Church, without acquiring the right of presenting oblations, or of receiving the communion: it corresponded to the fourth penitential station of the eastern Church. Those who had completed their penance in private, received absolution at any time; but, with the exception of the solemnities, in the same manner as the public penitents. The priest and deacons took part, as in the other sacraments, so also in the administration of the sacrament of penance: they imposed their hands, together with the bishop, on the persons to be absolved. But, for the first four centuries, no priest was permitted to absolve penitents at the public sacrifice: they could exercise this power only in private dwellings, in cases of emergency, or by the special commission of the bishop. We learn from St. Cyprian, and from the synod of Elvira, that when no priest could be found, deacons were empowered to impose hands, to grant the peace of the Church, and to administer the holy eucharist. In such cases, sincere repentance, and the desire to receive the absolution of the priest, were considered equivalent to the same. Thus, it is recorded of Serapion, who had fallen in the persecution of Decius, that upon his death-bed, the communion was given to him, although he had not previously obtained absolution. According to the earlier practice of the Roman Church, all those who died suddenly, without absolution or reconciliation, were deprived of the communion, and, consequently, of the prayers of the Church: but in Africa, and in Gaul, and after the sixth century in Rome also, a milder discipline was introduced, which conceded to all those who had died before the termination of their penance, the rights of those who had departed in the communion of the Church.

IV. The bishop could shorten the term of the penitential exercises, or mitigate their severity, in the same manner as the apostles had done. This abbreviation or mitigation was afterwards known by the name of *indulgence*, or a remission (the extent of which was defined by the grant) of those penitential works which had been imposed upon the sinner to atone for his offence against God. This favour was granted sometimes to those who displayed an extraordinary fervour in their exercises of penance, and to those who could obtain a recommendation to the bishop, from the martyrs. In the second century, the custom arose of conceding to the martyrs who had suffered torture, or who awaited in their dungeons the crown of their sufferings,—the privilege of granting to persons, with whom they were connected, letters of recommendation, by which the bishop was induced, in consideration of the glorious merits of the holy sufferers, to accord the desired remission to the favoured penitents. In the persecution of Decius, this custom grew in Africa into a dangerous abuse, for the martyrs granted their letters of recommendation, in the form of testimonials of peace and communion, and with such inconsiderate profusion, that whole crowds of those who had fallen, sought, in virtue of these letters, to be admitted to ecclesiastical communion, and to the sacraments, without any previous probation or penance. One of the confessors, Lucian, went so far as to declare, in his own name, and in the name of the other confessors, that he had forgiven the sins of all the fallen, and had granted them peace: he wrote in almost a threatening tone to St. Cyprian, requiring him to preserve peace with the holy martyrs. The African bishops, supported by the Church of Rome, opposed with firmness this relaxation of ecclesiastical discipline: St. Cyprian wrote, on this occasion, his book *On the Fallen;* and two synods, at Rome, and at Carthage in 251, ordained, that no hopes of peace should be given to the fallen, until they had first merited them by a long and serious repentance. But the second synod of Carthage decreed, that when a new outbreak of the persecution was feared, all the fallen should be admitted to reconciliation; and we know, that both at Rome and at Carthage, many received the peace of the Church for this cause, without any course of penance. As according to the doctrine of the Church, as it is fully explained by St. Cyprian, reparation was made by the works of penance, not so much to the Church, as to God himself; that by them he was appeased, and the conscience of the penitent purified; an indulgence, or a partial remission of these exercises was, therefore, a remission founded on the power of the Church, in the merits of Christ, and on the intercession of his martyrs, of the satisfaction due to the Divine justice.

When, after the commencement of the fourth century, the severity of discipline began more and more to decrease, indulgences became more frequent, and in the *Penitential* of Theodore, archbishop of Canterbury, it is directed, that the penitent should be permitted to approach the holy communion after a year or six months of penance.

SECTION XVI.

EXTREME UNCTION.—ORDERS AND MATRIMONY.*

THE sacrament of Extreme Unction, or of the anointing of the sick, (*unctio sacra, oleum sanctum,* ἅγιον ἔλαιον) which, according to the apostolical narration contained in the epistle of St. James, possesses a physically healing property, and also, but principally, the virtue of the remission of sins, as being the completion and perfection of penance, is often mentioned by St. John Chrysostom, by Victor of Antioch, by Cæsarius of Arles, and by many others: it is spoken of in the biographies of the saints, and in the history of St. Gregory of Tours. Pope Innocent I, in his epistle to Decentius, declares this anointing to be a sacrament, which, therefore, like the other sacraments, could not be administered to those who had not been reconciled by penance. In the west, only oil blessed by a bishop has ever been employed in the administration of this sacrament: the form of the blessing of the oil of the sick, is found in the sacramentary of St. Gregory the Great. In the east, on the contrary, priests performed this rite, in the seventh

---

* J. Morini, Commentarius de SS Ecclesiæ Ordinationibus; Amstelod. 1709, folio —(Gibert) Tradition de l'Eglise sur le Sacrement de Mariage; Paris, 1725, 3 vols 4to.—E. von Moy, " Das Eherecht der Christen bis zur Zeit Carls des Grossen," (Law of Marriage amongst Christians, to the time of Charlemagne); Regensburg, 1833.

century, as we learn from Theodore of Canterbury. This sacrament was conferred partly before and partly after the reception of the communion, and frequently by several priests, as is the practice even now in the Greek Church: but examples, in which it was conferred by only one priest, are not wanting. It was not administered to all. Children, neophytes, whose sins had just been remitted by baptism, persons who lived in a state of uninterrupted penance or unsullied purity of life, were not accustomed to receive it; for as this sacrament was considered a part of penance, it did not appear that such persons stood in need of a particular penitential work on their death-beds. Hence it is recorded as an act of humility of some saints that they received this sacrament upon their death-beds, for which their friends could see no necessity.

The sacrament of Holy Orders (*ordinatio, sacramentum antistitis, benedictio presbyterii*, χειροτονια) had been always since the times of the apostles administered by the imposition of hands, to impart the Holy Ghost to the person ordained. At the consecration of a bishop, it had been the usage, since the third century, not only to impose hands, but also to place the book of the gospels on the head of the new bishop. But the anointing, of which pope Leo makes mention, was unknown in the east, in Africa, and probably also in Spain. At the ordination of a priest, the bishop and all the priests present imposed hands: the anointing of the hands was not customary in the east nor in Rome, before the ninth century: but it had been previously introduced into Gaul. Deacons were ordained by the imposition of the hands of the bishop alone. The subdeaconship was not conferred, like the deaconship or priesthood, in the sanctuary before the altar, but in the sacristy or diaconicon, and without the imposition of hands. The inferior orders were given by presenting to the persons who received them, the instruments or signs of their ministry: to the subdeacon were presented the sacred vessels; to the acolythe, the lamps; to the exorcist, the

lector, the lectionary; and to the porter, the keys of the church.

The universal degradation of the state of marriage throughout the empire of pagan Rome, will naturally lead us to expect that the strict principles which the Church had received from Christ and his apostles regarding it, would encounter the most violent opposition, and that they would have to gain the ascendancy by degrees and after many severe combats. First, the unity of matrimony was so inviolably maintained by the primitive Church, that not only was any connexion with any woman other than his lawful wife never permitted to a man, but even second marriage after the death of one spouse was looked upon as allowed indeed, but as something defective or to be avoided. The Catholics were, however, far removed from the doctrine of the Montanists, who unconditionally rejected all second marriages; but there were some amongst them, such as Athenagoras and Origen, who loudly expressed their disapprobation of them; whilst others, St. Ambrose, St. John Chrysostom, and St. Jerome, endeavoured to dissuade the faithful from them. In some countries of the east, a particular canonical penance was laid upon those who had been twice married: they were for ever excluded from the ecclesiastical state, nor could they receive any portion of the alms of the Church. The solemn ecclesiastical benediction was not given in second marriages, nor could the bride wear the nuptial veil or garland. A third marriage was considered by many as unlawful, a fourth was declared by the apostolical constitutions as no better than a state of public infamy, and was always condemned by the oriental Church.

The dissolution of marriage by letters of divorce, which were granted to the Jews by the Mosaic law, on account of the hardness of their hearts, was prohibited by Christ and by his apostle St. Paul; and in the very first ages of the Church, the Christian conviction of the indissolubility of matrimony was most clearly and most firmly expressed, with from the declarations of

Hermas and Athenagoras. But in later times, the tradition of this indissolubility, as it was preserved in the Churches of Rome and of Africa, was the only one that could be followed with security. In other Churches, there was, for a period, a doubt, or permission was granted to dissolve the matrimonial bond, and to marry again, in case of adultery. The causes of this variation were many: in some places there arose a doubt as to the signification of the words of our Lord, recorded by St. Matthew (ch. v. and xix.): or it was even supposed that our Saviour had here positively excepted one case, in which a dissolution would be lawful: or a sufficient distinction was not made between a separation and interruption of matrimonial society, and an entire dissolution and annihilation of the contract. Again, as separation was granted by the imperial laws, which until the time of Justinian required no other cause than the mutual consent of the parties, the ecclesiastical power, in these countries, despaired of being able to enforce the severity of its own discipline. Many of the fathers, St. John Chrysostom, Ambrose, Gregory Nazianzen, and Jerome, condemned these laws, and declared them to be irreconcileable with the laws of the Church: but after the third century, we find no doctor of the Church, in the east, positively defending the absolute indissolubility of matrimony: the forty-eighth of the Apostolical Canons, indeed, prohibits in general the marriage of a woman who had been separated from her husband, under pain of excommunication. But as early as the time of Origen, there were bishops who permitted second marriages during the life of the divorced party; and the testimonies of Asterius, St. Epiphanius, and St. Basil, leave no doubt that the theory and practice of the east allowed to the man at least the right to marry after a divorce. When the laws of Justinian declared that the marriage bond was broken, by adultery, by high-treason, by an attempt against the life, or false testimony by one against the other party, the Church in the east seems to have given to the innocent party the p   of   marriage, at least in the case of adultery: and when the Trullan synod of 692, adopted two canons opposing the discipline of the Orientals, the forty-eighth of the apostolical and the seventeenth of Mileve, it proved by its adoption of the decision given by Basil, one of the bishops present, that it did not strictly enforce the doctrine of the indissoluble nature of matrimony.

In the west, on the contrary, this was unalterably maintained at Rome, and in Africa, as we learn from the declarations of the popes Innocent and Leo, and from the canon of the synod of Mileve, in 416, which latter declared, that according to the discipline of the gospel and of the apostles, no man, who had been forsaken by his wife or divorced from her, could marry again during her life-time. St. Augustin expressed himself strongly in the same sense, but confessed that there was an obscurity around the words of our Saviour. In Spain, the council of Elvira forbade the divorced woman to marry again, but was not so severe with regard to the man. In Gaul, the discipline was doubtful and varying: the synod of Vannes in 465, and of Agde, in 506, seem to grant the right of second marriage to the man, after the crime of adultery committed by his wife. The first synod of Arles gave on this subject only a counsel, that the man should abstain from a second marriage after a divorce: but a synod at Nantes (it is uncertain in what year, probably in 658) renewed the ancient law, that no man should presume to marry, as long as his wife, from whom he had been divorced, should live. That in Gaul and Britain, the dissolution of the matrimonial bond was not unfrequent, during the seventh century, is evident from the formulas of Marculphus and from the capitularies of Theodore of Canterbury.

Marriage with infidels was prohibited by most ancient fathers, and with heretics by the synod of Elvira: in a later age, these marriages were tolerated; they had never been considered as invalid. In Gaul, and in Spain, in the sixth and seventh centuries, marriage with Jews was forbidden under pain of excommunication, until a legal union should take place. Marriage with relatives descending in a right line was considered invalid by nature: in the collateral lines, it was forbidden, for a long time, even by the civil law: first cousins were forbidden by the Church to intermarry; and still more strictly was this prohibition extended to uncles and nieces. The ecclesiastical law, preventing the marriages of cousins, which was first made in the beginning of the fourth century was frequently renewed. In the time of St. Gregory the Great, the impediments of relationship extended to the seventh degree, according to the method of calculation then in use. The impediments of spiritual relationship, which was a species of adoption by the sponsors of the person baptized, was introduced or confirmed by a law of Justinian. From the time of the council of Chalcedon, and after the decrees of the popes Innocent and Leo, the entrance into the monastic state, and into the state of consecrated virgins, formed another impediment.

According to the most ancient Christian usage, the matrimonial contract was consecrated by the prayers of the Church, and the blessings of its priests. Tertullian extols the happiness of a marriage which, being solemnized by the Church, and sealed by the oblation of the holy sacrifice, is proclaimed by the angels in heaven: he expresses, on the other hand, the strong disapprobation in which those marriages were held which were not celebrated before the face of the Church. The validity of marriage, however, was not considered to depend on the ecclesiastical benediction. As a sanctifying power was attributed to this benediction, the fourth council of Carthage ordained that the newly-married persons should, through respect to the same, preserve themselves for a short time in continence. At the blessing, the spouse was covered with a purple veil and a crown was placed on her head: the blessing was given during the mass: both parties presented offerings and received the holy communion. After the benediction, their hands were bound together with white and red bands, as a sign of their indissoluble union. The marriage deed was confirmed or sealed by the bishop

SECTION XVII.

DISCIPLINE OF THE SECRET.*

As our Lord, in the exposition of his doctrine, employed a degree of reserve, and concealed in part from the multitudes, who could not comprehend his words, those mysteries of the kingdom of God which he unveiled to his disciples; as he observed also a certain economy even towards his apostles, revealing to them his mysteries only by degrees, so it was the right and duty of the primitive Church to remove from the stranger and the incipient believer, whose mind was not prepared for them, the knowledge and the view of her sacred mysteries. She did so, that she might not expose them to the misunderstanding, to the derision and to the blasphemy of the faithless, that she might not shock the mind of the catechumen, who could not comprehend them; and that she might at the same time fill his soul with a reverence for them, and with an ardent desire to be made acquainted with them. This discipline of the secret regarded both the dogmas and the rites of the Church. St. Basil distinguishes in the doctrine of the Church, the dogmas (δογματα) which were kept in secret, and the expositions (κηρυγματα) which were delivered in public: by the latter he understands the practical doctrines and precepts of morality; by the former the mysteries of faith, and in particular the mystery of the Trinity. That this dogma, which more than any other was exposed to greater misunderstanding and to more certain blasphemy was concealed from the pagans, we learn from the bishop Archelaus, in his *Disputation with Manes*. But after the Arian controversies this secrecy could not be strictly observed, and it was now no more than a pious wish, which St. Gregory Nazian-

---

* Schelstrate, De Disciplina Arcani; Romæ, 1685, 4to — De Moissy, Méthode dont les Pères se sont servis en traitant des Mystères; Paris, 1683, 4to.— Toulin, Dissertatio De Disciplina Arcani, 1756.

zen expressed in one of his discourses, that even in the heat of controversies with unbelievers, a degree of secrecy should be preserved. The forms of the profession of faith, and even the Lord's Prayer, were still preserved in secrecy, and were known to the catechumen only a short time before his baptism; and St. Ambrose warns the faithful against an imprudent revelation of either. But a particular object of this discipline was the administration of the sacraments. At the administration of baptism only the faithful could be present: catechumens were excluded by the first council of Orange: the same prudence was observed at confirmation, and pope Innocent I, in his epistle to Decentius, mentions not the form of words which accompanied the anointing, "lest he might seem to betray it." Sacred orders, according to a canon of the council of Laodicea, could not be conferred in presence of the *hearers*, the class of catechumens known by that name. But more anxiously than all others were preserved the doctrine of the eucharist and the celebration of the holy sacrifice. The apologists of the second and third centuries, Athenagoras, Minucius, Tertullian and Origen, who in answer to the calumnies of the pagans had so many opportunities to expatiate on this doctrine of their Church, dared not to break through the silence imposed upon them: St. Justin, in his apology addressed to the emperor and the senate, proceeded further than any other, in revealing the doctrine of the eucharist, in the attempt to refute the horrid accusations, that the Christians in their assemblies feasted on human flesh, and to infuse into the minds of the persecutors milder dispositions towards his brethren. Hence those allusions, which so often occur in the discourses of the holy fathers, particularly of St. John Chrysostom, "the initiated know what I mean," "the faithful understand me." In writings, which might easily fall into the hands of the unbaptized, similar precautions were adopted, and the fathers employ in them the expressions "the holy symbols,—the figure —the image," for the body and blood of Christ; and St. Epiph.

rist, adduces the words of consecration in a manner that could be understood only by the initiated, "this is my *that*" (τουτο εστι μου τοδε). When St. John Chrysostom, in his epistle to pope Innocent, relates the sudden entrance of soldiers into the church, he says that the sacred blood of Christ was cast upon the ground: Palladius, narrating the same fact, but in a work intended for the public, speaks only of the pouring out of the symbol. When the Arians caused the accusation against St Athanasius, that he had broken an eucharistic chalice, to be examined in the presence of pagans, the pope Julius and the synod of Alexandria, of the year 339, spoke with reluctance of such an unheard of profanation of the mystery. It was objected to heretics, particularly to the Marcionites by Tertullian, that they did not observe the discipline of the secret. When paganism had entirely or almost entirely fallen away, and when all or nearly all were baptized in their infancy and grew up as Christians, this discipline, which was no longer necessary, gradually disappeared.

SECTION XVIII.

CHURCHES.—ALTARS.—IMAGES.—THE CROSS.*

The first religious assemblies of the Christians were held in private houses. In the second century they possessed edifices appropriated to the Divine worship; but not to excite the suspicion of the pagans, these

---

* Pomp. Sarnelli, Antica Basilicografia; Napol. 1686, 4to —Jo. Ciampini, Synopsis, Hist. De Ædificiis a Constantino Magno extructis; Romæ, 1693, folio.—Ejusdem, Vetera Monumenta; Romæ, 1690, tom. i. ii., folio —God. Voigt, Thusiasteriologia; Hamburg, 1709 — Thiers, sur les Principaux Autels des Eglises; Paris, 1688.—Munter, Sinnbilder and Kunstvorstellungen der Alten Christen, Altona, 1825, 4to.—P. Aringhi, Roma Subterranea, Paris. 1659, folio —(Bottari), Sculture e Pitture sacre estratte dai Cimiteri di Roma; Romæ, 1733-46, 2 vols. folio.—J. Molsner, De Cruce Christi, Ingolst. 1608, 4to.

buildings presented nothing on their exterior which could distinguish them from ordinary dwellings. They, therefore, bore no resemblance to the heathen temples, and hence the apologists could for a long time assert, that the Christians, unlike the pagans and Jews, had neither temples nor altars. We read that in the year 202, the church at Edessa was swept away by an inundation: in 236, Maximin caused all the churches of the Christians to be destroyed; in 261, an imperial decree commanded that their former sites should be restored to the bishops. At the commencement of the fourth century there arose many magnificent churches, which naturally excited the jealousy of the idolaters, so that in the persecution of Diocletian, which followed, their immediate demolition was determined. But under the more favourable sway of Constantine, churches, more magnificent than those which had preceded them, arose in every part of his dominions. In the fourth century, Rome had its forty basilicas, and in the east were erected many churches, splendidly adorned, at the expense of the emperor and of his mother, Helen. The pagan temples, which had not been destined for numerous assemblies, and were, on account of their comparatively contracted space, not adapted for Christian churches, were converted to that purpose less frequently than they would otherwise have been. But the emperors often converted the basilicas, (elegant and capacious buildings, erected as courts of justice and halls for public deliberations), into Christian temples: it was in this manner that the Lateran basilica was given to the Christians. Temples which were afterwards built after the model of these basilicas were known by their names. The greatest number and the most beautiful of the churches were raised by Justinian, particularly at Constantinople. Amongst these was the church of St. Sophia, at the consecration of which the emperor boasted, that he had surpassed in magnificence the splendour of Solomon at the dedication of the temple of Jerusalem. Four hundred clerics, and one hundred porters, were appointed to the service of the church of St. Sophia. In 606, the

Pantheon, which had been built by Agrippa in the Field of Mars at Rome, and which was now presented by the emperor Phocas to pope Boniface IV, was dedicated as a Christian church in honour of the blessed Virgin, and of the holy martyrs. Churches (*ecclesiæ, dominica, κυριακαι, προσευκτηρια,* and after the fourth century, *templa, basilicæ*), were for a long period built in the form of a ship, and generally pointed to the east. After the time of Constantine, they assumed the shape of a cross, and sometimes an octangular form. The vestibule (ναρθαξ, προναος) had a court surrounded by pillars, and in the centre a vase of water for ablutions: this with its entrance was called the exterior narthax. The proper, interior vestibule was the space alloted to the catechumens, penitents and infidels. From this space, there was a passage by the "great" or "royal" gate into the centre, the ship or nave of the church, the place of the advanced penitents and faithful: here was the ambone, or elevated station for the lectors and singers. The two sexes had here their distinct places, separated by curtains or by partitions of wood: on the side of the women, the consecrated virgins and widows were divided from the others. In oriental churches, the women occupied tribunes. The sanctuary (βημα, αγιον, *presbyterium, chorus*), was generally raised by a few steps above the nave, and separated from it by partitions of wood: only the clergy could enter within it: a curtain hung before the altar. At the back of the sanctuary (the *apsis*), were the seats of the clergy, in a semicircle, divided into two parts by the episcopal throne. The altar—so it was called by the most ancient fathers, who nevertheless declared before the pagans that they had no altar (none like theirs)—stood in the centre of the choir, and was of the form of a table supported by four columns; at first, it was generally of wood, but after the fourth century of stone: in larger churches, it was surmounted by a canopy.* For a long time, (and it is so now in the

---

* This description of an ancient church will be familiar to all those who have seen and examined the venerable basilica of St. Clement, at Rome.

east) each church had only one altar: we first read of a greater number in the epistles of St. Gregory the Great, when he mentions the thirteen altars which Palladius, bishop of Saintes, erected in his church in honour of the apostles. On one side of the altar was the oblationary or prothesis, a vessel placed there to receive the offerings of the faithful.

Near the Church were the baptistery and secretarium or great diaconicum: in the choir was a smaller one, in which the clergy vested. In the greater secretarium, now called the sacristy, were deposited the sacred vessels and vestments, and the treasures of the church: it was sometimes so spacious, that synods were held therein. Schools were attached to many churches, and also libraries, which contained not only liturgical books, but copies of the Scripture and of the Dyptics. The consecration of churches appears to be almost as ancient as the churches themselves, for immediately after the persecution of Diocletian, it was universally practised, and with the greatest solemnity. It was customary for several bishops to assemble; and hence, on the occasion of a consecration, synods were frequently held. The festival sometimes continued through several days, and was afterwards commemorated every year. Altars were also dedicated, and according to the synod of Adge, in 506, they were consecrated, when of stone, with the sacred chrism. The form of consecration, as contained in the sacramentary of St. Gregory, was accompanied with many ceremonies, and consisted of six different acts. Every altar was either raised over the tomb of a martyr, or relics were placed in it at the consecration. The figure of the crucifix, was, after the fifth century always placed in the church, not on, but over, the altar: hence the canon of the synod of Tours, in 506,—that the body of the Lord should be preserved on the altar under the figure of the cross. Votive figures, or figures in silver or of gold, of limbs which had been healed by the intercession of the martyrs, were suspended in the churches, even as we now see them, as early as the fifth century. Wax tapers and lamps burned in the churches, in the fourth century, during the day: on solemn festivals great numbers of them were lighted. They were placed not upon the altar, but around it, or in chandeliers suspended from the roof. In many churches, they continued to burn through the day and night.

The primitive Christians, amongst some of whom the Jewish horror of all representations of the human form was strong,—whilst amongst others a dread of idolatry, and of all that might lead them back again to it, was not less powerful,—had no statues or pictures in their churches. The first representations, which they used, were symbols of Christ and of Christian faith and hope: these were a fish, a ship, a lyre and an anchor, and were carved on seal-rings, sarcophagi and lamps. Tertullian tells us that our Saviour was represented as the good shepherd, on chalices.

The synod of Elvira prohibited, as paganism was then living and powerful, Christian churches to be adorned with images, "for it was not proper, that that which was honoured and adorned, should be painted on walls:" this prohibition appears to have in view, principally, figures of Christ. The introduction of certain figures into the churches, would have been incompatible also with the then prevailing discipline of the secret. Even towards the close of the fourth century, St. Epiphanius thought that a curtain, which he saw in the church of Anablatha, in Palestine, which bore upon it a figure of Christ, or of a saint, ought not to be suffered to exist. But in his time, the use of images in churches had begun greatly to prevail; and in a fragment of one of his letters (if it, indeed, be genuine), he states that his blind zeal against the "unscriptural" use of figures, even in private dwellings, had met with universal opposition from the bishops and clergy. St. Gregory of Nyssa makes mention of the representations of the sufferings of martyrs in churches dedicated to them; and St. Paulinus of Nola caused the Scriptural history, and the sufferings of some of the martyrs, to be painted in his churches of Nola and Fundi: he represented, also, the Trinity, under symbolical forms; Jesus Christ as a

by those words which were heard from heaven, when his beloved Son was baptized in the Jordan. St. Ambrose writes, that he imagined he recognized in a vision of the night, the countenance of St. Paul, as he had seen it in paintings. Several of the fathers, such as St. Nilus, a disciple of St. John Chrysostom, and St. Gregory the Great, desired that churches should be adorned with these representations: for, as they say, they are books adapted to the capacities, and capable of producing impressions on the minds of the people. Hence, St. Gregory reproves Serenus, bishop of Marseilles, because he had removed them from the churches of his diocese, and destroyed them, on which account many of his people had withdrawn themselves from his communion. As now all pagan ideas had been destroyed with paganism itself, and as there was no longer danger that the faithful would return again to idolatry, it was natural, when the representations of Christ and his saints were introduced into churches and private dwellings, that an external honour should be paid to these figures, given not to them as to themselves, but to the originals, the memory of whom they so powerfully awakened in the minds of the faithful. Thus, it is stated by St. Gregory, that it was the custom in his time, to kneel before the image of our Redeemer; not that it was once supposed that this figure was a deity, but that He might be adored, whose birth, sufferings, and death were thereby brought to the mind.

The ancient Church had no precise tradition, by which the form and countenance of our Redeemer had been preserved. If several of the fathers, St. Clement, St. Basil, St. Cyril of Alexandria and Tertullian, suppose that he was in nowise distinguished by corporal beauty, not even in an ordinary degree, their conjecture rests not upon tradition, but upon their interpretation of the well known passages of Isaias.* It was, therefore,

---

* "So shall his visage be inglorious amongst men, and his form among the sons of men ...his look was as it were hidden and despised, whereupon we esteem him not....we have seen him, and there was no sightliness that we should be desirous of him'. Is. 14, liii. 2, 3.

thought that the Divine nature manifested itself in the power of his glance, in the calmness and high dignity of his bearing, and of his countenance. The Trullan synod, in 692, ordained that our Saviour Christ should no more be represented in the form of a lamb, but always as man. It is not easy to determine when the figure of our crucified Redeemer was first represented: before the sixth century, we cannot produce, either from the east or from the west, one positive proof of the use of the crucifix: it appears that no more that a cross was used before that period. In the catacombs, the burial places of the ancient Christians of Rome, and the richest mines of ancient Christian art, there are continually found figures of Christ, of the blessed Virgin, of the apostles Peter and Paul, of the other saints and martyrs; Christian symbols also, crosses, paintings from the Scriptural history, and from the acts of the martyrs; representations of baptism and of the agapè; but no figure of the crucifix has hitherto been discovered.

That the Christians of the earliest ages revered the cross, is proved by the accusations made by the pagans, and renewed by the apostate Julian, that "they adored that which they deserved to suffer." Crosses were also, in an early age carved upon sarcophagi and lamps. After the time of Constantine, who raised crosses in public places, and stamped them on his coins, the zeal of the faithful to venerate this sign of their redemption rapidly increased, and that the faithful venerated them on their knees we know from the example of St. Paula, related by St. Jerome. A more particular veneration was of course given to the cross on which our Redeemer suffered, and which was discovered by the empress Helen, the mother of Constantine. Particles of it were carried to every part of Christendom: they were encased in gold, and worn around the neck by the faithful, as a protection against evil. St. Gregory of Nyssa and St. Paulinus possessed particles of this kind. Over that portion, which remained at Jerusalem, and which, according to St. Paulinus, never decreased, a priest (σταυρο ,ιλαξ) was placed as guardian.

SECTION XIX.

THE FEASTS AND FASTS OF THE CHURCH.*

The primitive Church taught her children, that every day of the year should be consecrated to God; that the whole life of a Christian should be considered and sanctified as a continual festival. In this sense, according to a most ancient form of speech, each day of the week was named a *feria*, a holiday. But this did not prevent the Church from dedicating certain days of the week and of the year to particular devotion, as memorials of the great events of her religion, and as means of elevating the minds of the people, whom the uniform recurrences of ordinary life might otherwise sink deep in spiritual sloth and indifference.

Sunday (κυριακη, *dominica*) which is probably the "day of the Lord" mentioned in the Apocalypse, was dedicated to the Lord from the time of the apostles, as the day on which our Saviour, by his resurrection, sealed the great work of our redemption. As it was a day of joy, it was the custom never to fast on that day: public prayers were said standing, a practice which a canon of the council of Nice confirmed as a law. But we discover in the first century no trace of the transfer of the Judaical Sabbath laws to the Sunday: Tertullian expresses only a wish, that the ordinary occupations of life should be interrupted on the Sunday. Constantine, who made the observance of the Sunday the object of civil law, which extended even to pagans, prohibited mechanical employments and judicial proceedings, but permitted agriculture. The synod of Laodicea, commanded the cessation of labour on the Sunday only "as far as it were possible to Christians." Later imperial

---

* Guyeti, Heortologia; Paris, 1657, folio —Ad Baillet, Histoire des Festes, in his Vies des Saints; Paris, 1707, 4 vols. folio —Prosp. Lambertini (Benedict XIV.) Comment. De Jesu Christi ejusque Matris Festis; Patav. 1752. folio —Thomassin. Traité des Jeûnes de l'Eglise; Paris, 1680.

laws prohibit all public games on Sundays: by degrees the observance of this day became more strict in the Greek Church, and was established in England according to the principles of his country, by Theodore, archbishop of Canterbury; he wished to prohibit all domestic employments and travelling. The synod of Orleans, in 538, had, on the contrary, expressed its opinion, that such a law agreed with the judaical rather than with the Christian dispensation, and thought that it was sufficient to abstain from agriculture, and from all labour that prevented the Divine worship. The synod of Macon, in 585, prohibited agriculture under pain of corporal punishment. Not only Sunday, but Saturday also, was observed with solemnity in a great part of the Church, namely in many oriental communities, which were composed at first chiefly of Jewish converts. The observance of this day, which was considered as a feast of thanksgiving for the creation of the world, was traced to the apostles; and was so far similar to the observance of Sunday, that the public prayers of the day were recited by the people standing: but manual labour was never forbidden. Fasting was prohibited in these churches on Saturday, and as it became a peculiar practice of the Marcionites to fast on this day, the faithful were commanded, by one of the apostolical canons, not to imitate them, under pain of excommunication. In the Roman and Alexandrian Churches, this solemnity of the Saturday was not known, and even in Syria, where it was chiefly observed, Ignatius had warned those who were most zealous for the practice, that the council of Laodicea had forbidden the cessation from labour on that day: this festival appears to have ceased at Cyprus in the time of St. Epiphanius. In direct opposition to this practice, the Churches of Rome and of Spain commanded, that Saturday should be observed as a day of fasting, in memory of the passion of our Lord: at Milan, in Gaul, and in a part of Africa, it was neither a festival nor a fasting day. This variation gave scandal to many, particularly to those, who like Cassian, came from the east into the west, and it was on this occasion that St.

Ambrose gave the counsel always to conform to the different customs of different places,—to fast at Rome on Saturday and not to fast at Milan.

Wednesday and Friday had been, from the times of the apostles, station days, that is, days of fasting and of public prayer. The fast of these days was called a half fast, because it ended at three in the afternoon, three hours earlier than in the time of solemn fast, and in the west, it was for a long period rather an ecclesiastical custom than an obligatory law. In the Greek Church, the precept of fasting on every Wednesday and Friday of the year, with the exception of the Dodecahemeron (the twelve days between Christmas and the Epiphany) and the three weeks of the Prosphonesima, Apocreos and the Tyrophagus, has been preserved: in the west, this fast was a free practice until the ninth century. Constantine commanded that Friday as well as Sunday should be universally observed as a day of solemnity, in commemoration of the sufferings of our Divine Redeemer, and it was soon established as a general usage to suspend on that day all legal and judicial proceedings.

The fast which preceded the solemn feast of Easter (τεσσαρακοστη, *quadragesima*), was, if not an apostolical law, certainly a practice descending from the times of the apostles. But in the second century an uniformity in this practice was far from prevailing. Some observed only one day, others two or more days in the week, as public ecclesiastical fasts: on these days the holy sacrifice was not offered, nor was the kiss of peace given: the rest was left to the free will of the faithful. As late as the fifth century, a fast of only three weeks was known in some churches. But in the west, in Africa and in Egypt, the fast had been extended, early in the fourth century, to six weeks, during which, as the Sundays were not numbered, there were thirty-six days of fasting. In the fourth century also, the quadragesimal fast of the east continued for the same length of time, with this exception that there the faithful commenced their fast in the seventh week before Easter, to compensate for the six days, on which no one fasted. The custom of abstaining from meat on the Sundays of Lent was of early introduction. Abstinence from flesh and wine, and the late hour at which the meal was taken, formed the peculiar character of the ecclesiastical, but particularly of the quadragesimal fast: the fervour of the faithful was often content to make this meal a *xerophagy*, that is, a meal at which only dry, uncooked food, was eaten. In Asia Minor and in Syria, the xerophagy, which consisted of bread and water, or at most of herbs and lentiles, was universally observed. The Trullan synod, of 692, introduced such an uniformity, that the quadragesimal fast was a continued abstinence from flesh, fish, eggs, milk, wine, and oil. Less severe was the discipline of the west: the xerophagy was prescribed only on Good Friday; and the canons of the eighth synod of Toledo were the first which prohibited the use of flesh-meat on fasting days, under pain of ecclesiastical punishments. A voluntary fast of an entire day was termed *superpositio* (ὑπερθεσις), and was practised particularly in the holy week. During the season of Lent, festivals of martyrs were not solemnized: a canon of the Laodicean synod forbade the celebration of nuptials, and the festivities of birth-days: the imperial laws prohibited the infliction of corporal punishment upon criminals in the time of fasting. In the works of St. John Chrysostom we find a series of sermons for every day in Lent.

Only the Friday and Saturday of holy week were at first dedicated to the commemoration of the passion and death of our Lord: the Wednesday was, however, soon added, and before the end of the third century, the whole of the week before Easter, now called in the oriental Church "the great week," was occupied in devotion to these most sacred mysteries. The entire week was passed in severe fast, in mortification and vigils: all labour and worldly employments were suspended during this and the following week. The Thursday was dedicated in a particular manner to the memory of the institution of the holy eucharist; and as it was a festival of rejoicing, it was thought allowable to interrupt the fast on that day: this custom was abrogated by the council of Laodicea, whilst in Africa it was tolerated. In the west it had been customary since the fifth century to consecrate on this day the sacred oils used in the administration of the sacraments. From the time of Tertullian the sufferings and death of our Lord had been commemorated on the 25th of March, although that could hardly have been the day on which they occurred: but this and the feast of the resurrection were in an early age made moveable festivals, so that the former always fell on a Friday, the latter on a Sunday: they were named the pasch of the crucifixion, (πασχα σταυρωσιμον), and the pasch of the resurrection. (πασχα αναστασιμον).* Good Friday had been from the apostolical times a day of prayer, of religious labour, and of mortification: it afterwards became a festival of greater repose and of holy joy. In the east its solemnities began on the preceding night, during which the history of the passion was read to the faithful. In the Roman Church it was the practice (as it is still), to offer public prayers, on this day, for unbelievers, for Jews, heretics, and schismatics: after these followed the act of the adoration of the cross. On Saturday evening commenced the great vigil of Easter-day, which was continued until day-break of the following morning: the faithful were consequently in the Church from the setting to the rising of the sun. The religious exercises of this vigil were, on account of the shortness of the time, anticipated by degrees on the morning of Saturday. Amongst these were the last scrutiny of the catechumens, the blessing of the paschal candle, the symbol of the resurrection, which is described by Ennodius; and in the seventh century was introduced, into the whole of the Latin Church, the reading of the prophecies from the Old Testament, which were adapted to baptism, and the consecration of the baptismal water. Baptism was then administered, and the mass, which belonged particularly to the commencement of the paschal time, was celebrated for the neophytes at the fourth watch of the night, the hour of our Lord's resurrection. Easter Sunday (κυριακη μεγαλα), was observed as the most solemn and most joyful festival of the year: the faithful embraced and kissed each other, repeating the salutation, "The Lord is risen, he is truly risen!"

During the entire week after Easter, (called by the Greeks διακαινησιμος, and by the Latins *hebdomas alba*, "the white week," on account of the white garments worn by the neophytes), the celebration of Easter and of baptism was continued: imperial as well as ecclesiastical laws prohibited all legal actions, and all servile occupations. On the Sunday (*pascha clausum*, αντιπασχα), the neophytes put off their white robes, and joined for the first time the body of the faithful. The day was thence called also *dominica in albis* (that is *depositis*), or *dominica post albas*, the Sunday after the white garments.

The whole space of fifty days after Easter was considered from the beginning a time of festivity, sacred to the remembrance of the resurrection of the Lord, and of its effects upon man: during this period the holy sacrifice was daily offered: the faithful communicated every day: there was no fast, and all prayer was said standing. Tertullian alluded to these days, when he says that the Christians had more festivals than the pagans. The feast of the ascension (εορτη της αναλειψεως, and in Cappadocia, ἡ επισωζομενη, *the day of salvation*), which was always celebrated on the fortieth day after Easter, was one of the four most ancient festivals of the Church. As the Christian had succeeded to the Jewish pasch, so the feast of Pentecost (πεντηκοστη, or more definitely, ἡμερα του πνευματος), in commemoration of the descent of the Holy Ghost, took the place of the Jewish festival of the weeks and first fruits. The primitive Christians regulated this festival as they did the festival of Easter, according to the computation of the Jews, and it was not until they abandoned the fourteenth of the month Nisan, in their calculation of Easter, that they celebrated Pentecost always on a Sunday.

The Ember fasts, or the fasts of the four seasons of the year, were introduced into the Roman Church about the middle of the fifth century.* The summer fast was in the week following the feast of Pentecost; the autumnal in September, and the winter in December: the fast of the spring quarter occurred in Lent. It appears to have been the object in Rome to substitute the obligation of these fasts in the place of the weekly fasts, which were now only partially practised: for about this time the station fast, particularly that of Wednesday, began gradually to fall away. This institution, originally Roman, was extended by degrees, but slowly, to the other Churches of the west. In the east a fast was observed in the week after Pentecost, as prescribed in the Apostolical Constitutions.

The feast of the Epiphany was instituted in the east, and not later than the fourth century, in commemoration of the baptism of our Lord, when he was declared, by the Father and the Holy Ghost, to be the Divine Son and Messias. On this day or on the vigil, there was solemn baptism of catechumens throughout the east, in Egypt and in a part of Africa: immediately before the administration of the sacrament, the baptismal water was blessed. With the baptism of our Saviour, his first miracle, wrought at Cana, was joined in commemoration. In the west, this festival was dedicated principally to the manifestation of Christ to the first of the heathens, or to the adoration of the three Magi, a feast which was celebrated in the east on the day of the Nativity. St. Augustin defended the feast of the Epiphany, as the manifestation to the Magi, against the Donatists, who rejected it. In the west, therefore, as St. Peter Chrysologus, and Maximus of Turin remark, three events of our Saviour's life, to all of which the name Epiphany was applied, were celebrated in this festival—the baptism in

---

* In German the Ember seasons are named *Quatember*, evidently a contraction of the Latin words *Quatuor Tempora*, the four seasons of the year. Is not our own word *Ember* an abbreviation of the German word, and not derived, as we are told, from the practice of sprinkling ashes or embers on the head at these seasons?

the Jordan, the adoration of the kings, and the firs miracle.

The festival of the Nativity of our Lord appears to have been introduced later than the festival of Easter, of Pentecost or of the Ascension, and was, therefore, as St. Augustin remarks, for a long time, of less solemnity than the others. This was occasioned by the uncertainty of the birth-day of our Lord : some placed it in May, others in April, and others on the sixth of January. In Palestine and Egypt, the festivals of the birth and of the baptism of our Lord were celebrated on the sixth of January as late as the fifth century. The Latin Church, following the guidance of Rome, solemnized the nativity on the 25th of December : the churches of Constantinople and of Antioch united with it : in 430, the festival of this day spread over the entire east. The conjecture, that this feast was placed, in Rome, on the 25th of December, to give a Christian direction and signification to the pagan festival, sacred to the returning sun, which fell on this day, is founded on the remark of St. Ambrose, that the Christian and pagan festivals of the sun occurred together. The fast which preceded this feast was first instituted in Gaul, in 462, by Perpetuus, bishop of Tours, and was confirmed by the synod of Macon, in 581. It commenced on the day of St. Martin, and was practised thrice in each week. The first day of January was observed in some churches, from the sixth age, as the octave-day of the nativity, and in Spain from the middle of the seventh century as the feast of the Circumcision : in earlier times, to withdraw the faithful from all participation in the dissipating heathen festivities of the new year, it had been appointed a day of fasting.

The feast of the Purification of the blessed Virgin, or of the Presentation of our Lord in the temple ($\dot{v}παπαντη$), was celebrated, by order of Justinian, on the 2nd of February. In Rome, pope Gelasius had instituted it, in place of the pagan Lupercalia, and in the seventh century it had become universal in the Church. The festival of the Conception of our Lord, or of the Annunciation (ἐυαγγελισμος) began by degrees to be observed on the 25th of March: the Trullan council of 692, is the first that makes mention of it in the east. In Spain, the synod of Toledo, in 656, transferred it to December, on account of its frequent concurrence with the solemnities of Easter. In the Greek Church, the feast of the Transfiguration of Christ (της μεταμορφωσεως) arose in the seventh century.

That in the ancient Church, there was a day of general commemoration of all the apostles, we learn from a law of the emperor Valentinian, which commanded all law courts to be closed on this day. In the east this feast was celebrated on the 30th of June: in the west, the festival of St. Peter and St. Paul, which occurred on the 29th of June, and was observed on the same day in the east, appears to have taken the place of the former feast. The memory of the martyrs was, at first, solemnized in the churches in which they had lived and suffered: no festival of a martyr had then extended to the universal Church. The feast of the first martyr, St. Stephen, did' not spread generally into the east and west, before the fourth century. Ordinarily the day of the martyr's death, called indeed his birthday (*natalitia*, γενεθλια) was thus observed:—The festival commenced with the vigil, on which hymns and psalms were sung, and prayers recited. The sermon contained the praises of the saint, the acts of whose martyrdom were read in public: a public meal, given by the rich to the poor, concluded the celebration. A law of Constantine ordained, that the feast of a martyr should be observed with all the solemnities of Sunday. The very ancient festival, and which is spoken of by St. Augustin as such, of St. John the Baptist, was the only one that was celebrated on the day of the saint's nativity. In the east, there was a yearly festival of all the martyrs as early as the fourth century. Feasts of saints, who were not "spouses of blood," were instituted in the east, in the beginning of the fourth age; in the west somewhat later: the first in the west was that of St. Martin of Tours, at the end of the sixth century. In memory of the episcopacy of St. Peter at Rome, a festival *(natale Petri de Cathedra)* was instituted in that city in the fourth century, and in the sixth had been introduced into Gaul. Among the festivals peculiar to individual churches, we find, in the fourth century, the day of the consecration of the bishop, and of the dedication of the church *(encænia)*, and some other days in relation to particular events. The Rogation days, in the fifth week after Easter, (which were three days of fasting with processions and public prayers), were first instituted, in 469, by Mamertus, bishop of Vienne. Their observance was enjoined by decrees of synods, first in Gaul; it was extended soon after to the neighbouring countries, and finally, in 795, to Rome. Similar to this was the institution, occasioned by the public calamities of the times, of the "great Litanies," which were introduced into Rome by St. Gregory the Great, and which were ever after yearly recited in public, on the 25th of April.

SECTION XX.

DAILY PRAYER.—HONOUR PAID TO THE SAINTS AND TO THEIR RELICS.—BENEDICTIONS.—ECCLESIASTICAL HOSPITALITY.—BURIALS.—EXCOMMUNICATION.

From the age of the apostles, certain hours of the day had been dedicated to prayer and to the singing of psalms. In the Apostolical Constitutions, the faithful are required to unite in prayer six times in the day,— at the rising of the sun, in supplication to God that he would bless them during the day; at the third hour, at which our Lord was condemned to death; at the sixth hour, when he was crucified; at the ninth, when he died; in the evening, to implore the grace of God on their repose; and at the first crowing of the cock, to thank him for the returning morning. They were to assemble to offer up these prayers either in the church or in private dwellings; and, when public prayer was impossible, each one was to recite them alone, or companies of two and three were to be formed. Tertullian and St. Cyprian mention the third, sixth, and ninth hours (corresponding to our nine, twelve, and three), as the times of solemn prayer. But the faithful assembled principally at the prayers of morning and of evening, even on days which were not liturgical, that is, on those days when the holy sacrifice was not offered. The morning prayer commenced whilst it was yet dark, before the aurora, with the sixty-second psalm : to this were added, in some churches, prayers for the catechumens, for the energumeni, for the penitents, and other classes of men : a prayer of thanksgiving by the bishop, and his blessing, closed this first hour of daily adoration. Prayers at night were continued, even after the persecutions had ceased, particularly on vigils preceding festivals. At the first three watches of the night, according to the Roman division, that is, in the evening, at midnight, and at the first crowing of the cock, three psalms were sung: at the fourth watch, matins were sung, together with the psalms of praise or lauds. After the fifth century, this last watch was the only one that was continued, but the psalms of the others were then united with the matins. In many churches, during this nightly devotion, which was protracted until the morning, a general confession of sins was made : the psalms were then chaunted by the people in two choirs, and at break of day the fiftieth psalm ended the watch. The evening song commenced with the hundred and fortieth psalm ; this was succeeded by the prayers which accompanied the exercise of the morning, and by the blessing of the bishop. Lessons from the sacred Scriptures, and doxological hymns, were frequently joined with the psalms. During the fourth and fifth centuries, the people seem still to have assisted in great numbers at the evening prayer, and at devotion before sunrise. The public prayer, and the chaunting of psalms at the hours of tierce, sext, and none, were introduced into only a few churches, and did not there continue long;

for, in the fourth century, they were confined to cloisters: the devotion of prime was first instituted in the monastery at Bethlehem, whence it soon passed to others in other countries.

As the Christians of antiquity always believed that the saints, reigning with God in Heaven, could, by virtue of the communion of spiritual goods, and of that mutual assistance which all the members of the Church may render to each other, employ their intercession to obtain for them the graces and blessings of God, they considered it most salutary to invoke the saints to intercede in their behalf. Thus, according to the narration of St. Gregory of Nyssa, the holy martyr Justina, in the third century, invoked in her sufferings the powerful assistance of the mother of God: thus it is related in the acts of the martyrs, SS. Trypho and Respicius, who suffered under Decius, that the Christians, who collected their relics, recommended themselves to their intercession. The fathers of the fourth century, SS. Ephraem, Basil, Gregory Nazianzen, Chrysostom, Augustin, and others, not only frequently, and directly, speak of the invocation of the saints; they represent it, moreover, as a prevailing custom of the time, and gave examples of it themselves to the faithful in their prayers. As a proof of its prevalence in the earliest times, we might cite the objections of the pagans and heretics, particularly of the Manichees, the former of whom accused the Christians that they honoured dead men, instead of the immortal Gods; whilst the latter asserted that the Catholics had only substituted the martyrs in the place of the idols.

Similar to the honour given to the saints, was that which was given to the angels. The form of an invocation, to implore the assistance of an angel, is found in the works of Origen. The superstitious, and pagan, rather than Christian reverence, which was paid to the angels by the sect of the Angelicals, was condemned by the council of Laodicea.

The relics of the saints were collected by the Christians, and preserved and honoured by them with devout respect. The community of Smyrna, in their epistle to the Christians of Philadelphia, say that they had collected together the relics of the blessed martyr Polycarp; that they esteemed them more than gold and precious stones; and that they preserved them, that they might assemble yearly together in the place where these treasures were deposited, to commemorate the death of their holy bishop. To justify the respect which was shewn to relics, the fathers appealed to the Scripture; in which they found the example of the dead man, who was restored to life by contact with the bones of the prophet Eliseus; of the sick who were healed; and of the devils that had been cast out by the handkerchiefs and girdles which had touched the body of St. Paul. They believed that a power of blessing resided within the relics, which they imparted by touch to other things, to the vessels and linens in which they were preserved. In the writings of these early times are related many miraculous cures which were effected by relics. St. Augustin relates that he had been an eye-witness to many which were wrought at the discovery of the bodies of St. Gervasius and Protasius, by St. Ambrose at Milan, and to others which were effected by the relics of St. Stephen in Africa. Gaudentius, bishop of Brescia, undertook a journey into Cappadocia to obtain relics for his diocese; and it frequently happened that whole cities contended for the possession of the bodies of saints. St. Gregory the Great remarks that to those who sought for relics from Rome, cloths, which had been sanctified by being applied to the relics or tombs of the apostles, were sent.

To the most ancient actions of the Church, even those of the apostolic times, belong the Benedictions; by which certain things were sanctified for sacramental uses, were freed from that curse which was cast upon all creatures of this earth by the first sin, and were consecrated to the service of the faithful as the organs of a higher power. From the first century the baptismal water, and the oil of confirmation, and of the sick, were blessed by the sign of the cross and by prayer. Besides the baptismal water, we can trace another holy water in the Church, as far back as the beginning of the fourth century: the form of the blessing, in which a healing power, and the power of driving away demons, are ascribed to the water, is found in the eighth book of the Apostolical Constitutions. Whether this water were at first distinct from the baptismal water, or whether the latter were used for the purposes to which the other was afterwards applied, cannot be determined. That oil was also blessed and employed in the same manner is evident from the same constitutions. The blessing of fruits, and of meats, arose from the oblation of firstlings, which were blessed by the bishops: the benediction of these things continued, even after the oblations to the altar ceased. The blessed bread or eulogies we have mentioned in another place. As the Church has received the power to renew all things in Christ, and to free them from foreign dominion, the dominion of the devil, the blessing of water, of salt, and of oil, was accompanied with exorcism, or was often itself in the form of an exorcism. In all these benedictions, the sign of the cross was used, and was, indeed, employed on every occasion by the primitive Christians, as we learn from Tertullian. They were accustomed to sign themselves with it principally on the forehead; and so constant was this practice, that many, according to St. John Chrysostom, were so accustomed to it, that they signed themselves, often without thinking of it, when entering a bath, or when lighting a lamp.

The Church provided with maternal solicitude for the wants of the poor, for orphans, and for exposed children: richer communities were accustomed to assist the exertions of others, more needy, in this work of charity, as we know that the Church of Rome often sent from the abundance of its alms to others, even distant communities. Hospitality was given with cheerfulness to every stranger who could prove by letters from his bishop that he was a member of the Catholic Church: the sick, even those infected with the plague, were carefully and kindly attended; and as soon as the

Church was left at liberty to display the benevolence of her spirit, the bishops erected in their dióceses houses for the reception of the sick, (called νοσοκομεια, *houses for the sick*, and also ξενοδοχεια, *hostels*), of the maimed, of the idiotic, and of the aged. Eustathius, bishop of Sebaste, appointed Ærius superintendant of a house of this kind, in Pontus: St. Basil erected and endowed a large hospital at Cæsarea; and St. John Chrysostom founded several at Constantinople: the council of Chalcedon ordained that the spiritual directors of these establishments should be always subject to the bishops. In smaller dioceses the poor found an asylum in the house of the bishop; hence we read, in the life of St. Augustin, that it was his custom to eat at the same table with the sick.

The conviction that the body of a Christian is the temple of the Holy Ghost, that it is made sacred by the sacraments, that it shall be hereafter renewed, and called to a participation of eternal glory, influenced the faithful with a respect and reverential care for the earthly remains of their departed brethren, to which idolatry had been a stranger. From the beginning they discontinued the pagan practice of burning the corpses of their dead, and deposited their deceased friends within the earth. The Christian emperors strictly prohibited the burning of the dead. The faithful often embalmed the bodies of their relatives, particularly of the martyrs, or they at least preserved them from corruption by anointing them with myrrh, that they might the more easily hold their religious assemblies in the subterranean galleries and passages of the crypts and catacombs in which the dead were interred. As the Christians knew of no contamination from the sight or touch of a corpse, they performed their burials, not like the pagans at night, but, after the persecution had ceased, in the open day: but after the fourth century, they accompanied them with torches. The body was washed, and decently, oftentimes richly, clothed, but more frequently enrolled in cloths of white linen: it was then exposed in the house or in the church, and was attended by persons who recited during their watchings prayers and psalms. The virtuous and honoured dead, were often borne to the tomb on the shoulders of bishops; an honour which was paid by the bishops of Palestine to the Roman matron St. Paula. The expenses of the funerals of the poor were defrayed by the Church, which in large cities maintained for this service its *paraboli* or *fossarii*. Those who conducted the corpse chaunted psalms, as prescribed in the Apostolical Constitutions; and at the grave prayers were said for the repose of the departed soul: if the burial took place in the morning, the holy sacrifice was offered with the same intention; in other cases it was offered on a following, generally on the third, day. The holy fathers reprehended immoderate and protracted mourning, and recommended the faithful rather to honour the dead by their alms to the poor. The first synod of Braga decreed that suicides should be deprived of ecclesiastical burial. The Christian places of sepulture (*areæ, cœmeteria, dormitoria*), were like those of the Jews and pagans, situated beyond the walls of the city: in the subterranean crypts there are often found sarcophagi of stone which have been embedded and cemented in the walls. Constantine the Great was buried in the church of the apostles at Rome, the first instance of the kind on record: he was followed by Theodosius and Honorius; and the custom now commenced of burying some persons at the stations of the martyrs, consequently in or near the churches or chapels dedicated to their memory. Burial in churches which were within the cities, was for a long time granted only to emperors and bishops; and several councils opposed themselves to the growing desire of the people to obtain for the dead a resting-place under the roof of the church.

The last means to which the Church had recourse to subdue the obstinacy of false teachers, and other grievous offenders, was total excommunication, ($παντελης$ $αφορισμος$), by which the guilty one was excluded from all ecclesiastical communion, was separated from the body of the faithful, and deprived of all the rights of a Christian. The Church received from Christ the power thus to act for its own preservation, and for the protection of its members against error and depravation. This excommunication, or anathema, was different from the minor excommunication which was inflicted only for a short time, and was willingly endured; whilst the former was employed only against incorrigible offenders, who were then left to their own reprobate sense, and were considered, in the words of our Lord, as heathens and unbelievers. St. Augustin, therefore, distinguished between the *deadly* and the *medicinal prohibition;* and many of the fathers viewed the former as a punishment which had succeeded to the pain of death, to which those were doomed, in the Mosaic dispensation, who contemned the law of God. He, upon whom the greater excommunication had been pronounced, was not permitted to enter a church; he was avoided even in civil affairs: the bishop, by whom he had been excommunicated, gave information to the neighbouring churches, particularly to those to which he might easily pass, and to the chief metropolitans, that he might be rejected by all. The fathers unanimously taught, that this extreme measure should be employed only in extreme cases, with the greatest prudence, and with the greatest evidence of guilt.

END OF VOLUME THE SECOND.

CPSIA information can be obtained
at www.ICGtesting.com
Printed in the USA
LVHW080631260620
659029LV00016B/258